Civil Penalties,
Social Consequences

Civil Penalties, Social Consequences

Edited by

Christopher Mele and Teresa A. Miller

Routledge
New York • London

Published in 2005 by
Routledge
270 Madison Avenue
New York, NY 10016
www.routledge-ny.com

Published in Great Britain by
Routledge
2 Park Square
Milton Park, Abingdon,
Oxon, OX14 4RN
www.routledge.co.uk

10 9 8 7 6 5 4 3 2 1

Library of Congress Cataloging-in-Publication Data

Civil penalties, social consequences / Christopher Mele and Teresa A.
Miller, editors.
    p. cm.
    Includes bibliographical references and index.
    ISBN 0-415-94823-1 (hardback : alk. paper)—ISBN 0-415-94824-X
(pbk. : alk. paper)
1. Ex-convicts—Civil rights—United States. 2. Ex-convicts—Legal status,
laws, etc.—United States. 3. Ex-convicts—United States—Social conditions.
4. Ex-convicts—Government policy—United States. 5. Civil penalties—
United States. I. Mele, Christopher. II. Miller, Teresa (Teresa Ann) 1962–
    HV9304.C52 2004
    364.8'0973—dc22

2004016642

For John, Laura, and Melissa, in memory of their mother, my sister Lisa.—CM

In memory of my mother, Dr. Henrietta T. Dabney, and her devoted employee, Carol Daniel. Carol perished unexpectedly on a dark, rainy road in rural Virginia making her way home from a correctional facility where she was visiting her long-incarcerated son.—TM

Contents

Acknowledgments

We are grateful for support, monetary and otherwise, from the Baldy Center for Law and Social Policy and the College of Arts and Sciences at the University at Buffalo. We are especially thankful to Laura Mangan, Ellen Kausner, and Ann Gaulin of the Baldy Center for helping us to plan and hold the "Locked Up, then Locked Out" conference in October 2002 and the Baldy Center's director, Lynn Mather, for her support of the publication of this volume.

We are indebted to our research and editorial assistants, Jane Morris, Andrea Volker, Emilie Broderick, Cindy Cooper, and Meghan Dyer at the University at Buffalo and Vaughn Browne at the University of Miami. We thank them for their many hours of research, reading, and editing. Our gratitude also goes to James Gardner and Laura Mangan for reading and commenting on earlier versions of the manuscript.

Finally, we wish to thank the authors whose work appears in this volume.

Introduction

CHRISTOPHER MELE AND TERESA A. MILLER

The impetus for publishing this collection surfaced in the final discussion of a two-day workshop on the subject of collateral civil penalties and consequences of felony convictions entitled "Locked Up, then Locked Out," organized by the two co-editors through the University at Buffalo's Baldy Center for Law and Social Policy in October 2002. Our purpose for holding the conference was to bring together sociologists, urbanists, criminologists, lawyers, legal scholars, and legal rights advocates in order to discuss the legal and social ramifications of collateral civil penalties.

We use the term *collateral civil penalties* to characterize a host of legal restrictions that have come to hinder, in very real ways, the life chances for a large number of disadvantaged individuals, their families, and communities in the poorest sections of U.S. cities. The term itself is both awkward and imprecise, as the "civil" and "collateral" nature of the penalties is contested by many, including ourselves. Nevertheless we use the term (1) because it is more accurate than other terms, such as *civil disabilities* or *collateral consequences*, that fail to adequately emphasize the punitive nature of the sanctions and (2) because it makes the irony inherent in the term that much more prominent.

As the terminology suggests, collateral civil penalties differ from the standard forms of punishment for criminal behavior, such as a prison sentence, probation, or parole, that are meted out by the criminal justice system; they are created and enforced by civil, not criminal, law and they are collateral in the sense that they apply to individuals, concomitant with a felony conviction. The penalties include sanctions on certain types of employment, housing, education, welfare eligibility, parental rights, and protections from deportation (for noncitizens). And although they legally apply to individuals,

1

their effects on earning an income and finding a place to live, among other basic necessities, are felt by entire families. Most of the new collateral penalties are tied to convictions for nonviolent drug-related crimes, and their effects are clustered within mostly poor, inner-city communities. Other penalties have since emerged or have been strengthened in the domestic version of the War on Terror, targeting particular immigrant communities.

In the recent past, the academic focus on this phenomenon has largely been the domain of legal scholars. Contemporary realities of mass imprisonment and the U.S. government's recent investment in internal security necessitate an interdisciplinary discussion that crosses the boundaries of law and social science. Since the advent of the Wars on Drugs and Terror, the volume of criminal convictions, incarceration rates, and the number of deportations have increased dramatically and the legislation imposing new collateral civil penalties or strengthening older ones has proliferated. As a result, collateral penalties have become not only more severe, but also "unhinged" from the traditional justifications for their imposition. Nonviolent, low-level drug offenders—the majority of those incarcerated under mandatory minimum and "three strikes" drug laws—are currently subjected to penalties upon release that more than hinder their ability to reenter society. Just as alarming, the consequences of these penalties have moved well beyond the individual ex-offender to families and entire communities. These developments demand an interdisciplinary perspective that this book seeks to provide.

The two co-editors come to this topic from very different academic backgrounds and experiences. As an urban sociologist studying mobilization among resident organizations in public housing projects in southeastern North Carolina, Christopher Mele routinely encountered collateral civil penalties in everyday fieldwork, thus seeing them "at work" but unaware of their legal or policy basis. As one example: a small number of African-American men would routinely assemble each morning at a street corner to wait for their girlfriends or wives, who were residents of a nearby housing project, to leave their apartments and cross the street to visit them. These men, who had been accused, arrested, or convicted of various criminal infractions, were barred from stepping foot on the project. For their female companions, the cost of permitting them to visit or stay the night was possible eviction under HUD's "One Strike and You're Out" regulations, which have since been expanded and toughened. In this case, a civil measure (the threat of eviction) was employed to reduce the risk of criminal re-offending. Yet its social consequences—divided families, the surveillance of intimacy, the stigma of past behavior, among others—were even more pronounced.

Teresa A. Miller first encountered collateral civil penalties in the late 1990s, researching the broader impact of mass incarceration and prison expansion.

As a legal scholar, she became interested in the vast proliferation of new penalties, and became increasingly intrigued by the emergence of a new regime of penalty that was linked, but not limited, to the already familiar "prison warehouse." However, the transparency of these legal and regulatory penalties to the ex-offenders, families, and communities they so dramatically impacted only became apparent to Miller in extended discussions with prisoners and ex-offenders in Western New York. Even though social service providers and criminal defense attorneys in particular were keen to get as much information as possible about the operation of these new penalties, the response of ex-offenders was notably muted. When Miller questioned these men and women about their knowledge of new collateral civil penalties, it was clear that, from their perspective, there was nothing new about them. For these men and women who were enduring the stigma of criminal records, any newly enacted restrictions upon their ability to obtain housing and employment, to receive public assistance and federal financial aid, and obtain a driver's license (among other things) were all part of the seamless barrier dividing the haves from the have-nots. In their eyes, these restrictions were just another facet of the exclusion, the "mark of Cain," that they and their families would bear for the rest of their lives.

Although the co-editors' paths to this work differ, both lead to the broader, and frankly chilling, reality that collateral civil penalties and their consequences reach far beyond their intended legal subject—the felony offender. To varying degrees and directly and indirectly, individuals, family members, associates, neighbors, and communities may feel the implications of such penalties. Barriers to employment, child rearing, and the choice of living spaces—though "attached" to the individual—have effects felt throughout the scales of social interaction, from immediate family to community. Collateral civil penalties are a means *to systematically regulate and control* the everyday lives of certain social groups—mainly women, minorities, and the urban poor. There is a need to study collateral civil penalties "from the ground up"; in other words, from the experiences of the people who must shoulder their effects daily, rather than from the perspective of lawmaking or legal categories.

About This Book

In planning for the conference and eventual book publication, the co-editors invited contributing authors with different backgrounds and credentials, in order to explore multiple and different perspectives on collateral civil penalties and their consequences. The contributors include legal advocates, social service providers, lawyers, legal scholars, criminologists, sociologists, a journalist, and a public defender. They bring to this volume a diverse wealth of personal and professional experiences. Given that the intended purpose was to invite dialogue among disciplines and between academics and practitioners, readers should not expect to find a single overarching definition or a consummate cataloguing of civil penalties and consequences. What the contributing authors do share is a fundamental interest (and concern) in bringing to the fore the mostly detrimental and unjust effects that these penalties have on particular populations.

In Chapter 1, Mele and Miller revisit the existing scholarship on collateral civil penalties, characterizing it as primarily the domain of legal scholars who have approached the subject from a top-down, legalistic standpoint. The War on Drugs and, later, the War on Terror brought unprecedented numbers of mainly poor minorities into contact with the criminal justice system and, hence, collateral civil penalties and their social effects. Taking the cue from more recent scholarship on civil sanctions, Mele and Miller argue that a more grounded approach to the subject is needed, one that sees collateral civil penalties are a means *to systematically regulate and control* the everyday lives of certain social groups—mainly women, minorities, immigrants and the urban poor.

Following the lead from the first chapter, Chapters 2 and 3 more fully examine the policies and associated collateral penalties and consequences of the Wars on Drugs and Terror. Jack Chin positions race in the center of his analysis of longer and harsher sentencing and the targeted civil penalties that follow incarceration. Such techniques follow a historical pattern of excluding and containing minorities. Hence, the War on Drugs, he concludes, is but the most recent occasion for the employment of traditional techniques of racial discrimination. Teresa A. Miller examines how the War on Terror capitalizes on the disproportionately harsh, "zero tolerance" regime of collateral civil penalties that emerged during the Drug War to manage the perceived risk that non-U.S. citizens, particularly Muslims and Arabs, pose to national security. Her analysis centers upon deportation, a harsh and potent collateral civil penalty to which non-U.S. citizens are uniquely vulnerable.

Chapters 4 through 10 each focus on types of collateral civil penalties and their wide-ranging consequences for increasing numbers of ex-offenders, their families, and communities. Christopher Uggen and Jeff Manza introduce perhaps the most widely known civil penalty: felony disenfranchisement. They estimate that the size of the disenfranchised population in the United States to be between 4 and 5 million people. They consider the broader effects that this exclusion of a startling number of persons has on civic life and outline the various disenfranchisement regimes across jurisdictions. In Chapter 5, Amy Hirsch takes us through the multiple and compounding sanctions and obstacles that confront women with felony criminal records. As an attorney with Community

Legal Services, in Philadelphia, Hirsch has grounded insight into the many ways that sanctions on employment, housing, and social welfare damage the life chances of women already abused by partners and, increasingly, by unfair legal and social policies. Stephanie S. Franklin continues this focus on the negative effects of civil penalties, focusing on barriers to family unity and reunification in Chapter 6. She brings her considerable experience as an attorney and activist to the analysis of the Adoption and Safe Families Act, demonstrating how its bureaucratic, rule-laden configuration unjustifiably separates families and keeps them apart, in spite of the Act's good intentions.

Among the more basic needs made difficult to attain by severe civil penalties is housing, as Elizabeth L. Curtin amply notes in Chapter 7. Curtin is an adult correctional services director whose work includes solving the housing problems of persons released from prison. The obstacles to housing for ex-offenders, she notes, are personal as well as social and market supply–related as well as bureaucratic. The presence of collateral sanctions serves only to worsen an already difficult situation. In Chapter 8, Christopher Mele turns to public housing, exclusively. He examines the Department of Housing and Urban Development's One Strike and You're Out policy, which allows for the eviction of leaseholders on the basis of the criminal behavior of their dependents, other tenants, or their guests. He asks what such a draconian policy means for tenants who conform to its underlying premise: that they monitor and control the behavior of their associates inside and outside their homes. The immediate, everyday effects of social control and surveillance upon offenders and their families are the focus of William Staples's contribution, Chapter 9. Drawing on his interviews with 23 individuals under house arrest, Staples explores how entire households become involved in surveillance and monitoring. The day-to-day disruptions (monitoring phone calls, visits, etc.) that house arrest entails have collateral consequences for entire households, including additional tension and stress within the home. Interestingly, family and friends who do not want the person under house arrest to fail the program, often end up functioning as additional monitors of his or her everyday behaviors. Like Mele, Staples concludes the social space of the household becomes fully implicated in systems of surveillance and social control.

Social exclusion and surveillance are two of the more pervasive effects that collateral civil penalties have on disadvantaged individuals, families, and communities. Following the passage of the USA Patriot Act in 2001 and the selectively tightened enforcement of certain existing immigration laws, increasing numbers of noncitizens accused of criminal conduct face another, more decisive civil sanction: deportation. With the subtitle, "How Many People Without Rights Does It Take to Make You Feel Secure?," immigration law scholar Daniel Kanstroom maps out the contemporary legal and social terrain for noncitizens in which rights and tolerance are fast eroding. Kanstroom explains how immigration law has largely become a national regulatory system designed to manage the conditions of entry and residence of people defined as noncitizens. A key purpose of that regulation—including the use of deportation—is the social control of minorities, dissidents, and others deemed suspicious or dangerous.

Both Chapters 11 and 12 delve into the underlying legal problems associated with the implementation and enforcement of collateral civil penalties, albeit from different perspectives. In Chapter 11, Nora Demleitner challenges the claim that collateral sanctions are needed as precautionary measures to protect the public from the threat of ex-felons' re-offending. In her examination of deportation and weapons possession penalties, she finds the use of mandatory collateral sanctions excessive. An unnecessarily harsh application of sanctions is neither grounded in a rational calculation of risk to society nor in the interest of rehabilitation of offenders. The enforcement of deportation, for example, is currently justified for reasons of domestic security. Yet the laws in play were enacted in 1996 and connected to (and legitimized by) the War on Drugs. Demleitner calls for more discretionary approaches to deploying sanctions, which consider, among other factors, the severity of the crime and the ex-offender's immediate circumstances. Chapter 12 is co-authored by Lucian E. Ferster, an assistant public defender in Miami, and Santiago Aroca, a journalist and recent law graduate. In the first half of the chapter, Ferster outlines the legal bind that defendants find themselves in when negotiating pleas for alleged criminal offences. In short, defendants are typically unaware of collateral civil penalties that are attached to a conviction. If such a plea means avoiding jail time, collateral penalties, even when made known, become a distant and trivial concern. Yet, as Ferster makes clear, penalties do matter, sooner or later. This is made abundantly obvious in the second half of the chapter, in which Aroca recounts a Florida family's demoralizing and exhaustive attempts to overcome the nearly insuperable employment obstacles imposed by collateral civil penalties.

The final three chapters speak to the possibilities of reforming or abolishing collateral civil penalties. Patricia Allard sets the tone in Chapter 13. In order for meaningful and comprehensive reform to take place, we need first to institute a rights-centered framework, in which basic human needs (housing, employment, healthcare, etc.) are, indeed, elevated to the status of rights, not privileges. In doing so, the already-thin legitimation for the existence of collateral civil penalties evaporates, making way for a more-just postpenal reintegration of offenders, their families, and even entire communities. The final two chapters deal with civil sanctions in Canada and South Africa, partly to provide U.S. law makers, practitioners, academics, and other readers a real (and achievable) sense of difference elsewhere. Debra Parkes takes us through the Canadian experience in banning prisoners from voting in Chapter 14. In 2002 the Supreme Court of Canada rejected prisoner disenfranchisement, and Parkes uses this ruling to ask larger questions about the relationship between offenders and society. By adopting a perspective based on the unassailable rights of individuals, Parkes calls for a notion of citizenship that includes, rather than excludes, offenders. The benefit of this inclusiveness is an improved reintegration of offenders, one in which communities accept the premise that ex-offenders can be returned to the mainstream and that it is desirable to do so. In Chapter 15, Dirk van Zyl Smit presents the case of the civil disabilities of former prisoners in South Africa. A prominent feature of the apartheid era was the systematic legal exclusion of segments of the population from participation in civil society. Van Zyl Smit points out that, with the demise of apartheid, many of old legal disabilities remain intact. The fundamental basis for change and the improvement of conditions for ex-prisoners, however, is the South African Constitution, which provides the legal means for former prisoners to assert rights. Again we see reform efforts cast not in piecemeal fashion but in an overarching declaration of human rights. Without overtaxing a comparison with the current situation in the United States, one can see the lessons of South Africa's past as foreboding or its future as promising.

1

Collateral Civil Penalties as Techniques of Social Policy

CHRISTOPHER MELE AND TERESA A. MILLER

In this chapter, we describe first the ways in which collateral civil penalties were originally conceived as "disabilities" and how scholars have since examined their unstated purpose as an extension of punishment, their seemingly official invisibility, and their unfairness toward individuals who suffer under them. Following, we put forward a more sociological approach in which we examine penalties as techniques deployed as part of a default social policy that has evolved from the demise of the social welfare state and the rise of carceral regulation of the poor. This perspective informs our understanding of the more recent penalties linked to the Wars on Drugs and Terror, to which most of the authors in this volume refer. Finally, we address the limitations and possibilities of efforts to reform or undo collateral civil penalties in the United States and abroad.

From Civil Disabilities to Collateral Civil Penalties

In their original conception, collateral civil penalties served limited, focused purposes. The older term, *civil disabilities,* broadly referred to civil sanctions that denied certain categories of people, including ex-felons, participation in certain activities that define civic life, such as voting, holding public office, or serving on juries. Although sanctions presented obstacles to individuals attempting to reenter civil society, most were acknowledged as a "deserved" consequence of and as proportional in severity to an individual's breach of

9

the social contract. Other disabilities were largely precautionary measures, employed to protect the public from the possibility of ex-felons further breaching laws. These penalties tended to be explicitly connected to the original criminal culpability of the offender. Hence, individuals who committed crimes linked to their professions were denied the licenses to resume practice. Most states continue to revoke licenses for a number of occupations and businesses for persons convicted of certain categories of felonies. Attorneys, for example, are automatically disbarred for felony convictions in New York and several other states (Morvillo 1999). The Securities and Exchange Commission routinely revokes the registrations of investment advisors, brokers, and other securities industry personnel who have been convicted of securities violations. Physicians, accountants, and other licensed professionals, may have their licenses revoked at the state level (Morvillo 1999). In some states, public employment is denied to convicted felons (Olivares, Burton, and Cullen 1996).

The idea of civil sanctions as simply "disabilities" became unsustainable in light of drastic changes in the social welfare and criminal justice policies enacted since the late 1970s. The shift toward penal management of poor, mostly minority and immigrant populations and the concomitant criminal justice policies emanating from the Wars on Drugs and Terror since the early 1980s have brought historically unprecedented numbers of persons in contact with the U.S. criminal justice system.[1] In addition, legislation linked to the Wars on Drugs and Terror have put into practice new and harsher collateral civil penalties that are grossly disproportionate and noticeably disconnected from the felony crimes committed (as discussed later in this chapter). These developments have prompted legal scholars, criminal justice scholars, activists, and social service practitioners to reconsider the more benign "disabilities" as civil penalties with collateral consequences. This conceptual shift is reflected in more recent analyses of the punitive aspects of collateral civil penalties for individuals, their seeming "invisibility" at various stages of the criminal justice process, and the lamentable consequences of these penalties for poor, mostly minority individuals.[2]

The proportional relationship between the type of felony and the severity of civil disability that follows has always been tenuous at best.[3] Disenfranchisement is a prime example of disproportionality between the crime and the civil sanction. The growth of mass incarceration and the highly contested U.S. presidential election in 2000 have made this fact even more apparent to scholars, activists, and practitioners. The traditional rationale for disenfranchisement, such as fear of ex-felons corrupting the "purity of the ballot box" through electoral fraud or the questionable moral probity of felons as jurors, has always been specious.[4] The state-by-state proscriptions against the ex-felon vote challenge the legitimizing principle that disabilities are proportionally linked to the types of crimes committed. As a practical matter, mass incarceration has made the issue of felony disenfranchisement more salient and visible, affecting election outcomes and electoral representation of particular communities and not simply the constitutional rights of individuals (see Chapter 4).

When certain collateral civil penalties bear little or no relation to a criminal act either in kind or severity, it is no longer tenable to consider them simply civil consequences of criminal conviction. In the current period, multiple and compounding collateral civil penalties—denial of welfare benefits, federal student aid, and subsidized housing, among others— follow conviction for certain kinds of felonies, such as drug possession or sales. They function to continue *criminal* punishment (already heightened by federal sentencing guidelines and mandatory sentencing requirements) in *civil* form. In their penal function, collateral civil *penalties*, as opposed to *disabilities*, blur the boundaries between criminal law (required to abide defendants' constitutional procedural rights and traditionally concerned with individualized justice) and civil law (regulatory, administrative, and procedural) (Klein 1999). In the case of noncitizen criminal offenders, for example, the use of the government's deportation power (construed however dubiously as a civil sanction) to banish a noncitizen criminal offender from the United States by virtue of an "aggravated felony" or other criminal offenses, wholly avoids constitutional procedural protections that would otherwise be triggered if the criminal alien were a U.S. citizen. Even civil restrictions on professional employment licensing are increasingly disproportionate to the felony crime to which they are attached. In many states, licenses are required for automobile dealers, private security guards, boat pilots, stock salespersons, bail bondsmen, barbers and cosmetologists, nurses, midwives, embalmers, dental hygienists, social workers, and food inspectors, among many others (see, for example, Walter 1994). Civil licensing restrictions can effectively obstruct ex-felons from employment in a number of these professions.

Sociolegal and criminal justice scholars, as well as legal advocates and service providers, have also raised questions of individual justice and fairness regarding the expansive use of civil collateral penalties. In the criminal justice literature, collateral civil penalties are viewed as yet another barrier to successful reintegration of ex-prisoners and as a likely contributing factor to high recidivism rates among ex-offenders. Legal scholars have tended to focus on the manner in which these penalties abridge constitutional rights, which are inherently limited to individuals (and not groups at large). Advocates for legal reform have called for standardized procedures to notify criminal defendants of collateral civil penalties and their consequences in plea negotiations and deals (ABA Criminal Justice Standards 2002).

Other individual remedies include efforts to expunge criminal records, seek clemency, and obtain pardons on a case-by-case basis.

Another thread in the legal studies literature concerns itself with the concealed character of collateral civil penalties, of which there are several different aspects (Mauer and Chesney-Lind 2002; Travis 2002). First, judges, prosecutors, and defense attorneys are not required to inform defendants of collateral penalties and their consequences in criminal proceedings (as discussed more fully in the chapter by Ferster and Aroca).[5] As a result, the accused are often unaware of penalties and the harsh consequences to which they become subject after conviction. Second, these penalties tend to "kick in" automatically and without formal notice, often after criminal punishment. As such, they undermine the principle that an individual's debt to society is paid upon completion of his sentence.[6] Third, collateral civil penalties are enacted in civil legislation, rather than the more high-profile criminal sentencing legislation (such as mandatory minimum sentences, "three strikes" laws, and federal sentencing guidelines) with its pronounced emphasis on punishment. Penalties tend to be enacted with limited public knowledge and virtually no public debate, thus enhancing their "invisibility." Fourth, the forms that penalties take vary significantly from state-to-state (as statutes, regulations, administrative rules, court decisions, etc.). Consequently, a key policy motive of this scholarship is to require full disclosure of collateral civil penalties in criminal proceedings. Another notable research and policy focus is the substantial legal inconsistency across jurisdictions regarding the individuals to whom such penalties may apply and for how long (Kuzma 1998; Olivares, Burton, and Cullen 1996). Efforts to catalog the wide range of collateral civil penalties at both the state and federal levels expose the urgent need for reform of criminal plea bargaining and sentencing procedures (ABA Criminal Justice Standards 2002).

Seeing Collateral Civil Penalties at Work

It should be noted that the apparent invisibility of collateral civil penalties can be partly attributed to the top-down analytical approaches (most) legal scholars have taken to date. Top-down, predominantly legalistic approaches necessarily emphasize the formal distinctions within the binaries of civil/criminal, legal sanction/social consequence, and citizen/noncitizen, in which the former (i.e., civil, legal sanction, and citizen) are analytically privileged over the latter in the pairings. While imperative, such approaches, alone, cannot capture how collateral civil penalties "adhere" to individuals, families, and communities, and that their consequences are neither *ad hoc* nor willy-nilly, but systematic and targeted.

Increasingly, scholars and practitioners (including many whose writings appear in this volume) have addressed this topic from different angles, expanding the scope of inquiry to see penalties "at work" in the homes, neighborhoods, and communities of the growing numbers of persons who come in contact with the criminal justice system. These newer approaches track the implementation of collateral civil penalties and catalog their effects at the ground level, where they are made meaningful to everyday experiences of exclusion from employment, housing, social services, federal financial aid, and banishment from civil society and, for some, the nation's borders. Indeed, it is no longer feasible to address collateral civil penalties from an exclusively formal, legal, top-down perspective; the contemporary realities of mass incarceration and the release of thousands of prisoners each year, which disproportionately involve certain populations, require grounded, interdisciplinary approaches.

It is no accident that legal rights advocates, practitioners, and social service providers were among the first to address the crucial social, political, and economic ramifications of collateral civil penalties for families and entire communities. At least 95% of all prisoners in state facilities will be released from prison at some point (BJS 2003). The demographic scope of the rhetoric and policies associated with the Wars on Drugs and Terror is clearly narrow and sharply focused. Between 1984 and 1999, for example, the number of defendants charged with a drug offense in federal courts increased from 11,854 to 29,306 (BJS 2002). Poor women of color, many of whom are heads of households, have been the target of severe drug-related criminal and civil laws and regulations enacted since the 1980s. Incarceration rates for women of color increased exponentially in the 1980s and 1990s (Goldfarb 2002; Mauer 1999:125). As a result, large numbers are being released from prisons only to encounter substantial impediments to their ability to find work, receive public benefits, secure housing, and have their parental rights recognized (see the chapter by Hirsch and the one by Franklin). As a comprehensive report issued by the Center for Law and Social Policy documents, individuals—particularly women of color—who have served prison time for certain (mostly drug-related) felonies face multiple and compounding collateral civil penalties with devastating consequences to family unification and stability (CLASP 2002). Others, such as Hagan and Dinovitzer (1999) and Hagan and Coleman (2001) have addressed the unprecedented numbers of ex-offenders who are reentering communities and the challenges collateral civil penalties pose to family life.

There is a clustering of collateral penalties and their consequences among poor, mostly minority, populations in core, inner-city communities, where the War on Drugs has been most focused and concentrated.

Hence, entire communities, not only individuals and families, are implicated directly and indirectly in an expansive criminal justice system. Released prisoners are concentrated in states with large prison populations: California, New York, Texas, Florida, and Illinois accounted for nearly half of all releases from state prisons in 2000 (BJS 2002). Within these states, returnees are concentrated in mostly impoverished neighborhoods within cities (Lynch and Sabol 2001: 16; Clear, Rose, and Ryder 2001). Given that the massive prison population generated by the War on Drugs is disproportionately drawn from these communities, the problems associated with the return of ex-offenders are amplified when collateral civil penalties are imposed (Travis, Solomon, and Waul 2001; Clear, Rose, and Ryder 2001; Lynch and Sabol 2001). Civil penalties negatively affect reintegration and contribute to high recidivism rates *at the community level* (Petersilia 2003; Travis and Petersilia 2001).

From angles other than atop, therefore, collateral civil penalties are quite visible in their implementation and in their effects: penalties affect poor, mostly minority populations who encounter them as yet another obstacle to basic necessities and participation in civil society. Ground-level approaches suggest that collateral civil penalties heighten and amplify many of the existing obstacles to securing housing and employment and to family reunification that an ex-offender faces. In the following section, we argue that this systematic and focused deployment of collateral civil penalties serves to regulate and manage the everyday lives of ex-offenders, their families, and communities.

Collateral Civil Penalties and Social Policy

The chapters in this volume document the range of more recent and severe collateral civil penalties that were mostly enacted or strengthened in the 1980s and 1990s and have increasingly affected the families and communities of ex-offenders (and not the ex-offenders or people directly supervised by the criminal justice system, exclusively). In this section, we take the position that these penalties constitute a set of techniques used to manage, regulate, and isolate poor, mostly minority urban communities. We initially describe the recent drift in policy toward the urban poor, highlighted by the dismantling of social welfare and the intensification of criminal justice supervision and management as the foundation of social policy. We then discuss how this deliberate drift toward a carceral administration of the poor is enshrined in recent social policies—particularly drug and security policies—that affect mostly minority, disadvantaged, or at-risk populations. Finally, we enumerate the ways in which collateral civil penalties function as effective techniques for management and social control.

Penal-Welfare Arrangements
The expansion of collateral civil penalties and the reinforcement of existing ones since the 1980s are best understood within the framework of governance and social policy toward the poor and disadvantaged.

> . . . both "penal" and "welfare" modalities have changed their meaning. The penal mode, as well as becoming more prominent, has become more punitive, more expressive, more security-minded. . . . The welfare mode, as well as becoming more muted, has become more conditional, more offence-centered, more risk conscious (Garland 2001: 175).

Systems of criminal justice and social welfare have been historically intertwined—in what David Garland (2001: 28) has termed the "penal-welfare arrangement"—for the purposes of governance of the poor. In the early-twentieth century, social welfare reforms were gradually implemented partly in response to the rapid growth of impoverished, so-called dangerous classes. The state expanded its obligations beyond punishment and control of the poor to include efforts at social reform and welfare as well (Garland 2001: 39). New Deal–era programs for the regulation of the poor, from Work Relief to Social Security, became progressively institutionalized in the post–World War II social welfare state. Civil Rights–era legislation removed some of the egregious formal barriers to racial equality and full citizenship, leading to desegregation (particularly of schools and public spaces). Antidiscrimination legislation facilitated class mobility for many Blacks, for example, yet the urban ghetto remained a space of class containment for mostly poor minorities. The War on Poverty arguably may have been the apogee of social welfare in the United States, given its considerable successes in areas of education, job training, and childhood poverty. Yet these gains and others have been downplayed in an unflappable revisionist critique in which the urban crisis, crime, and social disorder are touted as evidence of the failures of both the criminal justice system and the welfare state.

The root causes of the drift toward the more penal and away from the welfare side of the arrangement are many and complex and have been documented at length elsewhere (Garland 2001 and 2001a; Wacquant 2001; Beckett and Western 2001). Urban labor markets have undergone dramatic restructuring since the 1970s, with low-wage part-time employment replacing semiskilled unionized manufacturing jobs (Massey and Denton 1993; Wilson 1997). Urban political and fiscal crises accompanied the decline of decently paying jobs, further segregating and isolating mostly minority groups in impoverished enclaves within cities. Federal, state, and local governments, embroiled in their own financial crises and under the increasing control of conservative politicians, declined to bail out cities and further enhanced the economic and social insecurity of their disadvantaged residents. Instead, the state embarked on the long trek to dismantle social welfare through a volatile mix of legislation and rhetoric. Federal spending on workforce education and job training for low-income people was drastically slashed in the 1980s and has not been anywhere near restored (Katz 1989); the federal curtailment of welfare funds, income benefits, and child welfare services has been steady over time.

In conjunction with the retrenchment of social welfare came the systematic expansion of criminal justice remedies to the intractable social problems plaguing cities. Whereas this expansion and its correlate of mass incarceration have been covered exhaustively by scholars from many disciplines, it is important to note here a few key points relevant to changes in how the urban poor came to be regulated and governed. In the wake of diminished social welfare programs, aggressive policing practices and the increased severity in the length of prison sentences and conditions of confinement have formed the basis for social policy bent on order-maintenance (Websdale 2001; Harcourt 2001). The warehousing of particular populations emerged as a strategic solution to the complex web of social and economic problems that afflict cities in particular (Mauer 1999). Loic Wacquant has convincingly noted the parallel between the prison and the urban ghetto in the era of mass incarceration, pointing out the porous boundaries and the increasing social and cultural similarities between the two (Wacquant 2001 and 2002). Prisons and ghettos have become more alike, not only in terms of nearly identical cohorts of inhabitants but also in the techniques of social control, denial of individual rights, and expansive surveillance. Both systems function to regulate the conduct of the urban, mostly minority poor, and incarceration, in particular, has taken on an "extra-penalogical" function that was once the domain of social welfare (Wacquant 2001).

Jonathan Simon and other proponents of what has become known as the *new penology* characterize the shift toward heightened punitiveness within the criminal justice system and the retreat from social welfare–based modalities as a *severity revolution,* contrasting starkly with the humanity revolution out of which the idea of rehabilitation emerged in the late-nineteenth century (Simon 2001). The severity revolution marks a fundamental transformation in the discourse, objectives, and techniques of criminal justice, leading to contemporary penal practices that view crime as a problem of managing high-risk categories and subpopulations (Feeley and Simon 1992). In contrast to the traditional discourse of individualized justice and personal transformation, criminal justice professionals now speak in terms of managing risk. The objectives of criminal justice have moved away from the rehabilitative ideal that once dominated the penal system toward the goal of managing high-risk subjects by containing and incapacitating them. The rehabilitative ideal was abandoned, and managerialism was embraced, as the public, inundated with crime discourse sanctioned by government and mass media, came to perceive the persistence of Black and Latino urban poverty (and criminal recidivism) both as relentless and as an indictment of a penal system premised upon personal transformation (Simon 1998).

Techniques, such as surveillance and containment, are grounded in the assumption that maintaining order among high-risk populations outweighs any deleterious consequences to individual constitutional rights or collective forms of social justice. Simon noted that the abandonment of transformational goals led to the displacement of evaluative norms rooted in real communities. In contrast to the old penal-welfare arrangement in which criminal justice decision makers (probation officers, parole officers, sentencing judges) were attuned to signals from members of the criminal offender's community with a stake in his past or future conduct (e.g., people in a position to either fear or control the offender), the operational parameters of the new managerial system are largely self-referencing (Simon 1998). The new managerialism takes its cues from internally generated measures such as drug tests and compliance with a technocratic web of administrative rules seemingly designed not to promote the reintegration of the ex-offender, but to frustrate her ability to stay out of prison (and, therefore, remove herself from the stigmatized category of "managed population").

Drug and Security Policies
The penal-focused, risk-conscious approach to social policy toward the poor has reached its apex in the Wars on Drugs and Terror, and most of the chapters in this volume focus on the recent, more severe collateral civil penalties that flow from drug and security policies.[7] Some of the harshest penalties emerged from the Anti-Drug Abuse Act of 1988.[8] The severity and sheer magnitude of collateral civil penalties that attach to nonviolent drug convictions exceeds that of any other category of crime (see Chapter 2), even crimes of violence such as murder, rape, and kidnapping (Demleitner 2002: 1033). The act created a host of grave consequences. It mandated the detention and deportation of non-U.S. citizens convicted of "aggravated felonies," and limited avenues of relief from these consequences that were traditionally available (see Chapter 11).[9] It authorized federal and state court judges to deny all or selected federal benefits to individuals convicted of drug possession or distribution (Musser 2000: 1). Another provision of the act created what has since become known as the *one strike* policy,

mandating that public housing authorities evict tenants whose household members or guests (or other persons under their control) engage in drug-related criminal activity (see Chapter 8).

The Anti-Drug Abuse Act's theme of civilly punishing individuals convicted of drug crimes was broadly embraced by subsequent civil legislation regulating aspects of civil society as diverse as education, parenting, and the receipt of welfare benefits. Under welfare reforms enacted in 1996, individuals with a felony conviction involving the possession, use, or distribution of a controlled substance became permanently banned from receiving welfare benefits, such as cash assistance and food stamps.[10] According to the Sentencing Project, the ban on Temporary Aid to Needy Families (TANF) assistance exacerbates poverty conditions for about 92,000 women, 70% of whom are mothers (Allard 2002). In 1998, Congress amended the Higher Education Act of 1965 to deny any student with a past conviction involving the possession of sale of a controlled substance eligibility from grants, loans, or work-study funds for a specified period of time ranging from one year to indefinitely (Musser 2000: 7). Not surprisingly, the penalty primarily affects low-income students and has little effect on individuals with the means to pay college tuition without financial aid.

Even where civil penalties are not triggered by a drug conviction per se, legislation passed within the Drug War's "get tough" era often restricts ex-offenders' basic abilities to maintain a family, earn a living, and put a roof over their heads (see Chapter 7). The 1997 Adoption and Safe Families Act (ASFA) modified existing child welfare law ostensibly to improve the welfare of foster children who languished in the system while the state made "reasonable efforts" to reunite these children with their parents (see Chapter 6). Eleven percent of the women incarcerated in the United States are forced to hand their children over to the foster care system. By drastically reducing the amount of time for reunification, and by mandating that states terminate the parental rights of a parent whose child has been in foster care for 15 or more of the last 22 months, ASFA virtually ensures that women sentenced to the lengthy terms required by mandatory minimum sentencing laws will permanently lose their children. The average term served by all women who are incarcerated is 18 months (Travis, Solomon and Waul 2001: 40). Furthermore, public housing laws require that public housing agencies and providers of Section 8 (and other federally assisted) housing deny housing to convicted sex offenders subject to sex offender registration, and permit such agencies and providers to deny housing to individuals with drug-related convictions, convictions for crimes of violence, or other crimes (Legal Action Center Fact Sheet, 2000). Housing authorities and private landlords who participate in subsidized housing programs, such as Section 8, have the right to obtain the criminal records of all tenants and applicants (Travis, Solomon, and Waul 2001: 35).

Collateral civil penalties matured as techniques of management and social control under the War on Drugs. New penalties were legislated—and, more importantly, deployed—without obvious and proportional connection to the felonies to which they are tied. In the short term, penalties proved useful as civil measures to contain and manage segments of the urban poor alongside mass incarceration. Their utility as social management techniques has been further tested in the recent flurry of security policies stemming from the War on Terror (see Chapters 3 and 10).

Collateral civil penalties are undoubtedly linked to the War on Terror; but not because Congress passed a flurry of legislation after the attacks on the Twin Towers and the Pentagon, imposing collateral penalties on convicted terrorists. To the contrary, immigration legislation passed years before the attacks embraced the criminal justice system's severe treatment of drug offenders and the poor. As the criminal justice system created punishments that got tough on *all* convicted drug offenders, immigration law adopted harsh consequences for those convicted drug offenders who were not U.S. citizens. Under immigration reforms enacted in 1996, these so-called "criminal aliens" could be detained and deported (many retroactively), and denied relief from detention and deportation based upon individual mitigating circumstances. And because these harsh measures were characterized by courts as regulatory, rather than punitive, the U.S. Constitution did not stand in the way.

In the years between 1996 and 2001, the immigration system bought into the severity revolution that was occurring within the criminal justice system. Some describe it as the "criminalization" of immigration law, while others describe it as a convergence between the criminal justice and deportation systems (Kanstroom 2000). Either way, the two systems interacted in a manner that produced outcomes that were unprecedented (even unintentional at times) in their harshness. For example, criminal sentencing enhancements for past offenses combined with immigration law's enhanced "aggravated felony" designation to mandate the detention and deportation of non-U.S. citizens with mere misdemeanor convictions on their criminal records. These outcomes helped to advance not only the War on Drugs—a crime-fighting agenda—but the reform of the welfare state as well—a social reform agenda.

The most significant immigration reforms enacted by Congress during this era dramatically enhanced collateral civil penalties pertaining to non-U.S. citizens. Two major immigration laws enacted in 1996—the Anti-Terrorism and Effective Death Penalty Act (AEDPA) and the Illegal

Immigration Reform and Immigrant Responsibility Act (IIRAIRA)—subjected non-U.S. citizens with criminal convictions prior to the enactment of the legislation to mandatory detention and deportation without the traditional avenues of relief previously available for detainable and deportable aliens. Previously, only limited categories of serious felony convictions subjected non-U.S. citizens to detention and deportation (e.g., murder, drug trafficking, and firearms trafficking). However, the 1996 legislation greatly expanded the litany of crimes subjecting foreigners to detention and deportation. Now a misdemeanor conviction of at least one year for a crime as minor as a first-time shoplifting conviction subjects a non-US citizen to detention and deportation. This expansion of the types of crimes mandating detention and deportation applied to all categories of non-U.S. citizens, including lawful permanent residents (or "green card holders") long privileged as aliens on the fast track to citizenship. It also applied retroactively so that noncitizens convicted of crimes that would not subject them to deportation before 1996 faced deportation if the crime became (re)classified as an "aggravated felony" under AEDPA and IIRIRA.

By the time the tragic events of 9/11, 2001 occurred, immigration law had already enhanced the collateral civil penalties for noncitizens convicted of crimes in the United States. The nation's urgent response to terrorism capitalized on immigration law's utility as a mechanism for crime control and social control to confront the "hypercrime" of terrorism. Indeed, the scope of the War on Terrorism has been expanded to include incarcerating and removing noncitizens with past criminal offenses. For example, the Department of Homeland Security (DHS) initiated Operation Predator in July 2003 to apprehend and purge from the nation's borders noncitizens with past sex offenses. By November 2003, Immigration and Customs Enforcement had made 1,300 arrests. Asa Hutchinson, a high-ranking DHS official commented that taking these ex-offenders off the streets made America safer, and the arrests represented "the broad mission that has to be carried out in the Department of Homeland Security." He further commented that the detention of these ex-offenders was facilitated by the grouping of government resources under the umbrella of homeland security.

Collateral Civil Penalties as Techniques of Management and Control
Collateral civil penalties broaden and extend social regulation emanating from the criminal justice system to poor, minority populations *as a whole,* and the civil statutes directly reference eligibility and ineligibility for social welfare benefits. The focus on the management of populations blurs otherwise important distinctions between the innocent, the accused, and the convicted and between the individual (accused, convicted) and the collective

(implicated) in a modern criminal justice system. Civil collateral penalties constitute a strategy of regulation and control in conjunction with the criminal justice system, through the civil extension of punishment beyond time of incarceration and, by further extension, to larger numbers of persons (families, friends, and neighbors) not directly under the supervision of the criminal justice system.

Hence, collateral civil penalties further connect and simultaneously expand the coherent collaboration of an expanded criminal justice system, civil laws, and statutes and shrinking social welfare into a new social policy—not articulated as such but acting as default urban policy bent on management, regulation, and social control of disadvantaged and undesirable groups. Civil penalties redefine the status "offender" to apply beyond the prison (and the purview of the criminal justice system) to include civil society and beyond the sentence to a permanent condition. As we have mentioned, the consequences of civil penalties also reach far beyond individuals who have come into direct contact with the criminal justice system to include their families and communities. The use of civil measures as a means of social control is effective because a larger portion of the population is *administratively* targeted in the construction and enforcement of the sanctions themselves. As such, the extension of collateral civil penalties is a legal element of the state's replacement of social-welfare treatment of poverty with penal management. Civil penalties act in tandem with the twin processes of social welfare contraction and mass incarceration which have vilified poor, mostly urban communities (see Wacquant 2001).

The enactment of collateral civil penalties also directly involves institutions *unrelated to criminal justice* in the management and social control of targeted populations. These include private and governmental employers, private landlords and local public housing authorities, immigration authorities, adoption agencies, and colleges and universities. All become complicit in the denial of eligibility of persons (and, by extension, their families if head of household) based on their criminal records, as dictated by the civil penalties. Federal and state governments readily share conviction records and other information with these institutions for the purpose of enforcing collateral civil penalties (background checks, credit reports, immigration status, etc.), further implicating them into the expanded criminal justice–diminished social welfare–civil law triad of social control. Collateral penalties add to the pervasiveness of control of vulnerable populations by enlisting nonwelfare and nonpenal institutions in social regulation and management. In addition, there is enhanced cooperation among public institutions (the FBI and DHS or the FBI and HUD).

Collateral civil penalties are also an effective tool of social control because they compel individuals and families to modify a much wider range of behaviors than simple compliance with criminal laws. The chapter by Staples and the one by Mele show how even the most mundane everyday practices of entire families—answering the telephone, inviting a friend for a visit—become implicated in the enforcement of penalties ostensibly aimed at individuals. Taken together (or more precisely, experienced together, as they often are by affected individuals and their families), employment, education, social welfare, and housing sanctions, among others, compel disadvantaged populations to take certain jobs and not others, to live in particular neighborhoods and types of homes and not others, to work rather than attend school, and to rely on families and charities for emergency assistance rather than the government. Neither mass imprisonment nor diminished social welfare alone or together can accomplish a similar degree of control. Primarily because they appear invisible to all but those affected, collateral civil penalties can dramatically alter and shape the political, social, and economic conditions of the mostly minority and poor persons they affect. This further intensifies residential geographical exclusion and marginalization of employment opportunities.

Possibilities and Limits of Reform

The recent increase in the number and kinds of collateral civil penalties marks the end of societal responsibilities to (re)integrate offenders as full citizens (native or naturalized) with full rights and responsibilities. Rather, collateral civil penalties function as a means to control risk behavior and to reduce the exposure of the "general population" (the so-called law-abiding citizenry) to ex-offenders. Part of social control is a process of "othering," as certain populations are systematically denied access to full participation in civil society and labeled with pariah status. This departure within criminal justice systems is not necessarily apparent in other "Western-model" nations in Europe and Canada, or former colonial states, such as South Africa (see Chapters 14 and 15).

In the United States, there have been some notable recent reversals in the overall trend in which collateral civil penalties pose as social policy toward the poor. As of June 2004, 17 states exercised their ability to opt out of the lifetime ban on cash assistance and food stamps for individuals with felony drug convictions. Welfare departments may no longer deny benefits on the basis of a drug felony conviction alone and are required to refer persons to drug and alcohol treatment if appropriate and available. Reentry courts, modeled on drug courts, are being introduced in a limited number of state courts with select groups of offenders. These courts have the potential to reduce some of the harm collateral civil penalties impose on ex-offenders by coordinating the delivery of services to released offenders. They also call for prison staff, parole officers, and court officers to evaluate and address the myriad needs of recent ex-offenders in their communities.

Piecemeal legal reforms that occur mostly at the state level are important because their impact upon individuals is most likely to be felt within their local communities. Yet a comprehensive, more meaningful reform requires politicians, activists, and academics alike first to adopt a more holistic, systemic view of collateral penalties and their consequences as put forth in this volume. Seeing how collateral penalties affect communities as well as individuals leads to an equally broad reform focus in which questions of social justice are addressed.

Although constituted as civil, the penalties arguably affect rights (housing, employment, use of public space) rather than entitlements. In her chapter in this volume, Patricia Allard calls for rights-centered reform efforts, which define the effects of collateral penalties as a violation of human dignity. From there, she argues that a discourse of rights needs to be fully asserted and that current civil penalties violate basic human rights by constructing shelter, employment, and social participation as privileges of an increasingly smaller part of society.

Efforts to implement a rights-based agenda for the reform of collateral civil penalties and their social effects face daunting challenges. Rights-based reform requires individuals, communities, and institutions to accept the premise that ex-offenders and, by extension, their families are *peers with rights* and should, in principle, be welcomed back as full participants in civil society. Such a dramatic change in mindset rests on an undoing of decades of a political rhetoric of social exclusion aimed at larger numbers of disadvantaged persons.

References

ABA Criminal Justice Standards. 2002. "ABA Criminal Justice Standards on Collateral Sanctions and Disqualification of Convicted Persons." Third edition.

Allard, Patrica. 2002. "Life Sentences: Denying Welfare Benefits to Women Convicted of Drug Offenses." Washington, D.C.: The Sentencing Project.

Beckett, Katherine and Bruce Western. 2001. "Governing Social Marginality: Welfare, Incarceration, and the Transformation of State Policy." *Punishment and Society* 3, 1: 43–59.

Bureau of Justice Statistics (BJS). 2002. "Federal Drug Offenders, 1999 with Trends, 1984–1999." www.ojp.usdoj.gov/bjs/.

Bureau of Justice Statistics (BJS). 2003. "Reentry Trends in the United States." www.ojp.usdoj.gov/bjs/.

Bureau of Justice Statistics (BJS). 2004. "Criminal Offender Statistics." www.ojp.usdoj.gov/bjs/.

Calmore, John O. 2001. "Race-Conscious Voting Rights and the New Demography in a Multiracing America." *North Carolina Law Review* 79: 1274–1280.

Center for Law and Social Policy (CLASP) 2002. "Every Door Closed: Barriers Facing Parents with Criminal Records." Washington, D.C.: The Center.

Clear, Todd R., Dina R. Rose, and Judith A. Ryder. 2001. "Incarceration and the Community: The Problem of Removing and Returning Offenders." *Crime and Delinquency* 47, 3: 335–351.

Currie, Elliot. 1998. *Crime and Punishment in America.* New York: Metropolitan Books; Henry Holt.

Demleitner, Nora. 2002. "Collateral Damage: No Reentry for Drug Offenders." *Villanova Law Review* 47: 1027–54.

Drug Policy Alliance. 2003. "New Jersey Leads Nation in Prison Admissions for Drugs, Says New Study Released Today." November 6. http://www.drugpolicy.org/news/pressroom/pressrelease/pr110603b.cfm.

Feeley, Malcolm and Jonathan Simon. 1992. "The New Penology: Notes on the Emerging Strategy of Corrections and it Implications." *Criminology* 30: 449–474.

Fellner, Jamie and Marc Mauer. 1998. *Losing the Vote: the Impact of Felony Disenfranchisment Laws in the United States.* Washington, D.C.: The Sentencing Project and Human Rights Watch.

Fletcher, George P. 1999. "Disenfranchisement as Punishment: Reflections on the Racial Uses of Infamia." *UCLA Law Review* 46: 1895.

Garland, David. 2001. *The Culture of Control: Crime and Social Order in Contemporary Society.* University of Chicago Press.

Garland, David. 2001a. "Introduction: The Meaning of Mass Imprisonment." *Punishment and Society* 3, 1: 5–7.

Goldfarb, Phyllis. 2002. "Counting the Drug War's Female Casualties." *The Journal of Gender, Race, and Justice* 6: 277.

Hagan, John and Ronit Dinovitzer. 1999. "Collateral Consequences of Imprisonment for Children, Communities, and Prisoners." In Michael Tonry and Joan Petersilia, Eds., *Prisons.* University of Chicago Press: 121–62.

Hagan, John and Juleigh Petty Coleman. 2001. "Returning Captives of the American War on Drugs: Issues of Community and Family Reentry." *Crime and Delinquency* 47, 3: 352–67.

Harcourt, Bernard. 2001. *Illusion of Order: The False Promise of Broken Windows Policing.* Harvard University Press.

Hench, Virginia. 1998. "The Death of Voting Rights: The Legal Disenfranchisement of Minority Voters." *Case Western Reserve Law Review* 48: 727.

Johnson, Robert M. A. 2001. "Collateral Consequences." *Criminal Justice* 16: 32.

Kanstroom, Daniel. 2000. "Deportation, Social Control and Punishment." *Harvard Law Review* 113: 1889.

Katz, Michael B. 1989. *The Undeserving Poor: From the War on Poverty to the War on Welfare.* New York: Pantheon Books.

Klein, Susan R. 1999. "Redrawing the Criminal-Civil Boundary." *Buffalo Criminal Law Review* 2: 679–721.

Kuzma, Susan M. 1998. "Civil Disabilities of Convicted Felons." *Corrections Today* 60, 4: 68–72.

Legal Action Center Fact Sheet, 2000. "Housing Laws Affecting Individuals with Criminal Convictions" New York: Legal Action Center:1-2, presented at The Enterprise Foundation's first annual "Ready, Work, Grow" National Workforce Conference, May 2000 in Baltimore, Maryland. http://www.enterprisefoundation.org/resources/ERD/resource.asp?id=1150&c=176&a=info&f=browse.

Lynch, James P. and William J. Sobol. 2001. "Prisoner Reentry in Perspective." Washington, D.C.: The Urban Institute.

Massey, Douglas S. and Nancy A. Denton. 1993. *American Apartheid: Segregation and the Making of the Underclass.* Harvard University Press.

Mauer, Marc. 1999. *Race to Incarcerate.* New York: New Press.

Mauer, Marc and Meda Chesney-Lind, Eds. 2002. *Invisible Punishment: The Collateral Consequences of Mass Imprisonment.* New York: New Press.

Morvillo, Robert G. 1999. "Consequences of Conviction." *New York Law Journal* 222, 110.

Musser, Robert W., Jr. 2000. "Denial of Federal Benefits to Drug Traffickers and Drug Possessors: A Broad-Reaching But Seldom Used Sanction." *Federal Sentencing Reporter* 12, 5: 1–7.

Olivares, Kathleen M., Velmer S. Burton, Jr., and Francis T. Cullen. 1996. "The Collateral Consequences of a Felony Conviction: A National Study of State Legal Codes ten Years Later." *Federal Probation* 60: 10–17.

Patillo, Mary, David Weiman, and Bruce Western (eds.). 2004. *Imprisoning America: The Social Effects of Mass Incarceration.* New York: Russell Sage

Parenti, Chrisian. 1999. *Lockdown America: Police and Prisons in the Age of Crisis.* Verso Books.

Petersilia, Joan 2003. *When Prisoners Come Home: Parole and Prisoner Reentry.* Oxford University Press.

Simon, Jonathan 1998. "Managing the Monstrous: Sex Offenders and the New Penology." *Psychology, Public Policy and Law* 4: 452–467.

Simon, Jonathan 2001. "Sanctioning Government: Explaining America's Severity Revolution." *University of Miami Law Review* 56.

Travis, Jeremy 2002. "Invisible Punishment: An Instrument of Social Exclusion." In Marc Mauer and Meda Chesney-Lind, Eds., *Invisible Punishment: The Collateral Consequences of Mass Imprisonment*. New York: New Press.

Travis, Jeremy and Joan Petersilia. 2001. "Reentry Reconsidered: A New Look at an Old Question." *Crime and Delinquency* 47, 3: 291–313.

Travis, Jeremy, Amy Solomon and Michel Waul. 2001. "From Prison to Home: The Dimensions and Consequences of Prisoner Reentry." Washington, D.C.: The Urban Institute.

Walter, Jeffrey T. 1994. "Validity and Application of Statute or Regulation Authorizing Revocation or Suspension of Driver's License for Reason Unrelated to Use of, or Ability to Operate, Motor Vehicle." *American Law Reports*, 5th Ed., 18: 542.

Wacquant, Loic. 2001. "Deadly Symbiosis: When Ghetto and Prison Meet and Mesh." *Punishment and Society* 3, 1: 95–134.

Wacquant, Loic 2002. "Four Strategies to Curb Carceral Costs: On Managing Mass Imprisonment in the United States." *Studies in Political Economy* 69: 19–41.

Websdale, Neil. 2001. *Policing the Poor: From Slave Plantation to Public Housing*. Boston: Northeastern University Press.

Western, Bruce and Katherine Beckett. 1999. "How Unregulated is the U.S. Labor Market? The Penal System as a Labor Market Institution." *American Journal of Sociology*, 104, 4: 1030–60.

Wilson, William J. 1997. *When Work Disappears: The World of the New Urban Poor*. New York: Knopf.

Endnotes

1. According to Bureau of Justice Statistics, as of December 31, 2001, there were an estimated 5.6 million adults who had served time in state or federal prison, including 4.3 million former prisoners and 1.3 million adults in prison. The percentage of the African-American male population incarcerated was 16.6%; for Hispanic males, 7.7%; and for white males, 2.6%. Among females, 1.7% of African-Americans, 0.7% of Hispanic, and 0.3% of whites were incarcerated (BJS 2004). See also Currie 1998; Parenti 1999; Patillo, Weiman and Western. 2004.

2. We choose to use the term *collateral civil penalties*, cognizant of the use of other terms. Some writers refer to these penalties as *civil disabilities*. This is an older term that harkens back to sanctions that historically denied married women and religious dissenters—in addition to ex-felons—from participating in society on par with their contemporaries. Other writers describe "disqualifications," focusing on rules that require offenders to desist from certain occupations and activities. Even when writers use the terms like *collateral sanction* and *civil disability* interchangeably, the more benign concept of disabling an ex-offender fails to capture the punitive dimension of laws, regulations, and policies that transform criminal offenders into social outcasts.

   Some writers use the terms *collateral penalties* and *collateral consequences* interchangeably. The distinctions between these terms are a bit tricky. To the extent that excluding ex-felons from important areas of civic and economic participation is seen as a consequence of a felony conviction, rather than a penalty, the same problem of emphasis exists. However, the penalties that obstruct an ex-offender's reintegration into social, economic, and political life are undoubtedly the "consequences" of a criminal conviction. Using the term *collateral consequences* also tends to address broadly the full range of effects of a criminal conviction without overly relying upon the formal legal category of collateral civil penalties. In other words, individuals released from prison experience obstacles to legitimate employment (for example) regardless of whether the employer is wary of hiring an ex-con or a regulation disqualifies him from hiring an ex-offender for the position. Thus, on one level, the difference between consequences and penalties is transparent to their subjects, and therefore unimportant.

3. The connection between certain felony convictions and restrictions on types of employment, for example, is questionable. A Drug Policy Alliance study of mass incarceration in New Jersey found that "there are 22 categories of jobs for which certain criminal convictions serve as an absolute bar to employment, including: bartenders and waiters in establishments where liquor is served, New Jersey Turnpike Authority employees and retail, and wholesale, manufacturing or distributing employees" (Drug Policy Alliance 2003).

4. Seeing the connection between disenfranchisement and race in terms of collateral civil penalties is one of many perspectives scholars have taken on this issue. See, inter alia, Fletcher 1999; Hench 1998; Fellner and Mauer 1999; and Calmore 2001.

5. Collateral civil penalties are another form of mandated sentence, but one that takes discretion away from judge *and prosecutor*. See Johnson 2001.

6. It is important to note that penalties may attach where the sentence is so light as to not involve incarceration (e.g., payment of fines, community service, probation, or a suspended sentence).

7. A third type of recent collateral civil penalty targets sex offenders and is exemplified by mandatory sex offender registration statutes. Many states now require persons convicted of certain felony offenses to register with a law enforcement agency. The federal passage of Meghan's Law requires states to adopt statutes for criminal registration and community notification of sex offenders. Given our interest in this volume is the immediate, direct, and tangible effects of collateral penalties on particular social groups, we do not include a discussion of sex offender registration penalties.

8. Pub. L. No. 100-690, 102 Stat. 4181 (1988).

9. Pub. L. No. 100-690, §7343(a)(4), 102 Stat. 4181,4470 (amending 8 U.S.C. §1252(a)(2) to provide for mandatory detention of criminal aliens). At the time, "aggravated felonies" were serious crimes involving murder, drug trafficking, trafficking in firearms or destructive devices, and any attempt or conspiracy to commit these crimes. ADAA §7342 (amending 8 U.S.C. §1101(a)).

10. The lifetime ban on welfare applies to all states unless a state legislature elects to either modify or opt out of the provision. As of June 2004, 17 states enforce the ban. Only 12 states have affirmatively opted out of the provision, and 21 states have modified it. "After Prison: Roadblocks to Reentry. A Report on State Legal Barriers Facing People with Criminal Records." (www.lac.org/lac/main.php?view=law&subaction=5).

2 [*]

Race, the War on Drugs, and the Collateral Consequences of Criminal Conviction

GABRIEL J. CHIN

One of the most important recent developments in the criminal justice system is the increasing imposition of sanctions for conviction "off-budget," covertly. These sanctions, often called *collateral consequences,* are not imposed explicitly as part of the sentencing process, but by legislative creation of penalties applicable by operation of law to persons convicted of particular crimes. Yet, collateral consequences may be the most significant penalties resulting from a criminal conviction.

Imagine, for example, an individual who possessed or sold a hard drug. Even in a tough-on-crime state, a first offender pleading guilty might receive a probationary sentence or a suspended term of incarceration.[1] Judges and prosecutors might not insist on incarceration in such a case, even though long sentences are authorized by statute, because actors in the trenches understand that low-level drug sellers are not cartel kingpins, but more typically users supporting their habits. Engaging in a consensual drug transaction is less reprehensible than robbery, rape, or murder. Thus, the formal sentence the individual receives at the plea might be insignificant.

[*]This chapter was originally published as "Race, the War on Drugs, and the Collateral Consequences of Criminal Conviction." *The Journal of Gender, Race and Justice,* 6, 2002: 253–76. It has been reproduced with the kind permission of the author and the Editors of the Journal.

The real sentence comes down like a ton of bricks in the form of a series of statutes denying convicted felons a variety of rights. The collateral sanctions begin with depriving them of the basic rights of membership in society: denying them the right to serve on juries or vote if they are citizens, and expelling them from the United States if they are not citizens. The sanctions also include deprivation of a wide variety of rights, benefits, and privileges.

The ton of bricks is invisible. Because these statutes are deemed "civil" and "regulatory," the individual need not be told by the court or defense counsel at plea and sentence of the full consequences of conviction. Even if the court or counsel wanted to explain, it would be very difficult to do so because laws imposing collateral consequences are dispersed in various codes, executive orders, and regulations. What is clear is that these collateral sanctions may make it impossible for convicted persons to be employed, to lead law-abiding lives, to complete probation, or to avoid recidivism.

Statutes imposing collateral consequences are formally race-neutral; they apply to any person regardless of race convicted of committing a particular offense. Yet, collateral sanctions are significant to the question of racial justice for several reasons. First, collateral consequences, such as felon disenfranchisement, were regularly used as a method of preventing African-Americans from voting during the Jim Crow era. Second, some categories of behavior, such as drug use, were criminalized in part because of their association with disfavored minority groups.

The tainted history of drug prosecutions and the use of collateral consequences as a technique of racial discrimination are troubling in the context of the modern criminal justice system. For all categories of crime, the best evidence of discriminatory prosecution exists for drug violations; although African-Americans are not more likely to commit drug crimes than are members of other races, they are much more likely to be arrested, prosecuted, convicted, and sentenced to prison. Moreover, drug crimes—rather than violent crimes or white-collar crimes—are associated with the greatest number and severity of collateral sanctions. The War on Drugs, then, is a new occasion for the employment of traditional techniques of discriminating against racial minorities.

The ultimate solution to the drug question is difficult, and this essay does not purport to address it as a whole.[2] Instead, it offers a modest reform. One central problem with collateral consequences is the unstructured and *ad hoc* manner in which they are identified and imposed. No one knows, actually, what they are—not legislators when they consider adding new ones, not judges when they impose sentence, not defense counsel when they advise clients charged with a crime, and not defendants when they plead guilty or are convicted of a crime and have no idea how their legal status has changed. Basic fairness requires first that collateral consequences be collected in one place, and second that persons charged with a crime be notified of what the consequences are when they plead guilty or are sentenced.

These simple changes would not directly remedy the deep racial disproportionality in the drug laws and their enforcement. On the other hand, bringing the concept of truth in sentencing to bear on collateral consequences would help individuals make decisions about whether to plead guilty or go to trial, and how to negotiate particular plea bargains. It would also help ensure that the laws are obeyed; individuals subject to legal requirements are more likely to obey them if they know what they are, yet some people pleading guilty or being sentenced will never hear about them. Fundamentally, legislatures that make decisions about sanctions to impose upon conviction might pause when they see what the penalties already are.

Collateral Consequences, Drug Regulation, and Jim Crow

Collateral consequences can be defined as penalties, disabilities, or disadvantages that occur automatically because of a criminal conviction, other than owing to the sentence itself.[3] Typical examples include disenfranchisement, loss of business or professional licenses, felon registration requirements, and ineligibility for public benefits. The varieties of collateral consequences are numerous and they are imposed by diverse sources of law. This essay focuses on disenfranchisement, particularly disenfranchisement resulting from drug convictions, because of its seriousness, pervasiveness, and the availability of evidence about the reasons for its adoption. Disenfranchisement is also important because the right to vote gives people the ability to influence the application of all other collateral consequences.

Section 2 of the Fourteenth Amendment attempted to protect African-American voting rights by reducing the representation in the House of Representatives of discriminating states.[4] Yet, Section 2 also recognized that disenfranchising convicts was permissible.[5] This raised the question of what the law required when states discriminated against African-Americans by providing for their disenfranchisement.

The historical record shows that criminal disenfranchisement was often adopted for discriminatory reasons. Until well into the middle of the twentieth century, racists felt it unnecessary to sugarcoat their views. Accordingly, the actual motivations of decision makers for various aspects of public policy are evident. Race-neutral felon disenfranchisement was an aspect of racial subordination in many parts of the South after Reconstruction. The Mississippi Constitutional Convention of 1890, which imposed a permanent disenfranchisement on those convicted of particular crimes that continues to this day, was described by the Mississippi Supreme Court in 1896 as follows:

> Within the field of permissible action under the limitations imposed by the federal constitution, the convention swept the circle of expedients to obstruct the exercise of the franchise by the negro race. By reason of its previous condition of servitude and dependence, this race had acquired or accentuated certain peculiarities of habit, of temperament, and of character, which clearly distinguished it as a race from that of the whites—a patient, docile people, but careless, landless, and migratory within narrow limits, without forethought, and its criminal members given rather to furtive offenses than to the robust crimes of the whites. Restrained by the federal constitution from discriminating against the negro race, the convention discriminated against its characteristics and the offenses to which its weaker members were prone. A voter who should move out of his election precinct, though only to an adjoining farm, was declared ineligible until his new residence should have continued for a year. Payment of taxes for two years at or before a date fixed many months anterior to an election is another requirement, and one well calculated to disqualify the careless. Burglary, theft, arson, and obtaining money under false pretenses were declared to be disqualifications, while robbery and murder and other crimes in which violence was the principal ingredient were not (*Ratliffe v. Beale* 1896).

Legal scholar Andrew Shapiro makes a compelling case that disenfranchisement by many other southern states was similarly motivated.[6] Indeed, in *Hunter v. Underwood* (1985), the Supreme Court unanimously held that Alabama's constitutional provision disenfranchising felons was unconstitutional because it was motivated by an intent "to establish white supremacy" (Hunter 1985: 229). A lawsuit pending in Florida makes the same argument with respect to that state's felon disenfranchisement provisions (*Johnson v. Bush* 2002).

Drug prohibition came about in the same period and for some of the same reasons. In America's first century, Americans were free to ingest what they liked because drugs were largely unregulated (Musto 1973). Although the full legal history of the creation of the drug laws has yet to be written, the decision to criminalize the use of drugs was driven in part by racial considerations. Yale professor David Musto, perhaps the best chronicler of the area, explained that "[i]n the nineteenth century addicts were identified with foreign groups and internal minorities who were already actively feared and the objects of elaborate and massive social and legal restraints" (Musto 1973: 5).

The most passionate support for legal prohibition of narcotics has been associated with the fear of a given drug's effect on a specific minority.

Certain drugs were dreaded because they seemed to undermine essential social restrictions that kept those groups under control; cocaine was supposed to enable blacks to withstand bullets that would kill normal persons and to stimulate sexual assault. Fear that smoking opium facilitated sexual contact between Chinese and white Americans was also a factor in its total prohibition. Chicanos in the Southwest were believed to be incited to violence by smoking marijuana. The occasion for legal prohibition of drugs for nonmedical purposes appears to come at a time of social crisis between the drug-linked group and the rest of American society. Public response to these minority-linked drugs differed radically from attitudes toward other drugs with similar potential for harm, such as the barbiturates (Musto 1973: 294–95).

Dr. Musto's view is well supported by the views before Congress when it enacted significant drug legislation. In the discussions that led to the Harrison Narcotics Act of 1914, many experts explained that the sexual integrity of the white race was imperiled by drug users. One testified as follows:

> In the Chinatown in the City of Philadelphia there are enormous quantities of opium consumed, and it is quite common, gentlemen, for these Chinese or "Chinks" as they are called, to have as a concubine a white woman. There is one particular house where I would say there are 20 white women living with Chinamen as their common-law wives. The Chinamen require these women to do no work, and they do nothing at all but smoke opium day and night. A great many of the girls are girls of family and the history of some of them is very pathetic. You will find those girls in their younger days went out with sporty boys, and they got to drinking. The next step was cigarettes. Then they go to the Chinese restaurants, and after they go there a couple of times and get a drink in them they want to "hit the pipe." They do it out of curiosity or pure devilishness. (Hearings Before the Committee on Ways and Means of the House of Representatives on the Importation and Use of Opium, 61st Cong. 11 [1910] ([testimony of Dr. Christopher Koch]).

African-Americans were also made dangerous by the use of drugs. An expert explained as follows:

> The colored race in the south, I have reason to believe, is very much perverted by cocaine. . . . A great many of the crimes that are committed in Pennsylvania (and from information received from other states, a great many of the crimes committed there as well) are traced directly to cocaine. . . . The colored people seem to have a weakness for it. It is a very seductive drug, and it produces

intense exhilaration. Persons under the influence of it have an exaggerated ego. They imagine they can lift this building if they want to, or can do anything they want to. They have no regard for right or wrong. It produces a kind of temporary insanity. They would just as soon rape a woman as anything else and a great many of the southern rape cases have been traced to cocaine. (Id. at 12.)

Hamilton Wright, the leading figure in drug control in the early Twentieth Century, reported as follows:

... cocaine is often the direct incentive to the crime of rape by the negroes of the South and other sections of the country; this problem required national regulation because the use of cocaine among the lower order of working Negroes is quite common. This class of Negro is not willing, as a rule, to go to much trouble or to send any distance for anything, and, for this reason, where he is known to have become debauched by cocaine, it is certain that the drug has been brought directly to him from New York and other Northern States where it is manufactured. (Message from the President of the United States on the Opium Problem, S. Doc. No. 61-377, at 49-50 [1910]).

Others agree that the history is tainted. For example, Professor Erik Luna concludes that drug regulation was the product of "functional racism," fueled by "racist drug propaganda" (Luna 1997: 493).

Contemporary Collateral Consequences

The history of drug policy and of collateral consequences reflects an unfortunate tendency to criminalize conduct thought to have been engaged in by minority groups, and to impose special punishments on those convicted of such crimes and not others. That tendency persists to this day. Of course, collateral consequences are not restricted to drug offenses. A person convicted of any felony will face severe collateral consequences. Felons lose many of the fundamental rights that are the hallmark of full citizenship. Felons cannot serve on federal juries, are disenfranchised in many states,[7] and are ineligible for the security clearance necessary for many jobs in government or with federal contractors. They may be imprisoned if they possess a firearm, and they cannot enlist in the military.

Congress created financial incentives for states to exclude those with criminal convictions from public housing and to enact sex-offender registration laws. The Adoption and Safe Families Act of 1997 prohibits individuals with certain criminal convictions from being approved as foster or adoptive parents. Yet, under current law, drug offenses are subjected to more and harsher collateral consequences than any other category of crime.

Those convicted of drug offenses are subject to a number of additional penalties. Federal law provides that as part of the criminal sentence for a drug offense, state judges as well as federal may deny "any or all" federal benefits to those convicted of drug possession or drug trafficking. "Federal benefits" include the issuance of any grant, contract, loan, professional license, or commercial license provided by an agency of the United States or by appropriated funds of the United States, but not earned retirement or health benefits. The Bureau of Justice Assistance lists more than 750 benefits potentially affected, including 162 by the Department of Education alone.[8]

If benefits are not removed as part of a sentence, they may be eliminated by other provisions of law that operate automatically.[9] Those convicted of felony distribution of a controlled substance are ineligible to participate in most federallyfunded health care programs; those with misdemeanor distribution convictions may be excluded in the discretion of the Secretary of Health and Human Services.

Those convicted of a state or federal felony involving distribution, possession, or use of a controlled substance are ineligible for Temporary Aid to Needy Families (TANF) and Food Stamps.[10] Persons convicted of a drug-related offense may not receive federal educational aid or the Hope Scholarship Credit. They are also ineligible for employment in certain federally regulated industries such as airlines.[11] Congress required states to revoke or suspend the driver's licenses of those convicted of drug felonies or suffer reduction of federal highway funds. Congress required public housing agencies and owners of federally subsidized housing to evict tenants if a member of the household is using a controlled substance or, in some cases, has used a controlled substance in the past.[12]

Deportation is a particularly significant collateral consequence imposed on noncitizens who are convicted of drug offenses. A noncitizen is deemed an "aggravated felon" if convicted of one or more of a number of crimes specified in the Immigration and Nationality Act. Aggravated felons are subject to removal with few if any grounds for relief or waiver. An odd feature of "aggravated felonies" is that they can be misdemeanors.[13] For example, "[i]llicit trafficking in a controlled substance" is an aggravated felony by statute, even if the conviction constitutes a misdemeanor under state law.[14] Another provision of the Immigration and Nationality Act makes deportable "[a]ny alien who at any time after admission has been convicted of a violation of . . . any law or regulation of a State, the United States, or a foreign country relating to controlled substances. . ." other than a single offense involving possession for one's own use of 30 grams or less of marijuana. Thus, any drug violation other than a minor marijuana offense can lead to deportation of a non-citizen.

The Supreme Court has recognized that being subject to enhanced or recidivist sentencing in a future prosecution is a collateral consequence of conviction (*Rutledge v. U.S.* 1996; *U.S. v. Morgan* 1954). The most severe forms of enhanced or recidivist sentencing are reserved for drug "dealers," those accused of manufacture, importation, or distribution of controlled substances, rather than mere possessors. The Federal Sentencing Guidelines define a "career offender" as a defendant over eighteen who is convicted of a violent crime or of a controlled substance offense, and who has two prior controlled substance offenses or violent convictions, or at least one of each (U.S. Sentencing Guidelines §4B1.1 2001). A "controlled substance offense" is a crime punishable by more than one year involving "manufacture, import, export, distribution or dispensing of a controlled substance" (U.S. Sentencing Guidelines §4B1.2(b) 2001). Drug convictions can even justify imposition of a death sentence. The federal death penalty statute deems it an aggravating factor if the defendant has two or more prior convictions for "State or Federal offenses punishable by a term of imprisonment of more than one year, committed on different occasions, involving the distribution of a controlled substance."[15]

None of this is to suggest that the imprisonment and fines imposed on convicted drug offenders are trivial. In 1998, 65% of those convicted of drug possession in state court and 71% of those convicted of trafficking were sentenced to incarceration (Durose 2001: 2). Yet the mean sentences were twelve months for possession and nineteen months for trafficking (Durose 2001: 4). Virtually all drug offenders convicted of crimes will return to society, where managing collateral consequences will be a continuing issue.

Racial Disparity in Drug Prosecutions
The raw numbers are shocking. At year-end 2000, over two million people were in prison, jail, or some other form of detention in the United States; of these, more than 1.3 million had been convicted of a crime and sentenced to a state or federal prison term, almost twice as many as had been imprisoned in 1990.[16] The prison population is not racially representative of the population as a whole. Although, according to the Census Bureau, African-Americans made up only 12.9% of the population in 2000, they were 46.2% of those incarcerated; the 12.5% of the population that was Latino or Hispanic made up 16.4% of the prison population (U.S. Department of Commerce 2001: 11).

Thus, 449 white males out of every 100,000 in the population were in custody pursuant to a sentence, compared with 1,220 out of every 100,000 Hispanic males and 3,457 of every 100,000 African-American males. The rates for women followed the same pattern; out of every 100,000 in the population, 205 African-American women, 60 Hispanic women, and 34 white women were imprisoned (U.S. Department of Commerce 2001: 11).

Collateral consequences, likewise, have substantial racially disparate effects. A study of felon disenfranchisement shows that 3.9 million adults are permanently disenfranchised, including 1.4 million African-American men. In ten states, one-fifth or more of African-American men are permanently disenfranchised (Fellner and Mauer 1998: 7–8). Of course, disparity in and of itself does not necessarily demonstrate discrimination. Michael Tonry offers an extremely accessible description of the best evidence about the explanation for the racial disparity (Tonry 1995: 49–80). Social scientists compare data on victim reports of the race of offenders with racial statistics regarding those arrested, convicted, and imprisoned to make rough estimates of disproportionality.[17] Although Professor Tonry acknowledges that "[o]fficial criminal justice records are at least as much an indicator of bureaucratic policies and officials' discretionary decisions as of criminal events" (Tonry 1995: 56), his review of the literature suggests that "most of the black punishment disproportions result not from racial bias or discrimination within the system but from patterns of black offending and of blacks' criminal records."[18] Tonry reports that there is a substantial although imperfect correlation between the races of offenders reported in victim surveys, and in the race of those arrested for particular categories of crimes. There is a reasonable correlation between the race of those arrested and those convicted, and the circumstances of the conviction and of the sentence. "Drug law enforcement is the conspicuous exception. Blacks are arrested and confined in numbers grossly out of line with their use or sale of drugs" (Tonry 1995: 49).

If drugs are the exception to the correlation between race and conviction, they are a big exception. About 25% of those in prison are incarcerated for drug offenses:64,904 out of 115,189 federal prisoners in 2001 (Bureau of Justice Statistics 2001) and 251,200 out of 1,189,800 state prisoners in 1999 (Beck and Harrison 2001: 11).

Although whites represent the vast majority of drug offenders, the races seem to have relatively similar appetites for illicit drugs. Although the specific substances the groups prefer vary, because of their size, whites are the largest users of every type of illicit drug, including "crack" cocaine. Yet whites seem less likely to be arrested; if arrested, less likely to be convicted; and if convicted, less likely to be imprisoned than members of other races. In 2000, over a million people were charged with drug crimes, 64.2% of them white, 34.5% of them African-American.[19] Yet, 53% of those convicted in state court for drug offenses in 1996 were African-American, and only 45% were white.[20] And 57.6% of those in state prison for drug offenses were African-American, 20.7% Hispanic, and only 20% white (Beck and Harrison 2001: 11).

Whites were disproportionately not prosecuted or acquitted and, even if convicted, disproportionately not sentenced to prison. Statistics for federal prosecutions, although less dramatic, show a similar effect: 67.2% of those arrested by federal authorities for drug offenses were white, 30.8% African-American (Sourcebook 2000: 399). 64.5% of those convicted in 1999 were white, and 33.3% were African-American (Sourcebook 2000: 427). 52.87% of those imprisoned were white, and 45.7% were African-American (Sourcebook 2000: 526).

Although the enormous disparity does not itself prove discrimination, it does call out for an explanation. Some have suggested that more African-Americans are serious or major drug offenders, more likely to be traffickers rather than mere possessors, for example, and that this explains the disparity. Yet for several reasons, the existence of a benign explanation seems doubtful. First, observers are entitled to be skeptical about the claim that there is a legitimate justification for the disparity when the government has made extra-ordinary efforts to resist disclosure of the actual reasons. Complying with the requests of the U.S. Department of Justice, the federal courts have made it quite difficult to obtain discovery of information that might demonstrate that decisions to prosecute were based on racial discrimination.

The key case is *U.S. v. Armstrong* (1996), where the Supreme Court reversed a decision holding that African-Americans charged with dealing crack cocaine should have discovery on a claim that they were being discriminatorily prosecuted. The Court held that the "showing necessary to obtain discovery should itself be a significant barrier to the litigation of insubstantial claims."[21] Given that discriminatory prosecution is itself a crime and in any event terminates the prosecution, one might assume that any prosecutor guilty of discrimination would conceal it. Thus, one cannot even get discovery without evidence, and one can rarely get evidence that will satisfy a court without discovery.

Courts are no more eager to allow discovery of legislative motivations than they are of the basis for prosecutorial decisions. A panel of the Sixth Circuit held that plaintiffs challenging Tennessee's felon disenfranchisement provision had failed to prove that it was motivated by discriminatory intent, and that "the further discovery requested by plaintiffs would be in the nature of a fishing expedition for unspecified evidence" (*Wesley v. Collins* 1986)—as with discriminatory prosecutions, governmental action is presumptively valid, and the information needed to overcome the presumption will be protected from discovery by the courts. We are left, then, with a racial disparity, naked denials that it is improperly motivated, and dogmatic resistance to disclosure of the actual facts.

What evidence does exist is hardly reassuring. The argument that African-Americans are more serious offenders does not explain why more whites are arrested for drug offenses in the first place. Obviously, arrestees are those whom law enforcement officials, after exercising their discretion with regard to allocation of resources, believe deserve to be targeted for legal action. If more whites engage in conduct worthy of arrest, it is difficult to see why fewer are convicted of crimes. Moreover, the argument that more serious offenses warrant more resources must be viewed in light of the fact that many collateral consequences were designed to be imposed on minor as well as major drug law violators. The Anti-Drug Abuse Act of 1988, which promised to make America drug-free by 1995, also introduced the concept of user accountability. The harsh criminal and civil penalties that fall disproportionately on African-Americans were, supposedly, aimed at even casual drug users.[22] If the laws are designed to sanction even the lowest-level offenders through conviction and collateral consequences, the unproven claim that whites are disproportionately low-level offenders is no answer.

In addition, the argument that African-Americans are targeted because they are disproportionately "drug dealers" has limited explanatory force because the definition of dealing is so broad that virtually all users are dealers. New York's definition of "sell" is typical. "'Sell' means to sell, exchange, give or dispose of to another, or to offer or agree to do the same" (N.Y. Penal Law §220.00(1) [McKinney 1999]; Uniform Controlled Substances Act 1994).

Thus, a person may be guilty of the felony of criminal sale of a controlled substance based on a noncommercial transaction of a minimal amount.[23] Similarly, federal law provides that "[t]he terms 'deliver' or 'delivery' mean the actual, constructive or attempted transfer of a controlled substance or a listed chemical, whether or not there exists an agency relationship," and that "[t]he term 'distribute' means to deliver." Thus, a defendant is guilty of "distributing" drugs simply by transferring them to another person. Under these formulations, the federal courts of appeal have held that "[s]haring drugs with another constitutes 'distribution'" (U.S. v. Hester 1998) even if "no commercial scheme is involved."[24] Handing a single marijuana cigarette to another person makes the actor a drug dealer; as the Court of Appeals of Alaska explained, "non-commercial transfers of small quantities of marijuana must be deemed to fall within the ambit of the prohibition against distribution" (Wright v. State 1982).

The courts of many other jurisdictions agree that "a sharing, or even a gift, of a controlled substance is enough to constitute a distribution."[25] Accordingly, even if more African-Americans are charged with "trafficking," that does not necessarily justify the differential outcomes because almost any user can be charged with trafficking. The definition of "trafficking" under the Immigration and Nationality Act also makes this clear.

The statute defines as an aggravated felony "illicit trafficking in a controlled substance . . . including a drug trafficking crime (as defined in section 924(c) of Title 18)" (8 U.S.C. §1101(a)(43)(B) 2000).

Section 924(c) defines a drug trafficking crime as "any felony punishable under the Controlled Substances Act (21 U.S.C. 801 et seq.), the Controlled Substances Import and Export Act (21 U.S.C. 951 et seq.), or the Maritime Drug Law Enforcement Act (46 U.S.C. App. 1901 et seq.)" (18 U.S.C. §924(c)(2) [2000]. Most courts have read this provision to include any felony under state or federal law, which is punishable either as a felony or misdemeanor under one of the statutes listed in Section 924(c).[26] As a result, simple possession of a controlled substance, even marijuana, if a felony under state law, can constitute "drug trafficking" (*U.S. v. Hernandez-Avalos* 2001; *U.S. v. Restrepo-Aguilar* 1996).

The conclusion that African-American offenders are targeted is not necessarily to conclude that law enforcement officers are motivated by simple anti-black animus, however. The problem is that the prevalence of drug use creates the necessity for discriminatory prosecution. Criminologist Alfred Blumstein reports that "[d]rug offenses are profoundly discretionary in terms of who gets arrested; where police patrol; and in the aggressiveness of police, prosecution, and sentencing policy that is targeted at drug offenders" (Blumstein and Wallman 2000). Professor Blumstein is clearly correct; the National Household Survey on Drug Abuse reports that 11.2% of non-Hispanic whites, 10.9% of non-Hispanic African-Americans, and 10.1% of Hispanics age 12 and older had used a controlled substance in the past year; this represents nearly 30 million potential defendants, only a fraction of whom could possibly be investigated or charged (Substance Abuse and Mental Health Services Administration 2001). There is always room in prison for one more rapist, armed robber, or murderer, but given the pervasive drug exposure of the American population (the lifetime rates of illicit drug use were approximately triple the one-year rate), full enforcement would be impossible, intolerable, and in principle undesirable.

Police officials and prosecutors who are not consciously racist might nevertheless reasonably conclude that there are many grounds to focus on African-American drug offenders rather than to pursue cases on a race-neutral basis. Focusing on African-Americans, at least on the streets of the inner city, is easier than going after whites where investigations might be more complicated. Targeting economically disadvantaged groups helps ensure that there will be few costly and difficult trials because the poor are less likely to be able to hire quality counsel. Prosecuting the disadvantaged for drug offenses scores political points rather than generating political backlash.

The focus on the poor is ironic because it is reasonable to assume that targeting the wealthy would be much more effective. Alfred Blumstein has written scathingly of the pointlessness of the approach of incarcerating low-level drug dealers:

> The futility of the strategy is clear from basic criminological theory. Incapacitation cannot work because the offender removed from the street does not take his crime off the street with him; his transactions are replaced by a substitute as long as the demand remains. Similarly, deterrence fails (even where large numbers are indeed deterred) as long as there is a queue of replacements to substitute for those deterred (Blumstein and Wallman 2000: 757).

One wonders what the deterrent effect would be of a full-force effort to investigate and prosecute participants in the drug networks at the elite prep schools, colleges, and corporations. If average Janes and Joes saw the children of the rich and powerful (and the rich and powerful themselves) subjected to the full force of the law for drug crimes that large segments of the population commit, then that might create real deterrence. By contrast, when drug users seem to be tracked, depending on race and class, to prison for some and to treatment (or just being allowed to grow out of it) for others, any moral message that drug prosecutions might otherwise have had is lost.

The Failure of Legal Challenges

Putting history and current practice together paints a bleak picture. The drug laws were initially created as a part of Jim Crow. Similarly, during the segregation era, collateral consequences such as felony disenfranchisement were gerrymandered to target African-Americans. Now, drug laws are freighted with the harshest and most numerous collateral consequences. And although the drug laws are systematically unenforced, the resources seem to be disproportionately aimed at African-Americans. Thus, the drug laws and collateral consequences associated with them continue to serve the purpose of keeping minorities in a particular relationship to the larger society.

Based on this history and practice, the drug laws and the collateral consequences that flow from them might seem to be promising targets for legal action, but courts have been extremely reluctant to grapple with the apparent injustices. As discussed earlier, it is very difficult to get discovery on a claim of selective prosecution. Even when discovery is allowed to proceed,[27] courts seem extremely reluctant to allow discovery or to grant relief.

Some courts refuse to find discrimination unless the plaintiff identifies cases not prosecuted that are virtually identical to the defendant's (*U.S. v. Smith* 2000). Of course, there will always be some differences between one case and another, so this approach comes close to a universal excuse. Some cases demand evidence of discriminatory intent, a matter very difficult to prove (*U.S. v. Green* 2000). Plaintiffs also lose for inconsistent reasons; one court denied discovery because the demonstration of racial prejudice did not extend to the agency as a whole but only to the particular police officer, which is "not enough" (*State v. Smith* 1997); another rejected a claim where the defendant's evidence went to the agency as a whole, but not to the particular "officers who allegedly stopped and searched him" (*Chavez v. Illinois State Police* 2001). Even when courts express doubts, as did one panel when it noted that a particular case selection system "unnecessarily invites a substantial risk of selective prosecution" (*U.S. v. Jones* 1999), they generally feel constrained to deny relief.

Courts also deny claims for allegedly neutral reasons that themselves raise the specter of unfairness. Thus, one court upheld a prosecutorial decision to enforce the drug laws vigorously in particular neighborhoods because there was more crime there (*U.S. v. Daniels* 2001). The court failed to acknowledge that police focus on a particular neighborhood is self-justifying because, given thirty million or more drug violators in any given year, once resources are invested in any neighborhood, drug defendants will be found.[28] Another case rejected a defense argument that methamphetamine dealers, who are largely white, were not targeted whereas crack dealers, who are largely African-American, were targeted; the court justified its position with the observation that the penalties for distribution of five grams or more of crack were higher than for distributing five grams or more of methamphetamine (*U.S. v. Davis* 2000). Going after more serious sentences was a legitimate prosecutorial decision. This begs the question, of course, of why sentences for crack are so high compared to other substances. Stiff sentences for crack cocaine as opposed to powder cocaine or other drugs could be another form of discrimination against African-Americans, motivated by the assumption that this is the type of crime that they are more likely to commit. Although some commentators have made the argument that this is the case,[29] in court the argument has not prevailed. In 1994, U.S. District Judge Clyde Cahill found the 100-to-1 disparity between sentences for crack cocaine and powder cocaine to be unconstitutional because of the racist origins of the drug laws. "Panic based on media reports which incited racial fears has been used historically in this country as the catalyst for generating racially biased legislation" (*U.S. v. Clary* 1994); "[h]istorically, a consortium of reactionary media and a subsequently inflamed constituency have combined to influence Congress to impose more severe criminal sanctions for use of narcotics once they become popular with minorities" (*U.S. v. Clary* 1994: 774). Judge Cahill's decision was promptly appealed and reversed.

Courts are also reluctant to invalidate apparently race-based collateral consequences. In *Williams v. Mississippi* (1898), the U.S. Supreme Court upheld Article XII, Section 241 of the Mississippi Constitution, disenfranchising certain felons, in spite of the unambiguous legislative history showing that it was aimed at disenfranchising African-Americans (*Williams v. Mississippi* 1898). The Court reasoned that because the provision was neutral on its face, it did not offend the 14th Amendment. A century later, in *Cotton v. Fordice* in 1998, the Fifth Circuit upheld the provision again. By 1998 the court had recognized that discriminatory legislative intent would invalidate a statute and that the taint, the court concluded, had been purged by the provision's revision and reenactment in 1950 and 1968 by the legislature and the voters (Cotton 1998: 391–92). The claim that the political structure of Mississippi was sufficiently racially neutral during the 1950s and 1960s that it could legitimize an earlier unconstitutional act must have been offered tongue-in-cheek. Mississippi was a deeply segregated society. Two of the most memorable incidents of the Civil Rights era—the assassination of civil rights workers Michael Schwerner, Andrew Goodman, and James Cheney and the Mississippi Freedom Democratic Party's shaming of the Democratic convention in Atlantic City—were based on Mississippi injustices in this period. Mississippi's denial of African-Americans' right to vote, to serve on juries, and to enjoy equal access to public accommodations is spread upon the records of the (law) reporters. Nevertheless, the decision stands.[30]

Conclusion: A Proposed Reform

The history and practice of both drug laws and collateral consequences raise deep questions about the wisdom of current policy. Yet, direct assaults have not proved particularly effective. For example, the U.S. Sentencing Commission reported in 2002 that "[t]he 100-to-1 drug quantity ratio was established based on a number of beliefs about the relative harmfulness of [crack cocaine and powder cocaine] and the relative prevalence of certain harmful conduct associated with their use and distribution that more recent research and data no longer support."[31] That is, once again, it appears that a law that bears most heavily on African-Americans was based upon false stereotypes. Yet, Congress has repeatedly rejected recommendations of the U.S. Sentencing Commission that the crack cocaine/powder cocaine disparity be reduced (U.S. Sentencing Commission 2002: 12–13). Similarly, a blue-ribbon panel headed by former presidents Carter and Ford recommended eliminating felon disenfranchisement upon release, but the report has thus far had little effect.

If systematic reform is not on the immediate horizon, it would be worthwhile at least to find a way to help achieve fairness in individual cases and to get policymakers to focus on the issues. One way to help accomplish that would be to reform the way collateral consequences are imposed. Most state legislatures attempt to make the punishment fit the crime, but this task is impossible if no one knows what the punishment is. Perhaps there are so many collateral consequences, and perhaps they are imposed so arbitrarily and inconsistently, because they are not dealt with in the systematic way that incarceration and fines are. As a first step, collateral consequences should be brought into the criminal justice process, as described in the following.

Codification

Because collateral sanctions are often difficult to find, consequences collateral to a particular offense should be consolidated and collected in a single section of a jurisdiction's code. The difficulty in locating all of the widely dispersed statutes imposing collateral penalties undermines the fundamental purpose of notice and fairness behind criminal codes, and indeed, written law of any kind. A prosecutor, defense lawyer, judge, or private citizen should be able to determine the full legal consequences of violation of a particular provision of the criminal code simply by reading it.

Notice

All consequences resulting from the fact of conviction of a particular offense should be included as part of the sentence or judgment imposed by the court. This will provide notice of what the actual sentence is in the particular case, and enable the sentencing judge to tailor the sanctions to the particular offense and offender. Before an offender pleads guilty or is sentenced, he or she should be informed of the full range of mandatory consequences of the conviction. This will not only make court proceedings fairer with respect to that individual, it also makes compliance more likely; offenders are more likely to follow rules if they know what they are.

These proposals may seem anticlimactic because they hold out no hope for immediate substantive change. However, they might help policymakers think about the issues. Only by understanding what the law is actually doing can legislators evaluate whether the effects are what the legislature is seeking, and whether the goals of the laws are being achieved. If taken in conjunction with the racial history of the drug laws, some legislatures might conclude that the collateral consequences are too severe.

Cases Cited

Chavez v. Illinois State Police, 251 F.3d 612, 646 (7th Cir. 2001)

Cotton v. Fordice, 157 F.3d 388 (5th Cir. 1998)

Hunter v. Underwood, 471 U.S. 222 (1985)

Johnson v. Bush, 214 F.Supp.2d 1333 (S.D.Fla. Jul 18, 2002), aff'd in part, rev'd in part and rem'd in part by *Johnson v. Governor of State of Fla.*, 353 F.3d 1287 (11th Cir. 2003)

Ratliffe v. Beale, 20 So. 865, 868 (Miss. 1896)

Rutledge v. United States, 517 U.S. 292, 302 (1996)

State v. Smith, 703 A.2d 954, 958 (N.J. Super. Ct. App. Div. 1997)

U.S. v. Armstrong, 517 U.S. 456 (1996)

U.S. v. Clary, 846 F. Supp. 768, 776 (E.D. Mo.), rev'd, 34 F.3d 709 (8th Cir. 1994)

U.S. v. Daniels, 142 F. Supp. 2d 140, 144 (D. Mass. 2001)

U.S. v. Davis, 194 F.R.D. 688, 690-91 (D. Kan. 2000)

U.S. v. Green, 108 F. Supp.2d 1169, 1170-71 (D. Kan. 2000)

U.S. v. Hernandez-Avalos, 251 F.3d 505, 507- 08 (5th Cir. 2001)

U.S. v. Hester, 140 F.3d 753, 761 (8th Cir. 1998)

U.S. v. Jones, 36 F. Supp. 2d 304, 312 (E.D. Va. 1999)

U.S. v. Morgan, 346 U.S. 502, 512-13 (1954)

U.S. v. Restrepo-Aguilar, 74 F.3d 361 (1st Cir. 1996)

U.S. v. Smith, 231 F.3d 800, 810-11 (11th Cir. 2000)

Wesley v. Collins, 791 F.2d 1255, 1262-63 (6th Cir. 1986)

Williams v. Mississippi, 170 U.S. 213 (1898)

Wright v. State, 651 P.2d 846, 849 (Alaska Ct. App. 1982)

Statutes Cited

Adoption and Safe Families Act of 1997, Pub. L. No. 105-89, 111 Stat. 2115 (1997)

Anti-Drug Abuse Act of 1988, Pub. L. 100-690, 102 Stat. 4181 (1988)

N.Y. Penal Law §220.00(1) (McKinney 1999)

Uniform Controlled Substances Act of 1994

U.S. Sentencing Guidelines §4B1.1 (2001)

21 U.S.C. §§801-904 (1994)

References

Allard, Patricia. 2002. "Life Sentences: Denying Welfare Benefits to Women Convicted of Drug Offenses." Available at http://www.sentencingproject.org/news/lifesentences.pdf.

Allard, Patricia and Mark Mauer. 2000. "Regaining the Vote: An Assessment of Activity Relating to Felon Disenfranchisement Laws." Available at http://www.sentencingproject.org/pubs/regainvote.pdf.

Beck, Allen J. and Paige M. Harrison. 2001. "Prisoners in 2000." Bureau of Justice Statistics Bulletin 1 August.

Blumstein, Alfred. 1982. "On the Racial Disproportionality of United States' Prison Populations." 73 *J. Crim. L. & Criminology* 1259.

———. 1993. "Racial Disproportionality of U.S. Prison Populations Revisited." 64 *Colo. L. Rev.* 743.

Blumstein, Alfred and Joel Wallman. 2000. *The Crime Drop in America*. New York: Cambridge University Press.

Bureau of Justice Statistics 2001. *Sourcebook of Criminal Justice Statistics 2000* Online 526 tbl.6.51 (28th ed. 2001), at http://www.albany.edu/sourcebook/1995/pdf/t651.pdf.

Burton, Jr., Velmer S. et al. 1987. "The Collateral Consequences of a Felony Conviction: A National Study of State Statutes," 51 *Fed. Probation* 52.

Calmore, John O. 2001. "Race-Conscious Voting Rights and the New Demography in a Multiracing America." 79 *N.C. L. Rev.* 1253, 1277–80.

Chin, Gabriel J. Forthcoming. "Rehabilitating Unconstitutional Statutes: An Analysis of *Cotton v. Fordice, 157 F.3d 388 (5th Cir. 1998)*." 71 *U. Cin. L. Rev.* 421.

Chin, Gabriel J. 2004. "Reconstruction, Felon Disenfranchisement, and the Right to Vote: Did the Fifteenth Amendment Repeal Section 2 of the Fourteenth Amendment? 92 *Geo. L. J.* 259.

Chin, Gabriel J. and Richard W. Holmes Jr. 2002. "Effective Assistance of Counsel and the Consequences of Guilty Pleas." 87 *Cornell Law Review* 697.

Cole, David. 1999. *No Equal Justice: Race and Class in the American Criminal Justice System*. New York: New Press.

Duke, Steven B and Albert C. Gross. 1993. *America's Longest War: Rethinking our Tragic Crusade Against Drugs*. New York: Putnam.

Durose, Matthew R., et al. 2001. "Felony Sentences in State Courts, 1998." Bureau of Justice Statistics Bulletin 2.

Dvorak, Richard. 2000. "Cracking the Code: "De-Coding" Colorblind Slurs during the Congressional Crack Cocaine Debates." 5 *Mich. J. Race & L.* 611, 662–63.

Fellner, Jamie and Marc Mauer. 1998. *Losing the Vote: The Impact of Felony Disenfranchisement Laws in the United States*. Washington, D.C.: The Sentencing Project and Human Rights Watch.

"The Death of Voting Rights: The Legal Disenfranchisement of Minority Voters." 1998. Case W. Res. L. Rev. 727.

————. 2002. "One Person, No Vote: The Laws of Felon Disenfranchisement." 115 *Harv. L. Rev.* 1939.

Husak, Douglas N. 1992. *Drugs and Rights.* New York: Cambridge University Press.

Kennedy, Randall. 1988. "*McCleskey v. Kemp:* Race, Capital Punishment and the Supreme Court." 101 *Harv. L. Rev.* 1388.

Luna, Erik. 1997. "Our Vietnam: The Prohibition Apocalypse." 46 *DePaul Law Review* 483: 490–493

Mauer, Marc. 1999. *Race to Incarcerate.* New York: New Press.

Musser, Jr., Robert W. 2000. "Denial of Federal Benefits to Drug Traffickers and Drug Possessors: A Broad- Reaching But Seldom Used Sanction." 12 *Fed. Sent. R.* 252.

Musto, David. 1999. *The American Disease: Origins of Narcotic Control,* 3rd ed. New York: Oxford University Press.

Office of the Pardon Attorney. 1996. "Civil Disabilities of Convicted Felons: A State by State Survey." October.

Olivares, Kathleen M. et al. 1996. "The Collateral Consequences of a Felony Conviction: A National Study of State Legal Codes 10 Years Later." 60 *Fed. Probation* 10.

Poulin, Anne Bowen. 1997. "Prosecutorial Discretion and Selective Prosecution: Enforcing Equal Protection after *United States v. Armstrong.*" 34 *Am. Crim. L. Rev.* 1071.

Shapiro, Andrew L. 1993. "Challenging Criminal Disenfranchisement under the Voting Rights Act: A New Strategy." 103 *Yale L.J.* 537, 537–42.

Sklansky, David. 1995. "Cocaine, Race and Equal Protection." 47 *Stan. L. Rev.* 1283, 1288–89.

Substance Abuse and Mental Health Services Administration. 2001. "Summary of Findings from the 2000 National Household Survey on Drug Abuse."

Tonry, Michael. 1995. *Malign Neglect: Race. Crime and Punishment in America.* New York: Oxford University Press.

Travis, Jeremy. 2002. "Invisible Punishment: An Instrument of Social Exclusion." In Marc Mauer and Meda Chesney-Lind, Eds., *Invisible Punishment: The Collateral Consequences of Mass Imprisonment.* New York: New Press.

U.S. Dep't of Commerce 2001. *Profiles of General Demographic Characteristics 2000.* Available at http://www.census.gov/prod/cen2000/dp1/2kh00.pdf.

U.S. Sentencing Commission 2002. Report to Congress: Cocaine and Federal Sentencing Policy 91. Available at http://www.ussc.gov/r_congress/02crack/2002crackrpt.htm.

Wilbanks, William. 1987. *The Myth of a Racist Criminal Justice System.* Monterey, CA: Brooks/Cole.

Endnotes

1. See Durose et al. 1998. 29% of those convicted of drug trafficking received probation; id. at 7 table 17, noting that only 43% of those convicted of trafficking who had one felony conviction received a prison sentence.

2. A number of sources offer general background on the war on drugs. See, e.g., Duke and Gross 1993 and Husak 1992.

3. See generally, "ABA Standards for Criminal Justice: Collateral Sanctions and Disqualification of Convicted Persons" (3d ed. 2004). Available at http://www.abanet.org/crimjust/standards/collateral_toc.html. Chin and Holmes 2002. See also Office of the Pardon Attorney 1996; Olivares et al. 1996; Burton et al. 1987.

4. *U.S. Const. amend. XIV, §2.* But when the right to vote at any election for the choice of electors for the President and Vice President of the United States, Representatives in Congress, the Executive and Judicial officers of a State, or the members of the Legislature thereof, is denied to any of the male inhabitants of such State, being twenty-one years of age, and citizens of the United States, or in any way abridged, except for participation in rebellion, or other crime, the basis of representation therein shall be reduced in the proportion which the number of such male citizens shall bear to the whole number of male citizens twenty-one years of age in such State.

5. Id.

6. See Shapiro 1993. See also Calmore 2001; "The Death of Voting Rights" 1998 and 2002.

7. See Fellner and Mauer. 1998; Allard and Mauer 2000; Shapiro 1993; cf. *Buckley v. Am. Const. L. Found.*, 525 U.S. 182, 231 (1999) (Rehnquist, C.J., dissenting) ("[T]he idea that convicted drug felons who have lost their right to vote under state law nonetheless have a constitutional right to circulate initiative petitions scarcely passes the laugh test."). The Supreme Court upheld the constitutionality of felon disenfranchisement in *Richardson v. Ramirez, 418 U.S. 24 (1974)*. But see Chin 2004.

8. Bureau of Justice Assistance, Denial of Federal Benefits Program and Clearinghouse (Fact Sheet) (1997) (discussed in Musser 2000).

9. Many of these laws allow states to opt out, however. See, e.g., Travis 2002 (identifying states opting out of various federal collateral consequences applicable to benefit programs).

10. *21 U.S.C. §862a(A) (2000)*. States were authorized to opt out of this ban and many did. 21 U.S.C. §862a(d)(A) (2000). See generally Allard 2002.

11. *49 U.S.C. §44936(b)(1)(B)9xiv)(IX)(2000)* Stating that airlines may not employ persons convicted within the last ten years of illegal possession of a controlled substance punishable by a maximum term of more than one year; 49 C.F.R. §1542.209 (d)(26)(x); 49 C.F.R. §1544.229 (d)(26)(ix)(2002) preventing persons from working as baggage handlers who have been convicted of possession of a controlled substance that is punishable by imprisonment for more than 1 year; see also 49 U.S.C. §44710(b)91)(2000) allowing for revocation in certain instances of the airman certificate of persons convicted under a law relating to possession of a controlled substance.

12. *42 U.S.C. §13662(a) (2000)*. See also *42 U.S.C. § 1437f(d)(1) (B)(iii) (2000)*. Public housing leases must provide for termination based on "any drug-related criminal activity on or near such premises, engaged in by a public housing tenant, any member of the tenant's household, or any guest or person under the tenant's control."

13. See, e.g., *Bockun v. Ashcroft,* 283 F.3d 166, 171 (3d Cir. 2002); *United States v. Robles-Rodriguez,* 281 F.3d 900, 902-03 (9th Cir. 2002); *United States v. Urias-Escobar,* 281 F.3d 165, 167-68 (5th Cir. 2002); *United States v. Gonzales-Vela,* 276 F.3d 763, 766-67 (6th Cir. 2001); *United States v. Pacheco,* 225 F.3d 148, 154 (2d Cir. 2000). But see *United States v. Gonzales-Vela,* 276 F.3d 763, 768 (6th Cir. 2001) (Merritt, J., dissenting); *United States v. Pacheco,* 225 F.3d 148, 158 (2d Cir. 2000) (Straub, J., dissenting).

14. As discussed, the concepts of "trafficking" or "dealing" are defined extremely broadly.

15. *18 U.S.C. §3592(c)(10)(2000)* (stating the aggravating factors for homicide). See also id. at §3592(d)(3) (aggravating factors for drug offense death penalty include prior serious drug conviction).

16. Beck and Harrison 2001. The remainder was in other forms of governmental detention, such as military, tribal, juvenile or INS custody. See generally Mauer 1999 (describing growth of prison population).

17. Every year, the National Crime Victimization Survey interviews approximately 50,000 households containing approximately 100,000 members to determine the incidence and nature of any serious criminal victimization they experienced; information sought includes the race of the assailant if the victim knows it. Available at http://www.ojp.usdoj.gov/bjs/cvict.htm#ncvs (last visited Oct. 4, 2002). The FBI's Uniform Crime Reports offer annual statistics about those arrested, including the race and charge. Available at http://www.fbi.gov/ucr/ucr.htm (last visited Oct. 3, 2002). The Bureau of Justice Statistics reports on convictions in state and federal court, including the race of the offender and the offense of conviction See, e.g., Durose, supra note 1. Finally, the Bureau of Justice Statistics reports on the prison population, breaking out the data by race and offense of conviction

18. Tonry at 49. Professor Tonry relies significantly on the work of Alfred Blumstein (1982 and 1993). It is important to note that Tonry's sophisticated analysis recognizes that past and present racism contributes to African-American poverty and thus may be criminogenic. He also recognizes, of course, that racial discrimination may often explain systematic disparities in particular regions, and of course in particular cases. A number of works argue that various aspects of the system are indeed racist. See, e.g., Cole 1999: 5 (arguing that the criminal justice system depends on racial and class inequality). But see Wilbanks 1987: 11 (arguing that the criminal justice system itself is not racist).

19. Extrapolating from 2000 Census data. U.S. Department of Commerce at 1 tbl.1, (Total population is approximately 281 million, including 35 million Hispanics, 36 million African Americans, and 217 million whites.)

20. Sourcebook, 2000 at table 5.41, at http:// www.albany.edu/ sourcebook/1995/pdf/t541.pdf. See also Durose, supra note 1, at 6 tbl.5 (53% of those convicted of drug offenses are African American, 46% are white).

21. See generally Poulin 1997.; see also Kennedy 1988.

22. Pub. L. 100-690, 102 Stat. 4181 (1988) at Title V (establishing or strengthening sanctions against users and possessors of drugs). See also 134 Cong. Rec. S16104-02 (Oct. 14, 1988) (remarks of Sen. Byrd) ("One whole title of the bill is devoted to what we call user accountability provisions which zero in on drug users."); id. at S15963-02 (remarks of Sen. Gramm) ("Clearly the intent of the user accountability effort is to say that if you are riding around in your Volvo smoking marijuana and you are arrested," you will lose federal benefits.); id. at H11108-01 (Oct. 21, 1988) (remarks of Rep. Wylie) (User accountability "means those who use drugs won't do so with impunity."); id. (remarks of Rep. McCollum) ("I am especially proud of those Members who worked so hard to make this concept of deterrence in the area of user accountability to exist, to be real, and to live in this legislation."). But see id. (remarks of Rep. Kastenmeier) ("While some elements of this concept are worth exploring, the potential for unfair treatment appears significant.").

23. See, e.g., *People v. Starling, 650 N.E.2d 387, 390 (N.Y. 1995)* ("By enacting a broad definition of the term 'sell' to embrace the acts of giving or disposing of drugs, the Legislature has evinced a clear intent to 'include any form of transfer of a controlled substance from one person to another'. . . . The statutory definition of that term conspicuously excludes any requirement that the transfer be commercial in nature or conducted for a particular type of benefit or underlying purpose").

24. *United States v. Ramirez,* 608 F.2d 1261, 1264 (9th Cir. 1979). There is a special rule for marijuana; the statute provides that noncommercial distribution of small quantities does not constitute distribution of a controlled substance. 21 U.S.C. § 841(b)(4) (1999). Of course, under the maxim expressio unius exclusio alterius est, this provision suggests that noncommercial sharing of other drugs, and commercial sharing of any drug including marijuana, constitutes distribution.

25. *Minor v. United States,* 623 A.2d 1182, 1186 (D.C. 1993) (quoting *Chambers v. United States,* 564 A.2d 26, 31 n.10 (D.C. 1989)). See also, e.g., *State v. Berger,* 480 A.2d 27, 29 (N.H. 1984) ("We have specifically defined sale to include a 'gift or offer' . . ."); *State v. Jackson,* 619 N.E.2d 1135, 1139 (Ohio Ct. App. 1993) ("Gifts of drugs are included in the statutory definition of 'sales' in trafficking offenses."); *Fontenot v. State,* 792 S.W.2d 250, 256 (Tex. App. 1990) ("[T]he concept of 'delivery' of narcotics includes sharing drugs with third persons, and is not limited to commercial ventures."). But cf. *State v. Ontiveros,* 674 P.2d 103, 104 (Utah 1983) (gift of marijuana did not constitute "distribution for value").

26. *18 U.S.C. § 924(c)(2) (2000).* See Navarro-Macias v. INS, 16 Fed. Appx. 468 (7th Cir. 2001); *United States v. Lugo,* 170 F.3d 996 (10th Cir. 1999). But see *Gerbier v. Holmes,* 280 F.3d 297 (3d Cir. 2002); cf. *Steele v. Blackman,* 236 F.3d 130 (3d Cir. 2001) (stating that a state misdemeanor drug conviction which would also be misdemeanor under federal law is not aggravated felony).

27. See *United States v. Bass,* 266 F.3d 532 (6th Cir. 2001); *United States v. Jones,* 159 F.3d 969 (6th Cir. 1998); *United States v. Tuitt,* 68 F. Supp. 2d 4 (D. Mass. 1999). Discovery may be more likely in civil cases. See, e.g., *Rodriguez v. California Highway Patrol,* 89 F. Supp. 2d 1131 (N.D. Cal. 2000); *State v. Williamson,* 763 A.2d 285 (N.J. Super. Ct. App. Div. 2000).

28. The necessity of discretion makes ominous the Supreme Court's suggestion that discrimination could be shown if similarly situated defendants of another race were "known to federal law enforcement officers, but were not prosecuted in federal court." *United States v. Armstrong, 517 U.S. 456, 470 (1996).* This puts a premium on willful blindness, because convenient ignorance defeats a discriminatory prosecution claim. Moreover, given the target-rich environment, anywhere law enforcement authorities choose to look will be fruitful.

29. See, e.g., Dvorak 2000; Slansky 1995.

30. See Chin, 2002 (criticizing reasoning and result of Cotton in more detail).

31. U.S. Sentencing Commission, Report to Congress: Cocaine and Federal Sentencing Policy 91 (2002) [hereinafter 2002 Report to Congress], available at http://www.ussc.gov/r_congress/02crack/2002crackrpt.htm. See also U.S. Sentencing Commission: Special Report to the Congress: Cocaine and Federal Sentencing Policy (1997), available at http://www.ussc.gov/r_congress/newcrack.pdf; U.S. Sentencing Commission, Special Report to Congress: Cocaine and Federal Sentencing Policy (1995), available at http://www.ussc.gov/crack/execsum.pdf.

3

By Any Means Necessary: Collateral Civil Penalties of Non-U.S. Citizens and the War on Terror

TERESA A. MILLER

Deportation as a consequence of a criminal conviction has become an important tool in the War on Terror. The Department of Homeland Security (DHS) has elevated apprehension and deportation of so-called "criminal aliens" to a high priority in its mission to flush out and expel from the United States foreigners with links to terrorist organizations. Yet the aggressive expulsion of non-citizen criminal offenders hardly seems intuitive as a key component of counter-terrorism. Particularly when expulsion is rarely based upon convictions even remotely related to terrorist activity.[1] Indeed the prioritizing of criminal alien removal did not come about solely in response to the horrific attacks that occurred on 9/11, 2001. Congress did not invent the collateral penalty of deportation after the attacks, as the first line of defense against terrorism.[2] As mentioned in Chapter 1, immigration legislation passed years before the attacks increasingly imposed deportation upon non-U.S. citizens with criminal records as the immigration system adopted the criminal justice system's severe treatment of drug offenders and the poor. As the criminal justice system created punishments that "got tough" on *all* convicted felons—particularly drug offenders—immigration law adopted harsh consequences for those convicted offenders who were not U.S. citizens. Under immigration reforms enacted in 1996, these so-called criminal aliens could be detained and deported (many retroactively), and denied relief from detention and deportation based upon individual mitigating circumstances. And because these harsh measures were characterized by courts as regulatory, rather than punitive, constitutionally mandated criminal procedures did not apply.

By the time that the tragic events of 9/11, 2001 occurred, immigration law had already bought into the "severity revolution" (Kennedy 2000) that had swept through and transformed the criminal justice system under the War on Drugs. A series of ever-harsher immigration reforms had quadrupled the volume of non-U.S. citizens being deported on criminal grounds. The nation's urgent response to terrorism capitalized on immigration law's utility as a means of crime control and social control to purge from the nation hundred of thousands convicts and ex-convicts lacking U.S. citizenship in the name of maintaining homeland security. Public safety, traditionally within the purview of law enforcement, is now one of the many objectives of homeland security. ICE Acting Assistant Secretary Michael J. Garcia declared as crucial to ICE's public safety mission, "reducing the number of dangerous criminal aliens hiding in this country." (USCIS 2003). Through initiatives such as Operation Predator, the Absconder Apprehension Initiative, the Institutional Removal Program and the ICE Most Wanted List, the DHS utilizes the resources of the 22 federal agencies subsumed by it to target, apprehend and expel non-US citizens with criminal convictions.

The Criminal Alien Crisis

The federal government maintains a Ten Most Wanted list of fugitives. Photographs of the fugitives' faces-head shots- are published as part of the list. Some are mug shots taken during the booking process, with the familiar black letter board with white lettering held under the chin. Others are simply "official" photographs taken with shadow-throwing, high-contrast lighting that imparts an unflattering, even menacing, quality to its subjects. Below each of the ten headshots is printed the last name and first name of each man, followed his date and place of birth, a government-issued number for identification, and finally the relevant crime (or crimes). The men pictured represent several different ethnic backgrounds, but the overwhelming majority are men of color, in varying shades of brown. These men are not wanted by the FBI. They have not escaped from prison, nor are they fleeing from (criminal) prosecution. The men depicted are sought by Immigration and Customs Enforcement's Office of Detention and Removal. They are on ICE's list of the Ten Most Wanted criminal aliens.[3]

What distinguishes these men from the fugitives from justice the FBI seeks to apprehend is that they are "wanted" for violating a civil order of removal.[4] They are fugitives only in the sense that they cannot presently be located, and thus the removal orders against them cannot be executed. The crimes listed are not crimes from which these men have fled prosecution. They are past convictions, for which most of them served time. Nevertheless, immigration authorities have embraced federal law enforcement's most public and visible demarcator of criminal dangerousness as a means to publicize and apprehend these aliens.

Criminal aliens are the Willie Hortons of the War on Terror.[5] Their persistent presence in the United States has been characterized as a "national crisis" and cited as prima facie evidence of a broken immigration system (Norwood 2003). Their liberty is lamented and their apprehension is celebrated (U.S. Department of Homeland Security 2002). Their harsh treatment across the board undermines the validity of concepts such as rehabilitation, individualized justice and fairness. They are not fugitives from justice. They have not escaped from criminal custody. Most have served time in prison, and were subsequently released, ostensibly having paid their "debt to society." Some are long-term lawful permanent residents who were too young to remember when they came to the United States. Others have entered the country recently without documentation. Some are repeat offenders with a record of serious crimes, and others have a single conviction from the remote past. What they have in common is that they all violated civil orders of removal. They are fugitives in the limited sense of having fled an administrative process. All are the subject of intensive, focused efforts to expel "dangerous criminal aliens" from the United States notwithstanding individual mitigating circumstances. And although the stated agenda of the DHS is to remove "dangerous" criminal aliens, it contradicts the agency's "zero tolerance" policy of actively pursuing the removal of *all* criminal aliens, even those with minor, remote offenses where rehabilitation is evident.

This chapter will explore the role of criminal aliens in the debate over immigration reform from the late 1980s to the present and the construction of criminal aliens within the War on Drugs and the War on Terror. It will discuss how immigration reforms of the past two decades embraced the severity revolution that took place in the criminal justice system during the War on Drugs. It will further explain how that embrace led to the harsh treatment of all non-U.S. citizen ex-offenders' including expanded grounds for detention and removal, drastically reduced grounds for relief from detention and removal, and diminished judicial review of deportation orders. Immigration law's embrace of the severity revolution has also led to unprecedented outcomes that are at odds with traditional notions of civil regulation and fairness to noncitizens. Finally, this chapter will analyze how the Department of Homeland Security has capitalized on the diminished rights of removable noncitizens to selectively ferret out and remove immigrants considered risky, dangerous, and undesirable in furtherance of its broad mission to combat terrorism.

First, I will define criminal aliens and describe the shift in the treatment of criminal aliens that took place during the War on Drugs. I will emphasize the particularly harsh treatment of aggravated felon and discuss the creation of the category as well as the repeated expansion of the category to encompass virtually every convicted non-U.S. citizen ex-felon. Second, I will describe how the immigration system's severity toward aggravated felons has led to unprecedented harshness and occasionally unintended consequences. These consequences include a lack of uniformity in removal law due to the reliance of federal immigration law on state criminal law and the indefinite detention of unremovable criminal aliens. Third, I will describe how the mandate of securing the homeland has become so expansive as to encompass the apprehension, detention, and expulsion of many lawful permanent residents and other non-U.S. citizens with past convictions for relatively minor criminal conduct. I contend that so conceived, homeland security is simply reproducing in immigration policy the type of "broken windows" law enforcement that has filled U.S. prisons without regard to the crime rate.

The Changing Regime of Collateral Civil Penality in the War on Drugs

Pre-Drug War Treatment of Non-U.S. Citizens with Criminal Convictions

Deportation is arguably the earliest collateral civil penalty applied in the United States. Prior to the American Revolution, Britain's practice of transporting convicts to the Colonies engendered bitter resentment expressed in legislation excluding foreigners with criminal convictions from emigrating. That historical aversion to foreign criminals survives in the form of immigration laws excluding non-U.S. citizens with foreign convictions, and deporting non-U.S. citizens with post-entry criminal convictions. This chapter is concerned with the latter.

In the decades immediately preceding the 1980s and 90s, non-U.S. citizens with criminal convictions were treated with far less harshness. Their treatment conformed to well-established principles of criminal justice that prioritized fairness, process, rehabilitation, and individualized justice. Serious offenders were punished more harshly than minor offenders. Noncitizens who committed criminal offenses soon after they came to the United States received harsher treatment than those whose convictions were remote. Judges weighed individual considerations in determining whether to deport the criminal offender or grant relief from deportation.

And the notion that criminal offenders could be transformed or rehabilitated in prison (and therefore come out less likely to offend and less "dangerous" than when they went in) still held some sway.

The harshest penalties were limited to those noncitizens who were repeat offenders or received criminal convictions soon after coming to the United States. Prior to the sweeping reforms in immigration law that began in 1988, the broadest category of crime for which a noncitizen could be deported was a crime involving moral turpitude. Noncitizens who committed crimes in the United States could be deported if they were (1) convicted of a crime involving moral turpitude that was committed *within five years after entering* the United States and sentenced to confinement or actually incarcerated for one year or more; or (2) convicted of two unrelated crimes involving moral turpitude at any time after entry, regardless of confinement (Harper 1975: 582). Thus, if a non-U.S. citizen committed a single crime involving moral turpitude seven years after coming to the United States, he was not deportable. And even if he committed a second crime not involving moral turpitude one year later, he would not be subject to deportation.

Furthermore deportable criminal aliens were afforded exemptions and liberal grounds of relief from deportation. For example, as long as the conviction was not for a drug offense, the noncitizen was exempt from deportation if the sentencing judge made a recommendation to the Attorney General that the alien not be deported.[6] And a noncitizen criminal offender could get relief from deportation if he was a close relative of a U.S. citizen or a permanent resident.

Even noncitizen offenders convicted of serious offenses were eligible to have their deportation suspended if they were physically present in the United States for at least ten years, could prove good moral character, and establish that their deportation would result in exceptional hardship. The latter criterion was met when a deportable alien financially supported dependent children who were U.S. citizens and had resided in the United States continuously for sixteen years (Matter of U., 5 I and N. Dec. 413, August 1953).

Other classes of deportable aliens were similarly treated with less harshness. Although illegal entrants (also referred to as *illegal aliens*) were deportable, their unauthorized entrance into the United States was a civil violation of immigration regulations, not a criminal offense. Therefore, they were not treated as criminal aliens. And asylum seekers who violated the criminal law by falsifying documents in order to leave their home countries were generally not criminally charged in deference to international agreements discouraging the punitive treatment of refugees who cause good cause for their illegal entry or presence (Mailman and Yale-Loehr 2003).

Prior to 1986, although criminal aliens could be deported for crimes involving controlled substances and certain weapons offenses, in addition to moral turpitude crimes, in reality deportation proceedings were rarely commenced (Taylor and Wright 2002). The Immigration and Nationality Act provided, with narrow exceptions, that noncitizens who were incarcerated could not be deported until they were released from prison. Lack of resources and infrastructure to track down deportable criminal aliens and enforce their deportation generally resulted in the deportation of only a fraction of criminal aliens (Miller 2003: 633). Indeed, at the time, some *U.S. citizen* ex-offenders were arguably treated more harshly. Although criminal aliens lived with the threat of the government commencing deportation proceedings, U.S. citizen ex-offenders in some states were stripped of rights that criminal aliens had never gained by virtue of their lack of citizenship (e.g., disenfranchisement, disqualification from holding public office, and disqualification from jury service).

In sum, prior to 1988, noncitizens with criminal convictions in their past were deportable for only a limited category of crimes. They were subject to detention only in a narrow range of circumstances and were afforded liberal relief form detention on the basis of a wide range of personal considerations (Harper 1975: 612–13). This would all change during the War on Drugs.

The War on Drugs Redefined the Criminal Alien
During the War on Drugs, the distinction between criminal offenders with U.S. citizenship and those without became increasingly significant in terms of the collateral civil penalties to which they were subject. Although both were subject to harsh sentencing and harsh conditions of confinement consistent with the "tough-on-crime" philosophy, the latter—the non-U.S. citizen criminal offender—was subject to additional penalties by virtue of his vulnerable citizenship status.

Although in the decades immediately preceding the Drug War, immigration laws could, and often did, impose hardships on noncitizens who were excludable and deportable for a variety of reasons, in the two decades immediately following the Drug War's inception, immigration laws and policies concerning *all* immigrants would become far more restrictive. No one factor accounts for the shift; however, changes in social welfare policies, economic woes, rising crime rates, higher rates of migration to the United States, "compassion fatigue," rising political resistance to "bilingualism," and a burgeoning international drug trade have all been cited as contributing to less-favorable public attitudes toward immigration (Miller 2003). Influenced by growing intolerance of inner-city and border crime, immigration laws and policies concerning criminal aliens changed dramatically as well, becoming harsh and punitive.

It is impossible to tease out the factors that predisposed Congress to crack down on criminal aliens from the factors contributing to a harsher approach, in general, toward refugees, illegal immigrants, visa overstayers, and others. By the late 1980s, the problems of unpredictable refugee waves, public perceptions of high social welfare demands of undocumented workers, and high levels of legal immigration seemed inextricable from the escalating domestic crime problem. The Mariel boatlift fiasco—wherein the United States took in over 100,000 "illegal" aliens from Cuba (many of whom were Cuban prisoners) in a chaotic and disorderly wave of immigration—was a refugee crisis that had a significant impact on the crimes rate in South Florida. Undocumented Mexican immigrants who crossed the border illegally to work in the United States began to carry packages for drug traffickers to fund their journey North as the risks and costs of crossing a more heavily patrolled border area increased. Thus, labor migration became entangled with drug smuggling (Lytle 2003). Immigration restrictionists placed much of the blame for new waves of organized ethnic crime in the 1980s—including Asian gangs, the Russian Mafia, and Columbian drug rings—on legal and illegal immigration (Lutton and Tanton 1994).

What is clear, however, is that the War on Drugs and its "get tough" posture toward a complicated problem of addiction, poverty, urban decay, postindustrial economic decline and social welfare were salient to lawmakers faced with a crisis of rising legal and illegal immigration rates and a declining ability to accommodate new immigrants. Zero tolerance of the *least desirable* immigrants was not hard for politicians to embrace at a time when nonviolent, low-level drug offenders were receiving long prison sentences under mandatory minimum sentences and sentencing guidelines that removed the discretion of judges to moderate the penalty on the basis of individual equities. Scholars have frequently observed that the War on Drugs targeted urban centers and the Mexican border in its campaign to get drugs off the streets. It is no coincidence that collateral civil penalties that proliferated during the War on Drugs likewise have had an inordinate impact in urban areas and border regions. Nor is it coincidental that immigration reform became a major platform for crime control. Indeed, the two immigration reforms that would increase removals of noncitizen criminal offenders to unprecedented levels—the aggravated felon classification and the Institutional Hearing Program—(dwarfing by large margins all previous campaigns to remove criminal aliens) were enacted in the Anti-Drug Abuse Act of 1988.

The Mythical Aggregated Felon Designation
The Anti-Drug Abuse Act of 1988 created a new category of crimes for which a noncitizen can be deported: aggravated felonies. At the time, this new category of crimes was limited to serious, often violent, offenses: murder, drug trafficking, and firearms trafficking. The new designation of

"aggravated felon" was significant because the penalties that were (gradu-ally) attached to it were the harshest penalties to which criminal aliens have ever been subjected. It has "brought ruin to more aliens than any other ground for deportation" (Wingerter 2001). Subsequent waves of legislation have vastly expanded this category and attached additional penalties to it.

The Immigration Act of 1990 expanded the definition of "aggravated felonies" to crimes of violence for which the sentence is at least five years.[7] Four years later, the Immigration and Technical Corrections Act expanded the definition to include additional firearms and explosives offenses, some theft or burglar offenses, some types of fraud, prostitution, and a few other offenses.[8]

The *Antiterrorism and Effective Death Penalty Act* (AEDPA) of 1996 expanded the scope of existing aggravated felonies related to gambling, transportation for purposes of prostitution, alien smuggling, passport fraud, and other forms of document fraud, and expanded the definition to include new offenses involving obstruction of justice, perjury, or bribery offenses for which a sentence of at least five years or more may be imposed; commercial bribery, forgery, counterfeiting, and vehicle trafficking offenses for which a sentence of at least five years or more may be imposed; offenses committed by an alien ordered previously deported; and offenses relating to skipping bail for which a sentence of two or more years may be imposed.[9]

Five months later, the *Illegal Immigration Reform and Immigrant Responsibility Act* (IIRAIRA) expanded the definition of aggravated felonies once again, to include new offenses such as rape and sexual abuse of a minor,[10] and lowered the sentence length and monetary amount thresholds involved in many crimes defined as aggravated felonies.[11]

The aggravated felony designation has grown so broad as to encompass many crimes involving moral turpitude. Consequently, after 1996, a nonci-tizen who commits a crime involving moral turpitude is punished more harshly than under the old law. For example, under the old law a non-U.S. citizen convicted of shoplifting and given a suspended sentence was not deportable unless he had two convictions, and could be eligible for relief from deportation. Under the new laws, that individual would be deported and barred from relief (Morawetz 2000).

With a conviction for an aggravated felony comes a host of other prob-lems. First, detention is mandatory. The Anti-Drug Abuse Act of 1988 pro-vided that aggravated felons, including lawful permanent residents, would be subject to mandatory detention without bond. The IIRIRA subse-quently provided for the mandatory detention of virtually all criminal aliens subject to deportation. And because immigration detainees are con-fined in county jails, federal lockups, and immigration service processing centers, they are locked up with, and treated like, prisoners. Second, since 1996, aggravated felons are deportable retroactively. In other words, noncitizens (including long-term lawful permanent residents) who committed relatively minor crimes long ago are being deported for past offenses that were not deportable crimes at the time of conviction. Many a noncitizen convicted of a minor crime long ago with the assurance that they would not be deported has since been arrested, detained, and deported as an aggravated felon. Third, although habeas corpus review is still available to aggravated felons to challenge removal orders on the basis of legal (but not factual) error, they have no other judicial recourse for challenging their order of removal. Fourth, removal precludes an aggravated felon from being eligible for reentry for the next twenty years, and substantially increases future penalties for reentry after removal, and it bars all aliens—even those who are lawful permanent residents who have lived in the United States their entire lives—from cancellation of removal (i.e., relief from deportation) (Lancaster 2003).

The Institutional Removal Program

The Institutional Removal Program (IRP) was initiated under the Anti-Drug Abuse Act of 1988 in an effort to address what was considered a gaping loophole in criminal alien deportation procedures, and primarily an issue of federalism. Because the overwhelming majority of convicted criminals serve their time in state correctional facilities, state correctional agencies normally released offenders to parole authorities for noncustodial supervision without regard to their citizenship status. Offenders who served their full term of incarceration were often simply released without aftercare. In either event, the (now-defunct) Immigration and Naturalization Service (INS) had no effective procedure for deporting non-U.S. citizens after their release from prison. Subject to deportation by federal immigration authorities, these non-U.S. citizen ex-offenders often dropped off the radar screen, frequently coming to the attention of immigration authorities only when attempting to reenter the country after having crossed the border. The IRP attempted to close the loophole by establishing procedures for deporting criminal aliens straight from prison, thus eliminating the need for subsequent immigration detention, and ensuring expeditious removal at the end of the term of criminal incarceration. The IIRIRA expanded the program to cover most non-U.S. citizens deportable on criminal grounds. Later, the Immigration Act of 1990 strengthened the program by requiring states to notify federal immigration authorities of state convictions.

The aggravated felon designation (making many more—even minor—criminal offenders subject to deportation) in conjunction with the IRP (coordinating state correctional authorities and federal immigration authorities) substantially accelerated deportation statistics. Whereas only 1,100 criminal aliens were removed in 1988, by 1996 that number had increased tenfold. By 1997, an estimated 24,000 criminal aliens were removed (Morris 1997: 1322).

Conceptual Links Between the War on Drugs and the Criminal Alien "Crisis"
It doesn't take a great stretch of the imagination to understand how the War on Drugs so influenced immigration strategies and how the immigration system, in turn, adopted the mechanisms of the severity revolution occurring in crime control. First, the War on Drugs and the immigration "crisis" were conceptually linked. Urban centers and the southern border were the main targets of the campaign to get drugs off the streets (Lytle 2003). Both areas contained high levels of immigration-related activity regarded as problematic (e.g., illegal border crossing, drug couriering, ethnic gang activity, and inner-city welfare dependency). Second, many of the same lawmakers that enacted harsh federal sentencing guidelines and other tough-on-crime measures as part of the War on Drugs were charged with passing harsh, new immigration reforms, only a few years later. Thus the criminal alien "crisis" was not only conceptually linked to the War on Drugs, but also spearheaded by many of the same lawmakers who had already demonstrated a willingness to use harsh measures to reform a criminal justice system widely perceived as broken.

Impacts and Unintended Consequences
The harshness of the immigration regime under the War on Drugs took a zero-tolerance approach to criminal aliens that drastically increased in the volume of immigration detainees and the number of criminal alien removals. In this regard, Congress achieved its goal. In 1984, 1,000 noncitizens were deported on criminal grounds (Gallagher 2001). In 1992, the INS reportedly deported 16,841 criminal aliens, a figure representing a 25% increase over 1991, and a 50% increase over 1990 (Los Angeles Times 1992). In 1995, the INS removed 33,842 criminal aliens (DHS Office of Immigration Statistics 2002). In 1998, the INS removed 60,965, and in 2001, 71,994 criminal aliens were removed (DHS Office of Immigration Statistics 2002), representing an increase of over 400% in just under a decade.

Despite the success of the zero-tolerance approach to criminal aliens as reflected in increased removals, the reforms strained existing notions of fairness to immigrants and even produced unintended consequences. Some criminal aliens ordered removed cannot be deported to their countries of origin because either the United States has no repatriation treaty with the country of origin and the country will not agree to accept the alien or the country of origin no longer exists. Under the 1996 immigration reforms, most of these individuals are subject to mandatory detention. They may languish for years in immigration detention facilities. A 2001 U.S. Supreme Court decision[12] held that indefinite detention was unconstitutional, found that six months past an initial removal of 90 days was a reasonable time to effect deportation, and placed the burden on the government to demonstrate that removal was imminent after the reasonable time had passed or release the alien. Nevertheless, immigration authorities have been accused of frequently delaying past six months, "suspending" the removal period for detainees, and placing the burden on detainees to show efforts to secure their own removal, in situations where that individual has never failed to cooperate with removal efforts. (Ammon 2002). Counsel for aliens subjected to prolonged detention charge that the government's "pattern and practice is to place a burden of proof on detainees to show cooperation, without regard to the length of time for which the detainee has already been detained after entry of an order of removal." (Ammon 2002).

Another unanticipated consequence stems from the haphazard manner in which the immigration enforcement system and the criminal justice system interface. Margaret Taylor and Ronald Wright noted that with regard to criminal aliens "Neither of these bureaucracies wins plaudits for its efficiency or its humane treatment of the people caught up in the cases. One system is profoundly troubled; the other is a disaster. Criminal defense lawyers and immigration attorneys might disagree about which system deserves which label." (Taylor and Wright 2002). There is a great deal of variation in the immigration consequences for state criminal convictions because of varying state standards and definitions. Existing variations in state substantive criminal law and sentencing schemes result in a pronounced lack of uniformity across states in determining whether an individual is deemed to have committed an aggravated felony. State convictions for crimes such as statutory rape (which may fall within the "sexual abuse of a minor" aggravated felony classification) and driving under the influence (which appears to fall within the "crime of violence" aggravated felony classification)[13] commonly produce varying immigration consequences that result in the detention and deportation of some non-US citizens, but not others (Bennett 1999).

By Any Means Necessary: Criminal Severity Toward Criminal Aliens in the War on Terrorism

Intensified Scrutiny of Criminal Aliens Under the War on Terror
Although immigration reforms enacted to address potential acts of terrorism predated the attacks of 9/11, the massive scale of the destruction and

the extensive loss of life served to shift these reforms into high gear, propelled in part by massive public support for effective antiterrorism measures, even at the expense of civil liberties. Antiterrorism policy was implemented on many domestic fronts, including the preventive detention of Arab and Muslim men immediately after the attacks and the use of material witness warrants to confine suspected terrorist sympathizers. By the time the attacks occurred, Congress had already enacted immigration reforms that embraced an unyieldingly severe approach to non-U.S. citizens with past criminal convictions that facilitated their swift expulsion. After the attacks—which were carried out not by illegal immigrants or noncitizens with criminal convictions, but lawfully admitted aliens—the nation's urgent response to terrorism capitalized on immigration law's demonstrated utility as a mechanism for crime control and social control. Arab and Muslim communities were the immediate and primary focus of law enforcement efforts to investigate the suicide attacks and to prevent further attacks from occurring. Immigration law—with its broad powers to detain and question non-U.S. citizens—facilitated the criminal investigation. Indeed, many Middle Eastern–looking immigrants—increasingly concerned about being "disappeared" off the streets by the government—felt that immigration authorities were using strict compliance with the letter of the law as a pretext for questioning people about terrorism (Kirchgaessner 2001).

Despite the immediate mobilization of immigration powers to detain and expel Muslim and Arab non-U.S. citizens, it was not a foregone conclusion that the War on Terror would more broadly intensify immigration scrutiny of criminal aliens. A number of factors contribute to the zero- tolerance approach to criminal aliens under the War on Terror. First, as government officials reviewed the 9/11 attacks in hindsight, they became more convinced that persistent vulnerabilities in the enforcementof immigration law permitted the hijackers to operate "beyond the radar" of government scrutiny. According to this logic, the hijackers would have been removed as aliens out of compliance with their visas had the government more aggressively enforced strict compliance with the letter of immigration law.

Second, the Drug War's zero tolerance of undesirable non-U.S. citizens furnished a ready tool for purging a new type of undesirable foreigner. Recall that in the 1980s and 90s the immigration system implemented a social policy of removing undesirable noncitizens by deporting those with criminal convictions. The focus was on noncitizens, who were undesirable because they were ex-offenders (and therefore considered to deserve severity), illegal aliens (popularly regarded as draining public coffers and taking jobs from U.S. citizens), or refugees (posing welfare and crime problems in unpredictable waves of migration). 9/11 focused attention upon legal aliens (who entered the U.S. with permission, usually a visa) who fall out-of-status (i.e., over-stayed their visas or failed to comply with the tems of their visas, like for example, dropping out of school after entering with a student visa). The extra scrutiny of visa holders and other legal aliens was prompted by revelations after the 9/11 attacks that four of the nineteen hijackers were holders of student visas who were out of compliance with the terms of their visas. After 9/11, legally admitted aliens who had fallen out of compliance with the terms of their visas joined the growing list of "criminal aliens."

Third, the threat of terrorist violence on a massive scale realigned immigration law enforcement to make national security its highest priority. Failure to comply with the letter of immigration was now scrutinized through the lens of national security. After 9/11, even minor infractions of immigration regulations and civil orders that were once considered benign have taken on new meaning. Consequently visa overstayers, illegal aliens, refugees, and criminal aliens are all considered potential threats to national security, and therefore treated as if they were presently dangerous. For example, the sweeps of noncitizen airport workers immediately after 9/11—Operation Tarmac—that involved 106 U.S. airports and identified a total of 4,271 undocumented aliens were conducted in recognition of the fact that undocumented workers at airports pose a "serious security risk" (Interpreter Releases 2003: 1; Interpreter Releases 2003: 2). Although many were employed in custodial, maintenance, food service and other non-sensitive, low-wage jobs, once identified, these airport workers were processed for removal by ICE. Those who falsified documentation to get work (e.g. misrepresenting their immigration status on a job application) were criminally charged and prosecuted, then deported as criminal aliens. After 9/11, the Department of Homeland Security implemented a new policy and security initiative—Operation Liberty Shield—requiring that asylum seekers from 33 countries where al Qaeda or related terrorist groups operate be detained across-the-board until their asylum claims are decided (Mailman and Yale-Loehr 2003). The process can take as six months or more. The DHS officials justified the policy in part by noting that at least three individuals who committed, or conspired to commit, acts of terrorism in the United States were originally admitted as asylum applicants (Drew and Liptak 2003).

Even when asylum seekers have no connection to a "terrorist country," concern for national security reconfigured the previous policy. For example, in 2003, federal prosecutors in South Florida began criminally charging Haitian refugees—long-familiar to the United States as individuals fleeing an unstable political regime in their home country—for entering the United States with falsified documents (Mailman and Yale-Loehr 2003). Although they are technically in violation of immigration law, they have not traditionally been treated as such. The United States has generally elected not to charge asylum seekers with false documents criminally, in recognition of the fact that falsifying documents is frequently one of the few means by which individuals persecuted by the government can escape.[14] These practices—detaining and criminally charging some asylum seekers—contrast sharply with the earlier, more sympathetic and humanitarian treatment afforded asylum seekers by virtue of their claims of persecution in their home countries and the hardship fleeing that persecution typically entails.

Fourth, not long after the attacks, the Bush administration, through the Office of National Drug Control Policy, began a campaign against narco-terrorism[15] that publicized and promoted the idea that the terrorism was linked to casual drug use. The most memorable aspect of the campaign was a series of television commercials that ran during the 2003 Super Bowl that portrayed American teenage drug abusers as "terrorists." The highly criticized media campaign was eventually withdrawn, and the U.S. Drug Enforcement Administration has yet to definitively establish that Osama bin Laden financed the 9/11 attacks with proceeds from opium sales. However, the message that drugs trafficked across U.S. borders are linked to the funding of terrorist organizations remains a cornerstone of the War on Drugs after 9/11, and provides powerful justification for importing zero-tolerance law enforcement from the drug war into immigration policy and other areas of regulation concerned with flushing out terrorists.

Rehabilitating Discredited Crime and Immigration Policies

The treatment of criminal aliens has become more severe after 9/11 as the War on Terror perpetuates the aggressive removals of the vastly expanded population of non-U.S. citizens considered to be "criminal aliens." The threat such individuals present to society has—in post–9/11 America—been recast in light of the War on Terrorism. For example, in 2002 the Department of Justice inaugurated a new law enforcement program, the Absconder Apprehension Initiative, that uses federal law enforcement agents to track down, interrogate, and prosecute fugitives from the removal process. Although it appears to be yet another mechanism for broadly enforcing strict compliance with immigration laws, in actuality, the program initially focused on 6,000 Muslims and Arabs as "priority absconders." Agents were directed to "use all appropriate means" to enlist the cooperation of these "priority absconders," including offering reward money and discussing the availability of S-visas (so-called "snitch" visas) in exchange for intelligence on terrorism (Interpreter Releases 2002).

The Absconder Apprehension Initiative illustrates how the War on Terrorism is rehabilitating old, discredited policies of the 1980s and 90s.

First, the mobilization of law enforcement agents, particularly state and local police who tend to have greater contact with immigrant communities "on the street" to arrest and apprehend immigration law violators was for many years discouraged. Municipalities, and even police officers, felt that such an arrangement would make immigrant communities distrustful of police officers and discourage them from reporting crimes. Second, the initiative—focused as it was on Muslim and Arab men—encouraged racial profiling, and enforced the impression that the government considers young Arab men to be suspicious and inherently dangerous.

The treatment of asylum seekers similarly rehabilitates former, discredited immigration policies. For example, the War on Terror has treated asylum seekers more harshly after 9/11 even when they have no connection with terrorism and have not committed a crime. A little over a year after 9/11, then INS announced a new policy of detaining all Haitian refugees arriving by sea (commonly referred to as *boat people*). The memorandum announcing the policy justified it, in part, as promoting the War on Terror by preventing the diversion of "key resources of the Coast Guard and the Department of Defense" from their primary mission of "protecting the homeland and fighting the War on Terrorism" (Bender's Immigration Bulletin 2002).

The most obvious revival of a discredited law enforcement policy is the racial profiling the government participated in, and condoned, after the attacks. Middle Eastern–looking men and women were searched and interrogated by members of the National Guard before boarding commercial aircraft, and in some instances, denied permission to board. Middle Eastern men were being "disappeared" off the streets by law enforcement agents and detained incommunicado in sweeps conducted across the country to immobilize terrorist networks and prevent future attacks. Every Middle Eastern– looking man was a potential terrorist, regardless of citizenship status. Ironically, a broad consensus had emerged on the eve of 9/11 that racial profiling was morally wrong and ineffective as a law enforcement mechanism. Indeed, shortly after his inauguration, President Bush attacked racial profiling in an address before a joint session of Congress and called for its demise of profiling. Yet, after the attacks, Bush's resolve crumbled as he argued in favor of the use of racial profiling to combat terrorism. As law professor Morgan Cloud observed, "the 9/11, 2001 terrorist attacks resurrected religious and racial profiling from the scrap heap of discredited constitutional doctrines to which it had only recently been discarded" (Cloud 2003: 272). Guidelines issued by the Justice Department took the position that profiling was prohibited in "traditional" law enforcement but acceptable in efforts to safeguard the nation from the threat of terrorism (Cloud 2003: 373).

The War on Terrorism has more broadly recast the War on Drugs in a light favorable to antiterrorist initiatives by defending drug law enforcement procedures that have become useful in combating terrorism. In the case *U.S. v. Alvarez-Machain*—recently argued before the U.S. Supreme Court—the U.S. government sought to rehabilitate law enforcement methods including kidnapping that were found to have constituted torts and violated basic human rights, and therefore exposed the government to liability. The Bush administration fought to overturn this holding and a subsequent award of damages against the government on the grounds that the case "has the potential to dramatically limit [the government's] power to fight the war on terror" (Totenberg 2004). As the government stated in one of its briefs, "kidnappings like this one are rare but they are necessary, particularly in the war on terror, and might be necessary one day if Osama bin Laden is found in a country that can't or won't extradite him" (Totenberg 2004).

The case emerged out of the U.S. government's indictment of Humberto Alvarez-Machain, a Mexican physician, for his alleged role in the murder and torture of a U.S. drug enforcement agent in Mexico. When Mexico refused to extradite the defendant, the U.S. government kidnapped him and brought him to the United States with the help of hired bounty hunters and a Mexican agent of the United States. The case was tried in 1992. At that point, the defendant had spent two years in pretrial detention. The judge ruled the evidence was insufficient for a conviction and dismissed the case. Alvarez-Machain returned to Mexico a free man, and promptly sued the United States under the Federal Tort Claims Act (claiming that Drug Enforcement Agency personnel have no authority to carry out arrests on foreign soil) and sued the Mexican agent of the United States under the Alien Tort Statute (claiming that his arrest was arbitrary and therefore violated international human rights law).

As the news media have observed, "what started out as a drug case for the U.S. government in 1990 . . . has been transformed into a terrorism case in 2004."[16] In June 2004, the Supreme Court reversed the Ninth Circuit's decision, thereby insulating the federal government from liability for exercising arrest power likely to be employed again within the context of counter-terrorism.

Broader Impact of the War on Terror on All Ex-Offenders

Criminal aliens are not the only ex-offenders for whom the impact of collateral civil penalties has been intensified under the War on Terror. Ex-offenders who lack citizenship are exclusively subject to detention and deportation and explicitly targeted by antiterrorism initiatives. Nevertheless, the impact of collateral civil penalties under the War on Terror extends to all ex-offenders. A clear example is the way in which criminal background checks have changed in the wake of the 9/11 terrorist attacks. A growing number of employers are conducting thorough criminal background checks of potential employees. Only a few years ago, ex-offenders could prove themselves on the job for a few months before the results of background check, required by many employers as part of the application process, were obatained. Since 9/11 security-conscious employers are refraining from extending employment offers until receiving the results of such background checks. As a result, ex-offenders are finding it harder to find employment and earn a living regardless of citizenship status (Abramson 2004). Since 9/11, the risk of terrorism seems to have brought into focus other risks, including the risk of criminal offending. That broader awareness of risk works against all ex-offenders in the context of job seeking.

Conclusion

After 9/11, national security and public safety are no longer discrete issues. The boundaries between defending U.S. sovereignty and policing criminal activity are increasingly merging. Justifications for policing immigration and policing crime are merging as well. Asa Hutchinson as much at stated this in a news conference unveiling the "Most Wanted Criminal Aliens" list. When asked whether the criminal aliens on the list posed a real threat to public safety in light of the risks posed by the most wanted al Qaeda members and other terrorists, Hutchinson responded: "[T]he Department of Homeland Security and ICE are not limited to a counterterrorism mission. We have broad responsibilities in law enforcement, and this [most wanted criminal aliens list] reflects that broad mandate." (U.S. Department of Homeland Security, 2003). He went on to say that the broad mandate of homeland security is assisted by the centralization of law enforcement, immigration, and anti-terrorism resources under the Department of Homeland Security. As the War on Terrorism evolves, it is reshaping the contours of criminal justice policies on many levels. The heightened scrutiny directed to criminal aliens has resulted in harsher treatment of citizens and noncitizens alike.

References

Abramson, Larry. 2004. "Background Checks" National Public Radio (*Morning Edition Transcript*), May 20.

Ammon, Elizabeth. 2002. "INS Flouts High Court on Prisoners, Critics Say," The National Law Journal, August 15.

Bender's Immigration Bulletin. "News: Boat People, aka Haitians, Threaten National Security?," vol. 7, no. 23 (December 1, 2002). 1510–11.

Bennett, Iris. 1999. "The Unconstitutionality of Nonuniform Immigration Consequences of "Aggravated Felony" Convictions." 74 New York University Law Review 1696–1740.

U.S. Department of Homeland Security 2003. "Asa Hutchinson Holds News Conference on the National Fugitive Operations Initiative." Press Release. May 14.

Brown, Steve and Chris Coon. 2003. "A CLEAR Solution for Criminal Aliens." *FrontPageMagazine.com*, November 18.

Cloud, Morgan. 2003. "Quakers, Slaves and the Founders: Profiling to Save the Union," Mississippi Law Journal v.79: 372–373.

Department of Homeland Security Office of Immigration Statistics. 2002. Aliens removed by criminal status and region and country of nationality: fiscal years 1993-2002, Table 46. http://uscis.gov/graphics/shared/aboutus/statistics/ENF2002list.htm.

Drew, Christopher and Adam Liptak . 2003. "Immigration Groups Fault Rule on Automatic Detention of Some Asylum Seekers," *New York Times* (March 31, 2003), p. B15.

Gallagher, Anna Maria. 2001. "Immigration Consequences of Criminal Convictions: Protecting Your Client's Immigration Interests in Criminal Proceedings," *Immigration Briefings*, no. 01-4: 2.

Harper, Elizabeth (ed.). 1975. *Immigration Laws of the United States*, 3rd Ed. (Bobbs-Merrill Co.: New York). 564–647.

Interpreter Releases 2002. "Deputy Attorney General Releases Internal Guidance for 'Absconder' Apprehensions, vol. 79, no. 8 (West Group, February 18): 261.

Interpreter Releases 2003:1. House Subcommittee Holds Immigration Enforcement Oversight Hearing, Sevis Hearing, vol. 80, no. 15 (West Group, April 14): 538, n. 5.

Interpreter Releases 2003:2. "Report and analysis of immigration and nationality law," vol. 80, no .45 (West Group, November 24.): 1612.

Kennedy, Joseph E. 2000. "Monstrous Offenders and the Search of Solidarity through Modern Punishment." 51 Hastings Law Journal 829: 832.

Kirchgaessner, Stephanie. 2001. "Some Immigration Lawyers Wary of INS Powers." *The Financial Times* (London Edition): 2.

Lutton, Wayne and John Tanton. 1994. *The Immigration Invasion* 61 (1994).

Lytle, Kelly. 2003. Constructing the Criminal Alien: A Historical Framework for Analyzing Border Vigilantes at the Turn of the 21st Century (Center for Comparative Immigration Studies), 1-8.

Lancaster, Kelly L. 2003. "Felony Drinking and Driving Convictions as Crimes of Violence Under 18 U.S.C. §16(B): What the Words Really Mean for Aliens." 37 *New England Law Review* 395, 401 (2003).

Los Angeles Times 1992. "S.D. Led in Criminal Deportations." October 30. Metro Desk: B5.

Mailman, Stanley and Stephen Yale-Loehr. 2003 "Detaining and Criminalizing Asylum Seekers," *Bender's Immigration Bulletin,* vol. 9, no. 9 (May 1, 2003), p. 763.

Morawetz, Nancy 2000. "Understanding the Impact of the 1996 Deportation Laws and the Limited Scope of Proposed Reforms." 113 Harvard Law Review 1936.

Norwood, Charlie 2003. "CLEAR Act Pointed to as Solution to Criminal Alien Crisis". Press Release. October 1.

Osborn, K. 2001. "DUI Get Aliens a Free Trip Home." Fox News, January 24, 2001.

Taylor, Margaret 2004. "Dangerous by Decree: Detention Without Bond in Immigration Proceedings." 9 Bender's Immigration Bulletin 906 (August 1, 2004).

Taylor, Margaret and Ronald Wright. 2002. "The Sentencing Judge as Immigration Judge." 51 Emory Law Journal 1131, 1134–35.

Totenberg, Nina. 2004. "Alien Tort Act," National Public Radio (*Morning Edition* transcript), March 30.

U.S. Citizenship and Immigration Services 2003. "ICE Unveils "Most Wanted" Criminal Aliens List". News Release. May 14, 2003. Available on the U.S. Department of Homeland Security website at: http://uscis.gov/graphics/publicaffairs/newsrels/mostwanted.htm

U.S. Department of Homeland Security. "L.A. ICE Agents Arrest one of Homeland Security's Most Wanted Criminal Aliens." Press Release. January 28, 2002.

Wingerter, Rex B. 2001. "Defenses to Removal Based on Criminal Convictions: INA Waivers." Immigration Briefings. No. 01-6 (June 2001) p. 9.

Cases Cited

Leocal v. Ashcroft, 2004 WL 2514904 (U.S.)

Matter of U., 5 I & N. Dec. 413, August 1953.

Zadvydas v. Davis, 533 U.S. 678 (2001)

Endnotes

1. Most criminal aliens are deported for drug offenses. Many criminal aliens are deported for relatively minor criminal offenses or offenses that are far in the past.

2. After the attacks, Congress specifically provided for the detention of suspected terrorists without bond in the USA PATRIOT Act. Rather than relying on the detention provisions of the PATRIOT Act however, the INS (later subsumed under the DHS) relied on the detention authority found in existing immigration legislation, including provisions for detaining criminal aliens, because they give more leeway to the executive branch. Margaret Taylor, "Dangerous By Decree: Detention without Bond in Immigration Proceedings," 9 Bender's Immigration Bulletin 906 (August 1, 2004).

3. A chart of the Ten Most Wanted Fugitive Criminal Aliens can be found on the Office of Detention and Removal website at: http://www.ice.gov/graphics/investigations/wanted/mostwanted.pdf.

4. I use the terms *deportation and removal* interchangeably. The 1996 immigration legislation introduces the term removal, but it hardly does justice to the experience of being forced to leave the country (often leaving family members behind), in effect banished, with no prospect of *legally* reentering the country for an extended period of time.

5. Willie Horton was a felon who committed a violent crime after being released from a Massachusetts prison through a furlough program. He was used by Republican presidential candidate George Bush to deride Michael Dukakis's legacy of liberal social policies and to legitimate Bush's "tough on crime" stance. Horton was repeatedly intoned in Bush's campaign rhetoric and became identified as the embodiment of the Democrats' inability to reform a "broken" criminal justice system. Recently, Republicans such as Charlie Norwood (R-GA) have spotlighted notorious noncitizen criminal offenders who committed crimes while subject to removal as paradigmatic of a broken immigration system. These offenders include the D.C. sniper John Lee Malvo, Armando Garcia (a deported Mexican national who reentered the United States and shot a sheriff's deputy during a traffic stop), Miguel Gordoba (a convicted child molester who failed to register as a sexual offender when he was released and cannot be located by immigration officials), and the 9/11 hijackers (some of whom had expired visas when they commandeered commercial aircraft and attacked multiple targets, killing thousands) (Brown and Coon 2003).

6. A noncitizen convicted at any time of a drug offense was deportable, notwithstanding a judicial recommendation against deportation. Aliens convicted of violating miscellaneous laws relating to espionage and subversive activities were deportable if convicted once within five years of entry or more than once at any time after entry.

7. Pub. L. No. 101-649, 104 Stat 4978 (November 29, 1990).

8. Pub. L. No. 103-416, 108 Stat 4305 (October 25, 1994).

9. Pub. L. No. 104-132, 110 Stat 279 (April 24, 1996).

10. Considered a misdemeanor in many states.

11. For example, IIRAIRA lowered the amount of funds involved in a money-laundering crime to be considered an aggravated felony from $100,000 to $10,000 and lowered to one year the sentence length required for many "crimes of violence" and theft offenses to be considered aggravated felonies.

12. Zadvydas v. Davis, 533 U.S. 678 (2001).

13. On November 9, 2004 the United States Supreme Court held that state "driving under the influence" (DUI) offenses which either do not have a *mens rea* (state of mind) component or require only a showing of negligence in the operation of a vehicle, are not "crimes of violence" for immigration purposes. Since the definition of aggravated felonies includes "crimes of violence" for which alien receives a sentence of at least one year of imprisonment, and deportation is mandated for all aggravated felons, the Court's ruling prohibits the deportation of non-US citizens with DUI convictions in states with no or low (negligent) mental state requirements. The Court did not reach the issue of whether convictions under state DUI statutes in which reckless use of force is an element of the crime are "crimes of violence" within the definition of aggravated felony. Furthermore, there is little likelihood of relief for those aliens deported for DUI convictions in states with no or low *mens rea* component prior to the Court's ruling.

14. Indeed until 9/11, the United States apparently deferred to Article 31(1) of the U.N. Refugee Convention, prohibiting member countries from penalizing asylum seekers who enter illegally,

as long as they come directly from the country whence they fled persecution, present themselves without delay to authorities, and show good cause for the illegal entry or presence (Leocal v. Ashcroft, 2004 WL 2514904 (U.S.)). Although the United States is not bound by the treaty because it is not self-executing, the federal government nevertheless generally refrained from criminally prosecuting asylum seekers arriving with false documentation before 9/11 (Mailman and Yale-Loehr 2003: 766).

15. *Narco-terrorism* refers to criminal activity, such as international trafficking in narcotics, and weapons and laundering money engaged in to support the pursuits of terrorist organizations, such as Hezbollah, al Qaeda, Hamas, and less-organized criminal, quasi-terrorist gangs.

16. Ibid.

4

Disenfranchisement and the Civic Reintegration of Convicted Felons

CHRISTOPHER UGGEN AND JEFF MANZA

This chapter addresses the political life of criminal offenders, with a particular emphasis on felon disenfranchisement. After a brief historical overview of voting restrictions on felons and ex-felons, we discuss the scope and likely political impact of disenfranchisement on state and national elections. The chapter then considers the question of the "civic reintegration" of large numbers of released offenders. This section draws on some recently collected interview and survey data regarding the political thoughts and attitudes of convicted offenders. The relationships among disenfranchisement, political participation, and recidivism are considered, as well as the merits of current procedures for the restoration of civil rights in some states. Finally, we discuss other barriers to democratic participation, taking stock of existing knowledge and suggesting some potentially promising future avenues of research.

Disenfranchisement and the Civic Reintegration of Convicted Felons

When criminologists talk about "citizens," they generally use the term in opposition to convicted offenders, placing criminals on one side of the ledger and law-abiding community residents on the other. Yet felons are *themselves* citizens, who occupy roles as taxpayers, homeowners, volunteers, and voters. This chapter explores the civic and political life of criminal offenders, with a particular emphasis on felon disenfranchisement. Although a well-developed research literature addresses socioeconomic (e.g., Sampson and Laub 1993; Uggen 2000) and family reintegration (e.g., Laub, Nagin, and Sampson 1998), the subject of reintegration into community life and civic participation has received comparatively little attention. In our view, civic reintegration represents a third reintegrative domain in which increased social participation may affect desistance patterns. If, as Shadd Maruna (2001: 7) contends, desistance is only possible when ex-offenders "develop a coherent pro-social identity for themselves," then prisoner reentry programs could facilitate this development by removing barriers to democratic participation. In fact, it is possible that developing a self-concept as a pro-social conforming citizen may be a key mechanism linking adult work and family roles with desistance from crime (Uggen, Manza, and Behrens 2004).

No account of this area would be complete without a historical overview of voting restrictions on felons and ex-felons, as well as a discussion of current legal challenges. We then turn to recent estimates of the scope and likely political impact of disenfranchisement on state and national elections. The topic that may be of greatest interest to the discussion of successful reentry is the question of the "civic reintegration" of large numbers of released offenders. To understand the political thoughts and attitudes of those most affected by these laws, we will draw here upon some recently collected interview and survey data. Next, other barriers to democratic participation are discussed, such as constraints on engaging in political discussions and demonstrations. Finally, we conclude by taking stock of existing knowledge and suggesting some potentially promising areas for research and policy.

Felon Disenfranchisement Law

Felon disenfranchisement refers to the loss of voting rights following a felony conviction. Almost all convicted felons in the United States face the temporary or permanent suspension of their access to the ballot. More generally, the idea of limiting the citizenship rights of criminals is founded on the liberal legal model and early Enlightenment notions of the social contract. For Thomas Hobbes [1651] (1962: 233), for example, "A banished man is a lawful enemy of the commonwealth that banished him; as being no more a member of the same." Employing a similar logic, Jean-Jacques Rousseau [1762] (1957: 32–33) argued that criminal offenders who violate the social compact must be separated from their fellow citizens:

> [E]very malefactor, by attacking the social right, becomes by his crimes a rebel and a traitor to his country; by violating its laws, he ceases to be a member of it and, in fact, wakes war upon it. The existence of the State then becomes incompatible with his; one of the two must therefore perish; and when the criminal is executed, he suffers less as a citizen than as an enemy. *The proceedings and the judgment pronounced in consequence, are the proofs and the declaration that he has broken the social treaty, and, consequently, that he is no longer a member of the State.* But as he is still considered as such at least while he sojourns there, he must be either removed by exile, as a violator of the pact, or by death, as a public enemy. [Emphasis added.]

For centuries, governments have punished criminals by restricting their fundamental rights of citizenship. States justify such sanctions as a form of retribution and deterrent to future offending. As Alexander Keyssar (2000) notes in *The Right to Vote,* his authoritative social history of the franchise, disenfranchisement of criminal offenders has long been imposed in English, European, and Roman law. In the United States, individual states began to incorporate felon disenfranchisement provisions into their constitutions in the late-18th and 19th centuries. Many of the more restrictive state laws were adopted in the era of the post-Reconstruction South, perhaps as part of a larger strategy of disfranchising African-Americans (Fellner and Mauer 1998). Some disenfranchisement laws also emerged in northern and southern states as anticorruption reform efforts, ostensibly to "preserve the purity of the ballot" *Washington v. State,* 75 Ala. 582 (1884).

Disenfranchisement Regimes

The recent explosion in rates of criminal punishment is well known to those of us studying reentry and reintegration. Nevertheless, it is important to note in this context that felon disenfranchisement constitutes a growing impediment to political participation primarily because of the rapid rise in the number of convicted felons since the 1970s. Seven times more people were imprisoned in state and federal facilities in 2000 (1,381,892) than were imprisoned in 1972 (196,429) (U.S. Department of Justice 2001; 1975). Other correctional populations have also increased in rate and number, with a quadrupling in the number of felony probationers (from 455,093 to 1,924,548) and parolees (from 160,900 to 712,700) from 1976 to 1999. Today, the United States incarcerates more of its citizens than most other advanced industrial societies (Mauer 1997a). Although many other nations currently disenfranchise some portion of their correctional populations, the United States is unusual in combining both high rates of criminal punishment and restrictive felon disenfranchisement laws. Within the United States, the correctional populations affected by disenfranchisement differ dramatically across the individual states. As of 2004, 48 of 50 states (all but Maine and Vermont) disenfranchise prison inmates, many more disenfranchise probationers and parolees, nine states bar some or all ex-felons from voting (Alabama, Florida, Iowa, Kentucky, Mississippi, Tennessee, Virginia, Washington [for those convicted prior to 1984], and Wyoming), three more disenfranchise some recidivists (Arizona, Maryland and Nevada), and another state requires a waiting period before voting rights are restored (Delaware). The following list summarizes the correctional populations affected by felon disenfranchisement in the United States. Although some within-category variation remains, the list illustrates a gradient, reading from top to bottom, of restrictiveness: states such as Maine and Vermont currently impose almost no restrictions and states such as Florida and Alabama disenfranchise felons for life, or until their rights are restored through pardon or clemency procedures:

No restrictions (2):
Maine, Vermont
Inmates only (13):
Hawaii, Illinois, Indiana, Massachusetts, Michigan, Montana, New Hampshire, North Dakota, Ohio, Oregon, Pennsylvania, South Dakota, Utah
Inmates, Parolees (4):
California, Colorado, Connecticut, New York
Inmates, Parolees, Felony Probationers (17):
Alaska, Arkansas, Georgia, Idaho, Kansas, Louisiana, Minnesota, Missouri, New Jersey, New Mexico, North Carolina, Oklahoma, Rhode Island, South Carolina, Texas, West Virginia, Wisconsin
Inmates, Parolees, Felony Probationers, some Ex-Felons (14):
Alabama, Arizona (recidivists), Delaware (5-year waiting period), Florida, Iowa, Kentucky, Maryland (violent recidivists), Mississippi, Nebraska, Nevada (recidivists and violent offenders), Tennessee (convictions pre-1986), Virginia, Washington (convictions pre-1984), Wyoming

Population Estimates

Although the Bureau of Justice Statistics provides head counts of the number of felons currently serving prison, probation, and parole sentences, the number of ex-felons currently residing in a given state is typically unknown.

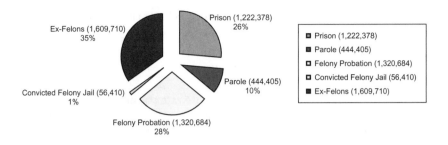

Figure 4.1 Estimated Distribution of Legally Disenfranchised Felons in the United States, 2000 (Uggen and Manza 2002).

Estimates of the size of the disenfranchised population therefore vary with the methodology used to compute the number of ex-felons no longer under supervision in states that disenfranchise ex-felons. In 1997, Marc Mauer of the Sentencing Project estimated the disenfranchised felon and ex-felon population at approximately 4.2 million (1997: 12). In an updated and expanded analysis, the Sentencing Project and Human Rights Watch reported in 1998 that approximately 4 million adults were disenfranchised, representing about 2% of the voting age population (Fellner and Mauer 1998). Uggen and Manza (2002), using a demographic life table method to calculate the ex-felon population, obtained higher estimates: approximately 4.7 million at year-end 2000. Based on these estimates and increases in correctional populations and releasees since 2000, it seems likely that between 4 and 5 million Americans are currently legally disenfranchised. Additionally, a large number of those in jail awaiting trial or serving time on misdemeanor convictions are "practically disenfranchised." Several hundred thousand jail inmates thus retain the legal right to vote, but lack access to a polling place on Election Day.

Figure 4.1 shows the approximate distribution of disenfranchised felons and ex-felons for year-end 2000 by correctional supervision category. Uggen and Manza include a very conservative estimate of the legally disenfranchised jail population, based on 10% of the inmate population at year-end 2000. Although the distribution is shifting continuously as states alter their disenfranchisement regimes, it remains the case that only a minority of disenfranchised felons are prison inmates. In 2000, almost three-fourths of those disenfranchised were either supervised in the community or ex-felons who had completed their sentences. The philosophical justification for disenfranchisement would appear to be stronger for current prison inmates than for those who have completed their sentence (ex-felons), or those otherwise deemed fit to maintain community ties (probationers and parolees). Even as the loss of voting rights is a powerful symbol of a felon's "outsider" status, their restoration provides a clear marker of reintegration and acceptance into a community of law-abiding citizens. In keeping with this logic, Congressman John Conyers (D-MI) and other have argued that voting rights should be restored as soon as inmates have been released from incarceration.

Perhaps more striking than the absolute rate or number of disenfranchised felons is their distribution by race and social class (Mauer 1999; U.S. Department of Justice 2001). African-American men are disproportionately affected, with over 1.4 million, or 13%, of the African-American male population disenfranchised owing to a current or former felony conviction (Fellner and Mauer 1998). Uggen and Manza (2002) find that in 15 states more than 10% of the total African-American voting age population (male and female) was disenfranchised in 2000.

Although it is more difficult to obtain reliable information on the social class distribution of the correctional populations affected by disenfranchisement, the *Survey of State Prison Inmates* data series shows that inmates have relatively low levels of educational attainment, with fewer than one-third having achieved a high school diploma in 1997 (U.S. Department of Justice 2000). Employment levels are also much lower than in the general population, with a slim majority holding a full-time job prior to their most recent arrest in the 1997 survey. In contrast, over three-fourths of males of comparable age in the general population held full-time jobs and 87 percent had attained a high school diploma or equivalency (Uggen and Massoglia 2003).

Current Legal Challenges

While many states implemented or altered their laws in the period immediately following the Civil War (Keyssar 2000), a century of relative inactivity in disenfranchisement provisions followed. The past 40 years, however, have witnessed the greatest changes in felon disenfranchisement law since the post-Reconstruction era (Behrens, Uggen, and Manza 2003). States once again began revising their laws in the 1960s and 1970s. In the past decade, a new flurry of legislative and judicial attention to felon disenfranchisement has occurred at both state and national levels. Although a comprehensive discussion of these cases and the legal issues they raise is beyond the scope of this chapter, we will briefly summarize some recent developments in this area.

Though some courts have overturned particular state disenfranchisement laws, most Constitutional challenges have been dismissed or otherwise unsuccessful, as courts have generally followed the 1974 United States Supreme Court decision in *Richardson v. Ramirez,* 418 U.S. 24, 56 (1974). *Richardson* ruled that felon disenfranchisement does not violate the equal protection clause of the Fourteenth Amendment, in part because Section 2 of that amendment appears to allow states to impose voting restrictions for "participation in rebellion, or other crime." While acknowledging the sovereignty of individual states and the legal issues raised by the *Richardson* precedent, the National Commission on Federal Election Reform (2001), headed by former presidents Jimmy Carter and Gerald Ford, recently argued against the disenfranchisement of ex-felons. The commission recommended that "each state should allow for restoration of voting rights to otherwise eligible citizens who have been convicted of a felony once they have fully served their sentence, including any term of probation or parole" (2001: 8).

A number of state court rulings have affected the voting rights of convicted felons. In New Hampshire, a 1998 state court decision barred the disenfranchisement of inmates, but in 2000, the New Hampshire Supreme Court reversed the lower court's ruling (*Fischer v. Governor*, 749 A.2d 321 (N. H. 2000)). The Pennsylvania state supreme court affirmed a lower court decision in 2000, overturning a disenfranchisement clause passed as part of the Pennsylvania Voting Rights Act of 1995 (*Mixon v. Commonwealth of Pennsylvania*, 783 A.2d 763 (Pa. 2001)). This clause, which prohibited ex-felons from registering to vote for five years following their release from prison, was also challenged in a federal district court (*NAACP v. Ridge*, U.S. Dist. LEXIS 11520 (E. D. Pa. 2000)).

Felon disenfranchisement has also faced challenges stemming from its disproportionate racial impact. Another case is currently pending in the Eleventh Circuit Court of Appeals, challenging the disenfranchisement of ex-felons in Florida as a violation of the Fourteenth Amendment's equal protection clause and the Voting Rights Act of 1965. In *Johnson v. Bush*, the plaintiffs argue that Florida's Reconstruction-era voting ban on those who had completed their sentences was adopted with discriminatory intent, as part of a strategy to reduce the political power of ex-slaves.

In addition to these lawsuits, several state legislatures have also overturned parts of longstanding disenfranchisement provisions for ex-felons, including Delaware (2000), Maryland (2003), Nevada (2003), and New Mexico (2001). Texas (1997) liberalized their disenfranchisement laws by removing a waiting period in which those who had completed their sentences were ineligible to vote before automatically regaining their voting rights after two years. In addition to changes in ballot restrictions for ex-felons, a number of states have begun to examine restrictions on probationers and parolees. Connecticut, for example, recently extended the franchise to felony probationers (Zielbauer 2001).

In contrast to these trends toward liberalizing disenfranchisement laws, however, other states have adopted more restrictive regimes. In both Utah (1998) and Massachusetts (2000), the electorate voted to disenfranchise state prison inmates who had previously been permitted to vote. In 2002, Kansas disenfranchised probationers. On a national level, proposed legislation to liberalize the voting rights of convicted felons has generally met with little success. For example, a bill introduced by Congressman John Conyers (D-MI) and Senator Harry Reid (D-NV) in the 106th Congress (the Civic Participation and Rehabilitation Act of 1999, H.R. 906) was unsuccessful in its attempt to secure voting rights for felony probationers, parolees, and ex-felons in all Federal elections.

Political Impact
Aside from the legal status of felon disenfranchisement, many observers have begun to consider its potential impact on political elections. Because felon eligibility rules are state-specific, several researchers have used state-level estimates of the size of the disenfranchised felon population to estimate the average impact of disenfranchisement laws across states. Using a sophisticated variant of this strategy, Miles (2000) finds that the felon disenfranchisement effect is small relative to its standard error and is not distinguishable from zero (cf. Hirschfield 1999). Specifically, Miles reports that neither a state's electoral participation rate, nor its likelihood of electing a Republican candidate, is significantly affected by legal restrictions on the voting rights of felons.

Uggen and Manza (2002), in contrast, develop an alternative approach, examining what would have happened in specific elections if disenfranchised felons had been permitted to vote and if their voting behavior mimicked the turnout and party preferences of those matched to them in the general population. They rely on censuses and surveys of prison inmates to determine the social characteristics of the felon population, the Current Population Survey's Voter Supplement Module to estimate turnout rates, and the National Election Study to predict voting intention. Combining these data sources, they estimate the net votes lost to disenfranchisement in closely contested presidential and U.S. Senate elections, and recompute vote returns after including these "lost felon voters."

Because felons are drawn disproportionately from the ranks of racial minorities and the poor—populations that have historically supported Democratic Party candidates—disenfranchisement laws tend to favor Republican candidates. Uggen and Manza's model predicted that the turnout rate among disenfranchised felons would have been substantially lower than among the general population, but that their strong Democratic Party preferences would have been a tipping point in a number of elections. They found that felon disenfranchisement would have altered the outcome of at least four, and likely six, recent U.S. Senate elections and four governor's races. Moreover, felon disenfranchisement may have affected control over the U.S. Senate. Assuming that Democrats who might have been elected in the absence of felon disenfranchisement had held their seats as long as the Republicans who narrowly defeated them, the Democratic Party would have gained parity in the 1984 Senate and would have maintained majority control of the U.S. Senate from 1986 to the present. Of course, this counterfactual analysis relied upon a *ceteris paribus* assumption: holding all else equal, changes in felon disenfranchisement law may have produced changes in the composition of the Senate.

In examining presidential elections, Uggen and Manza found that the Republican presidential victory of 2000 would have been reversed by a large margin had felons been allowed to vote, and that John F. Kennedy's Democratic presidential victory of 1960 would have been jeopardized had contemporary rates of disenfranchisement prevailed during that time. Today, disenfranchised felons and ex-felons make up more than 2% of the voting age population. Because the margin of victory in four of the last eleven presidential elections has been 1.1% of the voting-age population or less, felon disenfranchisement may be an important, and perhaps decisive, factor in future presidential races.

It should also be noted that a focus on national and state-level elections may understate the full impact of felon disenfranchisement. Because of the geographic concentration of disenfranchised felons and ex-felons in urban areas (Rose and Clear 1998), it is likely that such impact is even more pronounced in elections below the national level, such as state legislative and mayoral races. More targeted studies of local elections are needed, as well as better data on the effects of criminal sanctions on political participation.

Until recently, most observers considered felon disenfranchisement to be an interesting legal or philosophical issue, but one lacking strong political implications. As stated in a 1989 *Harvard Law Review*, "ex-felons are unlikely to constitute more than a tiny percentage of the population and thus are electorally insignificant" (Harvard Law Review Note 1989). Today, this is no longer the case. A confluence of high rates of criminal punishment and restrictive disenfranchisement regimes has created a situation in which the uncounted ballots of "lost felon voters" may be determining election outcomes.

Disenfranchisement, Reentry, and Reintegration

Disenfranchisement in Perspective: Does It Matter to Felons Themselves?
The meaning of disenfranchisement to those most affected by these laws is a critical issue in the analysis of barriers to democratic participation for criminal offenders. Uggen, Manza, and Behrens (2004; see also Uggen and

Manza 2004; Manza, Brooks, and Uggen 2004; and Manza and Uggen forthcoming) conducted 33 semistructured interviews with convicted felons in Minnesota. Of course, losing the right to vote is not the most pressing concern for most convicted felons. Nevertheless, we observed that disenfranchisement carried a sting for many and elicited an emotional response for some of our respondents. Steven (a pseudonym), a middle-aged probationer, put disenfranchisement into perspective with the other problems in his life as follows:

> On top of the whole messy pile, there it was. Something that was hardly mentioned, and it meant a lot. [Steven, male probationer, age 52]

Pamela, a female prisoner, similarly described disenfranchisement as "salt in the wound," explaining how the loss of voting rights is part of a larger package of restrictions that confounded her efforts to become a "normal citizen":

> I think that just getting back in the community and being a con-tributing member is difficult enough. . . . And saying, "Yeah, we don't value your vote either because you're a convicted felon from how many years back," okay? . . . But I, hopefully, have learned, have paid for that and *would like to someday feel like a, quote, "normal cit-izen," a contributing member of society,* and you know that's hard when every election you're constantly being reminded, "Oh yeah, that's right, I'm ashamed." . . . It's just like *a little salt in the wound.* You've already got that wound and it's trying to heal and it's trying to heal, and you're trying to be a good taxpayer and be a homeowner. . . . Just one little vote, right? But that means a lot to me. . . . It's just loss after loss after loss. And this is just another one. *Another to add to the pile.* . . . When I said salt in the wound, the wound's already there. Me being able to vote isn't going to just whip up and heal that wound. . . . It's like haven't I paid enough yet? . . . You can't really feel like a part of your government because they're still going like this, "Oh, you're bad. Remember what you did way back then? Nope, you can't vote. [Pamela, female prisoner, age 49; emphasis added]

These quotations make the point that voting rights are fundamental to conceptions of citizenship, even for those of us who take them for granted or fail to exercise them. If civic reintegration is a process of weaving offend-ers back into the social fabric, then restoration of voting rights is likely to help offenders begin to feel like citizens again and may even reduce the stigma associated with conviction.

Persons convicted of a felony form a very heterogeneous group. For example, those convicted of drug possession are likely to differ in important ways from sex offenders, burglars, or other offender groups. In discussing civil disabilities, felons express a clear desire for more *narrowly tailored* restrictions. Rita, a drug offender, made the case that disenfranchisement should only apply to election crimes:

> I didn't do anything that would affect how I voted or anything. It's not like I don't have a brain anymore.... And I really don't think it should go by the crime because that doesn't have nothing to do with it. [Y]ou know, *if you did something that had something to do with an election,* I could see it, but at least 99% of the people didn't have to do with an election. [Rita, female prisoner, age 41]

Manza and Uggen (forthcoming) also gathered survey data to learn more about the effects of criminal sanctions on political attitudes and behavior. In particular, we wished to determine whether the experience of punishment affects political efficacy, or the sense that one's individual efforts could influence government and policymaking. We included a battery of political attitude items on a recent wave of the Youth Development Study, a longitudinal survey of 1000 9th graders in St. Paul Public Schools begun in 1988 (Mortimer, 2003). By 1998, approximately 23% of the sample had been arrested and 7% of the sample had been incarcerated. We found that the young adults who had experienced criminal sanctions expressed significantly lower levels of political efficacy than those who had not been arrested or incarcerated. As Figure 4.2 shows, 57% of the former inmates agreed that "people like me have no say in what the government does," relative to 39% of those who had not been incarcerated. Similarly, a

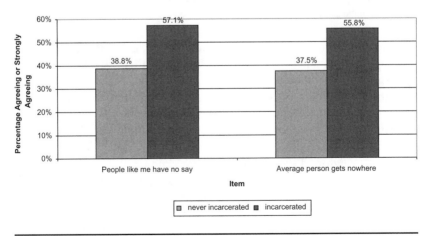

Figure 4.2 Political Efficacy by Incarceration History (Manza and Uggen, Forthcoming).

majority of the former inmates agreed that "the average person can get nowhere talking to public officials," relative to about 38% of the young adult comparison group.

Procedures for the Restoration of Civil Rights

If felons generally feel alienated from the political processes, formal mechanisms to restore their citizenship rights may encourage feelings of political efficacy and trust in government institutions. States that disenfranchise ex-felons beyond the duration of their sentence have generally established procedures and offices to administer clemency and restoration of voting rights and other civil disabilities. In Florida, for example, the Office of Clemency Administration is part of the state Parole Commission, providing support to the governor and cabinet members who make up the Board of Executive Clemency. Are such procedures impediments or facilitators of democratic participation? According to proponents such as Governor Jeb Bush, who heads the Florida Board, "it's an exhausting, emotionally draining process that can also be uplifting when people have changed their lives and turned things around" (Pfankuch 2001). Such statements suggest that some variant of these restoration processes may hold promise for reducing the stigma associated with a felony conviction in a "delabeling" (Trice and Roman 1970) or "deviant decertification ceremony." Conceivably, such procedures would ensure public safety while helping convicted felons to move on with their lives.

In practice, however, relatively few disenfranchised ex-felons are ever restored to full citizenship. Of approximately 600,000 ex-felons in Florida last year (Uggen and Manza, 2002), for example, only 1,067 were restored to civil rights (Kane and Hiaasen 2001). Critics charge that existing application processes are overly burdensome—requiring criminal records, bank statements, job history, and character references (Pfankuch 2001). Although automated restoration procedures exist in some states, a large proportion of convicted felons are ineligible for them because they owe outstanding fines, restitution, or court costs, or because they have committed multiple felonies or certain crimes from a proscribed list (Florida Parole Commission 2001).

Criminologists and sociologists have long noted the rehabilitative potential of deviant decertification or reintegration ceremonies (Braithwaite and Mugford 1994; Erikson 1964; Maruna 2001). As Kai Erikson observed in the 1960s, one is "ushered into the deviant position by a decisive and often dramatic ceremony, yet is retired from it with hardly a word of public notice. And as a result, the deviant often returns home with no proper license to resume a normal life in the community" (1964: 16–17). Unfortunately, existing procedures to restore the civil rights of convicted felons do not appear to perform this reintegrative function—too few individuals are restored to civil rights and the process is generally alienating rather than inclusive.

Other Forms of Political Participation

Participation in civic life, of course, entails more than voting. Many convicted offenders plan to volunteer time, coach youth sports, speak publicly about their crimes, or engage in some other form of civic participation (Uggen, Manza, and Behrens 2004). Although the impact of such civic participation on criminal behavior has yet to be established, some studies suggest that volunteer service may reduce offending (Nirel, Landau, Sebba, and Sagiv 1997; Uggen and Janikula 1999). Beyond formal disenfranchisement, however, felons and ex-felons face other barriers to civic participation. Susan, a woman in her thirties imprisoned for murder, told how her political discussions and interest in public affairs had waned:

> I was thinking about, like, getting involved with politics when I get out, and how I'd love to, and then I'm like, "Well, I can't vote," so it's so discouraging. Um, *I'm not gonna read this article on this candidate's views or, you know, I'm not going to research on it.* But then the only thing that motivates me is that the people around me don't know I'm an ex-con and can't vote, and so I don't want them to think I'm just like, lame and ignorant because *I can't participate in their political conversations.* So that's like my only motivation, and that's not a lot of motivation because, like, I mean being able to vote, my vote making a difference would be more motivation than the rare political conversation. Even if it's often, how important are they? [Susan, female prisoner; emphasis added]

Craig, a younger inmate classified as a sex offender, expressed interest in attending political gatherings when he was released. He was deterred from such political participation, however, because an arrest might jeopardize his conditional release status. He said that

> "a lot of times guys do come back on very minor stuff: I mean even if just doing stuff like participating in *peaceful marches.* You know I'm not talking about anything violent. But peaceful protests or, um, gatherings, but I mean from my understanding, how they go is a lot of times they just arrest everybody on the block. You know, it's like, You can't be here. *If I got arrested I'd come back to jail for five years and so I'm not about to go participate in anything like that....* I might feel also I'm putting my P.O. on the spot with maybe his superiors. Like, What's your kid do-, what's your guy doing at a march here? you know? So I, I wouldn't want to be pissing him off any ways like

that. . . . So yeah, it would stop me." [Craig, male prisoner; emphasis added]

The preceding excerpts show how offenders' criminal histories constrain their ability to participate in political demonstrations and even temper their political discussions with other citizens. Another way in which offenders appear to differ from other citizens is in their relationships with the police and criminal justice system. Many offenders' attitudes about the government are generalized from their experiences with our courts, corrections, and law enforcement personnel. If felons perceive that they have been treated unfairly, they may view other government institutions with distrust or hostility. In fact, according to Lawrence Sherman's (1993) defiance theory of offender responses to punishment, commitment to law-abiding behavior will be enhanced if offenders are treated in a procedurally fair and polite manner.

In the excerpt shown in Figure 4.3, we asked Scott, a young African-American probationer, whether he thought he had a say in what the government does (a standard political efficacy item, similar to the one reported in Figure 4.2). He responded to this global question by discussing his experiences with the police, referring to them as the "immediate government." In our view, this phrase aptly characterizes the centrality of the criminal justice system in convicted felons' views of the state. Although the presence and demeanor of the African-American officers who now patrol his neighborhood was encouraging to Scott, he still believed that government actors should be "watched and recorded." This excerpt suggests that one way to reduce political barriers to democratic participation is to improve relations between ex-felons and the "immediate government" they encounter in day-to-day life.

Survey data also show greater distrust of government and the criminal justice system among those with an incarceration history. Figure 4.4 shows that about 22% of those who had been incarcerated had great faith in the criminal justice system, relative to about 33% of the young adults who had never been incarcerated. Similarly, only about one-third of those who had spent time in prison or jail agreed that the government could be trusted to do what is best for the country, compared with half of those who had never been incarcerated. Consistent with Scott's remarks in the previous excerpt, we also find stronger intercorrelation of these trust items among those who have experienced criminal sanctions (Manza and Uggen, forthcoming).

How is Civic Reintegration Related to Recidivism?

The loss of voting rights affects offenders' views of themselves as deviant or conforming citizens. It is difficult to determine whether disenfranchisement

CU: Do you think that people like you have a say about what the government does?

SCOTT: *Um, I don't think that, I don't think that - I mean I just grew up and, grew up learning that, uh, you know learning about police ... I grew up where the police, you know, the police beat up, beat up people. And that didn't happen in every instance, you know, but you learn to not have trust, you know?*

CU: Mmhmm.

SCOTT: *Do you think, uh - asked me if I thought that, you know, that if people like me make a difference, right?*

CU: Or, or if you have a say about what the government does?

SCOTT: *I don't think I have a say about what the government does. They look good for a while, then they get elected and you hear all kind of junk.*

CU: When you mentioned - you connected this with the police and growing up, is that - Like when you think of the government do you think of the police?

SCOTT: *That's the immediate government right there.*

CU: The what?

SCOTT: *The immediate government.*

CU: The immediate government? Yeah. Okay. I've never heard that, that term, but it makes sense. Immediate government. I mean I've never heard anybody describe police like that.

SCOTT: *That's the way I grew up learning about them. You know I see black officers and people of color, you know, that are in the field. They talk to you. I don't know, man. It just – I don't want to feel like I'm saying that I'm prejudice or something, you know, cause I'm not , you know? But I mean I just grew up seeing a lot of things, you know, a lot of my friends from high school are all gone. Killed each other or police killed them. You know?*

CU: Yeah, So that - Well, let me get right into trust then. Do you think the government can be trusted to do what's best for the country?

SCOTT: *I think if - It's something like I think there need to be, like, restrictions ... there other things, other people doing other parts to make it, like, safe and so you can trust do. And I think it should be watched and recorded and stuff.*

Figure 4.3 Excerpt from Interview with Scott, a Minneapolis Felony Probationer, on Politics and Trust (Manza and Uggen, forthcoming).

has a direct effect on recidivism or desistance, although some researchers have tied shifting political attitudes (such as faith in government institutions) to trends in aggregate crime rates (LaFree 1998). It would be possible to compare recidivism rates *across* states with and without disenfranchisement laws, of course, but there is so much interstate variation in criminal justice system operations that these rates are not comparable. For example, the offender mix and administration of justice in a low-incarceration state such as North Dakota is unlikely to be equivalent to the offender mix and administration of justice in a high-incarceration state such as Louisiana. To circumvent some of these difficulties comparing states, we could compare recidivism rates *within* states that have changed felon disenfranchisement

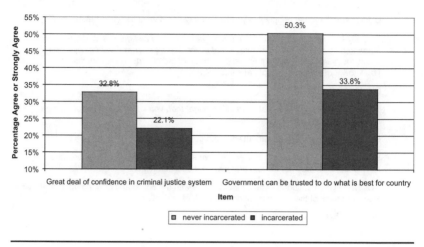

Figure 4.4 Trust in Government and the Criminal Justice System by Incarceration Status (Manza and Uggen, forthcoming).

laws. Unfortunately, it is also difficult to statistically control for other factors (such as the prevailing political climate and criminal justice practices) that may be responsible for changes in both legislation and recidivism. Moreover, definitions of recidivism vary over both time and locality.

Perhaps a better approach to testing these ideas is to craft an experimental pilot program designed to enhance the civic reintegration of released offenders. Such an intervention would be geared to establishing community ties, providing avenues for supervised volunteer service, and obtaining restoration of civil rights (if they are not automatically granted in the jurisdiction). Although it may be unrealistic to expect significant differences in recidivism rates from a short-term experimental program, it is likely that a civic reintegration initiative would affect intermediate outcomes such as voting and registration and attitudes such as political efficacy and trust in government. (We are grateful to Gary LaFree of the University of Maryland for these suggestions.)

Taking Stock

In the short time since the Sentencing Project's reports on felon disenfranchisement (Mauer 1997b; Fellner and Mauer 1998), we have learned a great deal about the political consequences of felon disenfranchisement (Miles 2004; Uggen and Manza 2002). Today, many states are reexamining their disenfranchisement laws and procedures for the restoration of civil rights. Nevertheless, we have only begun to understand the political life of convicted offenders. More research is needed to determine whethe civic reintegration can foster desistance from crime in the same way that adult social bonds to work and family reduce offending over the life course (Sampson and Laub 1993). Although there is no systematic body of evidence on the subject, some early studies suggest that facilitating the civic reintegration of offenders will ultimately hasten their desistance from crime (Uggen, Manza, and Behrens 2004; Uggen and Manza forthcoming).

References

Behrens, Angela, Christopher Uggen, and Jeff Manza. 2003. "Ballot Manipulation and the 'Menace of Negro Domination': Racial Threat and Felon Disenfranchisement in the United States, 1850-2002." *American Journal of Sociology* 109: 559–605.

Braithwaite, John and Steven Mugford. 1994. "Conditions of Successful Reintegration Ceremonies: Dealing with Juvenile Offenders." *British Journal of Criminology* 34: 139–71.

Erikson, Kai. 1964. "Notes on the Sociology of Deviance." Pages 9–22 in the *Other Side*, edited by H.S. Becker. New York: The Free Press.

Fellner, Jamie and Marc Mauer. 1998. *Losing the Vote: The Impact of Felony Disfranchisement Laws in the United States*. Washington, D.C.: Human Rights Watch and the Sentencing Project.

Florida Parole Commission. 2001. "Rules of Executive Clemency." Tallahassee, FL: Florida Parole Commission.

Harvard Law Review Note. 1989. "The Disfranchisement of Ex-Felons: Citizenship, Criminality, and 'The Purity of the Ballot Box.'" *Harvard Law Review* 102: 1300–17.

Hirschfield, Paul. 1999. "Losing the Prize: Assessing the Impact of Felon Disfranchisement Laws on Black Male Voting Participation." Paper presented at the Annual Meetings of the Law and Society Association, Chicago.

Hobbes, Thomas. [1651] 1962. *Leviathan. Or the Matter, Form and Power of a Commonwealth Ecclesiastical and Civil*. New York: Collier.

Kane, Gary and Scott Hiaasen. 2001. "Clemency Process Unfair to Blacks?" *Palm Beach Post*, December 23, 2001.

Keyssar, Alexander. 2000. *The Right to Vote: The Contested History of Democracy in the United States*. New York: Basic Books.

LaFree, Gary. 1998. *Losing Legitimacy: Street Crime and the Decline of Social Institutions in America*. Boulder, CO: Westview Press.

Laub, John, Daniel Nagin, and Robert Sampson. 1998. "Trajectories of Change in Criminal Offending: Good Marriages and the Desistance Process." *American Sociological Review* 63: 225–38.

Manza, Jeff, Clem Brooks, and Christopher Uggen. 2004. "Civil Death or Civil Rights? Public Attitudes toward Felon Disenfranchisement in the United States." *Public Opinion Quarterly* 68: 276–87.

Manza, Jeff and Christopher Uggen. Forthcoming. *Locking Up the Vote: Felon Disenfranchisement and American Democracy*. New York: Oxford University Press.

Mauer, Marc. 1997a. *Americans Behind Bars: U.S. and International Use of Incarceration, 1995*. Washington, D.C.: Sentencing Project.

———. 1997b. *Intended and Unintended Consequences: State Racial Disparities in Imprisonment*. Washington, D.C.: Sentencing Project.

———. 1999. *Race to Incarcerate*. New York: New Press.

Maruna, Shadd. 2001. *Making Good: How Ex-Convicts Reform and Rebuild Their Lives*. Washington, D.C.: American Psychological Association.

Miles, Thomas J. 2004. "Felon Disenfranchisement and Voter Turnout." *Journal of Legal Studies* 33: 85–12.

Mortimer, Jeylan T. 2003. *Working and Growing Up in America*. Cambridge, MA: Harvard University Press.

National Commission on Federal Election Reform. 2001. *To Ensure Pride and Confidence in the Electoral Process*. Charlottesville, VA: Miller Center of Public Affairs.

Nirel, Ronit, Simha F. Landau, Leslie Sebba, and Bilha Sagiv. 1997. "The Effectiveness of Service Work: An Analysis of Recidivism." *Journal of Quantitative Criminology* 13: 73–92.

Pfankuch, Thomas B. 2001. "Clemency Board Very Cautious in Restoring Rights." *Florida Times-Union*, Metro Section, June 3, 2001.

Rose, Dina R., and Todd R. Clear. 1998. "Incarceration, Social Capital, and Crime: Implications for Social Disorganization Theory." *Criminology* 36: 441–79.

Rousseau, Jean Jacques. [1962] 1957. *The Social Contract or Principles of Political Right.* New York: Hafner.

Sampson, Robert and John Laub. 1993. *Crime in the Making: Pathways and Turning Points Through Life.* Cambridge: Harvard University Press.

Sherman, Lawrence. 1993. "Defiance, Deterrence, and Irrelevance: A Theory of the Criminal Sanction." *Journal of Research in Crime and Delinquency* 30: 445–73.

Trice, Harrison and Paul M. Roman. 1970. "Delabeling, Relabeling, and Alcoholics Anonymous." *Social Problems* 17: 538–46.

Uggen, Christopher. 2000. "Work as a Turning Point in the Life Course of Criminals: A Duration Model of Age, Employment, and Recidivism." *American Sociological Review* 65: 529–46.

Uggen, Christopher and Jennifer Janikula. 1999. "Volunteerism and Arrest in the Transition to Adulthood." *Social Forces* 78: 331–62.

Uggen, Christopher and Jeff Manza. 2002. "Democratic Contraction? The Political Consequences of Felon Disenfranchisement in the United States." *American Sociological Review* 67: 777–803.

Uggen, Christopher, Jeff Manza, and Angela Behrens. 2004. "Stigma, Role Transition, and the Civic Reintegration of Convicted Felons." Pages 258–290 in *After Crime and Punishment: Ex-Offender Reintegration and Desistance from Crime*, edited by Shadd Maruna and Russ Immarigeon. Albany: SUNY Press.

Uggen, Christopher and Michael Massoglia. 2003. "Desistance from Crime as a Turning Point in the Life Course." Pages 311–29 in *Handbook of the Life Course*, edited by Jeylan T. Mortimer and Michael Shanahan. New York: Plenum Publishing.

Uggen, Christopher and Jeff Manza. 2004. "Lost Voices: The Civic and Political Views of Disfranchised Felons." Pages 165–204 in *Imprisoning America: The Social Effects of Mass Incarceration*, edited by Mary Pattillo, David Weiman, and Bruce Western. New York: Russell Sage Foundation.

Uggen, Christopher and Jeff Manza. Forthcoming. "Voting and Subsequent Crime and Arrest: Evidence from a Community Sample." *Columbia Human Rights Law Review*, vol. 36.

U.S. Department of Justice. 1973-2000. *Sourcebook of Criminal Justice Statistics.* Washington: Government Printing Office.

———.1975. "Prisoners in State and Federal Institutions on December 31, 1971, 1972, and 1973." *National Prisoner Statistics Bulletin* #SD-NPS-PSF-1. Washington: Government Printing Office.

———.2000. Survey of Inmates in State and Federal Correctional Facilities, 1997 [Computer file]. Ann Arbor, MI: Inter-university Consortium for Political and Social Research.

———.2001. Prisoners in 2000. Washington: Government Printing Office.

Zielbauer, Paul. 2001. "Felons Gain Voting Rights in Connecticut." *New York Times*, May 15, 2001.

Cases Cited

Fischer v. Governor, 749 A.2d 321 (N. H. 2000).
Mixon v. Commonwealth of Pennsylvania, 783 A.2d 763 (Pa. 2001).
NAACP v. Ridge, 2000 U.S. Dist. LEXIS 11520 (2000).
Richardson v. Ramirez, 418 U.S. 24 (1974).
Washington v. State, 75 Ala. 582 (1884).

5

Battered Women, Battered Again:
The Impact of Women's Criminal Records

AMY E. HIRSCH

Although women represent only a small fraction of the prison population, the absolute number and proportion of imprisoned women has increased dramatically in recent decades. Women differ from men with criminal records in several respects: they are more likely to have minor children and are more likely to have been custodial parents prior to incarceration; they are more likely to have been physically or sexually abused in childhood *and* adulthood; and they are more likely to have drug or alcohol problems as a result of the abuse they have experienced. For women with criminal records, the issues of parenting, of surviving and healing from physical and sexual assault, and of recovering from drug or alcohol addiction are critical. Although the strength and resilience of women who have survived repeated abuse should not be underestimated, the barriers imposed as a result of their incarceration and criminal records make it extraordinarily difficult for them to succeed after they are released, and ironically, make it more likely that they will be abused yet again.

This chapter first provides background information about women with criminal records, including their histories of physical and sexual assault, and then discusses the connections between the abuse they have experienced and their drug usage and criminal convictions. Next it looks at the findings from studies of survivors of trauma, and considers the implications of those findings for reentry policy. What is the impact of current policies on battered women? What would we do if we took seriously what we know about the violence that formerly incarcerated women have experienced and what is needed to heal from that violence?

What Do We Know about Women Who Have Criminal Records?

Almost 100,000 women were incarcerated in state or federal prisons at the end of 2002, representing 6.8% of all prison inmates. The rate of growth for women (4.9%) was twice that of men (2.4%) during 2002, and the total number of women prisoners has increased by 42% since 1995, compared to a 27% increase for men (Harrison and Beck 2003). "For women, the chances of going to prison were six times greater in 2001 (1.8%) than in 1974 (0.3%)" (Bonczar 2003: 1). In addition, 77,000 women were held in local jails, almost 12% of all jail inmates (Harrison and Karberg 2003). Women are a much larger proportion of individuals on probation (23%) and parole (14%) (Glaze 2003) and a larger proportion of the individuals being released from prison to parole (10%) (Hughes and Wilson 2003) than of individuals who are imprisoned. Approximately 60,000 women were released from state prisons in 2001 (Hughes and Wilson 2003).

No one knows how many women in the United States have criminal records. In addition to women who are currently incarcerated, currently on probation or parole, or have recently completed probation or parole, there are an unknown number of women with older criminal records, who are continuing to face barriers as a result of those records. The federal Bureau of Justice Statistics estimates that there are approximately 581,000 adult women who were incarcerated in a state or federal prison at some time between 1974 and 2001 (Bonczar 2003).

This statistic does not include women who were sentenced to probation or who were incarcerated in a local jail rather than in state or federal prison. Nor does it include women who were arrested but not charged, or charged but not convicted, and who encounter difficulties as a result of their arrest records.[1] Because so much more information is available about incarcerated women than about the larger universe of women with criminal records, most of the data included in this chapter focus on incarcerated women.

As with men, there are significant racial and ethnic disparities concerning incarceration of women. "Adult black females were nearly $2^1/_2$ times more likely than adult Hispanic females and $5^1/_2$ times more likely than adult white females to have ever served time in State or Federal prison" (Bonczar 2003: 5). One in 19 black women is likely to go to prison, compared with one in 118 white women (Bonczar 2003). Sixty-two percent of adult women on probation are white, 27% percent are black, and 10% percent are Hispanic; in contrast, 33% of women in state prison are white, 48% are black, and 15% are Hispanic (Greenfeld and Snell 1999).

Almost 70% of women state prisoners were convicted of nonviolent offenses (Harrison and Beck 2003); of women held in local jails, 88% were charged with nonviolent offenses (Greenfeld and Snell 1999). Thirty-five percent of mothers in state prisons and almost 75% of mothers in federal prisons were convicted of drug offenses; property offenses are the next largest category, accounting for 28% of mothers in state prisons and 10% of mothers in federal prisons (Mumola 2000). Nearly 75% of the violent offenses committed by women were simple assaults.

According to the Federal Bureau of Justice Statistics, 65% of women state prisoners report having minor children, and 64% of the women with minor children reported living with those children prior to admission (Mumola 2000). An even higher proportion of women held in local jails (70%), and of women on probation (72%), has minor children (Greenfeld and Snell 1999).[2] More than 1.3 million minor children are estimated to have mothers who are incarcerated, on probation, or on parole (Greenfeld and Snell 1999). Approximately 25% of incarcerated women are either pregnant while imprisoned or have given birth during the prior year (Barry, Ginchild, and Lee 1995).

As a result of the federal Adoption and Safe Families Act, states are moving very quickly to permanently terminate parental rights of incarcerated parents. The difficulties faced by incarcerated parents in arranging communications and visits with their children, communication with foster care agencies and child welfare authorities, participation in family service plans or court hearings, and in preventing termination of their parental rights, are enormous (Roberts 2002; Schneider 2002, Shapiro et al. 2001; see the chapter herein by S. Mecca Franklin).

Incarcerated women are overwhelmingly poor, with limited job skills and limited educations. They face multiple barriers in addition to their criminal records: mental and/or physical health problems, homelessness, alcohol or drug problems, and histories of physical and/or sexual abuse. Approximately 65% of women in state prison in 1997 did not have high school degrees (Harlow 2003). Although prison education programs have been shown to be cost-effective in preventing reincarceration, they were completely eliminated or sharply reduced in many facilities during the 1990s (Travis, Solomon, and Waul 2001; Center on Crime, Communities, and Culture 1997). About 40% of women in state prison were employed full-time prior to their arrest. Thirty-seven percent of women in state prison had incomes of less than $600 per month prior to arrest (Greenfeld and Snell 1999). Nearly 20% of mothers in state prison reported having been homeless in the year prior to imprisonment; 21% of mothers in state prison had incomes of less than $200, and 70% had incomes of less than $1,000 in the month prior to their arrest (Mumola 2000).

Twenty-four percent of women state prisoners were identified as mentally ill in a study by the federal Bureau of Justice Statistics, compared to 16% of men in state prisons (Ditton 1999). Research on admissions to a large Midwestern jail found that 33% of the women had been diagnosed with posttraumatic stress disorder (PTSD) (Teplin, Abram, and McClelland 1996). The proportion of individuals with mental illness is significantly higher among prison and jail inmates than in the general population (Ditton 1999; Steadman and Veysey 1997).[3] Almost 40% of mentally ill prisoners who are expected to be released within the next twelve months are not being given mental health treatment while incarcerated (Beck 2000). Multiple studies of mental health treatment in jails have determined that "discharge planning was found to be the weakest element of all programs for mentally disordered detainees" (Steadman and Veysey 1997: 5).

Women in state prisons and jails also have a wide range of physical health problems, including HIV/AIDS, tuberculosis, hepatitis, sexually transmitted diseases, asthma, diabetes, and injuries resulting from domestic violence and sexual assault, and may need prenatal or postpartum care. Significant problems with access to and quality of prison and jail health services are frequently reported (Stoller 2000; Veysey 1998). Forty-six percent of a sample of women jailed in Ohio reported their health as fair or poor, and 27% had been hospitalized within the past year (Alemagno 2001).

A very high proportion of incarcerated women have histories of drug and alcohol problems. Women in state prisons reported higher usage of drugs on every measure (ever used, using regularly, using in month before the offense, using at the time of the offense) than men in state prisons, with about 60% of women describing themselves as using drugs in the month before the offense. Twenty percent of women in state prisons with histories of drug usage reported receiving drug treatment while incarcerated (Greenfeld and Snell). Most women whose addictions result in criminal behavior are charged with nondrug crimes, such as prostitution and retail theft. For example, a federal study found that over 77% of the adult women arrested in Philadelphia tested positive for drugs in 1998 (Arrestee Drug Abuse Monitoring Program 1999), yet only 16% of the women arraigned in the Philadelphia criminal court system in September 1996 were charged with drug offenses (Hirsch 1999).

Women prisoners have experienced very high rates of prior physical and sexual abuse. A study of 150 women incarcerated in a maximum-security prison in New York found that 70% had experienced severe physical abuse and 59% had experienced sexual abuse during childhood or adolescence; 75% had experienced severe physical abuse by an intimate partner, and 36% had experienced marital rape or other sexual abuse by an intimate partner.

Seventy-seven percent had experienced physical or sexual assault by persons other than intimates. Ninety-four percent of the women had been physically or sexually attacked at least once during their lifetimes (Browne, Miller, and Maguin 1999). A study by the National Council on Crime and Delinquency found that 67% of the 151 women interviewed in state prisons in three states reported physical or sexual abuse as children, and 71% reported physical or sexual abuse as adults (Acoca and Austin 1996). In comparison, a nationally representative study of 8,000 women in the general population found that 51% had experienced some kind of physical assault, 18% had been sexually assaulted, and 55% had experienced physical or sexual assault during their lifetimes (Tjaden and Thoennes 2000).

A smaller, qualitative study of 26 women with drug convictions found that 21 (81%) of the women interviewed disclosed having been abused as children, adults, or both. Two of the other five women refused to talk about abuse. Eighteen (69%) of the 26 women disclosed having been physically and/or sexually abused as children; 17 (94%) of those 18 women also disclosed having been abused as adults. Fourteen (78%) of the 18 women who disclosed childhood abuse disclosed sexual abuse, 5 (28%) disclosed physical abuse, and one disclosed both sexual and physical abuse. Twenty (77%) of the 26 women disclosed having been battered by a boyfriend or husband. For 19 (90%) of the 21 women who disclosed abuse, jail or a women's drug and alcohol treatment program was the first place anyone had talked to them about the abuse they had survived or helped them try to deal with it (Hirsch 2001a). "[In jail] they had all different kind of classes—about being raped in the street, about being raped in your family. I needed both those classes" (Maria, interview, February 25, 1998). In a study of traumatic events and PTSD in an urban population of young adults, markedly higher rates of PTSD (80%) were found in women who had experienced rape than for other types of trauma, including physical assault (23%), seeing someone killed or seriously hurt (24%), or threat to life (24%) (Breslau et al. 1991).

Rates of abuse are much higher for women prisoners than for men. The Federal Bureau of Justice Statistics found that 57% of women in state prisons had experienced prior physical or sexual abuse, compared to 16% of men in state prisons (Harlow 1999).[4] In addition, almost 80% of women state prisoners with mental illness reported having been physically or sexually abused prior to incarceration—almost 70% reported prior physical abuse and almost 60% reported prior sexual abuse (Ditton 1999).

Many aspects of incarceration are particularly problematic for survivors of abuse. Being subjected to searches and physical restraints; lack of privacy while sleeping, showering, or using the toilet; and other conditions of confinement, including supervision by male guards, may all re-traumatize women inmates who have experienced prior physical or sexual assault (Veysey 1998; Human Rights Watch Women's Rights Project 1996).

> During incarceration, women diagnosed with mental illnesses who have histories of [being subjected to] violence are a particularly vulnerable group. . . . The jail is a highly coercive environment that is based on strict adherence to authority. It is also predominantly male, both detainees and staff. This kind of environment is extremely threatening to women with histories of abuse. The response to this perceived threat may be withdrawal, fighting back or extreme outbursts, and/or worsening of psychiatric symptoms or physical health problems (Veysey 1998: 375).

In addition to the problems that survivors of abuse experience as a result of the conditions of confinement, women are subjected to sexual harassment or assault by corrections officers or other staff (Parker 2002). In one study of over 1,200 complaints from women incarcerated in California's state prisons, "over 14% of the women in the sample experienced some form of sexual harassment from staff or doctors" (Stoller 2000). The federal Department of Justice has found several state prison systems in violation of the United States Constitution through sexual abuse of women inmates by guards (Human Rights Watch Women's Rights Project 1996) and filed civil rights lawsuits against two states' Departments of Corrections, resulting in settlement agreements concerning changes in rules and procedures (Layman, McCampbell, and Moss 2000).

Other cases have been filed against state and local corrections officials by public interest law firms, legal services programs, and the American Civil Liberties Union, seeking enforcement of existing policies, development of better policies, and damages for women who have been raped, sexually harassed, and assaulted. Not only have states failed to prevent rape and sexual harassment of women prisoners by staff, but also some states hold the women criminally liable for sexual conduct with staff "without reference to whether such contact was voluntary" (Human Rights Watch Women's Rights Project 1996: 41).

What Do We Know about the Effects of Trauma and Abuse?

There are clear connections between experiencing abuse and drug and alcohol usage, and connections among experiencing abuse, drug and alcohol usage, and women's criminal records. High rates of trauma and of PTSD are found among women with drug and alcohol problems (Fullilove et al. 1993). Women use drugs and alcohol to self-medicate the pain of the abuse they have experienced. "PTSD is likely to co-occur with depression and substance abuse, as survivors deal with unresolved and intense physical and psychic pain" (Bassuk, Melnick, and Browne 1998: 58). Many trauma survivors engage in high-risk activities or addictive behaviors as a way of asserting control over their situations, and muting, at least temporarily, intrusive memories and current experiences of abuse, and may have difficulty appropriately managing aggression (Bills and Bloom 1998). All of these results of trauma increase the chances of arrest.

A Federal Bureau of Justice Statistics study of prisoners found that women who had been abused were more likely to have used illegal drugs and alcohol regularly than women who did not report prior abuse (Harlow 1999). Childhood abuse is particularly devastating and is associated with early use of substances, school failure, delinquency, somatic symptoms often leading to self-medication with drugs or alcohol, relational difficulties, and teen pregnancy (Bloom 2002). A study comparing 206 inner-city women survivors of childhood sexual abuse to a matched group of 205 women found that the survivors of childhood sexual abuse were five times more likely to be arrested for drug offenses than members of the comparison group; the most extreme disparity between the two groups was for drug offenses (Siegel 1996).

Furthermore, for women experiencing domestic violence, advice to "just leave" is no more useful than "just say no" is for prevention of drug usage. "Leaving" is not a one-time event, nor is it the same as stopping the violence, which frequently escalates when a woman leaves or attempts to leave. The survival strategies of battered women vary, but there are some recurrent themes—financial resources and social supports, including family, friends, and shelters are extremely important in helping women to survive and escape abuse (Campbell et al. 2001).

> Thus a woman may be beaten again and again *not* because she likes it, has learned to be helpless, or fails to follow through when pressing charges, etc. Rather she is acting in a pattern that follows from a definition of battering as primarily an interpersonal, private matter between intimates. . . . For a woman, then, to leave a violent relationship and avoid killing either herself or her mate, requires external social resources, a "definition of the situation" that no longer targets *her* as the source of the problem, and her ability to combine these external and internal resources in an action plan that preserves her own and others' lives. (Hoff 1990: 78)

What Impact Do Current Reentry Policies Have on Battered Women?

All of the barriers faced by individuals with criminal records make it difficult for women to leave an abusive relationship, or to avoid further abuse. Mothers leaving jails and prisons report multiple reentry problems, including difficulty finding shelter, transportation, health care (including drug or alcohol and mental health treatment), employment or job training, and problems reuniting with their children (Alemagno 2001; Travis, Solomon, and Waul 2001; Johnston 1995). "The cumulative impact of these barriers is that every door is closed" (Hirsch et al. 2002: 8); the one door that remains open is returning to a relationship with a man who is abusive, but who "[takes] care of me. He was hitting me a lot, off and on the whole time we was together, but he took care of me" (Julie, interview on 5/12/98). A staff person from a battered women's shelter in central Pennsylvania describes women going "back to her abuser just for a home plan to get out of jail" (Donna 2001).

Denial of welfare benefits and bans on employment as a result of criminal records make it difficult for women to have an independent and legal source of income. In a study of women with drug convictions, 22 (85%) of the 26 women had work histories, but mostly in short-term, low-wage jobs, either in settings that would make it difficult to sustain their recovery from addiction (barmaids, strippers, dancers in topless bars), or in jobs they would be prohibited from performing as a result of their convictions (child care workers, nurse's aides, other health care workers). The other four women (15%) had only worked as prostitutes (Hirsch 1999). Eighteen (69%) of the 26 women disclosed having worked as prostitutes to get money for drugs and/or having traded sex for drugs.

Welfare benefits are an important resource in order for women to leave prostitution (El-Bassel et al. 1997). As the director of a needle exchange program explained, "[w]e see a lot of people having to scrounge to get money—collecting cans, shoplifting, sex work—there seems to be more of that when women lose benefits" (Julie Parr, interview, 12/3/98). Their lack of job skills, combined with employer reluctance to hire individuals with criminal records, and the loss of access to welfare-to-work programs for women who are barred from TANF because of drug convictions make it very difficult for women to find and sustain work, and increase the chances of a return to prostitution. In a vicious cycle, doing sex work entails a very high risk of physical and sexual assaults: a study of 130 prostitutes in San Francisco found that 82% had been physically assaulted, 83% had been threatened with a weapon, 68% had been raped while working as adults in prostitution, and 84% were or had been homeless. Eighty-eight percent wanted to leave prostitution; finding a safe place to live (78%) and job training (73%) headed the list of what they felt they needed in order to escape prostitution (Farley and Barkan 1998).

Current policies on access to housing make it very difficult for women with criminal records to avoid homelessness, let alone get a safe place to live (Landau 2002). Women who are unable to access housing are likely to stay in or return to an abusive relationship in order to have a place to live (Bassuk, Melnick, and Browne 1998), or to engage in "survival sex" in exchange for shelter (Alexander and Muenzenmaier 1998: 218). Staff members in women's drug and alcohol treatment programs describe women who have literally never had a safe night's sleep in their lives before arriving at the program (Wellbank 2003). Not being able to sleep because of abuse is a recurring theme in women's accounts of the violence they have survived. "I was afraid to go to sleep at home, because my mom's boyfriend came in and messed with me. I thought if I could just go to sleep—I only felt safe sleeping at school. So I went to sleep at school every day, and they yelled at me" (Wendy, interview on 4/28/98). Fear of being homeless as a result of being banned from welfare benefits because of drug convictions, and of being forced by a lack of alternatives to return to abusive relationships and unsafe living arrangements, was a recurring theme in interviews of affected women (Hirsch 1999). "I would die out there if I have to go back on the Avenue" (Donna, interview on 2/4/98).

Furthermore, loss of children—loss of custody, denial of visitation, or termination of parental rights resulting from imprisonment—is frequently described by women and by drug and alcohol treatment program staff as a trigger for relapse into active addiction, just as loss of children to the foster care system is considered a traumatic event (Fullilove et al. 1993).

What Are the Implications for Reentry Policy?

We have learned from trauma theory and the literature on survivors of trauma that safety, positive connections to other people, and access to helpful resources are of paramount importance in recovering from trauma (Bloom 1997). In the absence of other resources, women self-medicate the pain of trauma with drugs and alcohol, and develop survival strategies that unfortunately expose them to further violence and repeated trauma. If we take that information seriously, we need to radically rethink our policies on reentry from incarceration, and on the long-term consequences of criminal records.

"If I could get welfare, it would make a lot of difference to me. I wouldn't have to ask nobody for anything. I'd have something of my own" (Linda, interview on 6/25/98). Bans on welfare, employment, housing, and student loans not only create tremendous material hardship for women with criminal records, but they also create tremendous stigma and shame (Hirsch 2001b). Social disenfranchisement makes it harder for women to reduce drug usage or to maintain sobriety and to stay out of jail. Conversely, provision of benefits makes it possible for women to move forward with their lives. "Welfare helps us stay in touch with society" (Tanya, interview on 7/9/98). "[W]elfare benefits and subsidized housing . . . made it possible for me to survive and get my children back. Having my children back kept me strong and kept me from relapsing. The welfare benefits and low-cost housing made it possible for me to rebuild my life. Now I own a home and I have a steady job" (Donna 2001).

The extraordinarily difficult conditions of life for low-income women who are survivors of violence make accessing meaningful help very hard. Obstacles include the "the presence of extreme and unremitting stressors and the pervasiveness of community and family violence" as well as lack of safe housing, money, food, medical care, transportation, telephone service, and child care (Bassuk, Melnick, and Browne 1998: 58). Simply providing a woman with telephone numbers to call, or a suggestion that she seek services, is unlikely to be of significant use. Furthermore, any services that she is referred to, or required to attend as a condition of probation or parole, or as a condition of keeping or regaining visits with or custody of her children, need to be reassessed with the trauma she has experienced in mind (Bloom 2002). Alcohol and drug treatment and mental health programs need to be gender-specific and trauma-informed in order to adequately serve women (Alexander and Muenzenmaier 1998; Vesey 1998); gender-specific rape and assault prevention programs, aimed at men and women separately, are also needed (Bachar and Koss 2001).

Conclusion

This book focuses on what happens after individuals and families come in contact with the criminal justice system and the issues discussed here have implications for criminal justice policy further upstream. In addition to changes in reentry policy, we should be looking at wide-ranging changes in policy on arrests, prosecution, sentencing, and incarceration (Richie 2002; Chesney-Lind 1997). Mary Leftridge Byrd—currently deputy secretary for specialized facilities and programs of the Pennsylvania Department of Corrections, formerly superintendent of a women's prison in Pennsylvania, and past-president of the Association on Programs for Female Offenders—has proposed the creation of "family impact statements" to be considered during the sentencing of women defendants. Similar to a victim impact statement, it would explain to the court the offender's familial responsibilities and reveal what Byrd calls "the other cost of incarceration," the harm to her children. Byrd has also proposed creation of a "homework hotline" for incarcerated parents to communicate with their children (Martin 2003). Models of good parenting programs and of gender-specific, trauma-informed drug treatment programs in and out of prisons exist, as do good models of alternatives to incarceration that keep mothers and children together.

Every aspect of incarceration—ranging from a strip search to a directly observed drug test—should be reconsidered in light of its impact on women who have survived physical and sexual abuse, its potential for further traumatizing those survivors, and the extent to which it is really necessary for the maintenance of order (Veysey, De Cou, and Prescott 1998). Planning for release must also be informed by the reality of trauma. Development of safety plans for battered women prior to release is important "[b]ecause many women have few resources, simply leaving an abusive relationship is not possible" (Veysey, De Cou, and Prescott 1998: 53). In addition, conditions of probation and parole need to take into account the consequences of trauma, and the process of recovery from trauma and from addiction. Recognizing that relapse is "a part of recovery ... [allows] a positive drug screen to be used as an opportunity for growth" (Bloom et al. 2003: 187–88) rather than as a reason for reincarceration. Preventing the reincarceration of women for predictable relapses that are a part of the process of recovery and for technical violations of probation would significantly improve their likelihood of successful reentry.

Women with criminal records have been socially disenfranchised long before they enter the criminal justice system. The ways in which they are "locked out" upon reentry from incarceration simply reinforce and deepen their disenfranchisement, and increase the likelihood that they will return to abusive relationships, prostitution, and drug usage.

Acknowledgments The author thanks Sandra Bloom, June Axinn, and Jessica Robbins for helpful comments and suggestions and Laura Murphy for research assistance.

References

Acoca, Leslie and James Austin. 1996. *The Crisis: Women in Prison.* Oakland, CA: National Council on Crime and Delinquency.

Alemagno, Sonia A. 2001. "Women in Jail: Is Substance Abuse Treatment Enough?" *AmericanJournal of Public Health* 91: 798–800.

Alexander, Mary Jane and Muenzenmaier, Kristina. 1998. "Trauma, Addiction and Recovery." In *Women's Mental Health Services: A Public Health Perspective*, edited by Bruce Lubotsky Levin, Andrea K. Blanch, and Ann Jennings. Thousand Oaks, CA: Sage Publications: 215–239.

Arrestee Drug Abuse Monitoring Program. 1999. 1998 Annual Report on Drug Use Among Adult and Juvenile Arrestees. Washington, D.C.: National Institutes of Justice.

Bachar, Karen and Mary P. Koss. 2001. "From Prevalence to Prevention: Closing the Gap Between What We Know About Rape and What We Do." In *Sourcebook on Violence Against Women*, edited by Claire M. Renzetti, Jeffrey L. Edleson, and Raquel Kennedy Bergen.Thousand Oaks, CA: Sage Publications: 117–142.

Barry, Ellen with River Ginchild and Doreen Lee. 1995. "Legal Issues for Prisoners with Children." In *Children of Incarcerated Parents*, edited by Katherine Gabel and Denise Johnston. New York: Lexington Books: 147–66.

Barr, Heather. 1999. *Prisons and Jails: Hospitals of Last Resort.* New York: Correctional Association of New York and Urban Justice Center.

Bassuk, Ellen L., Sharon Melnick, and Angela Browne. 1998. "Responding to the Needs of Low-Income and Homeless Women Who Are Survivors of Family Violence," *Journal of the American Medical Women's Association* 53: 57–64.

Beck, Allen J. 2000. *State and Federal Prisoners Returning to the Community: Findings from the Bureau of Justice Statistics.* Washington, D.C.: U.S. Department of Justice, Bureau of Justice Statistics.

Bills, Lyndra J. and Sandra L. Bloom. 1998. "From Chaos to Sanctuary: Trauma-Based Treatment for Women in a State Hospital System." In *Women's Mental Health Services: A Public Health Perspective,* edited by Bruce Lubotsky Levin, Andrea K. Blanch, and Ann Jennings. Thousand Oaks, CA: Sage Publications: 348–67.

Bloom, Sandra L., Maggie Bennington-Davis, Brian Farragher, David McCorkle, Kelly Nice-Martini, and Kathy Wellbank. 2003. "Multiple Opportunities for Creating Sanctuary," *Psychiatric Quarterly* 74: 173–90.

Bloom, Sandra L. 2002. *The PVS Disaster: Poverty, Violence and Substance Abuse in the Lives of Women and Children: A Review of Recent Literature.* Philadelphia: Women's Law Project.

———. 1997. *Creating Sanctuary: Toward the Evolution of Sane Societies.* New York: Routledge.

Bonczar, Thomas P. 2003. *Prevalence of Imprisonment in the U.S. Population, 1974–2001.* Washington, D.C.: U.S. Department of Justice, Bureau of Justice Statistics.

Breslau, Naomi, Glenn C. Davis, Patricia Andreski, and Edward Peterson. 1991. "Traumatic Events and Posttraumatic Stress Disorder in an Urban Population of Young Adults," *Archives of General Psychiatry* 48: 216–22.

Browne, Angela, Brenda Miller, and Eugene Maguin. 1999. "Prevalence and Severity of Life time Physical and Sexual Victimization Among Incarcerated Women," *International Journal of Law and Psychiatry* 22: 301–22.

Campbell, Jacquelyn, Linda Rose, Joan Kub, and Daphne Nedd. 2001 "Voices of Strength and Resistance: A Contextual and Longitudinal Analysis of Women's Responses to Battering." In *Woman Battering in the United States: Till Death Do Us Part,* edited by Helen M. Eigenberg, Prospect Heights, IL: Waveland Press: 180–95.

Center on Crime, Communities and Culture. 1997. *Research Brief: Education as Crime Prevention.* New York: Open Society Institute.

Chesney-Lind, Meda. 1997. *The Female Offender: Girls, Women, and Crime.* Thousand Oaks, CA: Sage Publications.

Ditton, Paula M. 1999. *Mental Health and Treatment of Inmates and Probationers.* Washington, D.C.: U.S. Department of Justice, Bureau of Justice Statistics.

Donna. 2001. *Testimony of Donna.* Pennsylvania House of Representatives Health and Human Services Committee Public Hearing on House Bill 1401, June 15.

El-Bassel, Nabila, Robert F. Schilling, Kathleen L. Irwin, Sairus Faruque, Louisa Gilbert, Jennifer Von Bargen, Yolanda Serrano, and Brian R. Edlin. 1997. "Sex Trading and Psychological Distress among Women Recruited from the Streets of Harlem," *American Journal of Public Health* 87: 66–70.

Farley, Melissa and Howard Barkan. 1998. "Prostitution, Violence Against Women, and Posttraumatic Stress Disorder," *Women and Health* 27: 37–49.

Fullilove, Mindy Thompson, Robert E. Fullilove, III, Michael Smith, Karen Winkler, Calvin Michael, Paula G. Panzer, and Rodrick Wallace. 1993. "Violence, Trauma, and Post-Traumatic Stress Disorder Among Women Drug Users," *Journal of Traumatic Stress* 6: 533–43.

Glaze, Lauren E. 2003. *Probation and Parole in the United States, 2002.* Washington, D.C.: U.S. Department of Justice, Bureau of Justice Statistics.

Greenfeld, Lawrence A. and Tracy L. Snell. 1999. *Women Offenders.* Washington, D.C.: U.S. Department of Justice, Bureau of Justice Statistics.

Harlow, Caroline Wolf. 1999. *Prior Abuse Reported by Inmates and Probationers.* Washington, D.C.: U.S. Department of Justice, Bureau of Justice Statistics.

———. 2003. *Education and Correctional Populations.* Washington, D.C.: U.S. Department of Justice, Bureau of Justice Statistics.

Harrison, Paige M. and Allen J. Beck. 2003. *Prisoners in 2002.* Washington, D.C.: U.S. Department of Justice, Bureau of Justice Statistics.

Harrison, Paige M. and Jennifer C. Karberg. 2003. *Prison and Jail Inmates at Mid year 2002.* Washington, D.C.: U.S. Department of Justice, Bureau of Justice Statistics.

Hirsch, Amy E. 1999. *"Some Days Are Harder Than Hard": Welfare Reform and Women With Drug Convictions in Pennsylvania.* Washington, D.C.: Center for Law and Social Policy.

———. 2001a. "'The World Was Never a Safe Place for Them': Abuse, Welfare Reform, and Women With Drug Convictions," *Violence Against Women* 7: 159–75.

———. 2001b. "Bringing Back Shame: Women, Welfare Reform and Criminal Justice," *Temple Political and Civil Rights Law Review* 10: 417–33.

Hirsch, Amy E., Sharon M. Dietrich, Rue Landau, Peter D. Schneider, Irv Ackelsberg, Judith Bernstein-Baker, and Joseph Hohenstein. 2002. *Every Door Closed: Barriers Facing Parents With Criminal Records*. Washington, D.C.: Center for Law and Social Policy and Community Legal Services.

Hoff, Lee Ann 1990. *Battered Women As Survivors*. London: Routledge.

Hughes, Timothy and Doris James Wilson. 2003. *Reentry Trends in the United States: Inmates Returning to the Community After Serving Time in Prison*. Washington, D.C.: U.S. Department of Justice, Bureau of Justice Statistics.

Human Rights Watch Women's Rights Project. 1996. *All Too Familiar: Sexual Abuse of Women in U.S. State Prisons*. New York: Human Rights Watch.

Johnston, Denise. 1995. "Jailed Mothers." In *Children of Incarcerated Parents*, edited by Katherine Gabel and Denise Johnston. New York: Lexington Books: 41–58.

Landau, Rue. 2002. "Criminal Records and Subsidized Housing: Families Losing the Opportunity for Decent Shelter." In *Every Door Closed: Barriers Facing Parents with Criminal Records*. Washington, D.C.: Center for Law and Social Policy and Community Legal Services, Inc.: 41–51.

Layman, Elizabeth P., Susan W. McCampbell, and Andie Moss. 2000. "Sexual Misconduct in Corrections," American Jails November-December 2000.

Martin, Keith L. 2003. "Managing Female Offenders," *Graterfriends: A Publication of the Pennsylvania Prison Society* 22: 8–9.

Mumola, Christopher J. 2000. *Incarcerated Parents and Their Children*. Washington, D.C.: U.S.Department of Justice, Bureau of Justice Statistics.

Parker, Katherine C. 2002. "Female Inmates Living in Fear: Sexual Abuse by Correctional Officers in the District of Columbia," *Journal of Gender, Social Policy and the Law* 10: 443–77.

Richie, Beth E. 2002. "The Social Impact of Mass Incarceration on Women." In *Invisible Punishment: The Collateral Consequences of Mass Imprisonment*, edited by Marc Mauer and Meda Chesney-Lind. New York: New Press: 136–49.

Roberts, Dorothy. 2002. *Shattered Bonds: The Color of Child Welfare*. New York: Basic Books.

Schneider, Peter D. 2002. "Criminal Convictions, Incarceration, and Child Welfare: Ex-Offenders Lose Their Children." In *Every Door Closed: Barriers Facing Parents with Criminal Records*. Washington, D.C.: Center for Law and Social Policy and Community Legal Services, Inc.: 53–83.

Shapiro, Lauren, Lynn Vogelstein, and Jennifer Light. 2001. "Family Ties: Representing Formerly Incarcerated Women with Children in Family Court," *Clearinghouse Review: Journal of Poverty Law and Policy* 35: 243–59.

Siegel, Jane A. 1996. "Aggressive and Criminal Behavior Among Survivors of Child Abuse." Ph.D. diss., University of Pennsylvania.

Steadman, Henry J. and Bonita M. Veysey. 1997. *Providing Services for Jail Inmates With Mental Disorders*. Washington, D.C.: U.S. Department of Justice, National Institutes of Justice.

Stoller, Nancy. 2000. *Improving Access to Health Care for California's Women Prisoners*. Berkeley, CA: California Policy Research Center.

Teplin, Linda A., Karen M. Abram, and Gary M. McClelland. 1996. "Prevalence of Psychiatric Disorders Among Incarcerated Women: I. Pretrial Jail Detainees," *Archives of General Psychiatry* 53: 505–12.

Tjaden, Patricia and Nancy Thoennes. 2000. *Full Report of the Prevalence, Incidence, and Consequences of Violence Against Women: Findings From the National Violence Against Women Survey*. Washington, D.C.: U.S. Department of Justice, National Institutes of Justice.

Travis, Jeremy, Amy L. Solomon, and Michelle Waul. 2001. *From Prison to Home: The Dimensions and Consequences of Prisoner Reentry*. Washington, D.C.: Urban Institute.

U.S. Department of Justice, Bureau of Justice Statistics. 2001. *Use and Management of Criminal History Record Information: A Comprehensive Report 2001 Update*. Washington, D.C.: U.S. Department of Justice, Bureau of Justice Statistics.

Veysey, Bonita M. 1998. "Specific Needs of Women Diagnosed with Mental Illnesses in U.S. Jails." In *Women's Mental Health Services: A Public Health Perspective*, edited by Bruce Lubotsky Levin, Andrea K. Blanch, and Ann Jennings. Thousand Oaks, CA: Sage Publications: 368–89.

Veysey, Bonita M., Kate De Cou, and Laura Prescott. 1998. "Effective Management of Female Jail Detainees with Histories of Physical and Sexual Abuse," *American Jails* May/June: 50–54.

Wellbank, Kathy. 2003. Personal communication with author, March 27.

Endnotes

1. The criminal records systems maintained by the states contain information on more than 59 million individuals; the FBI has criminal records for more than 48 million individuals, and it is not known how many of these files are duplicative. In some states these records include arrests that did not result in criminal charges (U.S. Department of Justice, Bureau of Justice Statistics 2001). The federal reports on criminal record systems and data do not provide a breakdown by sex.

2. These figures may well reflect underreporting because incarcerated women may fear that their children will be placed in foster care if they divulge their existence.

3. Many observers attribute the high proportion of inmates with mental illness to the closing of state psychiatric hospitals and lack of community mental health services (Barr 1999, Steadman and Veysey 1977).

4. These results from the Bureau of Justice Statistics likely reflect under-reporting, because only two questions were asked, and respondents were required to identify the experiences as abuse. Estimates of abuse from the general population in polls using questions similar to those used by the Bureau of Justice Statistics (Harlow 1999) were much lower than the results from Tjaden and Thoennes' study described above.

6

A Practitioner's Account of the Impact of the Adoption and Safe Families Act (ASFA) on Incarcerated Persons and Their Families

STEPHANIE S. FRANKLIN

There has been a trend in the past 30 years to address crime with increasingly harsher sentences. Many who advocate for harshness justify such measures on the basis that they are "getting tough on crime." In the debate over the War on Drugs, many conservative ideologues believe that addressing crime and drugs with harsher sentences will deter crime and punish the "offender." However, this analysis is shortsighted. Those who support this belief fail to understand the impact that such policies have on communities and on the nation as a whole. When we, as a nation, penalize "offenders" with such severity, we dehumanize not only the individual, but also the community and the nation. Whereas the United States may possess material wealth, it falls short in the humane treatment of individuals and progressive social policy that incorporates "all" persons.

Our Constitution aims to treat all citizens within our borders as equal persons under the law, as granted through the Fourteenth Amendment to the Constitution. Supporters of our forefathers argue that this concept was the most ingenious instrument ever produced by a government, and is indicative of the Founding Fathers' timeless wisdom. Many people have attempted to achieve equal treatment but remain intentionally excluded from it.

They understand how the Constitution has been invoked to confer rights upon some and to strip others of their inalienable rights as human beings.

The U.S. Constitution sanctions punishment for crimes. The Eighth Amendment, however, bars cruel and unusual punishment. With the rapidly increasing growth of the prison population, it is clear that, in practice, incarcerated persons are subjected to excessive sentences that some say are "invisible" punishments; however, as much as they are considered invisible, the weight that they carry is clearly visible. Many people find "other" sentences imposed upon them as a result of their incarceration, such as the loss of welfare benefits, disqualification from public housing, disenfranchisement, and the loss of parental rights. This chapter will seek to explore and analyze the effect that the intersections of current criminal justice and child welfare policies have on incarcerated persons and their families.

Adoption and Safe Families Act

The Adoption and Safe Families Act, in conjunction with mass incarceration, has created a detrimental impact on the African American community, African American women, the poor and other women and communities of color, and women of color in particular. The Adoption and Safe Families Act was implemented as federal law in 1997 for the purposes of creating safe, stable, and permanent homes for children in the child welfare system (Adoption and Safe Families Act of 1997; AFSA). The law was enacted as a direct response to both the large number of children who lingered in the foster care system without permanent placement and national news coverage of children abused while in foster care (See AFSA 1997; Smith 2000). Implementation of ASFA mandated the state children and family services agency (hereafter, the Agency) to reunite families by focusing primarily on the safety and permanence of children in this system, and underscoring reasonable efforts to achieve this aim (see Family Preservation and Support Services Act of 1984). The Adoption and Safe Families Act's *reasonable efforts* language is crucial in achieving this purpose because states receive federal financial incentives by complying with this mandate (ASFA 1997; Baker 2001). The act calls for detailed and specific findings of efforts attempted by the Agency as mandatory predicates to receiving this funding (Ratterman 2001). Failure to provide evidence of reasonable efforts to achieve permanency plans results in states' receiving no monies for a child in care, which may or may not be replaced (Ratterman 2001). Rehabilitation and the possibility of receiving funding rest on the determination within which the Agency documents its findings of reasonable efforts. In addition, ASFA requires expeditious timelines within which the parent needs to work with the Agency in order to achieve reunification with the child. The act mandates that states file termination of parental rights petitions if a child has been out of the home for 15 of the most recent 22 months. It also allows states to waive reunification efforts of the Agency if aggravated circumstances exist, there has been a commission of an enumerated felony, and/or there is a finding of a prior involuntary termination of parental rights (Ratterman 2001; Smith 2000).

Implementation of ASFA and its Affect on Incarcerated Populations

A cursory reading of ASFA and its preamble may tempt readers and practitioners to believe that ASFA is a powerful tool to remedy chronic and complex problems in the child welfare system; however, critical analysis and daily practice will demonstrate that ASFA has had a devastating effect on the African American community, African American women, the poor, and other women in communities of color.

It is crucial that child welfare and criminal justice practitioners fully understand how their respective systems interact and how that interaction will affect individuals, families, and communities. Statistical data show that children of color, particularly African-Americans, are overrepresented in the child welfare system.[1] To no surprise, statistical data demonstrate that the same is evident in the criminal justice system.[2] Recent data show that the fastest growing incarcerated population is women (Ritchie 2002). Recent sentencing practices throughout the United States have placed stringent sentences on nonviolent offenders who are generally, of course, women of color (predominantly African-American). Children who are in the child welfare system usually come from single, female-headed households and, in some cases, their mothers or nonbiological female caregivers are incarcerated. With the imposition of harsh sentencing, most women who fall into this category receive sentences that exceed the length of time required by ASFA for reunification. So how does a mother who is incarcerated and sentenced to a time period that exceeds ASFA's mandatory termination filing requirement work with the Agency to achieve reunification? Generally, she does not, unless extraordinary circumstances exist.

The Adoption and Safe Families Act Timelines

The Adoption and Safe Families Act guidelines have expedited the time frame within which a parent can reunify with a child. The language statutory indicates that if a child has been out of the home "15 of the most recent 22 months," a petition to terminate parental rights must be filed by the Agency, unless a compelling reason not to file is documented (Ratterman 2001). This requirement is mandatory and sets a maximum time period, not a minimum. A state's failure to petition may jeopardize its monies received from the federal government.

Generally, incarcerated parents' sentences far exceed the statutory mandate set forth by ASFA to file petitions to terminate parental rights. It is impossible, at best, for a parent to work toward reunification with the child for several reasons. First, the ability to visit with a child while incarcerated is extremely difficult. The parent has no control over whether or not the current custodian will or is able to bring the child to visit at the jail or prison. Moreover, if the child is in the custody of the Agency, the Department is under no obligation to schedule visitation between the child and the parent. Even if the child is assigned to a worker who clearly understands the importance of contact maintenance between a child and its biological parent, limited access to resources, remote prison/jail locations, and restrictive prison visitation policies form substantial barriers to contact with the child.

Incarcerated parents are unable to telephone their children directly and must telephone persons in the community collect. This luxury is limited to those parents who have the financial means to do so. If the child is with a kinship care provider, phone contact is often at the discretion of the caregiver. If the child is in the custody of the Agency and is placed with someone other than a relative, the Agency cannot release the caregiver's telephone number or address to the incarcerated parent. The incarcerated parent must rely on the Agency to maintain telephone contact with the children. So, with caseworkers who are generally unavailable because of demanding caseloads and because of limited resources of social service agencies, this will almost never occur. In cases where the incarcerated parent is able to communicate with her child through letters, the purchase of stamps is a financial luxury. Currently, if the incarcerated parent has a job in prison, he or she generally makes approximately $1 a day, unless the individual works a skilled job.[3] In view of this, it is important to understand that every incarcerated individual is not able to get a job in prison, and the ability to purchase stamps rests solely upon the individual's financial situation, which also bars that parent from making financial contributions to the child's care and/or providing gifts to the child (another judicial consideration).

The attitudes of care providers are also a factor in determining whether or not an incarcerated parent has contact with her child. Some caretakers do not believe that children should have contact with a "criminal." If a child is very young, the parent is forced to communicate through the caretaker. Consequently, if the attitude of that care provider is negative, the parent will never learn of the welfare of his or her child. Additionally, courts and child advocates generally do not look favorably upon a child having contact with a parent in the criminal justice system; the system condemns parents regardless of what factors led to their incarceration. The courts' patriarchal view can strongly influence the road toward reunification and can supersede the parent's right to visit the child. Thus, in the eyes of the court, the failure of a parent to maintain a relationship with his or her child becomes a negative factor in termination of parental rights proceedings.

The Adoption and Safe Families Act is extremely detrimental to the parental rights of mothers and fathers incarcerated for a drug offense. Generally, as a part of recovery, the drug-abusing parent will relapse.[4] Most drug addiction counselors will state that relapse is a part of recovery; however, many courts and child welfare advocates will not consider this. A relapse can severely damage a parent who is on a positive road to recovery. Reunification with her child is tenuous because some advocates and judges will hold this against the parent despite the testimony of most expert addiction counselors. In addition, a drug-using parent's road to recovery generally takes much longer than the ASFA statute allows before the Agency files a petition to terminate parental rights.

Financial Incentives
Capitalism in the United States affects every crevice and fabric of our existence and can be a crucial factor in motivating many people to achieve numerous goals. Wealth is a compelling factor, I argue, in determining what child advocates and courts argue is in the "best interest" of a child in the child welfare system. The Adoption and Safe Families Act, as mentioned earlier, offers financial incentives to states to terminate parental rights and finalize adoptions. Again, as mentioned, the intent of ASFA was to provide safe, permanent, and stable homes for children in care and ASFA supporters believe that permanence is gained through adoption. As a result, financial incentives can drive state courts, caregivers, and child advocates toward adoption. Whether or not adoption constitutes permanence is a point of contention addressed later in this chapter.

Under its spending power, Congress has apportioned funds to states that meet a certain number of base adoptions (65 FR 4020-4093 2000). States receive $4,000 for each adopted child, plus an additional $2,000 for each child adopted with special needs (Welte 1997). For states with big cities and large numbers of children in care, this can mean an exorbitant amount of money to utilize in the system. The availability of funds also influences many care providers in their decisions of whether or not they are willing to adopt a child. Generally, an adoptive resource, who is a restrictive foster parent, can receive approximately $535 per month for a child with no special medical needs and can receive approximately $650 per month for a child with special needs.[3] However, the amount may vary based on the negotiation and skill level of the care provider and the assistance of a diligent caseworker. Not every foster parent receives the same amount of money for a child with or without special needs.

Financial incentives can push both states and prospective caretakers toward adoption at the expense of a parent's rights and may tear families and communities apart. Continuation of this behavior leads to the further disempowerment of communities of color and prevents many children—particularly those who are poor and African-American—from knowing and understanding their cultural identities. It is not my intent to limit the importance of money in providing care for a child in a capitalist country; however, it is essential that we understand some of the motives behind the push for adoption and whether they are in the best interests of children.

Reasonable efforts by the Agency are also tied to funding, and failure to specify these efforts can cost the child and the state monies while the child is in care (45 C.F.R. §1356.21(d)). There are three types of reasonable efforts: a) reasonable efforts to reunify the child with parent and thereby prevent placement, b) reasonable efforts to reunify families following placement, and, c) reasonable efforts to finalize a permanency plan (45 C.F.R. §1356.21 (b)(1), (2)). Only two of these efforts are tied to funding in which the court must make a judicial finding: reasonable efforts to prevent placement and reasonable efforts to finalize a permanency plan.

As one can see, the funding is solely tied to prevention of placement and finalization of a permanency plan. Efforts made by the Agency prior to the filing of a termination of parental rights petition are crucial in determining whether or not reunification with a parent will occur. The attitudes of caseworkers and other players in the child welfare system are crucial in determining whether or not a child will be reunified with a parent. For example, an incarcerated parent who has had no contact with a child for various reasons is a prime candidate for severance of his/her parental rights, whether or not contact with the child is within that parent's control. These considerations weigh heavily in determining whether or not a petition will be filed. If a petition is filed, this is a factor of consideration in the decision to terminate a parent's right. Therefore, pre-reasonable efforts are significant factors in determining whether or not a petition will be filed and whether or not a petition to terminate rights will be granted. In practice, it is best to prevent the filing of a petition to terminate parental rights because it appears that the chances for most parents, especially incarcerated parents, in defeating the petition are slim. Hence, the attitudes of caseworkers, child advocates, family courts, and other players are vital to determining the sustainability of a parent–child relationship. With so many barriers present for the incarcerated parent, the road to reunification appears to very bleak. The severing of parental ties, which last a lifetime, adds to the stress that incarcerated parents already feel.

Waiver of Reasonable Efforts
Presence of the following factors will waive the Agency's obligation to make reasonable efforts:

- Aggravated circumstances
    - Abandonment, sexual abuse, torture, chronic mental injury, or chronic physical harm
- Enumerated felony
    - Murder of another child of the parent, voluntary manslaughter, aiding, abetting, conspiring to commit such murder or voluntary manslaughter, felony assault
- Prior involuntary termination of parental rights

A judicial finding of the three circumstances above will certainly lead to termination, because no effort by the Agency is required in order to work with the parent toward reunification. A mother who has been in a domestic violence situation and subsequently has been convicted of one of the enumerated felonies will almost certainly lose her parental rights. Furthermore, some states, such as Maryland, mandate that parents who birth drug-exposed children be particularly vulnerable to termination proceedings (Annotated Code of Maryland, Family Law Article §5-313(d)).

It is clear that the aggravating circumstances are horrific, and the court must clearly weigh the harm to the child and the circumstances surrounding this harm in determining whether or not to pursue termination. A child who suffers on this level most certainly needs the protection of the court and to think otherwise would be truly unconscionable. The court has the obligation of showing by clear and convincing evidence that such circumstances occurred because of the act of the parent and the court must act responsibly in determining what is in the best interest of a child.

Lastly, involuntary termination is unconstitutional. Involuntary termination generally punishes a parent who refuses to consent to sever his or her rights and who exercises his or her constitutional rights to a trial and is unsuccessful. Exercising one's constitutional right to trial should not be used against an individual. Doing so suggests to parents that fighting for one child and failing to win will jeopardize future success in subsequent termination proceedings with other children in the system. Clearly, this prong to waive the Agency's reasonable efforts actions should be eliminated, and further scrutiny should be carefully and responsibly weighed before the court would make such a finding.

Other Considerations

It is clear that ASFA legislation is pro-child, and rarely sees the best interest of the child as the maintenance of the parent–child tie. Although this is a factor for consideration in a termination proceeding, it appears to me to hold little weight in practice. Not all children want to be adopted and many feel that legal separation from a parent is devastating. Some children in care understand adoption and are clear that this is not the road they want to travel. Strong biological or nonbiological familial ties to individuals, and for some, incarcerated individuals, are difficult for children to forego, and separation will have lasting and negative effects on the child. Many children who have been involved in the child welfare system are prime candidates for contact with the juvenile justice system and, subsequently, the adult criminal justice system. Ever-changing placements and foster parents are the only consistency that many of these children encounter in this system, and the legal severance of a child from his or her parent is the destruction of the last tie to family. Those in care sometimes find facing the decision whether or not to be adopted too complicated. Teens in care have a better understanding of adoption but those who are generally 10 years and younger have greater difficulty understanding the legal ramifications.[6] No matter how competent counsel is in explaining the consequences, the maturity level of the child may not sufficiently be developed to make that decision. Consequently, counsel is often compelled to make decisions for a child based upon current state law, which is in favor of termination.

Constitutional Considerations

The Universal Declaration of Human Rights was drafted with the intent of recognizing inherent dignities and inalienable rights of all members of the human family. Its recognition extends these rights equally and rests on the belief that honoring such rights will ensure global freedom, justice, and peace (Universal Declaration of Human Rights 1948). The International Covenant on Civil and Political Rights encompasses this belief and affirms the intent of the Declaration. Further, it includes the free enjoyment of social and cultural rights as derived by virtue of being human (International Covenant on Civil and Political Rights 1976). Moreover, constitutional protections afforded by the U.S. Constitution underscore these rights as well.

The Fourteenth Amendment of the U.S. Constitution guarantees that no state shall "deprive any person of life, liberty, or property, without due process of law, nor deny to any person within its jurisdiction the equal protection of the laws" (U.S. Constitution Amendment XIV). The fundamental right to parent has been established as a "liberty" interest under the Fourteenth Amendment of the U.S. Constitution and recognition of this interest has been cited in several U.S. Supreme Court cases, among them *Meyer v. Nebraska, Pierce v. Society of Sisters, Prince v. Massachusetts, Quillon v. Walcott, Parham v. J.R.,* and *Santosky v. Kramer.* Abrogation of this right can be accomplished only through a showing of compelling circumstances and may not occur without due process of law.

Termination of parental rights is arguably a violation of Section 16.3 of the U.N. Declaration of Human Rights, which states that "the family is the natural and fundamental group unit of society and is entitled to protection by society and the State." Clearly, the relationship between parent and child is constitutionally protected (*Parham v. J.R.*). As such, ASFA timelines serve as stringent impediments to the ability of a parent to reunify with her child in the face of incarceration and possibly drug addiction. These timelines are extremely short, and it often proves impossible for incarcerated parents to adhere to them. They create a dynamic that jeopardizes the constitutionally protected relationship between parent and child. Although courts have held that if a parent is determined to be unfit, the fundamental right of a parent can be abridged, but expeditious timelines and unfair practices can lead to termination of this fundamental right and thus constitutionally infringe on this special relationship between parent and child. Furthermore, it can be argued that the loss of parental rights as a result of incarceration is an 8th amendment violation in the sense that the punishment is cruel and unusual because the parent is serving a sentence for conviction of a crime and will lose their parental rights because of incarceration. Again, the use of ASFA timelines encroaches upon the fundamental right to parent, and specifically violates the Fourteenth Amendment's equal protection clause by being particularly harsh to those persons who fall within the incarcerated class and may suffer with addictions.

Balancing these interests against the best interest of a child must be considered. It needs to be stated that some children need to be removed from the parent because of physical abuse, neglect, abandonment, sexual abuse, and other atrocities. However, adoption is not always the answer for some children. Again, permanence is a concept that needs greater exploration by child welfare advocates and juvenile courts in determining what is in the best interest of the child. There is a class of children who are "unadoptable" and they generally include children with social, physical, behavioral, and mental health problems. Furthermore, even if parental rights are terminated, it does not mean automatic adoption of a child. Child welfare practices tend to hold foster care providers to a much lower standard in their assurances that they will adopt. Hence, courts move forward on termination of parental rights proceedings with assurances from preadoptive resources that they will adopt the child in their care, and subsequently it is not uncommon for the person to change her mind, thus leaving the parent childless and the child parentless. In short, legal orphans are created. Thus, the question becomes, "how do we achieve permanence for a child who has spent prolonged periods of time in the foster care system?"

Recommendations

States should consider subsidized guardianship for those who are committed to the long-term care of children in the foster care system. Caretakers who take custody and guardianship of a child may receive temporary cash assistance, if eligible, as a public entitlement for the child and subsidized guardianship can buttress these monies. This subsidy can equal the amount of monies received by foster parents who are adoptive resources. Presently, those who have custody and guardianship of a child in care are not entitled to the same monies that an adoptive parent receives. Generally these guardians receive medical assistance but the cash assistance is far less than the subsidy received by adoptive parents.

Utilizing subsidized guardianship as an option will preserve the natural rights of parents and create permanence for children. Generally, many foster parents, particularly kinship providers, travel the road of adoption because the monies are far greater than obtaining custody and guardianship. These providers are interested in obtaining the greatest financial support offered for these children, which is clearly reasonable in light of the cost of raising a family in a capitalist country. However, if other options were available, many care providers would avail themselves of these options. In addition, with respect to the issue of permanence, these caretakers are clearly committed to long-term care. And, generally, many children are unable to understand the legal complexities of adoption. Most children articulate that their primary concern is the ability to remain where they are, without full recognition or understanding of the finality of adoption. Some proponents who view adoption as permanent may argue that allowing subsidized guardianship will allow parents, who, in their eyes, are not committed to reunification, to enter in and out of the life of the child, thereby disrupting the child and foster family's life, in addition to costing the courts valuable time and resources. This action may occur; however, the court may, in its own discretion, decide whether or not it wants to entertain the petition of the parent, thereby limiting the possibility of this occurring.

Additionally, activists and advocates should address the shortened timelines that ASFA sets forth. Extending timelines within which a parent is able to work toward reunification" is also an excellent tool in balancing the interest of parent and child. Although I am not an avid supporter of any timeline, if, as a last resort this is the only remedy, it must be suggested.

Conclusion

The current state of both criminal justice and child welfare policies should be critically reviewed. We must understand that the preservation of family ties is essential to the growth of our individual emotional and psychological well-being. The parent–child legal relationship is not one to dissolve with haste. It is precious and needs to be recognized as such. Failure to do so will only expand the prison population and continue to perpetuate a history of racist and discriminatory practices.

Furthermore, what is in the best interest of a child needs to be viewed from a wider lens. Limited vision of this responsibility is hurting individuals, families, and communities, further disempowering them emotionally, politically, and spiritually. What is quite disturbing is that these policies clearly affect certain populations, especially African American women, women in communities of color, and the poor. We must stop this destruction of our community members and begin to see them as members of the human family who deserve to be treated with dignity and respect is our responsibility. Failure to do this will only hurt the nation and circumvent its growth, further disabling us and hindering our social progress.

The wisdom of our "forefathers" is revered, and yet it hasn't created a truly great society. It is my hope that the wisdom of our mothers and fathers today will lead us to greatness. Ultimately, the measure of a great society is the respect and social progress we make as a nation. Anything short of this is a travesty.

References

Baker, Debra Ratterman. 2001. *Making Sense of the ASFA Regulations.* American Bar Association, National Child Welfare Resource Center on Legal and Judicial Issues, Washington, D.C.

Ritchie, Beth E. 2002. "The Social Impact of Mass Incarceration on Women." In *Invisible Punishment: The Collateral Consequences of Mass Imprisonment,* edited by Marc Mauer and Meda Chesney-Lind. New York: New Press: 136–49.

Smith, Gail T. 2000. "The Adoption and Safe Families Act of 1997: Its Impact on Prisoner Mothers and their Children." December. http://www.c-l-a-i-m.org/pdf/impact.pdf.

Welte, Carmela. 1997. "Detailed Summary of the Adoption and Safe Families Act: Stresses Child's Safety in all Placement Decisions, and Provides Incentives for Adoptions." CASAnet Resources. http://www.casanet.org/reference/asfa-summary.htm.

Cases Cited

Meyer v. Nebraska, 262 US 320 (1923).

Pierce v. Society of Sisters, 268 US 510 (1925).

Prince v. Massachusetts, 321 US 158 (1944).

Quillon v. Walcott, 434 US 246 (1978).
Parham v. J.R., 442 US 584 (1979).
Santosky v. Kramer, 455 US 745 (1982).

Laws Cited

United States Constitution, Eighth Amendment, Fourteenth Amendment.
ASFA 1997, the Adoption and Safe Families Act of 1997.
Family Preservation and Support Services Act of 1984.
65 FR 4020-4093 (2000).
Annotated Code of Maryland, Family Law Article §5-313(d).
Universal Declaration of Human Rights (1948).
International Covenant on Civil and Political Rights (1976).

Endnotes

1. See generally, www.cwla.org/articles/cv0211minorities.htm
2. See generally, www.prisonpolicy.org/articles/notequal.shtm
3. I would like to thank the men and women I interviewed who are currently incarcerated in the eastern United States for graciously speaking with me and for being very open and honest about their current financial status while in prison. Without their stories I would not be able to express the hardship they encounter in working in a system that devalues their humanity and exploits them for their labor.
4. This information was obtained through the experience of being a practitioner and trying a significant amount of termination of parental rights cases in which the reason for the removal of the child was alleged drug abuse by the parent.
5. "Special needs" generally includes children with physical, psychological, and emotional needs. Oftentimes these children are on medication, receiving therapeutic intervention for physical, mental, and/or emotional issues.
6. This information was obtained through my experience as a practitioner.

7

Home Sweet Home for Ex-Offenders

ELIZABETH CURTIN

We are all familiar with such clichés as "home is where the heart is," "a man's home is his castle," "home, sweet home," and "there's no place like home." But for ex-offenders and their families, "home" is neither trendy nor cliché, but instead one of the most daunting issues they face during the reentry process. It can truly be classified as a collateral sanction or invisible punishment—perhaps not an "intended" consequence of the crime committed, but an all too real result of having done time.

For all of us, the search for housing can be an overwhelming task, especially in our large urban areas: which neighborhood do we want to live in? where are the decent schools for our children? how big a place do we want or need? what can we afford? Add on top of this the fact that you need a place to live and you need it *right now*, and there you have the reality facing the majority of the offender population as they exit state and federal correctional facilities.

Different ex-offenders have various levels of responsibility when it comes to housing. Beyond a roof over their own heads, many are responsible for other adult family members, significant others, or children. These family members or friends may have been staying with others and now expect to move back in with the returning offender. Or they may have been able to maintain a home and now expect the offender to help out. Regarding offenders' responsibilities for their children, some may have maintained custody of young children whereas others may be facing the process of reunification on a permanent or part-time basis. In either

111

case, the situation is impossible without a permanent address. Assuming responsibility for others is a healthy and natural part of relationships, but, for the returning offender, it also adds more pressure to an already stressful situation.

While experts estimate that approximately 10% of returning offenders are "homeless"—meaning they have absolutely no housing options other than the shelter system—there are many others who do not have stable or sober homes to return to. Although various studies find that most offenders leave jail or prison with an address to go to, the quality of many of these living arrangements is questionable at best. Sleeping on the couch in a friend's apartment in a high crime area or in a known drug hotspot is not an ideal situation for anyone, let alone for an ex-offender who has numerous barriers and temptations to confront and overcome. Temporary living arrangements, which by definition change every month or few months, are also not a stabilizing environment for successful reentry. Yet these are the only alternatives for many of these individuals, putting them in the same category as the "homeless" offenders: in need of safe and adequate housing options.

Issues and Barriers

Those who work in the field often see a last-minute scramble among offenders to secure postrelease housing. This is not always due to individual procrastination; it is just as likely that their expected housing fell through. Often, they believe they can live with a parent, a girlfriend or a cousin, or a friend, only to have those plans fall through at the last minute. Family members and friends may be reluctant to house ex-offenders. This is understandable, given the preincarceration criminal behavior and concerns over repeating it. The family member or friend indeed may have been through this before, hearing promises of changed behavior and new attitudes, only to be disappointed when the promises were broken. The end result for the offender is an added urgency to find housing and limited choices with such short notice. A case in point illustrates this problem:

> Recently, one of our staff picked up a client being released from the County House of Correction. This young man had a reasonable discharge plan, including living with his grandmother who had regularly visited him during his incarceration. When they arrived at the house, the grandmother was on the porch and told her grandson that she did not want him there. The situation escalated into a shouting match, with the offender in the street, the grandmother on the porch, all of this at 8:30 on a cold morning in a heavily populated neighborhood. Fortunately, our staff member was able to calm

the man down, help him to come up with another option, and drive the man across the city to his stepfather's home, where he was taken in. Here was a returning offender who thought he was all set. Speculating about what could have happened if the client had been alone is not a pleasant thought.

The housing issue is even more pronounced for offenders released from state or federal correctional facilities that are often far removed from prisoners' home communities. Any efforts to secure housing prior to discharge have to be done by long distance, through family or friends, thus adding additional barriers to an already barrier-laden situation. If the offender is leaving a correctional facility on parole, the housing challenge is often more difficult, since the home must be approved by the paroling authority. In their approval process, parole personnel are often looking for obvious drug activity, other residents with warrants or criminal histories, other residents on probation or parole, etc. These understandable concerns limit the options for the returning offender and the release may be delayed while housing is being worked out and approved by a parole officer.

Returning offenders need a stable, sober housing situation and they need it immediately. Without a permanent address, the real and perceived barriers to successful reentry, including finding and maintaining employment, reuniting with family and children, and taking care of treatment needs, are heightened. Indeed, a community "that does not concern itself with the housing needs of returning prisoners finds that it has done so at the expense of its own public safety" (Bradley and Oliver 2001: 1). The types of barriers ex-offenders face finding housing can be categorized as affordability, accessibility, and criminal history.

Affordability

The rise in home prices and the drop in affordable rentals have reached crisis proportions in the United States, especially in large cities. If an offender has not had the opportunity to participate in a work release or a prerelease program, he or she has probably not been able to put aside any money for housing expenses. In large cities, where the majority of ex-offenders live, rents have skyrocketed. The monthly rental for an average (3-room, 1 bathroom) one bedroom apartment in San Francisco costs nearly $1,500; in Boston, it is over $1,300; in New York, it is around $1,200; and in Washington, D.C., it is close to $1,300 (Runzheimer International 2002). A recent scan of rentals in the Boston Globe found the least expensive apartment to be a studio, advertised at $750/month without utilities, and only three listings for furnished room rentals, which ranged from $120/week to $150 per week (*Boston Globe* 2003: D 13).

Initial rental costs, first and last months' rent plus security deposits, can be exorbitant.

If an ex-offender has a family to return to, he or she has probably not been able to contribute financially to housing needs while incarcerated and may not be able to do so immediately upon release. Many offenders end up imposing on family and friends for a place to stay, putting a strain on even the closest of relationships. Usually as the last resort, some offenders are released from prison with no alternative other than the homeless shelter system. According to a 1997 study conducted by the McCormick Institute of Public Affairs at the University of Massachusetts Boston, 7% of the shelter population consists of offenders who have come directly from jail or prison (Hayes et al. January 2000: 10). Another 22% of shelter guests were incarcerated within the previous year (Hayes et al. 2000: 10). These data point out two disturbing facts: the high number of offenders released from correctional facilities with no housing plan in place and the number of offenders who lose their housing within the first twelve months after release. The incidence of lost housing is attributable to several factors, not the least of which is inability to afford high rents.

The shelters themselves present several barriers for the returning offender. There may literally be "no room at the inn"; shelters are often filled beyond capacity, especially during the winter months. Shelters may simply feel too much like prisons, prompting the ex-offenders to opt for the streets instead. To stay in a shelter that is funded through Housing and Urban Development (HUD), an individual must be homeless for at least 24 hours, meaning they cannot have spent the previous night in any residence. If there is one thing that all of the reentry research agrees upon, it is that the first 24 hours after release are critical to the ex-offender's successful reentry. "The moment of release presents mixed opportunities: it can be an occasion for a joyful family reunion or a first chance to resume old habits" (Nelson, Deess, and Allen 1999: 5). Having to spend a night on the streets in order to be admitted to a homeless shelter is not exactly a "joyous occasion."

Accessibility

There are no longer many cheap lodging or rooming houses in our cities, which used to provide reasonably priced rooms and allowed time for a person with a job to save up for his or her own apartment. What happened to the rooming houses? Most have been converted into market-rate apartments and condominiums, or are simply not profitable enough for property owners to keep them in business. The number of lodging houses in Boston, for example, is down by 90%—from 10,000 to 1,000—over a ten-year period (Community Resources for Justice 2001: 18).

Many offenders, and indeed many low-income individuals, do not own automobiles, requiring them to live in areas with access to public transportation. This usually limits them to living in or near larger urban areas. Certain kinds of employment options are also more plentiful in large urban areas. A report from the Urban Institute's Justice Policy Center found that the highest concentration of returning offenders is in just a few of our larger states; five states account for just under one-half of released offenders (Lynch and Sabol 2001: 15). The same report also found that offenders are returning to "core counties" within those states, with core counties being those that include the main city of a metropolitan area (Lynch and Sabol 2001: 15). Unfortunately, these metropolitan areas are also where housing costs are usually the highest.

This puts many offenders in the unenviable position of living with others—hopefully supportive family members—until they get on their own two feet. It often results in crowded living situations, and/or living with family and friends who may themselves have antisocial, pro-criminal tendencies and lifestyles. None of these situations is conducive to successful reintegration.

Criminal History

The use of criminal background checks has become a major barrier to an ex-offender's return to living and working in the community. For housing in particular, private landlords screen applicants based on criminal history, credit history, and work history, all of which present problems for the ex-offender population. Many have poor credit histories and their recent employment history is problematic. In competitive and expensive housing markets especially, the returning offender does not rise to the top of a landlord's list of desirable tenants.

A common myth is that all ex-offenders are permanently banned from public or subsidized housing. Local housing authorities require that any adult living in public or subsidized housing be named on the lease; therefore, all adults must follow the approval process. The federal government does require local public housing authorities to prohibit those with certain criminal histories from living in subsidized and public housing: 1) persons who have been evicted for drug-related activity (they are ineligible for three years unless they can demonstrate completion of an approved rehabilitation program); 2) persons with a lifetime registration requirement under a state sex offender registry program (they are permanently banned); and 3) those previously convicted of manufacturing or producing methamphetamine on the public housing premises (they, too, are permanently banned) (*Federal Register* 2001).

Although ex-offenders are frequently rejected upon first application based on their criminal records, there is an appeals process to pursue if they do not fall into one of these three categories. This is a time-consuming and bureaucratic endeavor but can result in approval for housing in the long run. Getting ex-offenders on the list for public housing, helping them through the appeals process, and providing advocacy for them can be very effective. Unfortunately, in most situations, they are not linked with the necessary assistance for long enough to see them through this process, which can take not just months, but years. For example, the average prerelease center has residents for a maximum of six months—nowhere near enough time to get them through the entire housing application and appeals process.

Existing Housing Practices

There are a variety of community-based residential programs for individuals with specific needs, including ex-offenders with those same special needs. For those with serious addiction, mental health, and physical health problems, these options may be an appropriate and effective housing option and a first step to reintegration into society. Programs of this type typically provide treatment services geared to the specific needs of their target population and comprehensive case management services to help their clients' transition to more-independent living arrangements.

One example is the SPAN program in Boston, which operates specifically for ex- offenders who are HIV-positive and serves approximately 60 individuals each year. With Emergency Shelter Grant funding from HUD, SPAN secures housing for returning offenders through a network of treatment programs, halfway houses, and some low-income housing units. They provide a range of counseling, case management, and transportation services to assist their clients to achieve stable living situations.

Even though these need-specific, community-based programs are indeed valuable, they also present limitations for the returning offender. Many substance abuse programs and sober homes require a certain period of sobriety (from 90 days to twelve months) but do not consider jail time as counting toward "sober" time. This may leave the offender with no place to live while maintaining sobriety in order to gain acceptance into these programs. Demand far exceeds the supply of spaces in these programs, resulting in long waiting lists, possibly rendering the returning offender homeless or leaving him or her to stay in jail longer while waiting for a bed to become available. Some programs understandably require that residents contribute financially to their room and board, which again presents a problem for the ex-offender with no financial resources at the time of release. Finally, most programs in this category do not want an all-offender population, further limiting the beds available.

Many correctional systems (county, state, and federal) operate prerelease or community corrections residential centers. Some are run directly by the correctional systems themselves, and others are contracted out to private nonprofit or for-profit agencies. Although residents are still under the authority of the correctional system in either case, these programs provide a period of structured transition from incarceration into the community. Typically, residents are required to work or attend a training program or school, as well as to participate in treatment activities and perform community service work. These programs emphasize planning and preparation for the next phase, which is release from correctional authority to life as an independent citizen. They provide an opportunity for the offender to work, save money, and secure appropriate housing. Several limitations of these programs include the following: the resident must be cleared by institutional classification to be admitted, even "minor" rule infractions can result in being returned to custody, and the scarcity of available beds limits the number of eligible offenders who can participate.

As previously mentioned, the homeless shelter systems are often the last choice among ex-offenders. Some shelter systems are reaching outside of their usual offerings to address this situation. One example is the Census Reduction for Ex-Offenders (CREO) program in Boston, operated by Community Resources for Justice. With funding from an Emergency Shelter Grant through the Department of Housing and Urban Development (HUD), CREO was created to keep offenders out of the shelters by providing transitional beds. The program focuses on housing and employment, provides funds for rental assistance and housing start-up goods, and allows residents to stay for an average of three months. This is a fabulous resource, but let's put it into context. The previously mentioned McCormick Institute of Public Affairs (University of Massachusetts) study estimates that Boston's shelters serve over 1,400 guests per year who come directly from prison (Hayes et al. 2000: 10). But CREO is only funded for 10 beds—5 for men, and 5 for women—and serves an average of 40 individuals per year.

Some cities and states have ordinances that regulate affordable housing. For example, in Massachusetts there is an affordable housing law, which requires that all municipalities set aside at least 10% of their housing stock for low- and moderate-income units. This is a step in the right direction, but it needs much work; the law has been on the books for 30 years and the 10% goal is far from realized. Cities and towns have resorted to innovative ways to skirt the law—through creative counting of units and creative definitions of "affordable"—and to practice what is commonly referred to as *snob zoning*, which prevents additional low/moderate units from being established.

Possible Solutions

The solution to the ex-offender housing crisis is as complex as the problem itself. Nonetheless, there are political, social, cultural, and economic remedies that we can attend to in the short term. Advocates for the offender population need to take advantage of any and all opportunities to present this issue to elected officials and community leaders. Another cliché, "don't do the crime if you can't do the time," could be amended to "don't do the crime if you can't do the time, and do the time, and do the time," because that is often the enduring result of conviction for certain types of felonies. These offenders continue to be "punished" by not being able to gain access to or to afford reasonable housing in the communities of their choice. From a public safety point of view, it is worth noting that the majority of offenders *do* get released. Do we want to see them released to stable homes or to the streets? Those concerned about social justice for the returning offender population should actively support leaders and officials who are knowledgeable about housing issues and the implications for ex-offenders. We need to speak up, and speak loudly, against those who discriminate against these individuals—communities with "snob zoning," landlords who reject ex-offenders as renters, and builders and communities who skirt affordable housing regulations.

Although they have been practiced in many areas with mixed results, we need to revise and support efforts to increase housing subsidies, rent vouchers, rent control, and programs of rental stabilization. The construction of new housing and the preservation of existing units must be a *priority*, especially for metropolitan areas. Creative initiatives to increase the housing stock also need exploration and support.

There is a creative new rent subsidy program in Missouri, operated by the St. Vincent De Paul Society of St. Louis. "From Release to Rent" will provide ten ex-offenders with rental assistance for up to one year, in decreasing increments as they transition back into society and are able to survive on their own. As those involved with the program state, it is less expensive than incarcerating these individuals for a year and it can set them up for success.

Although much progress has been made in recent years, we need to maintain pressure on our correctional facilities to start the discharge planning process the minute an inmate enters the door, especially at our jails and houses of correction where they are doing short time. Correctional staff must be given the resources, tools, and training to assist ex-offenders with finding appropriate housing.

We have to develop a persuasive means to convince communities to accept their offenders back into society. Just as the offenders have the responsibility to return to their communities as law-abiding and contributing citizens, communities too have the responsibility to allow them to do just that.

One of the most difficult aspects of working on behalf of returning offenders is the frustrating and discouraging experience of siting residential programs—neighborhood residents object, mayors object, zoning boards object—anyone who has been through this process has horror stories to tell. And, in most of the potential locations, the services are not for outsiders that anyone is trying to move in. They are the sons and daughters and mothers and fathers *from that very* neighborhood.

We need to bring back rooms for rent and lodging houses. For the non-profit community, building affordable transitional housing is a challenge but it is not impossible. In 1998, the Fortune Society in New York was able to purchase the shell of a former boarding school and an adjacent lot in uptown Manhattan for affordable ex-offender housing. This effort was spurred by their strategic planning committee, which identified the lack of safe housing as one of the most pressing needs of their ex-offender clients. In 2002, the Fortune Academy began providing emergency and long- term housing to ex-offenders. The model allows staff to track and assist residents in the move from the emergency phase with three to five residents in a room, to longer-term doubles if necessary, and to single units for those with increased stability but continuing need.

Several of the models already mentioned could, and should, be expanded. The SPAN and CREO programs in Boston serve approximately 100 individuals each year. But there are over 21,000 offenders released in Massachusetts each year (Massachusetts Department of Correction 2000), and if a conservative 10% figure is used for those who are homeless, then we need to be able to serve at least 2,000 individuals. This is not a call for massive group homes, which end up being community-based institutions. Instead, it is a call for a variety of small- to medium-size units (10 to 50 residents), which means multiple locations in metropolitan areas.

The days for nonprofits or government agencies to go it alone are long gone. Housing specialists and developers need to link up with correction, probation and parole, faith-based communities, and with other facets of our communities. If each partner contributes a part (funding, resources, manpower, or expertise) of the necessary whole, the job can get done without the infusion of the dreamed-of multimillion-dollar 20-year grant. The Hampden County Sheriff's Department in Springfield, Massachusetts, for example, has collaborated with Honor Court, a work therapy recovery program. Honor Court provides the housing and the services of its program; the Sheriff's Department provides staff and programming; and returning offenders, probationers, and parolees benefit from this structured environment for their transition back to society. Residents pay a portion of their wages for room and board (up to $350/month) and the rest is reserved for their permanent housing needs.

Conclusion

The literature on offender reentry clearly tells us that the "port of entry," where the offender goes immediately upon release, is a key determinant of success. The first 24 hours to the first month are fragile times for ex-offenders. How they fare during that time often determines their likelihood of successful reintegration and becoming constructive rather than destructive members of their communities. For their sake, for our sake, and for the sake of public safety and common decency, we have to attack this issue of housing with vigor, or we will continue to pay the price—lives lost in the cycles of crime, violence, poverty, and social disenfranchisement.

References

Boston Globe. 2003. *Boston Globe* Classified Section. December.

Bradley, Katherine H. and R. B. Michael Oliver. 2001. "No Place Like Home: Housing and the Ex-Prisoner." Policy Brief. Community Resources for Justice. Boston, MA.

Community Resources for Justice. 2001. *Returning Inmates: Closing the Public Safety Gap.* Boston, MA.

Federal Register. 2001. Vol. 66, No. 1011. Department of Housing and Urban Development, 24 CFR 982553. May.

Hayes, Michael et al. 2000. *A Preliminary Look at Boston's Homeless Population.* Center for Social Policy, McCormick Institute of Public Affairs, University of Massachusetts Boston. January.

Lynch, James P. and William J. Sabol. 2001. *Prisoner Reentry in Perspective.* Urban Institute Justice Policy Center. Washington, D.C.

Massachusetts Department of Correction. 2000. *Statistical Description of Releases from Institutions and the Jurisdiction of the Massachusetts Department of Correction during 1999.* September.

Nelson, Marta, Perry Deess, and Charlotte Allen. 1999. *First Month Out: Post Incarceration Experiences in New York City.* Vera Institute of Justice. New York.

Runzheimer International. 2002. "Apartment Rental Costs Nationwide." Rochester, WI.

8

The Civil Threat of Eviction and the Regulation and Control of U.S. Public Housing Communities

CHRISTOPHER MELE

> "We don't want to kick people out left and right. We're just saying you need to pay careful attention to who you have living with you and who you have visit you."
>
> —Director of the Housing Authority of East St. Louis, MO

Low-income individuals and families often wait years for apartments in public housing projects to become available. And when the day comes to sign the lease, soon-to-be tenants contractually agree to more than paying their rents on time, keeping noise down, and making sure their homes are neat and tidy: they agree to the impracticable task of full-blown monitoring of the activities of household members and their guests while at home, in school, at the mall, the pizza parlor, and just about anywhere else. Because, as public housing leases are required to stipulate: if a public housing tenant, any member of the tenant's household, or any guest or other person under the tenant's control engages in criminal activity or any drug-related criminal activity on or off premises, tenancy will be terminated.

Such is the fate of many, predominantly minority and female, public housing tenants: a grandmother whose daughter's houseguest is charged with drug possession in a project parking lot; a mother whose son, accused of assault, visits but does not live with her, and; a woman, beaten by her boyfriend, who calls the police and has him arrested for battering.[1] In all of these examples, tenants were evicted from their public housing apartments neither for participating in nor knowing about the alleged crime but for failing to prevent it. The no-fault eviction provision, now found in all public housing leases, was made mandatory in the Department of Housing and Urban Development's 1996 One Strike and You're Out policy and was upheld by the United States Supreme Court in 2002. The provision holds tenants liable for alleged criminal activities of third parties—household members and their guests—and, in doing so, obligates them to scrutinize the behaviors of anyone and everyone who enters their apartment.

As others have argued, the One Strike eviction policy is emblematic of the "zero tolerance" rhetoric that pervades contemporary antidrug criminal justice policy despite its apparent failure and, more importantly, its disastrous consequences mostly for poor people (Mock 1998; Piety 2003; Castle 2003; Moye 2003). According to the zero tolerance logic, the threat of eviction should deter drug activity within public housing projects, and spirited enforcement of the eviction policy will remove the threat of future infractions, hence making public housing communities safer. While in agreement with the critique of the HUD policy as a defensible form of punishment or deterrence, this chapter examines the threat of eviction from a different tack—that of compliance with, rather than the violation of, collateral civil penalties as part of a system of social control and regulation of poor, mostly minority urban communities.

My interest in this chapter is the set of obligations that public housing tenants are compelled to abide by in the signing of a lease—to scrutinize the behaviors of family members, their friends, and visitors within the home and outside of it. In total, these expectations form an "affirmative obligation" on the part of leaseholders to prevent criminal activities through the control of third-party behavior, hence implicating each tenant of public housing in a system of social regulation and control. I do not contend that such compliance is completely willing; indeed, the presence of real and negative consequences for violation of the policy means that it is compelled. Nonetheless, I contend there is much to be gained by a focus on the majority of people who do not violate certain civil legal prescriptions— that through their compliance, we can see the mostly pernicious ways the state has slipped control, surveillance, and regulation into ordinary everyday behaviors of specific populations.

In part one of this chapter, I outline the development of the U.S. Department of Housing and Urban Development's (HUD) One Strike and You're Out eviction policy as a particular collateral penalty with grave implications for the tenancy of poor, mostly minority residents of public housing.

Although the policy is applicable to public housing tenants exclusively, its range of affected persons within that cohort is wider than that of other collateral penalties: the penalty applies to persons *accused* of drug-related or other criminal activities, as well as those who may have been arrested, convicted, or incarcerated. Second, the penalty applies to *entire households* of public housing residents shown to be linked to (i.e., allowing entry to) persons who allegedly engage in drug-related or other criminal activities. Finally, *compliance* with the One Strike and You're Out policy has a regulatory effect on the social relationships and interactions of all public housing residents.

In the second half of this chapter, I explore in fuller detail the notion of compliance with collateral civil penalties, showing how anticipated conformity to civil laws functions as a means of social control and regulation of poor minorities. The deployment of certain forms of civil laws proves more amenable to social control and regulation than the application of criminal laws alone. Drawing on parts of the HUD eviction clause, I suggest in detail the ways in which expected compliance from public housing tenants plays into contemporary management of race, class, and gender relations, alongside similar systems of social control, including mass incarceration and the penalization of poverty through welfare reform.

The War on Drugs and the Eviction of Entire Households from Public Housing

With drug testing and searches now routine conventions, the War on Drugs rhetoric and accompanying moral panic have crept their way into the regulation of ordinary activities of the workplace and home, in schools, as well as on highways and in parks and other public spaces (Sandy 2003). The most severe and direct corollaries to the War on Drugs have been the passage of harsh federal and, increasingly, state criminal drug possession and distribution laws that carry substantial penalties and, consequently, the mass incarceration of particular segments of the population, namely poor, minority males and, more recently, females. Collateral penalties associated with the War on Drugs—denial of social welfare benefits, disenfranchisement, and employment and housing restrictions—amount to secondary effects, although with the expected release of more persons from jail and prison, these effects will soon prove critical to affected individuals, their families, and communities (as other chapters in this volume document).

The impetus behind many of these penalties is the Congressional passage of the Anti-Drug Abuse Act of 1988, which called for the suspension or termination of federal benefits, such as student loans, for individuals convicted of certain drug offenses. While the 1988 Anti-Drug Abuse Act's immediate effects were minimal, a string of policies, rulings, and laws related to housing, employment, and social welfare eligibility written in the 1990s draws directly from its mandate. This is no less true for HUD's current tactic in the War on Drugs in public housing: the intense screening of tenant applicants for drug-related activities and, as discussed in this chapter, the insertion of a drug-related activities eviction clause in tenant leases. The latter policy (explored fully below) originated in the 1988 Act, was toughened and expanded in amendments made throughout the 1990s, and, finally, was upheld by the Supreme Court's ruling in *Department of Housing and Urban Development v. Rucker*, 535 U.S. 125 (2002).

In the 1988 Act, Congress paid particular (arguably, exclusive) attention to drug-related criminal activities[2] that reportedly had overpowered community life in public housing projects. Congress found that "drug dealers are increasingly imposing a reign of terror on public and other federally assisted low-income housing tenants" and that "local law enforcement authorities often lack the resources to deal with the drug problem in public and other federally assisted low-income housing, particularly in light of the recent reductions in Federal aid to cities" (42 U.S.C. §11901). In order to address the problem, Congress directed HUD to require local public housing authorities[3] to include a drug-related activity eviction clause in a tenant's lease. The leases clause was to

> provide that a public housing tenant, any member of the tenant's household, or a guest or other person under the tenant's control shall not engage in criminal activity, including drug-related criminal activity, on or near public housing, and such criminal activity shall be cause for termination of tenancy. (42 U.S.C. §1437d(l)5 1988)

The reference to persons other than the leaseholder who may be engaged in criminal activities is remarkable not only in the legal sense, but also in its social consequences for tenants, as discussed later in this chapter. Tenants were to be made *civilly* liable for the alleged *criminal* conduct of other "covered persons" (guests or other persons under the tenant's control). In other words, the lease clause allowed for punishment (in the form of eviction) for criminal behavior (drug-related activities) to be extended beyond the individual offender to include those tenants with whom he or she is connected, however briefly (e.g., visiting).

The 1988 provision was reiterated and given sharper teeth in the Cranston-Gonzalez National Affordable Housing Act of 1990. The 1990 Act required each public housing agency to utilize leases that

> provide that any criminal activity that threatens the health, safety, or right to peaceful enjoyment of the premises by other tenants or any

drug-related criminal activity on or near such premises, engaged in by a public housing tenant, any member of the tenant's household, or any guest or other person under the tenant's control, shall be cause for termination of tenancy. (Cranston-Gonzalez National Affordable Housing Act, Pub. L. No. 101-625, 504, 104 Stat. 4181 1990; codified as 42 § U.S.C.A. 1437(l)(5).

Cranston-Gonzalez broadened the scope of criminal activity that threatens the health, safety, or right to peaceful enjoyment of tenants. The act further enhanced the discretion of local public housing authorities to determine what constitutes a threat to "the health, safety, or right to peaceful enjoyment of the premises by other tenants."

The Clinton administration raised the stakes in the War on Drugs and called on all local public housing authorities to adopt a One Strike and You're Out zero-tolerance policy to evict offending tenants. The use of evictions as an anti-drug tool was recognized as a national priority in the 1996 State of the Union speech. In March 1996, the Housing Opportunity Extension Act was signed into law, granting local public housing authorities increased powers to evict. The Extension Act added the abuse of alcohol to the list of actionable violations. Authorities were to administer leases that

provide that any criminal activity that threatens the health, safety, or right to peaceful enjoyment of the premises by other tenants or any drug-related criminal activity on or off such premises, engaged in by a public housing tenant, any member of the tenant's household, or any guest or other person under the tenant's control, shall be cause for termination of the tenancy. (42 U.S.C. §1437d(l)6 1996)

The Extension Act replaced the words "on or near the premises" with "on or off the premises," hence removing any geographical ambiguities as to where offending activities can or cannot take place: the provision applies to certain criminal activities by "covered persons" that occur potentially *anywhere at anytime.*

HUD produced a regulation of the One Strike policy the same year, drawing on the relevant statutes within the Anti-Drug Abuse Act of 1988, the Affordable Housing Act of 1990, and the 1996 Amendment (and fully drawing on the tougher 1996 amended provision). As a result of such prioritization, local housing authorities began to implement the policies in earnest, triggering alarm from housing and tenants rights advocates and some resident associations.

In 2001, HUD published its final rules to amend the regulations for public housing and other subsidized housing programs for low income, elderly, and disabled populations (Section 8 assisted housing, Section 221(d) 3 below market interest rate (BMIR) program, Section 202 program for the elderly, Section 811 program for persons with disabilities, and Section 236 interest reduction program) (HUD 2001).

As one would expect, legal challenges to the eviction clause were plentiful given the fact that it would make tenants liable for the alleged misconduct— that transpires ostensibly anywhere at anytime—by certain people other than the tenants themselves. In addition, tenants could be held liable regardless of their knowledge or ignorance of the criminal behavior in question. Finally, the eviction of public housing tenants is a civil, not criminal, procedure. In most cases, tenants abide by eviction notices because the costs of contestation (in money and time) are high. Given that tenants often feel powerless against local housing authorities, many of those faced with eviction view disputing an authority's ruling as pointless. Residents who opt to challenge an eviction are offered informal and administrative hearings in which the rules of evidence for an eviction finding are lax. In March 2002, the Supreme Court ruled in *HUD v. Rucker* that the eviction clause was constitutional and the policy now stands.

Before I discuss what the policy entails for compliance by the majority of public housing tenants, I briefly cover aspects of the Supreme Court's ruling pertinent to the use of civil law as a tool for social control and regulation.

Strict Interpretation and a Federal Policy of No-Fault Evictions

In *HUD v. Rucker*, the U.S. Supreme Court unanimously upheld the statutorily required lease eviction clause, overturning an earlier ruling by an *en banc* panel of the U.S. Ninth Circuit Court of Appeals that key parts of HUD's eviction regulations were inconsistent with the Congressional statute that authorized them. In particular, the Ninth Circuit judges, as well as a number of other judges (mostly dissenting) sitting on other federal courts and hearing similar cases prior to *Rucker*, took issue with the eviction of innocent tenants—those not accused or even aware of criminal activity but evicted owing to their association with an alleged offender. The case at hand, *Rucker v. Davis* 237 F.3d 1113 (9th Cir. 2001), involved the Oakland (California) Housing Authority's efforts to evict four of its tenants for violation of the lease provision in 1997 and 1998. The authority had sought to evict William Lee and Barbara Hill after their grandsons were charged with smoking marijuana in a parking lot near their apartments. In another occurrence, police arrested the daughter of a tenant, Pearlie Rucker, for possession of cocaine and paraphernalia three blocks from her mother's home. Police found cocaine on the person of Herman Walker's caregiver and, after two warning notices, the authority expected to evict him for violation of the lease. In each of these situations, the housing authority claimed the tenants had violated their leases because on-premise contacts with alleged wrongdoers had jeopardized the security of all residents.

The central issue in *Rucker v. Davis* (before both the Ninth Circuit and the Supreme Court) was the constitutional basis for evicting tenants who were in some way connected to "third-party" individuals accused of criminal activities but who were ostensibly innocent of any criminal wrongdoing themselves. Whereas the Ninth Circuit ruled that some fault or knowledge of the criminal activity on the part of tenants was required to be shown, the Supreme Court ruled it was not. In doing so, the Supreme Court relied on the landlord-tenant contract, hence reaffirming the use of civil law and procedure to punish and, as I later argue, regulate and control the conduct of public housing residents.

The appellate judges (and other, mostly dissenting judges in similar eviction cases) argued that the eviction liability standard should be fault-based, as intended by Congress in the original Anti-Drug Abuse Act of 1988 and all amendments to the lease clause made since. That is, a public housing authority must prove a tenant's knowledge of or some form of participation in an alleged infraction by "covered persons" (a member of the tenant's household, or any guest or other person under the tenant's control). A knowledge or fault-based interpretation of the eviction clause reads "under the tenant's control" to mean the tenant either knew of the guest's criminal activity or in some way had control over the guest. From this perspective, an opposing and stricter interpretation of the eviction clause would "impose too heavy a burden on the tenant, as the tenant cannot possibly know or control the conduct of every person who enters her household" (Mock 1998: 1516).

The Supreme Court rejected that reading and ultimately upheld HUD's preference for a no-fault eviction policy for all federally funded housing programs. The no-fault eviction policy holds all tenants strictly liable for third-party actions (alleged infractions or criminal behavior by guests or visitors of a tenant). A "strict liability" interpretation holds that a tenant may be held responsible for criminal activity by covered persons, regardless of the tenant's knowledge of or ability to control such activity. It maintains there is no provision in the clause or anywhere else in the lease that would make tenant knowledge of drug activity a necessary precondition for eviction.

The Court's legal basis for a strict liability interpretation of the eviction clause is predicated on two findings. First, Congress purposefully did not require HUD or local housing authorities to prove fault or knowledge of criminal activity on the part of persons to be evicted. The Court upheld HUD's reasoning that Congress determined that drug crime and criminal threats by household members and their guests were "a special danger to the security and general benefit of public housing residents" (U.S.H. Act, section 6(l)(5), 42 U.S.C. 1437d(l)(5).) For this reason, Congress specified that these types of criminal activities be grounds for termination of contract (tenancy) without the need for a separate inquiry as to whether such criminal activity constitutes serious or repeated lease violation or other good cause for eviction.

Second, the Court held that the government, in this instance, assumes the role of landlord and, therefore, standard procedures of landlord-tenant law apply. Since "contractual responsibility of the tenant for [specified] acts . . . is a conventional incident of tenant responsibility under normal landlord-tenant law and practice" the no-fault eviction ruling applies. In practice, therefore, an individual who signs a lease and enters into a legal contract with the landlord (the public housing authority) "should not be excused from contractual responsibility by arguing that tenant did not know, could not foresee, or could not control behavior by other occupants of the unit" (56 *Federal Register* 51560-01 1991).

It is important to reiterate that tenants are not evicted for the alleged *criminal* activities of a "member of the tenant's household, or any guest or other person under the tenant's control"; they are evicted for violating a clause in their lease that stipulates their removal should any "covered person" be accused or convicted of certain categories of criminal behavior. It is the relationship established between the leaseholder and covered person—however casual or formal, recent or stable—that is the basis for culpability: it violates a *civil* contract and is the grounds for eviction under property law.

Although each public housing authority is now required to include the eviction clause in a lease, the level of enforcement of the eviction clause is left up to the individual authorities. Section 578 of the Quality Housing and Work Responsibility Act (QHWRA) of 1998 (PL 105-276, 1998 HR 4194) authorizes local public housing authorities to obtain criminal history records from the FBI and state and local police departments. Apartment owners and landlords who participate in Section 8 programs may access this information from the local public housing authority. Local authorities may show discretion in enforcement on a case-by-case basis. They are granted leeway, for example, in deciding what constitutes serious criminal activity and in considering mitigating circumstances, such as participation in a drug or alcohol rehabilitation program. Alternatively, the minimal oversight by HUD and the limited legal resources of most tenants may lead to potential misuse of the clause by authorities resolute on "cleaning up" public housing.

Whereas local public housing authorities may or may not exercise discretion in enforcing eviction as civil punishment, it is apparent that compliance with the lease terms is expected. Given that the clause is a requirement in all tenant leases, all public housing residents are directly implicated by the Court's strict liability or "no-fault eviction" interpretation of the law. In *Memphis Housing Authority v. Thompson* (1999), the Tennessee Court of Appeals held that tenants have an "affirmative obligation" to ensure that household members, guests, or anyone else under the tenant's control do not engage in drug-related criminal activity on or off the premises. In order to be in full compliance with the eviction clause in their leases, lease-holders are required to scrutinize their own relationships and acquaintances and those of other household members.

Strict Liability, No-Fault Evictions, and Self-Governance of Public Housing Residents

Touted as "a new tool" in the War on Drugs, the eviction clause appears less a crime prevention technique than a tool designed to extend responsibility (and, more importantly, liability) for "community safety" from the traditional locus of institutions of law enforcement to the entirety of public housing tenants. Upon signing a lease, tenants are contractually obligated to control and monitor the sets of social relationships they and their guests engage in and to assume the risks associated with those relationships: that alleged criminal activities by covered persons (household members, guests, and others under a tenant's control) are legal grounds for eviction. Accordingly, tenant compliance with the eviction clause should produce and maintain the security desired by residents, housing officials, and society at large. The desired goal of security, however, serves only to legitimize the insidious efforts to implicate poor, mostly minority public housing residents in their own regulation and social control.

The eviction clause is indicative of a broader governmental shift toward the use of civil laws to regulate the conduct of particular social groups and to fix liability or risk for security within the confined spaces where they live (Anleu 1998; Cheh 1998; Buerger and Mazerolle 1998). The use of civil laws as a form of regulation differs from conventional disciplinary strategies of social control, such as traditional policing, that are organized around compliance with institutionalized authority, focused prevention of criminal acts and other transgressions, and social welfare-based efforts to address root causes of deviance. Drawing on Foucault's (1991) writings on governmentality, regulation takes the form of practices in which many and varying techniques—new security technologies, architecture and design of public space, restrictive covenants governing property owners, and innovative uses for existing civil statutes, among others—are deployed to manufacture, enhance, or preserve some predefined desire for security (Dean 1999: 19; Sanchez 1997). Such practices constitute a ". . . 'way of doing things,' or 'art,' for acting on the actions of individuals, taken either singly or collectively, so as to shape, guide, correct, and modify the ways in which they conduct themselves" (Burchell 1993: 267).

As part of governance, regulation and control are folded into routine and everyday behaviors and decisions; individuals are not to be policed or controlled per se, but are to be actively engaged in the policing, regulating, and controlling of themselves and others (cf. Hindess 2000: 119). Governance, as an art, therefore, does not presuppose a forcible compliance of those who are to be controlled; rather, it "brings about" their active participation in practices of regulation and social control. Regulation appears as an irresistible urge (folded in among others), not as an extrinsic form of coercion (Ericson and Haggerty 1997: 133). Legitimized by the call for enhanced security (a collective good), governance implicates individuals and families in the responsibility and liability for the management of risk (Valverde et al. 1999).

Collateral civil penalties are central to new forms of governance, given their hidden nature. They are less imposed upon individuals than encountered through the quite ordinary experiences of renting an apartment, finding a job, or attending school. In the case of public housing, the somewhat routine occurrence of signing a lease obligates leaseholders and entire households to participate in practices of regulation and control. These practices and their consequences are worth examining in some detail, as follows.

Congress, the Courts, and HUD Have Characterized Strict Liability, No-Fault Evictions as Empowering Public Housing Communities, Not Penalizing Individual Tenants

In the 1988 Anti-Drug Abuse Act, Congress specifically labeled drug crimes as a "special danger" to the security of a specific population: public housing residents. The act also pointed to the failure of direct and conventional policing of criminal behavior and described public housing tenants as uncooperative with law enforcement efforts to remedy the problem. This special mention in the law brought about an eviction policy in which the enhancement of collective security clearly trumps potential damage to individual rights of association. An Eleventh Circuit Court ruling concurs:

> While we acknowledge the potential for unfairness as a result of the Congressional authorization to evict ignorant tenants, we find that this is a necessary and just means of attaining a legitimate government objective. Public housing had deteriorated to unsafe and unlivable conditions, and Congress needed a remedy to eradicate the harmful element that had infiltrated these complexes. (*Burton v. Tampa Housing Authority*, 271 F.3d 1274 (11th Cir. 2001)

HUD views the threat of eviction as a necessary means to attain communities comprised of "responsible, law-abiding families." HUD also emphasizes the shrinking supply of public housing units (but not the underlying federal policies that have created the shortage), and describes the eviction policy as a practical solution to a problem of too much demand and limited supply: the eviction of some makes room for the desirable residents on long waiting lists.

More importantly, HUD portrays any weakness or failure to enforce the policy as *collectively* unfair: "By refusing to evict or screen out problem tenants, we are unjustly denying responsible and deserving low-income families access to housing and are jeopardizing the community and safety of existing residents who abide by the terms of their lease" (HUD 1996: 4). Following this reasoning, the preferred tenant is one disposed to scrutinizing social relationships and associations of "covered persons" for the larger, collective good of security and who is willing to gladly police and regulate whoever enters their home. Hence, techniques of regulating self are cast in terms of a larger social welfare of citizens, of their security and protection (Dean 1999: 20).

Strict Liability, No-Fault Evictions Implicate Individuals and Families in the Regulation and Control of "Who Belongs Where"

More critically focused criminologists, law and society scholars, and urban geographers and sociologists have written on the spatial aspects of governmentality within the past decade. Urban geographers and sociologists, for example, have explored the uses of security apparatuses and siege-oriented architecture to isolate and segregate "high-risk, urban" populations. Driven by the rhetoric of fear and crime, municipal governments, as well as private concerns (such as homeowner associations), have instituted zoning laws, "compacts," and an assortment of civil techniques to further spatially segregate the city's population by race/ethnicity and class (Merry 2001; Caldeira 1999; Davis 1990).

The eviction clause is a civil effort to spatially classify "who belongs where"—not at the scale of *neighborhood* but within the much smaller social space of the *home*. In shifting some of the responsibility for community security to the tenant, the geographical threshold between inside/outside and private/public spaces becomes the site of self-governance and regulation. In Court of Appeals decisions on public housing eviction, for example, there is considerable attention paid not only to the social relationship between a tenant and a "covered person" accused of wrongdoing, but also to *where that relationship takes place*. In *Chavez v. Housing Authority*, the El Paso, Texas, housing authority evicted a tenant whose son physically threatened two security guards, despite the tenant's claim that her son neither lived on the premises nor was a guest at the time of the incident. The Authority successfully argued that Chavez had occasionally permitted her son to stay overnight as a guest; hence, he could be classified as "under Chavez's control" when he engaged in criminal activity.

Under the eviction policy, tenants are civilly liable if they permit access to a guest in their home who engages in misconduct while on premises or later elsewhere. In legally implicating tenants in the responsibility and control over "who belongs where," HUD has erased the conventional (even practical) boundaries between a tenant's apartment, the housing complex at large, and beyond.

Strict Liability, No-Fault Evictions Implicate Individuals and Families in the Regulation And Control of Their Social Relationships and Those of Others

The Supreme Court–upheld, no-fault, strict-liability interpretation of the eviction clause obligates tenants to be thoroughly acquainted with those allowed in their homes and to monitor their conduct on and off the premises. Such a tall order may be impracticable for tenants to meet, and compliance requires heightened efforts at regulation and control of interpersonal social relationships, networks, and associations.

Abiding by the stipulations of the lease would appear to affect the character and quality of family relationships. Courts have said as much. In the *Chavez v. Housing Authority* case, in which the Authority evicted a mother for her association with (but not the misconduct of) her son, the plaintiff, Elfida Chavez, sued claiming violation of her First Amendment right to freedom of association and the equal protection and due process clauses of the Fifth and Fourteenth Amendments. The district court held that none of Chavez's constitutional rights were violated since she had permitted her son to occasionally stay over as a guest. The Court ruled that Chavez was not punished for the actions of her son but for failing to "ensure that her guests do not disturb or endanger others in her community," as stipulated in her lease. According to the Court, the "unintended and incidental effect on family relationships does not violate . . . [the] right of association" (*Chavez v. Housing Authority* 1992).

In this case, the "covered person" was a guest who happened to be the tenant's son, and the Court ruled that the parent–child relationship was not a determining factor in the public housing authority's decision to punish the tenant. Yet it is chillingly apparent that compliance with the eviction policy among the majority of residents has a direct bearing on their familial relations—that parents, children, and siblings are compelled, at the very least, to "modify" how they interact and associate with each other.

Regulation and social control are deeply insinuated in the most ordinary of microsocial relations—who visits for dinner or overnight? what is his or her conduct on or off the premises?—and the management of risks and their consequences becomes the responsibility of mothers, fathers, and teenagers. Likewise, otherwise innocuous visits from after-school friends, caregivers, and babysitters are fraught with risk. Here we see social regulation and control deeply insinuated in the most ordinary of behaviors.

A Strict Liability, No-Fault Eviction Policy Manages Risk by Transferring Aspects of Policing to Tenants Themselves

The emphasis upon governance of the conduct of populations (rather than the prevention and punishment of offensive behaviors) implies that government "also aims to affect . . . actions indirectly by influencing the manner in which [individuals] regulate their own and other's behavior" (Hindess 2000: 119). Through the deployment of civil law and penalties, regulation and social control appear "folded" into everyday life in the most commonplace and ordinary means (Hellegers 2000).

The eviction policy fully engages residents in "security" for themselves and their neighbors by "putting teeth" (the threat of eviction) into community-watch programs, touted to preserve law and order as a collective good. HUD field officers, local housing authority directors, and project managers call attention to the positive aspects of such engagement of residents. Active participation in so-called security efforts recognizes and elevates the status of the "responsible, decent" tenant (simultaneously casting suspicion on those who do not participate), enhances community pride and allegiance to place, and promotes a sense of self-reliance and individual stake ("ownership") in the success of community.

As part of governance, ". . . the emphasis on corrective disciplinary techniques is shifted with the rise of . . . techniques of self that seek to 'manage' risk in the 'self-interests' of predefined communities" (Pavlich 1999: 123). The lease provision stiffens the resolve of social regulation of self and others because, under the threat of eviction, tenants are *compelled* to police themselves and others. As a result, the requisite scrutiny of one's kin and friendship associations cultivates an individualist, self-preservationist ethic among tenants. To remain in compliance with the lease provision and avoid eviction, tenants must monitor the individuals who associate with members of their household, at any time or place (manage risk). Likewise, as indicated in some of the eviction proceedings, leaseholders need to be concerned with the surveillance of their household members and guests by other tenants in the project (keeping in mind that hearsay testimony is likely to be admitted as evidence in informal and administrative eviction hearings[4]). Through surveillance and control among residents themselves, the overall strategy of minimizing risk is in play.

As a Civil Provision, the Strict Liability, No-Fault Eviction Policy
Manages Risk More Powerfully Than Criminal Provisions Alone

As previously mentioned, the Anti-Drug Abuse Act of 1988 noted both the failure of law enforcement efforts to control drug-related crime in public housing projects and the willful lack of cooperation among residents with those efforts. The resulting eviction policy addresses both by using civil procedures that are legally less burdensome in comparison to criminal ones. In relying upon landlord–tenant law, the Supreme Court ruled there is no required demonstration of knowledge or participation in criminal activity in order to evict. While civil procedures are beholden to due process requirements, the admission of and weight attributed to certain kinds of evidence differs markedly from conventional policing and criminal law due to the different "rights" at stake.

Since eviction is a civil proceeding, HUD has instituted rules that state that a public housing authority does not have to wait until criminal prosecution is complete in order to evict a tenant, nor is the authority required to reverse an eviction order if there has been an acquittal or the criminal charges have been dropped. The bar for evidence in civil proceedings is much lower than in criminal ones. There is a need to provide preponderance of evidence in order to evict but the nature of that evidence is very different than that in criminal cases. Hearsay testimony or allegations from neighbors, for example, may be entered.

Arguments made in federal trial and appellate cases clearly acknowledge that the eviction policy's civil basis remedies the legal obstacles faced in conventional criminal procedures. In *Burton v. Tampa*, the judges noted that "speculative evidence at best, such as hearsay, gossip, and rumor" hamstring the efforts to show criminal culpability of tenants' knowledge or participation in criminal wrongdoing by covered persons. Such evidence rarely withstands scrutiny in criminal court. As a civil procedure, the eviction clause allows local public housing authorities to "evict an ignorant tenant [and] not only acts as a credible deterrent against criminal activity, it eliminates the need to happen upon the rare occurrence of joint wrongdoing, and diminishes the drug pusher's power of intimidation" (*Burton v. Tampa*, U.S. Court of Appeals, 11th Circuit). In this instance, civil law trumps criminal law as the technique best suited to eliminate "problems" and promote collective conformity.

As Rehnquist notes in the Supreme Court ruling in *HUD v. Rucker*, "strict liability maximizes deterrence and eases enforcement difficulties."

The implication is that criminal remedies to those social problems identified by the government as pressing are unwieldy and ineffective. Civil provisions are appealing, as they offer solutions to the collective security problem that criminal ones could not (Cheh 1998).

Conclusions and Implications

Although the cancellation of this lease and the eviction of Virgie Green is a civil penalty, the effect is just as devastating as a sentence for a criminal act. To do so in the absence of proof of any fault on the part of the defendant violates all of our concepts of fair play, equity, and justice. (Judge J. Ciaccio, dissenting opinion, *Housing Authority v. Green* 1995: 16)

The One Strike and You're Out policy redefines the notion of penalty from that of retribution for a particular act to a broader, social mandate in which specifically targeted groups (and *not* individual potential offenders) are compelled to behave in prescribed ways. The eviction clause threatens a civil sanction against entire households for the alleged criminal activities of individuals. It is, therefore, more than reasonable to consider it as *civil coercion*—"affirmative obligation"—for poor, mostly minority residents to monitor and control their own and others' choices of associations and relationships. The eviction clause, as the legal system finds, is a sanction—but less an effort to prevent certain undesirable activities than one to compel behaviors that the state finds necessary and desirable for the management of social order and stability.

What is asked of public housing residents is not asked of others who benefit from housing subsidies of different sorts. The eviction policy applies to one type of housing subsidy (publicly assisted for limited income persons and families) and not others, such as mortgage assistance programs and the exemption of mortgage loan interest from income taxes. The latter benefit largely nonminority middle and upper classes who are exempt from such scrutiny. As such, the policy targets the most economically disadvantaged persons and families with the smallest number of housing options. The median income of public housing residents is a mere quarter of that of residents in larger, surrounding communities. Of the roughly 1.1 million residents of federally subsidized housing owned by public authorities, 47% are black non-Hispanic and 19% are Hispanic. The highest percentages of public housing residents most affected by the lease clause obligations are women with children and senior citizens, many of whom are part- or full-time caretakers for children and teenagers. Households without children (a good many of which are headed by the elderly) amount to 58% of public housing tenant households (HUD 2000).

From a sociohistorical perspective, this form of civil coercion appears less an anomaly than a continuation of the practice of dismantling social welfare, with its correlates of isolation and marginalization of poor minorities (see Websdale 2001). In addition to longstanding political efforts to curtail social welfare, these same populations have been subjected to global political economic processes, including the loss of manufacturing jobs that are replaced with unstable labor markets; rising social and cultural stigmatization; and the fragmentation of social ties among individuals, families, and communities (Wacquant 2002: 223–28). In addition to these (or, more aptly, as an expression of them) is the recent deterioration of social citizenship among marginalized populations (van Kempen 2002). Theoretically, the right to access and participation in civil society applies to individuals universally, regardless of income. Recent legislation that has modified social welfare policies, however, has created "special categories" among the subsidized poor.

The Quality Housing and Work Responsibility Act of 1998 recasts subsidized housing recipients as privileged, but temporary, beneficiaries of financial support. The Act enshrines the rhetoric of public housing as drug-infested projects overrun with shiftless and lazy tenants addicted to years of lavish handouts from federal coffers. As a remedy, it calls on local public housing authorities to promote new initiatives to reduce the numbers of public housing tenants (through, among other ways, the demolition of existing units and the provision of temporary rent vouchers). The number of persons eligible to receive a housing subsidy is tightened not only along economic lines, but also moral ones (e.g., President George Bush's 2000 bid to promote marriage among low-income individuals as part of welfare reform). Hence, the newly defined and narrowed category of "eligible, worthy tenants" is in increasingly sharp contrast to the many in actual need of affordable housing.

For those deemed eligible to live in public housing, the length of their tenure depends upon adherence to stricter rules and regulations that are legitimated by larger political discourses on welfarism, the worthy poor, and drugs and crime. As I have argued in this chapter, compliance with the One Strike policy requires public housing residents to forego unfettered rights of association and privacy of social relations. Tenants modify their behaviors, scrutinize the most mundane of associations, and monitor the activities of a wide range of persons they come in contact with, familiar and unfamiliar. The HUD rule demands that tenants extend the sphere of personal responsibility far outside their homes, to the public realm. In turn, the cost of being poor, black, and a resident of public housing is a decreasing level of privacy over one's everyday life.

Acknowledgments

The author wishes to thank Judy Scales-Trent, Cindy T. Cooper, and Emilie Broderick for their critical and helpful comments.

References

Anleu, Sharyn L. Roach. 1998. "The Role of Civil Sanctions in Social Control: A Socio-legal Examination." *Crime Prevention Studies,* 9: 21–43.

Buerger, Michael and Lorraine Green Mazerolle. 1998. "Third-Party Policing: A Theoretical Analysis of an Emerging Trend." *Justice Quarterly,* 15, 2: 301–27.

Burchell, Graham. 1993. "Liberal Government and Techniques of Self." *Economy and Society,* 22, 2: 267–82.

Caldeira, Theresa P. 1999. "Fortified Enclaves: The New Urban Segregation." In *Theorizing the City: The New Urban Anthropology Reader,* edited by Setha M. Low. New Brunswick, NJ: Rutgers University Press, 83–110.

Castle, Caroline. 2003. "You Call That a Strike? A Post-*Rucker* Examination of Eviction from Public Housing Due to Drug-Related Criminal Activity of a Third Party." *Georgia Law Review* 37: 1435–69.

Cheh, Mary M. 1998. "Civil Remedies to Control Crime: Legal Issues and Constitutional Challenges." *Crime Prevention Studies,* 8: 45–66.

Davis, Mike. 1990. *City of Quartz: Excavating the Future in Los Angeles.* New York : Verso.

Dean, Mitchell. 1999. *Governmentality: Power and Rule in Modern Society.* Thousand Oaks, CA: Sage.

Ericson, Richard V. and Kevin D. Haggerty. 1997. *Policing the Risk Society.* Toronto: University of Toronto Press.

Foucault, Michel. 1991. "Governmentality." In *The Foucault Effect: Studies in Governmentality,* edited by Graham Burchell, Colin Gordon and Peter Miller. London: Harvester Wheatsheaf: 87–104.

Hellegers, Adam P. 2000. "Reforming HUD's 'One Strike' Public Housing Evictions through Tenant Participation." *Criminal Law and Criminology* 90, 1: 323–62.

Hindess, Barry. 2000. "Divide and Govern." In *Governing Modern Societies,* edited by Richard V. Ericson and Nico Stehr. Toronto: University of Toronto Press: 118–40.

Housing and Urban Development (HUD), The Department of. 1996. "'One Strike and You're Out' Policy in Public Housing." Washington, D.C.: The Department.

Housing and Urban Development (HUD), The Department of. 2000. "New Facts about Households Assisted by HUD's Housing Programs." *Recent Research Results,* October.

Housing and Urban Development (HUD), The Department of. 2001. "Screening and Eviction for Drug Abuse and Other Criminal Activity." *Federal Register,* Volume 66, Number 101, May 24: 28775–806.

Merry, Sally Engle. 2001. "Spatial Governmentality and the New Urban Social Order: Controlling Gender Violence through Law." *American Anthropologist* 103, 1: 16–29.

Mock, Nelson H. 1998. "Punishing the Innocent: No-Fault Eviction of Public Housing Tenants for the Actions of Third Parties." *Texas Law Review,* 7: 1495–1535.

Moye, Jim. 2003. "Can't Stop the Hustle: The Department of Housing and Urban Development's 'One Strike' Eviction Policy Fails to Get Drugs Out of America's Projects." *B.C. Third World Law Journal,* 23: 275–92.

Pavlich, George. 1999. "Preventing Crime: 'Social' versus 'Community' Governance in Aotearoa/New Zealand." In *Governable Places,* edited by Russell Smandych. Aldershot, UK: Ashgate Publishing: 103–32.

Piety, Tamara R. 2003. "The War on the Poor—News from the Front: *Department of Housing and Urban Development v. Rucker.*" *Tulsa Law Review,* 385: 385–403.

Renzetti, Claire. 2001. "One Strike and You're Out: Implications of a Federal Crime Control Policy for Battered Women." *Violence Against Women,* 7, 6: 685–97.

Sanchez, Lisa E. 1997. "Boundaries of Legitimacy: Sex, Violence, Citizenship, and Community in a Local Sexual Economy." *Law & Social Inquiry* 22, 3: 543–80.

Sandy, Kathleen R. 2003. "The Discrimination Inherent in America's Drug War: Hidden Racism Revealed by Examining the Hysteria over Crack." *Alabama Law Review,* 54: 665–93.

Valverde, Mariana, Ron Levi, Clifford Shearing, Mary Condon and Pat O'Malley. 1999. "Democracy in Governance: A Socio-Legal Framework." Report for the Law Commission of Canada on Law and Governance Relationships.

Van Kempen, Eva T. 2002. "Poverty Pockets and Social Exclusion: On the Role of Place in Shaping Social Inequality." In *Of States and Cities: The Partitioning of Urban Space*, edited by Peter Marcuse and Ronald van Kempen. Oxford University Press: 240–57.

Vrettos, Tara M. 2002. "Victimizing the Victim: Evicting Domestic Violence Victims from Public Housing Based on the Zero-Tolerance Policy." *Cardozo Women's Law Journal*, 9: 97–131.

Wacquant, Loic. 2002. "The Rise of Advanced Marginality: Notes on its Nature and Implications." In *Of States and Cities: The Partitioning of Urban Space*, edited by Peter Marcuse and Ronald van Kempen. Oxford University Press: 221–39.

Websdale, Neil. 2001. *Policing the Poor: From Slave Plantation to Public Housing*. Boston: Northeastern University Press.

Laws Cited

1988 Anti-Drug Abuse Act, PL 100–690, 1988 HR 5210.

Cranston-Gonzalez National Affordable Housing Act, PL 101–625, 1990 S 566.

"One Strike and You're Out," 42 USCA SS 1437d(l)6. The earlier "One Strike" was 42 USCA SS 1437d(l)5.

Quality Housing and Work Responsibility Act" is PL 105-276, 1998 HR 4194. Section 578 thereof was codified as 42 U.S.C.A. §13661.

The Public Health And Welfare Chapter 124, 42 U.S.C. §11901. 1988. Title 42.

56 Federal Register 51560. 1991. "Public Housing Lease and Grievance Procedures." HUD.

Cases Cited

Burton v. Tampa Housing Authority, 271 F.3d 1274 (11th Cir.2001).

Chavez v. Housing Authority of City of El Paso, 973 F.2d 1245 (5th Cir.1992).

Department of Housing and Urban Development v. Rucker, 535 U.S. 125 (2002).

Housing Authority of New Orleans v. Green, 657 So.2d 552 (La.App. 4 Cir.1995).

Memphis Housing Authority v. Thompson, No. 02A01-9812-CV-00356, 1999 Tenn. App. LEXIS 506 (Tenn. Ct. App. 1999).

Rucker v. Davis 237 F.3d 1113 (9th Cir. 2001).

Endnotes

1. In 2002, Congress passed the Lee Amendment to protect victims of domestic violence under HUD's "One Strike" policy. Between 1996 and 2002 (predominantly female) tenants were threatened with eviction for domestic violence and similar crimes in which they were the actual victim. See Renzetti 2001 and Vrettos 2002.
2. "Drug-related criminal activities" refer to the illegal manufacture, sale, distribution, use, or possession with intent to manufacture, sell, distribute, or use a controlled substance (42 U.S.C. §11901).
3. Public housing authorities are independent agencies established by local governments to own, develop, and manage public housing and other subsidized low-income housing programs funded and administered largely by the Department of Housing and Urban Development (HUD). There are about 3,200 public housing authorities in the United States and its possessions. Approximately 160 large, urban authorities manage nearly 60% of the entire U.S. public housing stock of 1.25 million units.
4. HUD encourages local public housing authorities to provide legal and other support to tenants who provide testimony in eviction proceedings: ". . . residents are more likely to testify if they understand that the program will benefit them" (HUD 1996: 9).

9

The Everyday World of House Arrest: Collateral Consequences for Families and Others

WILLIAM G. STAPLES

It's not just me doing the house arrest but they [his family] feel *they're* on house arrest . . . and that's unfair to them for what, you know, me being punished, their being punished also, by the phone ringing, by being woke up in the middle of the night, to make sure that I am up and I am on the phone so I don't get in trouble and have the police coming out here to get me.

—Jeff,[1] on living under house arrest

Jeff is a twenty-four-year-old white male who works as a plastics fabricator, one of the twenty-three people I have interviewed living under house arrest in the Kansas City metropolitan area. Jeff has been convicted of driving under the influence (DUI) and a number of misdemeanors, including violating the conditions of his parole. This is his second experience with house arrest. All together, he has spent more than a month being electronically monitored at home, this time following a three-month stint in a residential treatment center. Once on his own, Jeff now lives with his father and grandmother. Being under house arrest means that Jeff needs to respond to random phone calls from a Department of Corrections computer to verify that he is at home when he is scheduled to be. In order to do this, officials have installed a small, computerized unit in the house that is attached to their only phone line. The calls demand that Jeff complete a drill of answering the phone within the first three rings and blowing into an alcohol tester that is built into the machine. While he is doing this, the device takes his picture and compares it to a reference photograph stored on a central computer.

For Jeff, like many of the other house arrest "clients" I spoke with, a sentence to house arrest was characterized, for a variety of reasons, as "better" than the alternative of sitting in the county jail. Yet during our interview, Jeff also expressed frustration and anger at several aspects of his treatment by corrections officials, especially how his sentence to house arrest means that his family is being, in his words, "punished" for something he did. In fact, nearly everyone I spoke with reported that their spouses, lovers, immediate family, roommates, relatives, or others were affected, in various ways, by *their* sentence to house arrest. These secondary effects or "collateral consequences" (Mauer and Chesney-Lind 2002) ranged from the inconvenience of not being able to have alcohol in the house; to increased tension and stress in their relationships; to a nearly shared experience of the punishment, discipline, and control that are part of house arrest. These collateral consequences, I argue, are the result of inserting the law, or what Foucault called the "power to punish" (1979), into the social space of the household. Through an examination of these offender narratives, we can see how the penalty of house arrest is made meaningful within the everyday experiences of these individuals and within the complex web of affiliation they share with others. This approach is consistent with the "law in everyday life" perspective (Sarat 1998; Garth and Sarat 1998; Ewick and Silbey 1988) that considers law a social process and seeks to investigate how it actually operates in routine, everyday ways.

In this chapter I explore two general types of collateral consequences for the intimates, family members, and friends of the people whom I interviewed. The first type centers on what I call the *spillover effect,* or the disruptions to everyday family life that house arrest brings and the accommodations that have to be made in order to adapt to the bureaucratically ordered life of the offender. These disruptions include, among other things, the intrusion of frequent, random phone calls, especially at night, visits by corrections officials, the rearranging of schedules and activities, and the limits placed on the clients' participation in their roles and relationships as parents, partners, friends, and the like. But more than a mere imposition or inconvenience, these effects, changes, and adaptations often produce co-experiences such as stress, tension, and the feeling on the part of these significant others that they themselves are being disciplined and controlled by house arrest. After all, these intimates are often awakened by the same phone calls, they are there when officials visit their home, and their lives are impacted by a rigid confinement schedule set by strangers in a state bureaucracy. The second but related type of collateral consequence is what I call the *backup work* of family and others. Here we can see how significant others, through their actions and behaviors "supporting" those on house arrest, end up functioning as ancillary "watchers" for the program, surveilling the offenders themselves, and prodding them to stay in compliance with program demands (Donzelot 1979).

Doing Time at Home

The original and commonly used method of electronically monitoring someone at home involves deploying a small radio transmitter that is typically attached to the ankle of the offender. A monitoring box is placed in the home or apartment and the arrestee cannot stray more than about 150 feet from the box without triggering a violation that is recorded by a central computer. Sometimes called *tagging*, the idea is credited to a New Mexico district court judge who was supposedly inspired by the use of a similar device in a 1979 Spiderman comic strip (Klein-Saffran 1993). First used on nonviolent felony offenders who were on parole from prison, house arrest began to proliferate in the mid-1990s to include other populations and those at nearly every point in the justice process. Currently, house arrest programs tether more than 70,000 individuals to central monitoring systems in the United States (Harrison and Karberg 2003), and similar programs exist in Canada, United Kingdom, Sweden, the Netherlands, Australia, and New Zealand (Newman 1999).

House arrest with electronic monitoring emerged as one of the community-based "intermediate sanctions" associated with the "new penology" of the 1980s (Feeley and Simon 1992). This ideological and policy shift emphasized a new rationality centered on the sorting and classifying of offenders into finer categories of levels of risk and danger. Intermediate sanctions—including boot camps, intensive supervision, community service, work-release, restitution, day-reporting centers, and day fines—were conceived as incremental punishments (along a continuum with the extreme ends of probation and prison) and therefore better suited to those classified as lower risk and marginally dangerous.

The bulk of academic literature dealing with house arrest has focused on whether or not the treatment is effective at reducing recidivism and/or assessing its relative cost when compared with other sanctions (cf. Maxfield and Baumer 1990; Glaser and Watts 1992; Joplin and Stipak 1992; Lilly, Ball, Curry, and McMullen 1993; Sandhu, Dodder, and Mathur 1993; Jones and Ross 1997; Courtright, Berg, and Mutchnick 1997a, 1997b, 2000; Ulmer 2001). By contrast, I am interested in investigating the broader, social control implications of the use of this kind of technology and how it actually operates and is experienced in everyday ways. I see house arrest as one in a plethora of contemporary disciplinary practices and technologies—technologies that I contend are constituted by and indicative of conditions of postmodernity (Staples 1994, 2000). "Doing time at home," I argue, is a pastiche of old and new: a blending of the institutional confinement of the past and the more futuristic possibility of being monitored in everyday life. It is a virtual world where the values of order, authority, justice, discipline, freedom, consumption, work, and self-help are celebrated, simulated, and presented. Only a few studies (Holman and Quinn 1992; Payne and Gainey 1998, 2000; Maidment 2002) have marginally explored what offenders actually make of the experience of house arrest and only one (Ansay 1999) has studied the experience in-depth and considered the effects of the sanction on families and intimates. Ansay (1999) argues that house arrest programs tend to ignore the relationships and responsibilities of clients as family members and its use creates undo hardship for intimates who end up sharing the experience of the sentence. As Ansay (1999: 115) points out, all house arrestees are subjected to the same set of program rules and restrictions, yet their lived, domestic worlds are varied and complex. This counterpoint—between their official lives and identities as correctional clients and their familial lives and roles as husbands, wives, partners, parents, sons and daughters—must be constantly negotiated in an attempt to satisfy both sets of often competing demands. As the offender narratives presented here reveal, the disciplinary regime of house arrest produces important consequences for those significant others and intimates caught in the collision of these two worlds.

Studying House Arrest

Between August and October of 2001, I conducted face-to-face, open-ended interviews with twenty-three clients in a house arrest program in the metropolitan Kansas City area. While I waited in another room, program personnel asked clients if they were interested in participating in a study about house arrest, which was being conducted by a researcher from the University of Kansas. About one-third declined to participate. If they agreed, I would be introduced to the client and we would move to a private office at the facility. Informed-consent statements were proffered and I addressed any concerns or questions they may have had about the study before we began. Importantly, I assured them that I had nothing to do with the program or the staff and that anything they told me would not be identified with them personally. The interviews took approximately thirty minutes to conduct. I used an interview guide of about a dozen general questions centered on their experiences with house arrest. The interviews were taped and later transcribed. The final sample included twenty-three individuals, fifteen European-Americans (twelve males and three females) and eight African-Americans (one female and seven males). The mean age was thirty-three with a range of eighteen to seventy-four.

The house arrest program I studied had been operating for more than a decade by the time I visited it on a dozen occasions in 2001. It is located in the same building as the county Department of Corrections' 172-bed residential program in an isolated industrial area of the county. House arrest, as practiced by this community corrections department, is a highly structured program involving mandatory employment, educational and treatment programs, frequent drug and alcohol testing, and an offender fee payment that is touted by officials as an alternative to incarceration. Once assigned to house arrest, offenders sign a three-page, seventeen-point contract that outlines all the conditions and behavioral expectations of the program. Clients must develop a daily schedule of approved activities (e.g., work, school, AA meetings, doctors' visits). Weekly face-to-face meetings with their House Arrest Officer are required to review and update client schedules and to verify their compliance through various means (tests for drug or alcohol use, the collection of paycheck stubs, or the signed verification of attendance at required treatment programs). House arrest officers also meet with "collateral contacts" and make unannounced on-site visits to places of employment and residence. In addition, a computerized monitoring device, manufactured by Mitsubishi, is installed in the offender's home. The device functions to verify compliance with the house arrest contract by recording the offender's voice, taking his or her picture, and collecting breath samples for analysis. The house arrest officer determines the number of calls appropriate within a specific block of time and the system randomly calls the offender within those blocks.

When a call is made, a computer simulated human voice tells the person answering the phone that the call is from the house arrest department and a short pause gives the offender time to get to the phone in case someone else has answered. The system then instructs the offender to take his or her own photograph and to submit a breath sample through a straw inserted into the home monitoring unit. The photograph is displayed on a computer screen in the house arrest office next to a reference photo previously entered into the system so that staff can verify the identity of the person answering the call. The black and white photographs have a grainy, fish-eye-lens appearance and, because often taken at night, frequently show clients in a disheveled, sleepy state. The results of the alcohol breath test are recorded in the computer and are displayed on screen with the photo of the offender, which includes name, date, and time. If a violation occurs, the computer immediately places a second call. If the second call results in a violation, an alarm alerts staff at the house arrest office.

As many of the clients told me, there is little leeway for those violating the conditions of their house arrest contract. If a client does not respond to phone calls, there is a two-hour window to either call the house arrest office or show up in person. If offenders do not contact the office within this time frame, they are "violated" by their house arrest officer, meaning that they had broken their house arrest contract. Likewise, failing the in-home breathalyzer or having a "hot UA" (a positive urine analysis) following an office visit will result in an infraction. Program staff frequently call upon local law enforcement to conduct residence checks, to look for clients suspected of being "AWOL," to provide arrest and detention services, to investigate allegations of abuse in the home, or to verify whether an offender has been driving on a suspended license. The program requires offenders to pay a daily monitoring fee and all fees associated with the program, including drug testing. All the clients I spoke with were court-ordered to maintain full-time employment.

In the year 2000, 1,048 adult clients participated in the program, with about 80 to 100 individuals being monitored at any given time but with relatively high turnover; the typical house arrest sentence lasted between 30 and 90 days. Males accounted for 81% of the cases; 19% were females. The majority, 68%, were sentenced directly to the house arrest program. The remaining cohort was placed on house arrest as a condition of a bond (pending a probation violation hearing) either as an internal sanction of the Intensive Supervision Probation program or as part of a conditional release agreement from a residential/work release program. Felony offenders accounted for 34% of those (n = 361), 30% of which were DUI cases, 19% burglary/theft, and 18% drug possession. Of the misdemeanant cases served (n = 687), 50% were DUI, 18% were theft/larceny, and 16% were drug possession charges. Clients were charged $12.00 per day for the house arrest monitoring and $17 per drug test. The program collected more than $211,000 in "fees" from clients in 2000.

"It's That Damn Phone Again"

Nearly all the clients I spoke with reported the random surveillance phone calls from the Department of Corrections computer to be a constant source of irritation and problems for themselves and the people they lived with. The more time I spent with the house arrest clients and staff, the more I became convinced that the purpose of the random, nightly phone calls was not simply to verify that an offender was home or even to remind them that they were being monitored but also to create what Foucault (1979) called "docile bodies," in this case, through sleep deprivation. Many described themselves as physically exhausted and mentally anxious. As one client put it, "it's hell. Sometimes you get three calls at night and you got two, three hours of sleep and then you have to go into work at six-thirty in the morning.

It's going to suck." The few who did not report problems with the calls tended to be those who were on house arrest longer and had either adapted to the routine or, having "proved" themselves as lower risks, were now being subjected to fewer calls at night. Those who did not report problems for other residents of the same house lived alone or worked nights. A smaller number were well off enough to have multiple phone lines or lived in homes large enough to isolate themselves from the rest of the household. Consider the following examples.

Jeff, the young man I quoted at the beginning of this chapter, had a fair amount to say about his experiences on house arrest and the effects on his family. Like nearly all of those I interviewed, Jeff repeatedly stated that house arrest "wasn't that bad" but at the same time it was clear that he was angry and resentful about his and his family's treatment by corrections officials. As he put it, "they're invading your privacy. That's what it feels like." When I asked him for more details he told me that

> it's kinda irritating because there's other people, like my father, he works, so, it's kind of irritating for him to be sleeping at night and then his phone rings and then I have to get it. I don't think they have any consideration if you do stay with somebody else, and there's other people living in that household too, that work too, I don't think there's much consideration about that.

Thirty-three-year-old Rita, an African-American woman with an infant, is living with her mother-in-law and her male companion. Rita works as a housekeeper at a motel but tells me she has no car and is receiving cash assistance to buy food through the government's Women, Infants, and Children (WIC) program. She has been on house arrest for two weeks following a sentence to a residential treatment center for forging a check. Rita was one of the few people I spoke with who found house arrest to be a less than attractive option. In fact, given her difficulties, Rita told me that it would have been easier for her to just do another thirty days in the residential treatment center than to do the same time on house arrest. As she told me, "It's, to me, I, really, I'm making it because of my baby, I just had my baby, but other than that, it's *hard*! It's *hard*!"

As one of the poorest and most dependent people I spoke with, Rita's case tells me that house arrest may only "work" for those with some means. She continued: "It's really *hard*! For one, they call you, like every hour on the hour. . . ." And later, when I asked her whether others in the house were affected by her house arrest, she said

> Yeah, because the one, the phone keep ringin'. . . . And then with that one line thing, you know, they act like, she can't be on her own

phone; that's her problem. Yes, there's only one line. And, if they can't get through they think you got somebody holding the line for you so they ain't get through. But she be, they have to use that phone, I can't stop them from using their own phone. . . . They keep saying, "Why do they keep calling you back-to-back like that?" and stuff like that, they gettin' upset with me; I don't want them gettin' upset with me.

Jesse is a window salesman, white, and in his early thirties who travels a lot for his job and has a pregnant fiancée with two children at home. He has been convicted twice for DUI and has been on house arrest, "a little over 21 days." Jesse described his very hectic life. On the day we spoke, he told me he was going to try to negotiate with his house arrest officer for more hours at work because he fell behind financially. This occurred even though he was working the maximally allowed fifty hours a week:

Staples: Fifty hours a week and you are falling behind?

Jesse: I can only take like a five o'clock or eight o'clock appointment, or two o'clock; I've got kids and daycares, and picking people up from work; I did just have a car break down, uh, last week, so now we got just one car, trying to get somebody to, 'cause I'm on house arrest I can't do that, um. My fiancée is pregnant; she isn't real thrilled when she wakes up at 2:30 from a phone call.

I probed Jesse about the impact of house arrest on his family and if he thought of house arrest as a violation of his family's privacy, and he told me the following

You know, it probably could be but the fact that I messed up, I feel like I deserve it. Now the person that's sleeping right next to me, or my family that's getting, that's getting, hearing the phone call at 3:30 in the morning or 4:30, I'm mean, it's all odd hours. . . . I think it's a little bit of a privacy issue with the people I live with, my fiancée, the kids, um, but they'll tell me move the camera and the breathalyzer thing to another bedroom and sleep in another bedroom if you don't want that to happen.

I also spoke with Reggie, a deliberate-speaking African-American male in his thirties, married with two children. He is a small business owner charged with a rape he vigorously denies committing, who reluctantly agreed to plead guilty to the lesser charge of sexual assault.

Staples: How is house arrest like or not like being in jail?

Reggie: You know you say you have your rights, privacy, now my house arresting officer, they, she, came *to* my home, but she didn't come *into* my home. You see, the things these people have to take into consideration is that's not just *my* home, that's my other half's home, that's my kid's home. So, it's like because you put me under house arrest, that gives you the right to cross the line and disrupt their life, which isn't fair, it's not right.

Later, I asked him more about the effects on his family:

Reggie: Yeah, the phone ringing. . . . At night, she's sleeping. Yeah, well [long pause], a woman is a woman. Hell, I can leave the cap off the toothpaste and that causes tension, I mean. But her understanding what could have happened, as opposed to what is happening, which would you rather deal with, me not being here and you have the kids by yourself, and everything else by yourself? Or what, you rather me be here and just deal with these phone calls?

Ronald was seventy-four years old when I interviewed him and the oldest person I spoke with. A married, white male, he identified himself as a "city official" who was convicted of DUI. It was Ronald's first time on house arrest. On the day I spoke with him he was very relieved to have completed his three-week sentence and to have turned in his monitoring device to the office. When I asked him if being on house arrest had affected his wife of fifty-three years, he said:

I took a lot of guff from [her] 'cause she figured that she wasn't getting some of her phone calls. We're very active in church and other city affairs, of course. [Elaborates]. Oh yeah, it's affected her very definitely. [She] would say, "I hope you get off that damn thing" because, I know she was missing phone calls.

Justin is a white, twenty-year-old, who works on a landscape crew and lives with his parents. The morning I spoke with him his eye was badly injured and bandaged. He was originally assigned to a month of house arrest following a drug conviction but a "hot UA" got him another month. "Do you think your parents are affected by it?" I asked. "Definitely, definitely. I live with my parents and they don't sleep as well anymore, the phone ringing at four in the morning, six in the morning." [And later:] "Oh, of course they're affected by it. If you miss a call at two and three in the morning they're woken up and they got to deal with it." Similarly, Peter, a white eighteen-year-old who lives with his parents and was charged with DUI, identified the phone calls as a problem: "Absolutely, the phone calls. I mean, they call you in the middle of the night and if you have a spouse, or someone you're living with, that's definitely going to affect them because the phone rings and you got to get up and you know . . . yeah they're definitely affected."

Besides the phone interruptions, others I interviewed suggested that their being on house arrest necessitated that the household rearrange schedules and activities and make accommodations for them. For example, Rita told me:

> Rita: You know, sometimes the machine messes up the phones, the phone line, and you don't get no phone call in four hours. You gotta come back all the way out here and sometimes you don't have trans-portation to come out here when they want you to come, my mother-in-law works, you know, and it's hard for her to keep bring-ing me out here when they want me to come out here.

> Staples: So you don't have a car?

> Rita: Not me, no. So she does. And, to me it's hard, I can't, I can't do it. For real. You gotta come on out here see 'em when *they* want, it could be between 10 o'clock at night, two o'clock at night they want you to come all the way out here. You know, just like this morning, they called my house 6:30 this morning, sent the police to my house first, thinking I was gone. I told them I'm still here, it was the machine, for it to start back over you have to blow in it, that machine. The day I left they gave me a broken machine. . . . I got home, it did not work; so I have to come *all* the way out here; I had two hours to get back out here, if I didn't they were going to send the police to my house. [Elaborates] They have to keep bringing me out here, she has to get her, my mother-in-law, has to get her boyfriend to bring me out here, he's old, and, he gets upset, and he takes it out on her, and you know, I ask her, and she asks him.

Frank is a married forty-five-year-old African-American who is self-employed at odd jobs. Convicted of a DUI and only on house arrest a week or so, Frank was upset and agitated during most of our interview about his treatment by the court and the house arrest program. When I asked Frank how his wife was affected by his house arrest, he stated the following.

> I can't take her to work like I normally do because, they can't fix it where I can, like seven o'clock to eight, four to five, I can't take her to work and pick her up, that's making us spend more money! She got to spend at least $45 for parking now. . . . Normally, you know, what I was doing, I take her to work, I go cut grass, work on cars, and then I got back and pick her up at 4:30 and then we back at home. I can't even do that 'cause they said, Judge said I could, and they called the Judge back and said I couldn't.

Ronald, the older "city official," in discussing the effects on his wife, said, "Yeah, because she was free to come and go, and she also had to run the errands that I would have ordinarily [done]."

"The Whole Family Dynamic Thing"

Some of the clients related how being on house arrest restricted their ability to fully participate in or fulfill their roles as parents, partners, extended family members, friends, and the like. Of course, had they been sitting in jail, they could not have performed these roles at all. Yet, precisely because they are in the home but with restrictions on their activities means that others "do family" (Gubrium and Holstein 1990) around them as they sit on the sidelines. Not only is this a particularly difficult thing for the client to do, but it also means that others have to fill the void left by the clients' limited participation. Here are some examples.

Marge is a pleasant thirty-two year-old working-class white female. She is married with five children and works as a waitress, a job secured for her by the program. She was convicted of DUI and a probation violation and has spent nearly two months on house arrest. When I asked Marge if her being on house arrest had affected her family:

> Well, in a sense, yeah; when you're on house arrest you can't very well put down, you want to go to the park, or you know, you want to go out and do the family outing thing; it limits my activity with my family. . . . I have five children; I'm constantly busy, busy, busy, if you've lived your life that way, by a schedule, I mean it just totally turns your life upside down.

Barbara is a white thirty-six-year-old waitress with two children who lives with her mother-in-law. She had a very positive attitude the day I spoke with her. Convicted of a drug offense, she would spend more than three months on house arrest. I asked Barbara if she would describe for me what it was like living under house arrest:

> I have two small children and I don't have the freedom to take them places that they need to go or to go to their school activities and things like that. . . . It affects the whole family dynamic thing. Like, um, last week my son was sick. He had, uh, strep throat. And I had to call and you had to get permission to go to the doctor, and then while you're at the doctor you have to call them all the time, and then whenever you get home, of course, you have to call them. And then I had to find someone to pick up the prescription. . . . But I'm sure that they get tired of sitting at home all the time. You know, Dad will take them once in a while, but you know, dads aren't like moms I suppose much.

Frank, the self-employed African-American, told me that house arrest prevented him from helping his elderly grandmother and that other family members would have to cover for him, as follows.

> I have to go to Higginsville, Missouri. My grandmother is 94, I usually go down there every Sunday and help her. I can't even do that. They won't let me go down and help my grandmother. So you know, that's really hurting the whole family because now somebody else is going to have to try to get down there since I normally go down there every Sunday. And she depends on me to come every Sunday 'cause she knows I'll come every Sunday and now I can't.

Reggie, the African-American small business owner, works nights and takes care of his children during the day. He found that house arrest procedures intruded on his role as a parent. He seemed to resent how house arrest brought his family into contact with the justice system.

> Staples: Describe for me what it is like living under house arrest. How do you feel about it?

> Reggie: I'm fortunate because I have two small kids; I have a family; so being at home, it, actually works to my advantage, because during the day, I watch my kids while she works. So, I'm at home anyway; it's not like this is killing me, uh . . . and at night I work. I mean the only thing, the only thing that bugs me is, I could be taking a shower, I could be in the bathroom, uh, I could be changing one of my kids, I have to hit that phone when it rings. . . . I'm toying with my kids, or changing my kids, the phone rings, I know who it is, I gotta cut them off, run over here, deal with this phone thing. I felt really bad 'cause my son, he saw me blowing into this straw, and he doesn't know, he's only two, but I know. . . . And to see him looking at me and I'm blowing into this damn straw, I'm like, "hey man, don't you *ever*," that's what I tell him, and he doesn't understand, but just the mere fact that my son is watching me blow into this damn straw, it's kinda annoying, it's kinda irritating, it's kinda painful . . . he doesn't deserve to see that, I'm not going to hide it from him. My daughter, phone rings, I have to put her down, she's nine months. And go run to the phone, deal with the phone, be done with it.

Duane is a thirty-six-year-old African-American who works as a night grocer. He has a wife and three children. This is his first time on house arrest. He has been on it two weeks. He regretted not being able to help his family in a time of need: ". . . you can't take care of your main, your main family situations that, you know, may go on. You never know, you may get an emergency in the middle of the night, with your children or family members. Like I got a phone call the other night. My brother was in trouble, he uh, he uh, needed me to bail him out, out of jail. Couldn't leave the house to do that."

Twenty-year-old Jeff told me that house arrest was just something he had to do to get back to his "normal life" which included, ". . . going to my sister's house, and playing with my niece when I want. I miss that." Chuck is a twenty-one-year-old white male who manages a restaurant. Twice convicted of DUI, he had spent the last twenty-five days on house arrest. Asked if any of his friends knew that he was on house arrest, Chuck said: "Yeah, some of my friends know. Sometimes when they come over, you know, they want to bring some alcohol in and, you know, they can't. One night I got really mad cause this girl—I was like, 'get out'—and she brought something in and I said, 'that can't be in here' and then she like, 'I'm not taking it out,' and I'm like, 'well, just get out.' It kinda sucks. It puts me in an awkward position. So some of my friends, I'm like, 'I'm sorry guys,' you know."

"My Stress Level Was Just Out the Roof"

For many of these clients, the "no second chances" stance of the program, backed up by the very real threat of jail time if they "messed up," was a constant source of stress and anxiety (Holman and Quinn 1992). As Jesse put it: "It's nerve wracking though, 'cause every day, basically, they just hold it over your head." When combined with the weekly regimen of appointments, home and work visits, drug testing, and the challenge of successfully answering the random phone calls, it is little wonder that nearly all the clients I spoke with characterized house arrest as a stressful experience. Mark: "It's just really stressful." Barbara: "Ah, this time, this time around it's more stressful than the first time." Jesse: "I don't think of myself as being a high anxiety or stressful person at all, but this last three weeks, I mean I've been just . . . my stress level was just out the roof." Ronald: "I was very anxious . . . the whole time." Duane: "It's kind of, like I said, it's stressful, very stressful." Chris: "Well, uh, it can get stressful at times." Charles: "If you don't know exactly how this thing's going to play out, then that puts a little stress in your life."

Given the level of stress and anxiety reported by many of the clients, it is not difficult to understand how their emotional state would have a significant impact on the people that they lived with. This consequence took several forms. As is evident from some of the material quoted above, the stress experienced by clients caused pressure and strain in their relationships and their dealings with others. In addition, parents, family members, and loved ones reported worrying whether or not their wives or husbands, partners, and sons or daughters would make it home in time to get the call, pass their drug test, and, in the end, complete the program without getting sent to jail. And, as some of the clients informed me, house arrest was emotion laden for parents who lived within the household. Living with their sons or daughters under these controlled conditions, they were reminded of their child's troubles and, possibly, their own shortcomings as parents.

Mark is a well-dressed, very polite, and articulate African-American male in his early twenties who attends a local community college. He was convicted of driving while intoxicated and manslaughter, the result of a car wreck that killed one of his passengers. He served twenty-one days on house arrest following a stay in the residential treatment center. He was living with his parents in a well-to-do suburb. When I asked Mark if he thought his parents were affected by his house arrest, he responded thus.

> My Mom, she's affected because it's still a stress on her, because she worries about me so much, and then she's like, "Oh my god, the phone, the phone, the phone." And I'm like, "The phone probably isn't ringing," and she's saying "The phone" . . . and I mean it's always her protection. It's just how she is. Yeah, it worries her, it will be a stress off her when I get off of it, because it really is a stress, the whole situation has been stressful.

In my conversation with Jesse, the window salesman with the pregnant fiancée and two children, I asked him directly about the possibility of what I began to call the spill-over effect on his family:

> Staples: And you said also that it's affecting your family, your fiancée, in the sense there is a spill-over effect with the phone calls. Do they get kinda caught up in the whole anxiety of it do you think?
>
> Jesse: Uh, she does because so many times I've been pushing that, I need to be home at 1:30 or something, or whatever time it is, and I'm getting in the door at 1:31 and I'm flying to make it work. . . .
>
> Staples: So she knows your schedule, she knows that they are going to call, and she's waiting for you to come in. . . .
>
> Jesse: Right. She has gotten phone calls before, you know, where she sees it on the Caller ID, she can't answer the phone 'cause I'm not there yet cause I maybe get the second one cause I'm 10 or 15 minutes late, and she is just . . . expecting them to come pick me up any day and come put me in jail.

Duane, the thirty-six-year-old African-American who has a wife and three children, responded this way when I asked him about the effect of others in his family.

Yeah, um [pause]. I'm having to stay with my mom at this time . . . she says she's affected by the phone calls and all through the night and uh . . . just worrying about her son, if I'm going to be ok, you know. . . . My wife . . . wife and kids and like I said, they're also worried about me, you know.

Frank, the African-American who is self-employed, responded this way when I asked him, "Are there ways your wife might be affected by it? Is she worried about you getting the calls?"

Sure, she just wants to make sure that I get the calls 'cause, it's like, we both want to get through with this. But she, you know, the phone rings and either it's her sister or something and we're both just sitting there [shows a tensed up expression on his face] you know . . . she just had a blow-a-thing through her heart. Doctor got her off, doctor took her off that same evening I come and got it [the monitoring device].

Paul is a fifty-three-year-old white male who works as a shop floor manager. He had been on house arrest for just one week when we spoke following a stint in jail and a residential treatment center. He lives with his girlfriend, someone he was convicted of battering.

Staples: So, your girlfriend accepts that, uh, do you think there is a difference between accepting it and being affected by it? I mean . . .

Paul: Well, uh, she's made a couple of comments, early in the morning like, "it's that the damn phone again" and I'm like "Sorry honey. Hey, its part of the game, I gotta play it."

Staples: Well, but it's the impact of it, though, on families.

Paul: When you, you take it back home with you, then it's something else, 'cause they've had enough, too. You know, they've been down that road with me. It's time to let them go, too. And that phone ringing every hour. It reminds them this ain't over yet, you know. And, yeah, it comes up, conversations and stuff, you know, when's this gonna stop? It'll stop when they tell me it'll stop.

Derek is twenty-one, is white, and works as a carpet layer. He lives with his father now but previously with his mother. He had been on house arrest three different times for a total of five months. When I asked him if his parents were affected by the house arrest he said the following:

In a way, you know, it's a disappointment. She don't want to see her kids do wrong. It's a thing that all parents go through. They don't want to see their kids in jail, they'd rather see them on house arrest than in jail, but they really don't want to see them on neither. Like to see them stay out of trouble, so, I think for her it was a disappointment more than anything.

"Where Are You and What Are You Doing?"

The second but related type of collateral consequence is how significant others, through their actions and behaviors in "support" of those on house arrest, end up functioning as ancillary "watchers," keeping an eye on the offenders' behaviors and prodding them to stay in compliance with program demands. In this way, intimates are indirectly turned into agents of the state (Donzelot 1979) within their "deprivatized" (Gubrium and Holstein 1990) domestic life worlds. Clients reported that intimates woke them up when surveillance calls came, drove them to work when their licenses were suspended, acted as their emergency or "collateral contact" person, and berated them to "stay on the right track." From the perspective of officials, clients, and even significant others, these actions may be considered a positive contribution because this kind of "support" improves completion rates and helps keep clients out of jail. Yet, even if family members or partners gladly offer assistance, this backup work is still work—emotional, mental, and physical labor. It constitutes, therefore, a collateral consequence imposed on them simply because of their relationship and proximity to the offenders.

Jeff, the twenty-four-year-old plastics fabricator, described his father being woken up in the middle of the night by the phone calls and thus putting the father in the position of having to ". . . make sure that I am up and I am on the phone so I don't get in trouble." And when I suggested that family members might end up watching arrestees, Jeff said: "Right. Feels like you got a babysitter there, not just a machine but you also have your family, too." Barbara, the thirty-six-year-old waitress with two children who lives with her eighty-three-year-old mother-in-law, told me that the elder woman ". . . feels a sense of responsibility to kind of keep an eye on me and that kind of thing. And even though she doesn't have that legal responsibility, that's something that she feels personally."

Barbara went on to describe a situation in which she was having technical problems with the monitoring machine and the house arrest office could not reach her:

> So they called my aunt, who lives like thirty minutes from me, and made her come out to our house at ten o'clock at night. [She is] my emergency contact. So they came out and said, "They are having a problem getting a hold of you. You need to call them as soon as you can."

[And later] "My aunt's very good about it and very supportive because everybody, the alternative is being in jail, so at least I'm home, you know. But it just spills over into everybody in the family.

Julie, a white female in her thirties, who was a painter and now manages a fast-food outlet, likened her support group to a "big circle." She has three children and lives with her mother. Convicted on drug charges, this was her second time on house arrest; the first time was in another jurisdiction.

Staples: Tell me what it is like for you living under house arrest.

Julie: Yes, very nice. Um, I was able to be at home with the kids. [Elaborates] You learn to be accountable for yourself. Make sure other people know. And I think a lot that, letting the other people know, so that it's out there, you're used to letting people know where you're at. So the people that you know, like I have children. The school knows where I'm at all the time. Or say, like, my parents know where I'm at all the time. And my good friends that may help me out with my kids know where I'm at all the time. You know, it's like a big circle. Like in here [the Center] here, you have a little circle. And out there you're on your own circle. So you're . . . the accountability does really carry over a lot.

Staples: Do you mean that all those people know, would normally know where you are? But with house arrest it adds another group that knows what you're doing?

Julie: Like the house arrest people, exactly, 'cause you're like on the accountability thing. You've got to let all these people here know where you're at—the house arrest people. And like this one, everybody's got to know where you're at too, for the first two weeks. And it conditions you to be used to telling your people on the street where you're at.

Staples: Did those people know that you were on house arrest?

Julie: [Elaborates] They are trying to help me put it all behind me and making sure that I stay on the right track. I've got an excellent support group. A lot of people don't have that but I'm very fortunate that I do.

Staples [later]: Are the people in the house affected by you being on house arrest?

Julie: Well, my mom lives at a different house. They had two phones to get hold of me at, at my house. . . . And I also left them, as an emergency number. That has an answering machine on it, my mom's number. Just in case my phone . . . I wasn't able to get to it and, all they have to do is call my mom's house. So they tried both my phones and couldn't get a hold of me, so the number that I had listed was, you know, my emergency contact, my mom at a different house so they called her. She made sure and called me back. But see, and that's good because, like, they'd have, like, somebody else that they could call. That support group that calls me and says, "What are you doing?" People are bugging me in the middle of the night: "You're not being accountable, you're not being responsible." A big old slap in the face saying, "wake-up, hello." And you know, it helps to have people that do that.

Later in our interview, Julie told me about what happened one night when she forgot to bring the phone to bed with her.

I used to sleep with the cordless right here at my ear, so that I would hear it. One night I forgot to bring the phone to bed and it was in the other room and I almost "freaked." They ended up calling my cell phone and then they called my mom, my mom called me just as I was getting the message off of my cell. "Where are you and what are you doing?" I'm like, "I forgot and left the phone in the other room."

Dusty, a drug offender in his late twenties, told me that his brother looks after him: "I think my brother who I'm living with thinks, you know, this is my final draw and he knows when things come down like this I'm pretty responsible so, he feels pretty strong that I'll accomplish it pretty good." Patrick, a white twenty-year-old, was serving sixty days of house arrest. "I was on probation for residential burglary, then I got an MIP [minor in possession]." When I asked about his family members' involvement he said: "Yeah they do. Like, yeah, I look at my Dad and my little brothers, and they look out for me, you know. My Dad, well, he acts like he doesn't care but, like, he's like, 'You better be home or you're screwed.'" Twenty-year-old Justin responded this way when I asked him whether his parents are anxious about making sure he gets the phone and the like: "Very much so. They're almost as controlling as house arrest is to me. At least my mom is; uh, she's always nervous. My family's been very, very supportive. They've been that way throughout my entire life."

Conclusion

The purpose of this chapter has been to explore some of the collateral consequences associated with a sentence of house arrest for twenty-three individuals living within the Kansas City metropolitan area. In doing so, I have attempted to show how this form of punishment was made meaningful in the everyday lives and experiences of the clients interviewed as well those sharing their domestic worlds. From these offender narratives, I have identified two general types of collateral consequences for the intimates, family members, and friends of these house arrest clients. The first is a set of spillover effects. These include the disruptions to everyday family life that a sentence to house arrest brings as well as various forms of co-experiences for those sharing the social space of the household. The second but related type of collateral consequence identified involves the backup work of significant others. We can see how, through their efforts at "supporting" those on house arrest, intimates become caught up in the role of ancillary "watchers" for the program, creating a kind of collusion between the family goal of getting the offender off house arrest and the official goal of ensuring program compliance.

Proponents of intermediate sanctions, like house arrest, have argued that these new forms of punishment cost less than incarceration and provide more supervision than traditional probation. These sanctions, when coupled with rehabilitative strategies, such as substance abuse treatment and education and employment programs, also encourage and strengthen bonds to adult roles and attachments to work and family (Jones 1990; Morris and Tonry 1990; Petersilia and Turner 1990; Renzema 1992; Smith and Akers 1993). Yet it seems that none of the advocates of these sanctions anticipated the collateral consequences that might be associated with a sentence to house arrest. Nor have they taken into account how such consequences might actually *weaken* the bonds of family by disrupting the routines of domestic life and bringing stress and tension into already difficult lives. Only by examining the actual lived experiences of those sentenced to house arrest are we able to appreciate fully the extent of these ancillary effects.

References

Ansay, Sylvia J. 1999. "When Home Is a Prison Cell: The Social Construction of Compliance in House Arrest." Ph.D. diss., University of Florida.

Courtright, Kevin E., Bruce L. Berg, and Robert J. Mutchnick. 1997a. "The Cost Effectiveness of Using House Arrest with Electronic Monitoring for Drunk Drivers." *Federal Probation* 61: 19–22.

Courtright, Kevin E., Bruce L. Berg, and Robert J. Mutchnick. 1997b. "Effects of House Arrest with Electronic Monitoring on DUI Offenders." *Journal of Offender Rehabilitation* 24: 35–51.

Courtright, Kevin E., Bruce L. Berg, and Robert J. Mutchnick. 2000. "Rehabilitation in the New Machine? Exploring Drug and Alcohol Use and Variables Related to Success Among DUI Offenders Under Electronic Monitoring—Some Preliminary Outcomes." *International Journal of Offender Therapy and Comparative Criminology* 44: 293–311.

Donzelot, Jacques. 1997 [1979]. *The Policing of Families*. Translated by Robert Hurley. Baltimore: Johns Hopkins University Press.

Ewick, Patricia and Susan S. Silbey. 1988. *The Common Place of Law: Stories from Everyday Life*. Chicago: University of Chicago Press.

Feeley, Malcolm and Jonathan Simon. 1992. "The New Penology: Notes on the Emerging Strategy of Corrections and it Implications." *Criminology* 30: 449–74.

Foucault, Michel. 1995 [1979]. *Discipline and Punish: The Birth of the Prison.* Translated by Alan Sheridan. New York: Vintage Books.

Garth, Bryant G. and Austin Sarat, Eds. 1998. *How Does Law Matter?* Evanston: Northwestern University Press.

Glaser, Daniel and Ronald Watts. 1992. "Electronic Monitoring of Drug Offenders on Probation." *Judicature* 76: 112–17.

Gubrium, Jaber F. and James A. Holstein. 1990. *What is Family?* Mountain View CA: Mayfield Publishing Company.

Harrison, Paige M. and Jennifer C. Karberg. 2003. "Prison and Jail Inmates at Midyear 2002." *Bureau of Justice Statistics Bulletin,* U.S. Department of Justice Office of Justice Programs (April).

Holman, John E. and James F. Quinn. 1992. "Dysphoria and Electronically Monitored Home Confinement." *Deviant Behavior* 13: 21–32.

Jones, Peter. 1990. "Community Corrections in Kansas: Extending Community-Based Corrections or Widening the Net?" *Journal of Research in Crime and Delinquency* 27: 79–101.

Jones, Mark and Darrell Ross. 1997. "Electronic House Arrest and Boot Camp In North Carolina: Comparing Recidivism." *Criminal Justice Policy Review* 8: 383–403.

Joplin, Annette and Brian Stipak. (1992) "Drug Treatment and Electronically Monitored Home Confinement: An Evaluation of a Community-Based Sentencing Option." *Crime and Delinquency* 39: 158–70.

Klein-Saffran, Jody 1993. "Electronic Monitoring versus Halfway Houses: A Study of Federal Offenders." Ph.D. diss., University of Maryland.

Lilly, J. Robert, Richard A. Ball, David G. Curry, and John McMullen. 1993. "Electronic Monitoring of the Drunk Driver: A Seven-Year Study of the Home Confinement Alternative." *Crime and Delinquency* 39: 462–84.

Maidment, MaDonna R. 2002. "Toward a 'Woman-Centered' Approach to Community-Based Corrections: A Gendered Analysis of Electronic Monitoring (EM) in Eastern Canada." *Women & Criminal Justice* 13: 47–68.

Mauer, Marc and Meda Chesney-Lind 2002. *Invisible Punishment: The Collateral Consequences of Mass Imprisonment.* New York: New Press.

Maxfield, Michael G. and Terry L. Baumer. 1990. "Home Detention With Electronic Monitoring: Comparing Pretrial and Postconviction Programs." *Crime and Delinquency* 36: 521–36.

Morris Norval and Michael Tonry. 1990. *Between Prison and Probation: Intermediate Punishments in a Rational Sentencing System.* New York: Oxford University Press.

Newman, Graeme. 1999. *The Global Report on Crime and Justice.* Oxford, UK: Oxford University Press.

Payne, Brian K. and Randy R. Gainey. 1998. "A Qualitative Assessment of the Pains Experienced on Electronic Monitoring." *International Journal of Offender Therapy and Comparative Criminology* 42: 149–63.

Payne, Brian K. and Randy R. Gainey. 2000. "Understanding the Experience of House Arrest with Electronic Monitoring: An Analysis of Quantitative and Qualitative Data." *International Journal of Offender Therapy and Comparative Criminology* 44: 84–96.

Petersilia, Joan M. and Susan Turner. 1990. "Comparing Intensive and Regular Supervision for High-Risk Probationer: Early Results from an Experiment in California." *Crime and Delinquency* 36: 87–111.

Renzema, Marc. 1992. "Home Confinement Programs: Development, Implementation, and Impact." In *Smart Sentencing: The Emergence of Intermediate Sanctions,* edited by James M. Byrne, Arthur J. Lurigio, and Joan Petersilia. Newbury Park: Sage Publications: 41–53.

Sandhu, Harjit S., Richard A. Dodder, and Minu Mathur. 1993. "House Arrest: Success and Failure Rates in Residential and Nonresidential Community-Based Programs." *Journal of Offender Rehabilitation* 19: 131–44.

Sarat, Austin. 1998. *Crossing Boundaries: Traditions and Transformations in Law and Society Research.* Evanston, IL: Northwestern University Press.

Smith, Linda and Ronald Akers. 1993. "A Comparison of Recidivism in Florida's Community Control and Prisons: A Five-year Survival Analysis." *Journal of Research in Crime and Delinquency* 30: 267–92.

Staples, William G. 1994. "Small Acts of Cunning: Disciplinary Practices in Contemporary Life." *Sociological Quarterly* 35: 645–64.

Staples, William G. 2000. *Everyday Surveillance: Vigilance and Visibility in Postmodern Life.* Lanham, MD: Rowman & Littlefield Publishers.

Ulmer, Jeffery T. 2001. "Intermediate Sanctions: A Comparative Analysis of the Probability and Severity of Recidivism." *Sociological Inquiry* 71: 164–93.

Endnotes

1. The names used here are fictitious. The research protocol was conducted within the ethical and procedural guidelines set out by the Human Subjects Committee of the University of Kansas, the American Correctional Association, and the American Sociological Association.

10

Immigration Law as Social Control: How Many People Without Rights Does It Take to Make You Feel Secure?

DANIEL KANSTROOM

Introduction

Deportation for criminal conduct is generally described as a "collateral sanction." Technically, this means that deportation is not regarded as a punishment within the criminal justice system. Therefore, those who are subject to it do not have the rights of criminal defendants. They are not "punished" by deportation, but are simply undergoing a civil or regulatory process within the immigration law system of the United States. To deportees and their families, of course, this distinction is no more persuasive than the phrase "collateral damage" is to Iraqi civilians who are killed or maimed by U.S. bombs. The harm is the same, however it is named. Moreover, the deficiency of the term *collateral*, when applied to deportation, is not only that it depreciates the harm. It also misleads us as to the nature of the system.

According to *The American Heritage Dictionary of the English Language* (Fourth edition, 2000), the adjective, "collateral" has four primary, potentially relevant meanings:

1. Situated or running side by side; parallel.
2. Coinciding in tendency or effect; concomitant or accompanying.
3. Serving to support or corroborate: collateral evidence.
4. Of a secondary nature; subordinate: collateral target damage from a bombing run.

This chapter questions the understanding of deportation as a "collateral" sanction under any of these definitions. Its thesis is that deportation, far from being a concomitant, regulatory aspect of immigration law, also serves as an efficient, powerful, and large-scale system of social control, primarily of poor people of color. Its post-9/11 use against certain people (Muslims, "Middle-eastern" men, etc.) is the most recent manifestation of a well-established U.S. pattern. Moreover, many of the specific legal measures used against noncitizens in the current regime, such as detention without bond, zero tolerance for minor infractions, and lack of judicial review, derive from laws and practices originally aimed at nonpolitical "criminal aliens." The deportation system thus links the "War on Crime" to the War on Terror and illustrates how a harsh mechanism of social control based on fear—domestic or international—tends to grow, to generalize, and to affect hundreds if not thousands of innocent people. All of this occurs with virtually no effective restraint from the constitutional legal system.

The Realm of the Rightless in the "Nation of Immigrants"

Nobody knows for sure how many foreign-born people actually live in the "nation of immigrants," but it is a very large number. As importantly, they live in many respects without the rights that U.S. citizens routinely accept as constitutional heritage. They are subject to harsh, punitive sanctions that are deemed by law to be "noncriminal." They may be deported by the operation of retroactive laws. They may be incarcerated upon mere accusation, with no right to bail—potentially for many months or years—while their cases wend their way through an underfunded, Kafkaesque system. They may be permanently separated from home and family by agency orders without judicial review. And so on. The U.S. government has used this system as a central part of its post-9/11 program to increase so-called national security. When we consider how many people, especially people of color, have been affected by this strategy and how little seems to have been accomplished in terms of real security, we might well question the vision of our nation-state and the security implicit within it.

The realm of the potentially rightless is bigger than you might suspect.[1] The (now-defunct) U.S. Immigration and Naturalization Service[2] (INS) calculated that more than 11 million persons immigrated legally to the United States from 1991 through 2002, as lawful permanent residents (Fiscal Year 2002 Yearbook of Immigration Statistics). Many millions more entered legally as temporary nonimmigrants. Most of these people have left as required by law; but many haven't. Also, uncounted millions have entered without inspection. Thus, by the best estimates, between 7 and 10 million people now live in the United States without legal status. The INS estimated the number of undocumented persons in this country at 7 million in 2000.[3]

The foreign born, some of who are naturalized citizens, make up a significant percentage of the total U.S. population. Calculations by the U.S. Census Bureau in March 2002 indicated that a total U.S. population of some 282 million people, including more than 32.5 million who were foreign born.[4] More than 20 million foreign-born people were counted as noncitizens, but this number is probably low due to undercounting of the undocumented population.[5]

To understand immigration law as a social control mechanism, we must highlight the fact that the contemporary foreign-born population of the United States is mostly non-European, and mostly people of color. The largest number of foreign-born persons in the United States—52.2%—was born in Latin America, with 25.5% born in Asia, and 14% from Europe.[6] The foreign-born population is also, on the whole, much younger and much more urban than the native-born.[7] More than 80% of the foreign born are between 18 and 64 years of age. Among the native population, the number is 59.9%. Some 45% of the foreign born are in the 25- to 44-year-old bracket, compared with 23% of natives.[8]

The vast majority of foreign-born residents in the United States are relative newcomers. Some three-quarters of the noncitizens in this country have arrived in the last quarter-century; and nearly half, 48%, have entered the United States since 1990. Many have become U.S. citizens, but this tendency seems to have slowed significantly in the 1990s. Naturalization records show that 45% of those who entered in the 1980s had naturalized by 2002, whereas only 12.7% of those who entered in 1990 or later had done so.[9] Proponents of "family values" may also be interested to learn that family households with a foreign-born member were twice as likely to contain five or more people than is the case with native households.[10]

Place of birth and citizenship status are strongly related to poverty in the United States. In 2001, 16.1% of the foreign born lived below the poverty level, compared with 11.1% of natives. Naturalization makes a huge difference in the prospects of the foreign born, however. Those foreign-born persons who remained noncitizens were twice as likely to be poor as those who naturalized.[11]

These data are striking in that they demonstrate the existence of a large, discrete population, which, when compared with the majority, native-born population, is young, mostly people of color, newly arrived, and relatively poor. The data may be even more striking when one considers two other things: First, the so-called population universe analyzed by the Census Bureau excludes the institutionalized population, including most significantly those in correctional institutions. Second, the intimate connections between the foreign born and native born are much deeper and more common than one might think. A generally accepted conservative estimate is that more than one in five residents of the United States are either foreign-born or native-born children of immigrant parents. The Urban Institute determined in 1999 that 9% of all U.S. families were of "mixed status," meaning that they contained at least one noncitizen parent and one citizen child.[12] The percentage was estimated at 27% in California. As Donald Kerwin has noted, "measures designed to impact the undocumented can and do have an impact on (lawful permanent residents) and U.S. citizens, and those individuals are often children" (Kerwin, 1999 at 1215) Thus, many more than 32.5 million persons in the United States are personally affected by the conditions of the foreign-born population.

But it is the foreign-born who bear the brunt of immigration law. All noncitizens are subject to the immigration laws of the United States.[13] What does it mean to be "subject to immigration law" in the current environment? Ask Edna Borges.[14] Ms. Borges, 23 years old, has lived in the United States for more than two decades; she arrived here as a toddler. Her entire family lives in the United States, including its most recent addition, her baby daughter, Juliana, born in late July 2003. As a teenager, Edna unfortunately had gotten into some trouble and was arrested for shoplifting and possession of pepper spray. As these are among the most minor offenses in the criminal justice system, Edna pled guilty and was, in effect, placed on probation. But someone, probably a state probation officer, notified the immigration authorities and Edna was ordered to check in with them on a regular basis—every three months. This was an intimidating and inconvenient experience for her, but she did it without major incident until her August 2003 appointment.

Eight days after baby Juliana was born, and while she was still being breast-fed, Edna showed up at the Boston Office of the Bureau of Immigration and Customs Enforcement (part of the Department of Homeland Security and known by the chilly acronym ICE) for her routine appointment. Without warning, she was immediately arrested and sent to a jail in Dartmouth, Massachusetts, as an immigration detainee. She was not permitted contact with Juliana, who, she was informed, was refusing to drink formula. She was told that her next scheduled hearing date before an immigration judge was more than *one year* in the future—October, 2004—and that, as a "criminal alien" she not only would not be released but had no right to bail at all. As a flurry of publicity began to surround her case, and as lawyers, including me, rallied to her cause, a spokeswoman for the Department of Homeland Security offered a sad refrain: "We have no discretion once someone is convicted. It's that conviction that does it. . . ."[15]

Immigration law may be most generally described as a national regulatory system designed to manage the conditions of entry and residence of people defined as noncitizens. Recent events in the United States have demonstrated the inadequacy of this abstract and formal definition, however. We need a more functional one to account for what is really happening to many thousands of people.

Most broadly conceived, immigration law aims to control much of the demographic composition of the nation-state. This may be accomplished in two ways. First, by the border-control function, which seeks to prevent certain types of entries and to categorize, to count, and otherwise regulate permitted entrants. Second, immigration law controls the status of noncitizens and their possible transition to citizenship through naturalization. These are clearly matters of major importance, for obvious practical reasons, as well as for more abstract reasons, which remain particularly meaningful in a nation-state whose defining mythology is that of a nation of immigrants. Since 9/11, 2001, however, it has become abundantly clear that immigration law, especially in its internal enforcement guise, may also serve a very different function—that of social control of minorities, dissidents, and others deemed suspicious or dangerous. Stripped of its formalities, deportation law—the main prosecutorial element of immigration enforcement—is a tool with which government power is brought to bear against the most discrete and marginalized segment of society. With ever-increasing fury, and ever-decreasing potential for mercy, the enforcers of deportation law have aimed its power at noncitizens who have allegedly violated its ever more technical rules. In some cases, people have been accused of violating *both* criminal law and immigration law, a situation that renders them doubly marginalized and subject to two separate systems of punishment.[16] But in many other cases, they are accused of mind-numbingly technical violations that seem only to inspire government action because of the noncitizens' national origin, religious beliefs, or political opinions.

The magnitude of this system should not be underestimated. According to the Immigration and Naturalization Service, from 1991 through 2000, the total number of people compelled to leave the United States, either through formal removal processes or immigration law plea-bargaining, known as *voluntary departure,* has been nearly 23 million.[17] In 2001 and 2002 alone, the total number of formal removals of persons from the United States was over 326,000, whereas those who left pursuant to a grant of "voluntary departure" exceeded 2 million.[18] Thus, in the most recent two-year period for which statistics are available, the total number of so-called deportable aliens located by INS was 2,449,765.[19] One can only guess at the number of family members, both citizens and noncitizens, affected by these legal proceedings. But it clearly runs into many millions. The reasons that people have been ordered out of the United States are also telling. Among those caught within the interior—a category that necessarily includes many lawful permanent residents—by far the two most common grounds are illegal presence (i.e., present without authorization) and criminal grounds. The latter category has, since 1996, approximated 40,000 persons per year.[20] For these people, the linkage between the criminal justice system and the immigration control system is efficient and complete, with one important distinction: noncitizens in the criminal justice system retain the same constitutional rights as U.S. citizen defendants when they are criminally prosecuted. Immigration law, however, is a regime of vastly reduced rights, and in some situations, *devoid of* rights. Thus, when a person faces deportation, she will have no right to counsel if she is indigent, no jury trial, no ex post facto clause protection, no selective prosecution defenses, no exclusionary rule, and, in many cases, no bail and virtually no judicial review.

Post-9/11 Use of Immigration Law as Social Control

The government, of course, understands the civil/criminal distinction well and relies heavily on it. Immigration law enforcement was thus an immediate and central part of the government response to the 9/11 attacks.[21] Attorney General John Aschcroft, speaking to the U.S. Conference of Mayors in October 2001, stated his approach bluntly:

> Forty years ago, another Attorney General was confronted with a different enemy within our borders . . . when organized crime was threatening the very foundations of the republic. . . . Robert Kennedy's Justice Department, it is said, would arrest mobsters for "spitting on the sidewalk". . . . It has been and will be the policy of this Department of Justice to use the same aggressive arrest and detention tactics in the war on terror. Let the terrorists among us be warned: If you overstay your visa—even by one day—we will arrest you. If you violate a local law, you will be put in jail and kept in custody as long as possible. (OIG 2003: 12)

The Attorney General was as good as his word. But far more people than "the terrorists among us" have been affected. Indeed, the harsh use of immigration law as a tool of social control has recently meant the interrogation, arrest, incarceration, and deportation for thousands of people. Consider the widely reported case of Tarek Mohamed Fayad, an Egyptian dentist who came to the United States in 1998 to study (Senate Judiciary Committee Testimony 2001). On September 13, 2001, he was arrested after stopping at a gas station near his home in California. Four agents reportedly ordered him to lie on the ground. The INS "thinks you're illegal," they said. The officers searched his home, seized his passport and other papers, and then arrested him on the charge that he had violated his student visa status. Mr. Fayad was held in a Los Angeles jail. Four days after his arrest, when friends tried to post bond, they were told Mr. Fayad's bond had been "rescinded." One of his friends was himself detained and questioned for eight hours.

Soon thereafter, Mr. Fayad was interrogated by FBI agents and then transferred to Brooklyn, New York's, high-security Metropolitan Detention Center. Guards taunted him by calling him a terrorist. At night, he was awakened every half hour. He was held in the Special Housing Unit, where he was in a cell 23 hours a day. He had no access to newspapers, television, or radio. It wasn't until the end of October that he was allowed to go outside—at 7 A.M—for an hour. Neither his friends, family, attorney, nor the Egyptian Embassy could locate him until November.

Mr. Fayad's story may be shocking but it is certainly not unique. Immigration enforcement efforts have increased dramatically, with detention for the most minor violations (OIG 2003: 13) and zero tolerance as the order of the day for noncitizens. Thousands have been held in detention, many for technical violations that have often seemed to be pretextual. Some 762 persons, about whom there were at least some specific suspicions, were held by the INS in a scattered network of federal, local, and private detention facilities throughout the country. Their detention was a direct result of the so-called PENTTBOM investigation, led by the FBI (OIG 2003: 1–2). It is now clear that aggressive, wide-ranging government action swept many innocent people into the enforcement net. Noncitizens encountered at the scene of the arrest of a person "of interest to the 9/11 investigation" were detained "because the FBI wanted to be certain that no terrorist was inadvertently set free (OIG 2003: 16)." Indeed, even if the FBI could not determine whether it had an interest in a particular immigration detainee, the person was treated as "of interest (OIG 2003: 46)." The largest number of "interest" detainees came from Pakistan, Egypt, Turkey, Jordan, and Yemen. But more than 20 countries' nationals were ultimately included (OIG 2003: 21). Detainees were subjected to a "hold until cleared by the FBI" policy, which resulted in the *average* length of time from arrest to clearance of 80 days, with considerable numbers of people being held for more than six months (OIG 2003: 46). A government report describes one such case:

A Muslim man in his 40s . . . was arrested after an acquaintance wrote a letter to law enforcement officers stating that the man had made anti-American statements . . . [that were] very general and did not involve threats of violence or suggest any direct connection to terrorism. Nonetheless the lead was assigned to a special agent . . . and resulted in the man's arrest for overstaying his visa . . . he automatically was placed in the FBI New York's "special interest" category (OIG 2003: 64).

This man, according to the government report, was cleared of any terrorist links. He nevertheless languished in detention for more than four months before being deported (OIG 2003: 64).

While in such detention, a significant number of detainees were subjected to what a government report describes as "a pattern of physical and verbal abuse . . . by some correctional officers" as well as extremely restrictive conditions of confinement (OIG 2003: 142). A 2003 report by the Office of the Inspector General has cited dozens of recent cases in which department employees were accused of serious civil rights and civil liberties violations involving enforcement the USA Patriot Act (Report to Congress 2003). The report said that in the six-month period that ended on June 15, 2003, the inspector general's office had received 34 "credible" complaints of civil rights and civil liberties violations by government employees, including allegations that Muslim and Arab immigrants in federal detention centers had been beaten (Shenon 2003). "Credible" accusations had been made against agents of the FBI, the Drug Enforcement Administration (D.E.A.), and the Immigration and Naturalization Service. The inspector general's report said that, from December 16 through June 15, 1,073 complaints had been received, "suggesting a Patriot Act–related" abuse of civil rights or civil liberties. Although hundreds of the accusations were dismissed as "not credible or impossible to prove," 272 were determined to fall within the inspector general's jurisdiction, with 34 raising "credible Patriot Act violations on their face." In the 34 cases ultimately deemed credible, the accusations "ranged in seriousness from alleged beatings of immigration detainees to B.O.P. correctional officers allegedly verbally abusing inmates."

Why Was the Deportation Power So Easy to Use After 9/11?

Why did the Bush administration choose to use detention and deportation in this way? The answer is obvious: it was relatively easy (compared with using the criminal justice system), apparently efficient,[22] and without obvious immediate major political risk. These aspects of U.S. immigration law are among the most effective available enforcement tools in the government's arsenal. The harder questions are, *why* was the strategy so easy? Why did it seem so natural? What does it tell us about the United States?

To answer these questions fully, one must understand the nature and the history of U.S. government power over noncitizens, especially its power to detain and to deport.

It must be emphasized at the outset that the use of this power does *not* clearly indicate an anti-immigrant agenda per se. The Administration, to its credit, has taken pains to assert that the War on Terror should not be a "War on Immigrants." Indeed, even as Administration officials and elected representatives have sought ever-greater enforcement authority over noncitizens, they have, virtually without exception, also quite strongly rhetorically reaffirmed the "nation of immigrants" ideal.[23] But there can be little doubt that the United States has come to what I describe to my students as a Willie Loman moment (as in Arthur Miller's play *Death of a Salesman*): one in which *attention must be paid.*

Most attention should be paid to deportation and the concomitant powers to arrest and incarcerate. Deportation is the Sword of Damocles for noncitizens, and, for the most part, it is the power to deport that justifies the related powers to arrest and imprison. There are dozens of reasons why a noncitizen, whether undocumented or a long-term, lawful permanent resident, can be deported (see 8 U.S.C. §1227(a)). They range from the most obvious and largely noncontroversial—such as terrorism—to the mind-numbingly technical. This range, which is the result of years of accretion through very different historical periods, gives prosecutors great flexibility and enormous power.[24] Thus, as I often must warn my clients and my students, almost any noncitizen can be deported at almost any time if an immigration agent wants to look closely enough at his or her case. If these laws are not being used as a War on Immigrants as such, then how are they being used?

From a functional perspective, we can see three distinct uses.[25] First, extant law was used by a variety of law enforcement agencies to facilitate the surveillance, interrogation, arrest, and detention of certain noncitizens. This should have come as no surprise. Deportation law is an irresistible prosecutorial device. Anyone even remotely familiar with the immigration/deportation law system knew that arrests of noncitizens deemed suspicious or potentially dangerous could be based on an array of potential grounds of removal ranging from highly technical status violations (see, e.g., 8 U.S.C. §1227(a)(1)(C)(i); nonimmigrant status violators) to failures to report changes of address within ten days (see 8 U.S.C. §1227 (3)(A)) to:

> any alien who has engaged, is engaged, or at any time after admission engages in any terrorist activity . . . (see 8 U.S.C. §1227 (4)(B)). Or even any alien who has engaged, is engaged, or at any time after

admission engages in . . . any activity a purpose of which is the opposition to, or the control or overthrow of, the Government of the United States by force, violence, or other unlawful means. (see 8 U.S.C. §1227 (4)(A)).

Indeed, long before 9/11, 2001, a noncitizen might have been deported from the United States as "[a]n alien whose presence or activities in the United States the Secretary of State has *reasonable ground to believe* would have *potentially* serious adverse foreign policy consequences for the United States.[26]

As noted above, pre-hearing detention[27] and judicial review give the government much more leeway than when it arrests and detains citizens (see, generally, Kanstroom 2000). It was therefore no great surprise in late 2001 that unusually forceful steps were quickly taken within the broad parameters of existing immigration law.[28] The extent, however, stunned many observers. Beginning in the immediate aftermath of the attacks, the detention of hundreds of noncitizens such as Mr. Fayad proceeded amid nearly complete secrecy,[29] as many detainees were held on minor immigration charges without meaningful access to counsel. Removal hearings, historically open to the public, were permitted to be closed.[30] In mid-November 2001, the Administration publicly confirmed that neither the location nor the identities of post–9/11 detainees would be disclosed.[31]

Throughout 2002, the INS, before being dissolved and having its functions placed within the Department of Homeland Security,[32] enforced technical aspects of immigration law with highly focused zeal. Enforcement of long-ignored address-reporting requirements was undertaken with unprecedented vigor, especially against certain targeted groups.[33] The Absconder Apprehension Initiative sought to locate 314,000 "absconders" from immigration proceedings, prioritizing young men of particular national origin.[34]

The Administration also deployed new techniques of streamlined immigration law enforcement. Thus, on November 9, 2001, the Attorney General established a program of ostensibly voluntary interviews of some 5,000 men who had entered the United States since January 2000 from countries where Al Qaeda was said to have a "terrorist presence or activity." Also, on June 13, 2002, the INS published a proposed rule in the *Federal Register* entitled, "Registration and Monitoring of Certain Non-immigrants" (67 *Fed. Reg.* 40, 581). In its summary, the INS stated that

> recent terrorist incidents have underscored the need to broaden the special registration requirements for nonimmigrant aliens from certain designated countries, and other nonimmigrant aliens whose presence in the United States requires closer monitoring, to require

that they provide specific information at regular intervals to ensure their compliance with the terms of their visas and admission, and to ensure that they depart the United States at the end of their authorized stay. . . .

The proposed rule sought to require certain nonimmigrants to make specific reports to the Immigration and Naturalization Service: upon arrival; approximately 30 days after arrival; every twelve months after arrival; upon certain events, such as a change of address, employment, or school; and at the time of departure from the United States.[35]

Affected people are photographed and fingerprinted, and also must submit to an interview, reportedly about a variety of questions including opinions and associations. Indeed, one Special Registration Worksheet reportedly prepared by INS for student visa–holders begins with two pages of innocuous questions, such as, what is your family (last) name? what is your place of birth? It then moves to more specific inquiries, including, "What courses are you enrolled in? What are the names of the class instructors? Are you currently enrolled in a full course of study?"[36] But, at the very end, come two questions that tell a great deal about what is really being aimed at:

1. What campus/social/religious/political groups are you a member of or associated with?

And the stunningly vague

2. Are you associated with anyone who is *potentially* dangerous to the United States? [emphasis added]

Failure to comply with the rule, or the discovery of immigration violations while registering, can result in arrest, detention, and/or deportation. The program focused on men from 20 countries, most of which are in the Middle East and have predominantly Muslim populations. The registration process, divided into three distinct waves, ultimately affected tens of thousands of nonimmigrants within the United States.[37]

These interviews included questions about immigration status, which, in many cases, have led to removal proceedings.[38] According to news reports, hundreds of people were arrested or detained for suspected visa violations by the INS when they attempted to comply with the rule by registering during the first round. As a result, the second and third deadlines have drawn much greater attention from the media and human rights observers. It has been reported that some 13,000 of the Arab and Muslim men who voluntarily came forward to register with immigration authorities—some

16% of the total—now face deportation proceedings, though almost none of them has been linked to terrorism (Cardwell 2003).

In addition to the effective use of the existing system, some statutory changes were also deemed necessary. The so-called USA Patriot Act,[39] proposed in its first form by Attorney General Ashcroft shortly after the attacks, was signed by President Bush on October 26, 2001. Among its many controversial provisions, the Patriot Act authorizes the Attorney General to incarcerate and detain noncitizens on the basis of suspicion alone. Title IV permits the detention of a noncitizen if the government has "reasonable grounds to believe" that the individual may be a threat to national security.[40] Such a person may be held for seven days pending the commencement of criminal or removal proceedings.[41] The Patriot Act also bars noncitizens from reentry into the United States for certain types of speech and associational activities that, if engaged in by citizens, would likely be deemed protected by the First Amendment.[42]

A variety of other law enforcement measures, such as material witness warrants, military tribunals, and specialized criminal law enforcement also targeted noncitizens. On November 13, 2001, for example, President Bush issued an executive order authorizing the creation of military tribunals to try those alleged to be involved in international terrorism. The order, unlike the similar order issued by President Roosevelt during the Second World War, was expressly limited to certain noncitizens.[43]

What does all of this tell us about the United States? Supporters of the various enforcement measures aimed at noncitizens invariably focus on the serious threat facing the United States. They argue that the citizen/noncitizen line is a perfectly rational basis for enforcement focus because the 9/11 attacks were perpetrated by noncitizens. Indeed, some supporters of the Administration's policies argue that it is both rational and fair to specifically target young Arab or Muslim males for the same reasons.[44] However, as noted above, Administration statements in support of vigorous action against certain noncitizens also affirm that the United States is a nation of immigrants and that newcomers will always be welcomed here. In the same sense in which it was once said that the constitution "is not a suicide pact,"[45] many now argue that the nation of immigrants requires strict controls on noncitizens if it is to continue to thrive.[46] The notion of liberty by security, articulated most famously in the past by Edmund Burke, seems especially appropriate to some in the immigration law context.[47]

Opponents of current policies initially raised pragmatic objections to the Administration's strategy—particularly that it was likely to alienate important constituencies whose support is needed to avoid future terrorist attacks.[48] But something much more fundamental is at stake in this debate. Thus, many commentators have argued that the harsh use of detention and deportation of noncitizens contradicts the United States's self-definition as a "nation of immigrants" insofar as that self-definition requires constitutional protections for noncitizens' rights to basic individual liberties, due process, and equal protection of law (see, e.g., Cole 2002). Put another way, many believe that we cannot legitimately style ourselves as a nation of immigrants consistent with our other proud constitutional traditions if we maintain a marginalized, potentially rightless population of noncitizens.

This argument has deep roots. As a dissenting Supreme Court justice in a foundational U.S. deportation case wrote of the deportation of Chinese workers more than a century ago:

> But even if that [deportation] power were exercised by every government of Europe, it would have no bearing in these cases. . . . Spain expelled the Moors; England, in the reign of Edward I, banished 15,000 Jews; and Louis IX, in 1685 . . . drove out the Huguenots . . . ; all the instances mentioned have been condemned for their barbarity and cruelty, and no power to perpetuate such barbarity is to be implied from the nature of our government, and certainly is not found in any delegated powers under the Constitution. (Fong Yue Ting, Field, J, dissenting)

A variant of this argument might accept some differentiation in employment and other matters between citizens and noncitizens, but rejects the "crude" rights deprivation in some post–9/11 actions, such as the initial military tribunal order.[49]

One side argues that the post–9/11 enforcement measures that target noncitizens are consistent with—perhaps essential to—the liberty and equality aspects of the nation of immigrants ideal, whereas the other sees a deep contradiction. Who is right? To put the questions more specifically: how sharply can a nation of immigrants focus law enforcement against noncitizens before its very self-definition is placed in jeopardy? How isolated from the basic norms of the rule of law may noncitizens be, especially where their liberty is concerned? What effect does such isolation have on the constitutional rule of law itself?

These questions have has been raised in the court challenges to harsh laws as well as in the realm of public discourse. It is in such cases that the connection between the "collateral" deportation sanction and the post–9/11th regimes becomes most clear. Edna Borges was separated from her baby because of a law passed in 1996 that had authorized the mandatory detention, with no right to bail, of certain noncitizens during their deportation proceedings. Indeed, many of the post–9/11 detentions were facilitated by harsh laws, passed in 1996, aimed at a group that many found impossible to defend—"criminal aliens." Following immediately in the aftermath of a major act of terrorism on U.S. soil, the Oklahoma City bombing, two 1996 laws, the Antiterrorism and Effective Death Penalty Act of 1996 (AEDPA; Pub. L. No. 104-132, 110 Stat. 1214 (1996); codified as amended in scattered sections of 8, 18, 22, 28, 40, 42 U.S.C.) (1999)) and the Illegal Immigration Reform and Immigrant Responsibility Act of 1996 (IIRIRA; Pub. L. No. 104-208, Div. C, 110 Stat. 3009-546 (1996); codified as amended in scattered sections of 8, 18 U.S.C.) (1999), implemented a wide range of exceptionally harsh mechanisms aimed at noncitizens. (The laws passed, of course, before it was proven that the terrorist act had been perpetrated by white American citizens.) The 1996 laws contained provisions for:

1. The elimination of judicial review of certain types of deportation (removal) orders (Immigration and Nationality Act [hereafter INA] §242, 8 U.S.C. §1252 (1999).
2. Major changes to many grounds of inadmissibility and deportation (INA §212, 8 U.S.C. §1182 (1999); INA §237, 8 U.S.C. §1227 (1999)).
3. Elimination and limitation of some discretionary waivers of deportability (INA §240(A), 8 U.S.C. §1229(b) (replacing §212(c) and former supension of deportation with more restricted forms of relief known as "cancellation of removal").
4. Dramatic, often retroactive, expansion of criminal grounds of deportation (INA §101(a)(43), 8 U.S.C. §1101 (a)(43) (adding retroactive aggravated felony grounds)).
5. Mandatory detention for certain classes of noncitizens (INA §236, 8 U.S.C. §1226 (listing rules governing apprehension and detention of aliens)).
6. Expedited deportation procedures for certain types of cases (INA §238, 8 U.S.C. §1228 (1999)).
7. Creation of a new system, with extremely limited judicial review, for the summary exclusion from the United States of certain noncitizens who lack proper documentation (INA §235, 8 U.S.C. §1225 (1999)).
8. Authorization for vastly increased state and local law enforcement involvement in immigration matters (INA §103 (a)(8), 8 U.S.C. §1103 (a)(8) (1999)).
9. A new type of radically streamlined "removal" proceeding—including the possibility of using secret evidence—for noncitizens accused of "terrorist" activity (INA §§501–507, 8 U.S.C. §§1531–1537 (1999)).

The 1996 laws were rightly criticized by many commentators for the devastation they have wrought on families, for their rigidity, for their retroactivity, and for their elimination of judicial review. In hindsight, we can also now see how these laws laid the groundwork for the detention and deportation of people like Mr. Fayad and Ms. Borges.[50]

When a constitutional challenge to the law brought by a long-term lawful permanent resident made it to the Supreme Court in 2003, the majority deprecated the constitutional problem. In the exercise of its broad power over naturalization and immigration, said the Court, citing a case from a very different context, "Congress regularly makes rules that would be unacceptable if applied to citizens." (*Matthews v. Diaz*, 426 U.S. 67, 79–80 1976)). Although the Fifth Amendment has been held to provide some procedural due process rights in deportation proceedings (*Reno v. Flores*, 507 U.S. 292, 306, 123 L. Ed. 2d. 1,113 S. Ct. 1439(1993)), detention during such proceedings has long been accepted as a "constitutionally valid aspect of the process." This principle, said Chief Justice Rehnquist, now includes even a case in which an individual challenged his detention on the grounds that there was *no finding whatsoever* that he was unlikely to appear for deportation proceedings (*Demore v Kim*, 123 S. Ct. 1708 (2003). In other words, Congress may now define an immigration law violation and at the same time mandate that anyone *accused of* that violation will not be released from *custody under any circumstances* until proceedings have been concluded.

This ruling provoked sharp controversy. Justice Souter, in dissent, was sufficiently moved to write in strong, accusatory prose:

> This case is not about the National Government's undisputed power to detain aliens in order to avoid flight or prevent danger to the community. The issue is whether that power may be exercised by detaining a still lawful permanent resident alien when there is no reason for it and no way to challenge it. The Court's holding that the Due Process Clause allows this under a blanket rule is devoid of even ostensible justification in fact and at odds with the settled standard of liberty. (*Denmore*, supra.)

These debates, though undoubtedly influenced by 9/11, are not new. Indeed, we are immersed in a time upon which we will look back(as we do to the McCarthy era, the Second World War Japanese internments, the Palmer Raids, the late–nineteenth century exclusion and deportation of Chinese laborers, and the Alien and Sedition Acts and see that the fabric of our national mythology[51] is being stretched in profound ways.

Conclusion

The post–9/11 enforcement actions have made clear that the truth about immigration law in the United States is infinitely more complicated than the often-repeated teleological morality tale of suffering, flight, entry, struggle, and inevitable success.

When entry is relatively unconstrained in times of great fear, then postentry control, regulation, and deportation of noncitizens become the almost inevitable governmental responses. The "nation of immigrants" myth has generally sustained open admission policies better than it has the postentry rights of noncitizens.[53] There are many reasons for this, the most obvious of which include the following: the greater numbers of entrants than deportees, the superior power of a positive idea versus a negative critique, and the political aspirations of those who repeat the myth. Another more subtle reason is that historically distinct rationales for deportation laws—which may be termed the *extended border control* and *social control* models—become conflated (see, generally, Kanstroom 2000). The latter models, which are always much more controversial because of their direct effect on civil liberties, may be legitimated by border control failures. Thus, criticism of the (former) INS for having issued apparently fraudulent student visas to 9/11 hijackers (see *Interpreter Releases* 2002) may support calls not merely for better controls on visa processes, but also for the arrest and deportation of noncitizens who may have innocently donated money to Hamas-affiliated charities or who protest U.S. foreign policy. The call for greater government efficiency also inspires action against societal groups with the least well-developed legal and political clout. Fear increases majoritarian group solidarity, and citizenship status is perhaps the least-controversial grouping available(as compared with qualities such as whiteness Christianity or Euro-Western cultural orientation. Ironically, the very openness of the United States to newcomers may seem to justify the use of the citizen/noncitizen line and the "collateral" deportation power as efficient tools of social control. Normatively, this may seem better than some of the alternatives (e.g., a closed society). But, as history reveals so clearly, it is not without its own substantial costs and risks.

Acknowledgments

The author wishes to thank the participants at the conference on collateral sanctions organized by the Baldy Center in 2002 who helped him to refine his thoughts on these matters. Thanks also to his students, James Coburn, Mary Holper, and Christine Zemina, for research assistance and to Emily B. Kanstroom for her helpful critique. He is most appreciative of support from the Robert J. and Catherine E. Muldoon Memorial Faculty Research Fund and Dean John Garvey.

References

Bork, Robert H. 1996. *Slouching Towards Gomorrah: Modern Liberalism and American Decline.* New York: Regan Books.

Cardwell, Diane. 2003. "Threats and Responses: The Immigrants; Muslims Face Deportation, But Say US Is Their Home," *New York Times,* June 13, A22.

Cole, David. 2002. "Enemy Aliens," *Stanford Law Review* 54: 053, 957.

Fiscal Year 2002 Yearbook of Immigration Statistics, BCIS, Table 1; http://www.bcis.gov/graphics/shared/aboutus/statistics/IMM02yrbk/IMM2002list.html.

Gonzalez, Roberto J. 2003. "Detentions Don't Make Us More Secure," *Mercury News,* January 16.

Interpreter Releases. 2002. "INS Explains Issuance of Student Visas to Terrorists" 79, 400, March 18.

Johnson, Kevin R. 2002. "The End of 'Civil Rights' as We Know It?: Immigration and Civil Rights in the New Millennium" *UCLA Law Review.* 49: 1481–1511.

Kanstroom, Daniel. 1993. "Wer Sind Wir Wieder: Laws of Asylum, Immigration, and Citizenship in the Struggle for the Soul of the New Germany." *Yale Journal of International Law* 18: 155.

Kanstroom, Daniel. 1993a. "The Shining City and the Fortress: Reflections on the 'Euro-solution' to the German Immigration Dilemma." *Boston College International and Comparative. Law Review* 21: 201.

Kanstroom, Daniel. 1999. "Crying Wolf or a Dying Canary?" *Review of Law & Social Change* 25: 435–477.

Kanstroom, Daniel. 2000. "Deportation, Social Control, and Punishment: Some Thoughts About Why Hard Laws Make Bad Cases." *Harvard Law Review* 113, (June): 1890–1935.

Kanstroom, Daniel. 2000a. "Deportation and Justice: A Constitutional Dialogue." *Boston College Law Review* 41 (July): 771–88.

Kanstroom, Daniel. 2003. "'Unlawful Combatants' in the United States: Drawing the Fine Line Between Law and War." *Human Rights* 30 (Winter): 18–21.

Katyal, Neal K. and Laurence H. Tribe. 2002. "Waging War, Deciding Guilt: Trying the Military Tribunals." *Yale Law Journal* 111.

Kerwin, Donald S. 1999."How Our Immigration Laws Divide, Impoverish, and Undermine American Families," 76 *Interpreter Releases* 31, 1213, August 16.

Lawyers Committee for Human Rights. 2003. "Imbalance of Powers, How Changes to U.S. Law & Policy Since 9/11 Erode Human Rights and Civil Liberties." March.

Lewis, Anthony. 1996. "Mean and Petty." *New York Times* April 12: A13.

Office of the Inspector General (OIG). 2003. "The 9/11 Detainees: A Review of the Treatment of Aliens Held on Immigration Charges in Connection with the Investigation of the 9/11 Attacks."

Popper, Karl. 1945. *The Open Society and Its Enemies.* London: Routledge.

Report to Congress. 2003. On Implementation of Section 1001 of the USA PATRIOT Act; July 17, 2003; Office of the Inspector General; http://www.usdoj.gov/oig/special/03-07/index.htm.

Schmidley, Dianne. 2003. "Current Population Reports" U.S. Department of Commerce, Economics, and Statistics Administration U.S. Census Bureau," February.

Schultz, Evan P. 2002. "Bad Precedent." *Legal Times,* June 17.

Senate Judiciary Committee Testimony. 2001. Attorney General Michael Boyle. December. http://www.aila.org/contentViewer.aspx?bc=9,576,971,978.

Shenon, Philip. 2003. "Report on USA Patriot Act Civil Rights Violations," *New York Times,* July 20.

Urban Institute. 1999. "All Under One Roof: Mixed Status Families in an Era of Reform." June.

Verhovek, Sam Howe. 2001. "A Nation Challenged: Civil Liberties; Americans Give In To Race Profiling," *New York Times,* Sept. 23: A1.

Endnotes

1. Noncitizens in the United States do retain important constitutional rights, including important versions of equal protection and free speech rights analogous but not identical to those of citizens. When they are subject to deportation or when they travel outside the United States, however, these rights become minimal and in many situations nonexistent.

2. The INS was dissolved as of March 1, 2003, and its functions were transferred to the newly created Department of Homeland Security (DHS). The primary mission of DHS is the prevention of terrorist attacks, the reduction of U.S. vulnerability to terrorist attacks, and the minimization of damage from such attacks. See Section 101 Homeland Security Act. Many commentators have expressed concern about how this over-arching mission will affect immigration services. See, e.g., Lawyers Committee for Human Rights 2003: 48. Immigration-related applications for benefits, such as permanent residence, are now handled by a new bureau: the Bureau of Immigration and Citizenship Services (BCIS). Enforcement functions of several border and security agencies including the U.S. Customs Service, Federal Protective Service, and INS were transferred into the Directorate of Border and Transportation Security within the Department of Homeland Security. As part of this transition, these agency functions were reorganized into the Bureau of Immigration and Customs Enforcement (BICE).

3. Estimates of the Unauthorized Immigrant Population Residing in the United States: 1990–2000, US Immigration and Naturalization Service, Office of Policy and Planning (Jan.2003), http://www.immigration.gov/graphics/shared/aboutus/statistics/Ill Report 1211.pdf. The Pew Hispanic Study Center offered a midrange estimate of 7.8 million in 2001 in "How Many Undocumented: The Numbers behind the US-Mexico Migration Talks," *Pew Hispanic Center Study* (2002) http://www.pewhispanic.org/site/docs/pdf/study frank bean pdf.). The Urban Institute estimate exceeds 9 million. See Urban Institute, "Undocumented Immigrants: facts and Figures," http://www.urban.org/urlprint.cfm?ID=8685 (January 14, 2004).

4. U.S. Census Bureau, Current Population Survey, March 2002, Ethnic and Hispanic Studies Branch, Population Division, issued February 2003. The report understates the foreign-born population in at least one regard: it includes as "natives" persons who were born in "a U.S. island area such as Puerto Rico or born abroad of at least one parent who was a U.S. citizen." See Schmidley 2003.

5. The Census Bureau report notes that some 11 million foreign-born persons had naturalized.

6. Id. at 2.

7. The percentage of the foreign born who live in nonmetropolitan areas is some 5.7%, whereas the percentage of natives who do so is 20.4%.

8. Id. at 3.

9. CPS naturalization percentage data include so-called nonimmigrants, such as students and temporary workers as well as some undocumented people, all of whom are ineligible to naturalize.

10. Id. at 4.

11. Id. at 6.

12. Urban Institute 1999; see also Kerwin 1999.

13. This is true even as to naturalized citizens who, under certain unusual circumstances may be "denaturalized."

14. I was involved as a consultant to the defense team in Ms. Borges's case. Normally, I would not use the real name of a client. However, Ms. Borges's case has already been widely reported in the press.

15. Amy Otten, quoted in Theo Emery, "Shoplifting Conviction Comes Back to Haunt Portuguese Mom." Associated Press, August 6, 2003. Due to the extraordinary efforts of her primary counsel, Susan Church, Edna Borges was ultimately granted cancellation of removal and then released from DHS custody.

16. See generally, Kanstroom 2000, 2000a, and 1999.

17. Fiscal Year 2002 Yearbook of Immigration Statistics. The category of "formal removals" includes deportations, exclusions, and removal proceedings (which were created in 1996 as a unified system to include both exclusions and deportations.)

18. Id. Table 62.

19. Id. Table 57.

20. Id. Table 64

21. The designation by the government of two U.S. citizens, Jose Padilla and Yaser Hamdi, as "unlawful combatants" raises a host of related problems beyond the scope of this chapter. See generally, Kanstroom 2003 and Schultz 2002: 51.

22. I write "apparently" because, to date, the strategy seems to have resulted in a very small number of prosecutions or even leads.

23. One of the leading Administration supporters of strict enforcement, Viet Dinh, Assistant Attorney General for the Office of Legal Policy, is an immigrant. His statements weave together the three critical elements of immigration, liberty, and security: "9/11 . . . was a shock for me personally because I did not know very much about terrorism. I did not know very much about America, to tell you the truth, being a newcomer to this country. . . . I fundamentally reject any notion that liberty and security are competing goals that must be balanced in this war on terrorism. Rather, we seek to protect liberty by providing security." "Life After 9/11: Issues Affecting the Courts and the Nation," 51 *Kan. L. Rev.* 219 (2003).

24. It would take some thought to find a serious problem in the United States for which noncitizens have not been "the usual suspects." Before 9/11, it was the Oklahoma City bombing. Through the late 1980s and early 1990s, it was crime. In California, it was crime plus social services and state fiscal problems. And so on and on it has been—back through the history of AIDS, the Mafia, the Red Scares throughout the twentieth century, the nineteenth century "Yellow Peril." Because this tradition is so venerable, immigration law has long provided authorities with an impressive array of enforcement tools. Many, though not all, of the relevant provisions were legacies from episodes of antiforeigner fear. See generally, "Reigning in the Terrorists" at 52–54.

25. Id. at 62.

26. See 8 U.S.C. §1227(4)(C), emphasis added. Important exceptions to the potential breadth of this ground are described in 8 U.S.C. §1182 (a)(3)(C) (exception for officials and higher standard required for beliefs, statements or associations that would be lawful within the United States).

27. As the Supreme Court has recently reiterated, detention during deportation proceedings is "a constitutionally valid aspect of the deportation process." *Demore v. Kim,* 123 S.Ct. 1708, 1717 (2003). See also *Wong Wing v. United States,* 163 U.S. 228, 235, 41 L. Ed. 140, 16 S. Ct. 977 (1896) (deportation proceedings "would be vain if those accused could not be held in custody pending the inquiry into their true character.").

28. Less than two weeks after the attacks, Attorney General John Ashcroft also presented the rather gracelessly named Mobilization Against Terrorism Act (MATA) to Congress. (The unfortunate association between this acronym and Spanish verb *matar* ("to kill") was noted by many observers.) (Press Release, Attorney General John Ashcroft (Sept. 24, 2001), available at http://www.usdoj.gov/opa/pr/2001/September/492ag.html.n17). Among other provisions, the proposal sought to "[enhance] the authority of the Immigration and Naturalization Service (INS) to detain and remove suspected terrorists by expanding the definition of terrorists to include those who lend support to terrorist organizations." This proposal, like virtually all immigration-related Administration statements, also contained a strong reaffirmation of the nation of immigrants ideal: suggesting in this case that the government's goal was to "protect the integrity of the United States borders without sacrificing the ability to welcome law-abiding visitors and legal immigrants."

29. The Attorney General issued an internal memo on October 12, 2001, which stated, "when you carefully consider FOIA [Freedom of Information Act] requests and decide to withhold records, in whole or in part, you can be assured that the Department of Justice will defend your decisions unless they lack a sound legal basis or present an unwarranted risk of adverse impact on the ability of other agencies to protect other important records."

30. The Attorney General's memo instructed immigration judges to hold certain hearings separately, to close these hearings to the public, and to avoid discussing the case or otherwise disclosing any information about the case to anyone outside of the immigration court. Indeed, judges were instructed not to confirm or deny whether such a case was, or is, on the docket or scheduled for a hearing.

31. On November 8, 2001, the Department of Justice announced it would no longer release the number of detentions. Although the Justice Department had subsequently released a list of the number of people charged with specific immigration violations and their countries of origin, many questions about the post–9/11 detainees remain unanswered, including the identities of all those detained, where they were held, etc. Hearings have also been veiled from public scrutiny. See Letter from U.S. Department of Justice, Office of Legislative Affairs to Senator Russell D. Feingold (Nov. 16, 2001).

32. See infra note 2.

33. On July 24, 2002, the Justice Department also issued a final rule allowing the authorization of state and local law enforcement officers to enforce federal immigration laws. The rule implements INA Section 103(a)(8).

34. Office of Deputy Attorney General, Subject: Guidance for Absconder Apprehension Initiative (Jan. 25, 2002). On July 12, 2002, the INS stated that 758 persons were arrested as part of this program. See 79 *Interpreter Releases* 1044 (July 15, 2002). The period of stay for visitors to the United States was also shortened from its prior 3–6 months to 30 days or a "fair and reasonable period," and most changes of status from visitor to student were prohibited by a proposed regulation in April 2002. Limiting the Period of Admissions for B Nonimmigrant Aliens, 67 *Fed. Reg.* 18065 (proposed Apr. 12, 2002). See also 67 *Fed. Reg.* 71 at 18062 (prohibiting attendance in school while change of status is sought). New security checks and reporting and fingerprinting requirements for students were put into place in May 2002, and a plan authorizing the Attorney General to order certain designated noncitizens to provide fingerprints, photographs, and other information was issued in June 2002. See "Registration and Monitoring of Certain Non-immigrants," 67 *Fed. Reg.* 40,581 (proposed June 13, 2002).

35. The rule became final on August 12, 2002, effective 9/11, 2002. 67 *Fed. Reg.* 52,584.

36. This is a requirement of the law for the maintenance of legal status.

37. Men over the age of sixteen years from the following countries were required to register as follows: November 15, 2002–December 16: Iran, Iraq, Libya, Sudan, and Syria; December 2, 2002–January 10, 2003: Afghanistan, Algeria, Bahrain, Eritrea, Lebanon, Morocco, North Korea, Oman, Qatar, Somalia, Tunisia, United Arab Emirates, and Yemen; January 13, 2003–February 21, 2003: Pakistan, Saudi Arabia.

38. The INS confirmed this practice in a subsequent memo, which stated that "officers conducting these interviews may discover information which leads them to suspect that specific aliens on the list are unlawfully present or in violation of their immigration status." See Memorandum from Michael A. Pearson, INS Executive Associate Commissioner (Nov. 23, 2001). A Department of Justice (DOJ) report on the initial round of interviews, dated February 26, 2002, stated that more than 2,000 men on the list were interviewed, approximately one percent of whom were found to be in violation of immigration laws. Three men were arrested on criminal charges. Kenneth L. Wainstein, Director, Final Report on Interview Project (Feb. 26, 2002). Despite this rather low success rate, the DOJ announced that a second round of interviews of some 3000 Arab/Muslim men would commence on March 20, 2002. Again, the interviewees were selected, not because of any particular individualized suspicion but apparently because of their nationality, ethnicity and religion. See generally Johnson 2002.

39 Uniting and Strengthening America by Providing Appropriate Tools Required to Intercept and Obstruct Terrorism (USA PATRIOT), Act of 2001, Pub. L. No. 107-56, 115 Stat. 272 (2001) (hereinafter USA PATRIOT Act).

40. See id. §412.
MANDATORY DETENTION OF SUSPECTED TERRORISTS; HABEAS CORPUS; JUDICIAL REVIEW
SEC. 236A. (a) DETENTION OF TERRORIST ALIENS—(1) CUSTODY—The Attorney General shall take into custody any alien who is certified under paragraph (3) . . .
(3) CERTIFICATION—The Attorney General may certify an alien under this paragraph if the Attorney General has reasonable grounds to believe that the alien—
(A) is described in section 212(a)(3)(A)(i), 212(a)(3)(A)(iii), 212(a)(3)(B), 237(a)(4)(A)(i), 237(a)(4)(A)(iii), or 237(a)(4)(B); or
(B) is engaged in any other activity that endangers the national security of the United States. Id. [emphasis added].

41. See id. §412:
(5) COMMENCEMENT OF PROCEEDINGS—The Attorney General shall place an alien detained under paragraph (1) in removal proceedings, or shall charge the alien with a criminal offense, not later than 7 days after the commencement of such detention. If the requirement of the preceding sentence is not satisfied, the Attorney General shall release the alien. Id.

42. See id §412:
Definitions Relating To Terrorism.

(a) GROUNDS OF INADMISSIBILITY- Section 212(a)(3) of the Immigration and Nationality Act (8 U.S.C. 1182(a)(3)) is amended—
(1) in subparagraph (B)—
(A) in clause (i)—
(i) by amending sub clause (IV) to read as follows:
(IV) is a representative (as defined in clause (v)) of—
(aa) a foreign terrorist organization, as designated by the Secretary of State under section 219, or
(bb) a political, social or other similar group whose public endorsement of acts of terrorist activity the Secretary of State has determined undermines United States efforts to reduce or eliminate terrorist activities;
(ii) in sub clause (V), by inserting 'or' after 'section 219,'; and
(iii) by adding at the end the following new sub clauses:
(VI) *has used the alien's position of prominence within any country to endorse or espouse terrorist activity, or to persuade others to support terrorist activity or a terrorist organization, in a way that the Secretary of State has determined undermines United States efforts to reduce or eliminate terrorist activities* . . . " Id. [emphasis added]. The Enhanced Border Security and Visa Entry Reform Act, signed by the President on May 14, 2002, deals with a range of post–9/11 security issues, including closer monitoring of student visa entrants, and limits on visa issuance to persons from certain countries, designated as state sponsors of terrorism. Enhanced Border Security and Visa Entry Reform Act, Pub. L. No. 107—173, 116 Stat. 543 (2002). See generally 79 *Interpreter Releases* 769 (May 20, 2002).

43. The term *individual subject to this order* shall mean any individual *who is not a United States citizen* with respect to whom I determine . . . that:
(1) there is reason to believe that such individual . . .
(i) is or was a member of the organization known as al Qaida;
(ii) has engaged in, aided or abetted, or conspired to commit, acts of international terrorism, or acts in preparation therefore, that have caused, threaten to cause or have as their aim to cause injury or adverse effects on the United States, its citizens, national security, foreign policy, or economy . . .
 . . . any individual subject to this order . . . shall . . . forthwith be placed under the control of the Secretary of Defense. . . . Detention, Treatment, and Trial of Certain Non-Citizens in the War Against Terrorism, 66 *Fed. Reg.* 57,833 (Nov. 13, 2001).

44. See generally Verhovek 2001, noting how, "for many Americans who say they have deeply believed that it was wrong for law enforcement officers to single out members of minorities for special interrogation or searches, the terrorist attacks on 9/11 have prompted a painful confrontation with the sudden anxieties they acknowledge feeling in the presence of one minority in particular. With all of the hijackers involved believed to have Arab backgrounds, these Americans say, officials have ample reason to zero in on that group" and that a CNN/USA Today/Gallup poll taken a few days after the 9/11 attacks showed that fifty-eight percent backed more intensive security checks for Arabs. One of the more extreme examples was Louisiana congressman, Rep. John Cooksey, who said in a radio interview broadcast statewide, "If I see someone come in and he's got a diaper on his head and a fan belt around that diaper on his head, that guy needs to be pulled over and checked." Mr. Cooksey later said he was referring to Osama bin Laden and, referencing the citizen/non-citizen line obliquely, "I never intended to disparage loyal Americans of Arab descent.").

45. *Kennedy v. Mendoza-Martinez*, 372 U.S. 144, 160 (1963). "We deal with the contending constitutional arguments in the context of certain basic and sometimes conflicting principles. Citizenship is a most precious right. It is expressly guaranteed by the Fourteenth Amendment to the Constitution, which speaks in the most positive terms. . . . The powers of Congress to require military service for the common defense are broad and far-reaching, for while the Constitution protects against invasions of individual rights, it is not a suicide pact. . . ." Id. at 159–60.

46. This approach to immigration law and policy has venerable roots. As President John Adams once put it:
"If we glory in making our country an asylum for virtue in distress and for innocent industry, it behooves us to beware, that under this pretext it is not made a receptacle of malevolence and turbulence, for the outcasts of the universe." Argument to the Grand Jury

of the County of Duchess New York (Sept. 22, 1798), in XI *The Works of John Adams* 223 (Francis Adams ed., 1850–56).

47. See Viet Dinh, Life After 9/11: "Issues Affecting the Courts and the Nation," 51 *Kan. L. Rev.* 219, 220 (2003) (citing Edmund Burke, "Speech at His Arrival at Bristol Before the Election in That City (1774)," as quoted in Bork 1996: 64. Dinh acknowledges his debt to Edmund Burke (though he cites Robert Bork, too) for this construct. As Burke put it more than two centuries ago, "[t]he only liberty I mean is a liberty connected with order; that not only exists along with order and virtue, but which cannot exist at all without them."

48. See, e.g., Gonzalez 2003: "The Justice Department's post–9/11 detentions and deportations of Arab and Muslim men are ill-conceived and ineffective national security strategies. Instead of protecting our country, such actions breed mistrust and fear among immigrants and xenophobia among the general public." Id.

49. As two scholars wrote of the Bush Military Tribunal order:

[A]lthough we might afford considerable deference to the President in treating aliens less favorably than citizens in the distribution of Medicare, social security, or other similar benefits, or even in matters of employment, there is little or no room for government by approximation when it puts people on one side or another of a crude line that makes the difference between giving them access to the fundamental protections of civilian justice—from indictment to a jury trial presided over by a judge not answerable to the prosecutor, not to mention access to an appeal before a tribunal independent of the prosecuting authority—and relegating them to a distinctly less protective, and frankly inferior, brand of adjudication (Katyal and Tribe 2002: 1259).

50. Agency practice, too, must be understood in a broader timeframe. Years before 9/11, 2001, INS was already recognized as the largest single federal law enforcement agency, employing more armed agents than any other agency, including the FBI. See "Federal Law Enforcement Statistics," U.S. Department of Justice, Bureau of Justice Statistics (2000) http://www.ojp.usdoj.gov/bjs/fedle.htm . See also "Strategic Objective: An Effective System of Justice," U.S. Gen. Accounting Office, *GAO Strategic Supplement 2002–2007*, (June 12, 2002), http://www.gao.gov/sp/strobj15.pdf; see also Lewis 1996. Following the terrorist attacks, its enforcement budget continued to grow, more than quadrupling in less than a decade, to $5.6 billion in 2002, from $1.6 billion in 1994. "Ten Year Display of Budget Authority and Positions," U.S. Department of Justice, Immigration and Naturalization Service, at http://www.usdoj.gov/jmd/2003summary/pdf/INS-BAR.pdf.

In early 1999, INS developed a comprehensive Interior Enforcement Strategy that envisioned the deportation of some 5 million persons over a five-year period. As INS put it at the time, the agency is now focusing its capabilities on the nation's interior, in areas that had previously not been affected by illegal immigration. To this end, INS developed a comprehensive interior enforcement strategy to systematically combat illegal immigration inside the United States by attacking its causes, not merely its symptoms.

The new strategy shifted INS focus from work-place raids to five priorities, to:
1. "Identify and remove criminal aliens."
2. "Deter, dismantle, and diminish smuggling and trafficking of aliens."
3. "Minimize immigration benefit fraud and other document abuse."
"Respond to community reports and complaints about illegal immigration and build partnerships to solve local problems."
"Block and remove employers' access to undocumented workers."

See Backgrounder, "Interior Enforcement Strategy," U.S.Department of Justice, http://www.immigration.gov/graphics/publicaffairs/backgrounds/inenfbgr2.htm (Mar. 29, 1999).

Since 1998, INS has focused most of its enforcement resources on the first of the above priorities: the removal of "criminal aliens." It is estimated that the agency devoted as much time and resources to that one priority as to all of the other listed priorities combined. See "Homeland Security, Challenges to Implementing the Immigration Interior Enforcement Strategy" U.S. Gen. Accounting Office, Testimony Before the Subcommittee on Immigration, Border Security and Claims, Committee on the Judiciary, House of Representatives, GAO-03-660T, (April 2003.)

51. I do not mean to imply anything pejorative by my use of the word "mythology." As I have discussed at greater length elsewhere, every nation-state has a distinctive mythology that seeks to define its character. See Kanstroom 1993 and 1993a.

52. I am thinking in this regard of Popper 1945.
53. As Francis Walker wrote in the *Atlantic* in 1896: "The first thing to be said respecting any serious proposition importantly to restrict immigration into the United States is, that such a proposition necessarily and properly encounters a high degree of incredulity, arising from the traditions of our country. From the beginning, it has been the policy of the United States, both officially and according to the prevailing sentiment of our people, to tolerate, to welcome, and to encourage immigration, without qualification and without discrimination."

11

A Vicious Cycle: Resanctioning Offenders

NORA V. DEMLEITNER

The high imprisonment rate in the United States and the concomitant high release rate of 600,000 individuals annually have focused efforts in recent years on the reintegration and reentry of offenders (Travis, Solomon, and Waul 2001). Among the many hurdles ex-offenders face upon release are locating employment and housing, reconnecting with family, establishing bank accounts, and applying for welfare benefits. Many of these tasks are difficult not only because of the offender's often long absence from the larger society but also because of his criminal record. Some forms of stigmatization of ex-offenders are legally mandated, others are socially condoned; only some forms of discrimination, for example in the employment area, are prohibited. Frequently, it is impossible for offenders to take certain steps generally considered crucial toward reintegration because of so-called collateral consequences, or collateral sanctions (Travis 2002).

Collateral sanctions prevent released offenders with drug convictions from receiving most public benefits, including federally funded housing and food stamps (Demleitner 2002), and bar them from receiving driver's licenses. Sanctions also prevent convicted sex offenders from moving into public housing. Collateral sanctions make it impossible for many ex-offenders to regain their children, and prohibit others from voting in local, state, and federal elections, sometimes for life (Fellner and Mauer 1998; see also the chapter herein by Uggen and Manza). While detailed studies do not exist, some of these sanctions obviously make reintegration immediately upon release from prison difficult, and lead the ex-offender quickly

185

back into a life of crime. To what extent the reimprisonment of parole violators is connected to such disabling collateral sanctions remains undetermined, however. Other collateral sanctions have a more long-term impact on ex-offender reintegration as they continue to exert the stigma of the prior conviction.

Despite their debilitating impact on ex-offenders' lives, courts have generally declined to find such collateral sanctions punishment for constitutional purposes, largely because legislatures justify them in terms of public safety rather than retribution. For that reason, protections otherwise available in the criminal justice system, such as the bans on double jeopardy and ex post facto legislation, do not apply.

Even though state and federal law hold out the promise of erasing criminal records, in many cases the process of doing so is lengthy, cumbersome, expensive, and leads only to partial restoration of full citizenship. State pardons, for example, do not necessarily prevent the imposition of federal restrictions on ex-offenders; sealed criminal records remain available to law-enforcement agencies; and even expungement may not guarantee a fresh start.

As long as collateral sanctions apply to ex-offenders, their violations may lead to further criminal punishment, and in some cases to draconian sentences. This chapter focuses on two very different types of such violations, both of which carry substantial penalties. First, deportation upon conviction of a criminal offense is one of the most dramatic and severe collateral sanctions in existence. Should a noncitizen deported because of the commission of a criminal offense attempt to reenter the United States without authorization and be caught, the maximum possible sentences range from ten to twenty years. Congress rationalized this legislation by arguing that such ex-felons constitute an on-going threat to the United States, and should therefore be banned from the country for a long time. Any attempt at reentry must be punished. Second, convicted felons caught with a dangerous weapon, a definition that includes firearms and ammunition, face prison terms under state and federal laws based on the assumption that such armed individuals always constitute a substantial threat to society. Should the offender have three or more prior qualifying convictions, the mandatory minimum federal sentence is fifteen years.

Even though the laws appear to advance important societal goals, in many cases they merely exacerbate the serious negative consequences of collateral sanctions for individuals, families, and communities and further burden the federal and state budgets with the cost of incarcerating nondangerous individuals. Because of the substantial length of potential maximum sentences in our sentencing regimes, the scope and breadth of collateral sanctions, and the use of mandatory sanctions for the violation of such statutes, the resulting punishments are too sweeping. This article suggests a narrowing of collateral sanctions to reorient them toward a risk-based analysis and a more targeted approach in prosecuting and punishing offenders who have violated collateral sanctions. Ultimately, the goal should be to focus on dangerous and potentially dangerous offenders. This implies in most cases the abolition of mandatory sanctions that merely allow for police and prosecutorial discretion in enforcement but do not make society safer.

Reentry of Deported Ex-Offenders

Since the late 1980s, Congress has substantially enlarged the category of noncitizens deportable upon the commission of criminal offenses. In addition, it has expanded the ban on reentry applicable to such deportees and has increased the penalties for reentry upon deportation. Combined with heightened enforcement, this has led to a dramatic rise in the number of deportations of criminal offenders and subsequent prosecutions for illegal reentry.

The Law

The interplay of two sets of laws—the expansion of deportation grounds for criminal offenders and the reentry penalties—creates the current legal situation. The 1952 immigration legislation created a maximum two-year imprisonment for deportees who reentered the United States. This law, with its maximum sentence exposure, remained in place until 1988.

Deportation on a wide variety of grounds has existed virtually since the beginning of this country. However, deportation on criminal grounds became more stringent through the Anti-Drug Abuse Act of 1988, which, for the first time, created the category of "aggravated felons." This term was reserved for a group of violent and serious drug offenders who would be subject to deportation, virtually without exception. This meant that these offenders were denied the opportunity to argue for suspension of deportation based on outstanding equities, such as their family connections in the United States.

The same legislation increased the penalty for deported noncitizens who reenter the United States and created a three-tier penalty structure (see 18 U.S.C. §1326(6)(2)). The law continued the maximum two-year imprisonment for reentry upon deportation but imposed a maximum five years for reentry for deported felons and a maximum fifteen years for deported aggravated felons. The penalty provisions also included a potential fine of up to $1,000, $10,000, and $20,000, respectively, which could be imposed instead of or in addition to an incarcerative sanction.

By 1994 Congress expanded the middle category, which had applied solely to felons also to those who had committed "three or more misdemeanors involving drugs, crimes against the person or both" (Violent Crime Control and Law Enforcement Act of 1994). In addition, believing that the existing penalties did not sufficiently deter foreign offenders from reentering, Congress increased the maximum penalty for deported felons and misdemeanants who reenter to ten and for aggravated felons to twenty years. Two years later, Congress added a non-concurrent ten-year term of imprisonment for reentering aliens whose removal had been based on terrorist activity. This provision, however, has solely symbolic value because even in the post–9/11 world, no noncitizen has been removed under that provision. Removals, even of individuals suspected of having terrorist connections, are usually based on criminal convictions or violations of the immigration laws.

The aggravated felon category was expanded in 1994 and then again in 1996.[1] Serious violent felons and drug traffickers are no longer considered to be the only aggravated felons; the category now includes those engaging in gambling offenses, prostitution, treason, (most) immigration document fraud, and gun-related crimes as well as burglaries. Under earlier definitions of "aggravated felon," the length of the sentence determined whether an offender was categorized as an aggravated felon. Under the recent changes, imprisonment requirements have been dramatically lowered and even removed for some crimes. Due to a change in terminology, probationary and suspended sentences are frequently counted as if they had been imposed as prison terms. For that reason, in cases of so-called crimes of violence, an offender is in a more advantageous position for immigration purposes when serving 364 days in jail rather than receiving a one-year (365 days) probationary sentence.

Under other provisions of the immigration act, the maximum possible sentence rather than the actual sentence imposed affects an offender's classification. Because of the high maximum sentences in most state and federal statutes, such a limitation excludes only the most minor offenses from being classified as "aggravated felonies." In addition, the Board of Immigration Appeals (BIA), the highest administrative appeals unit in the immigration area, has construed some crime categories broadly: felony *possession* of a controlled substance is an aggravated felony, as is indecency with a minor.[2] Courts have followed suit, holding even some misdemeanor offenses to be aggravated felonies, leading to automatic deportation. Determining the scope of the term *crime of violence* has caused federal courts particular difficulty, often leading to widely diverging results in different circuits.

The 1996 legislation also defines the term *conviction* broadly. It has been interpreted to cover even expunged convictions (Nafziger and Yimesgen 2003). Aggravated felons are deprived of virtually any form of relief from deportation. This means that deportation will occur independent of the length of time they have spent in the United States—and some arrived as very young children—their family ties, work history, aberrational character of the offense, or health issues. Only in very few cases—for example, in the case of torture in their home country—may deportations be suspended.[3] Combined with more aggressive enforcement of these deportation provisions in the wake of the 1996 legislation, the number of those deported for criminal offenses has increased dramatically (U.S. Department of Homeland Security 2003a). Of almost 149,000 deported noncitizens in 2002, nearly 48% (slightly over 71,000) were deported for criminal offenses. This constitutes a dramatic increase in the total number of deportations as well as a substantial rise in the deportations of criminal offenders over earlier years.

Some of those deported are career criminals, who likely have a long criminal history in their home country and the United States.[4] Among this group, some may have entered the United States only to commit crimes. How large these groups are, however, is virtually impossible to determine. For others, who arrived as young children and lived here since, their criminal history is restricted to the United States.

The ongoing threat these individuals pose to the United States is no different from that posed by offenders who were born here. Societal influences that may be (partially) responsible for the offender's criminal activities are linked to time spent in the United States, not the offender's country of citizenship. Even those who claim that genetic make-up rather than societal conditions are responsible for criminal behavior cannot blame the offender's country of citizenship. They are reduced to arguing for a decrease in overall immigration to keep the offender and his family out of the United States long before the initial onset of criminality. Finally, some offenders who are being deported are not career criminals but have committed an offense on a single occasion whether out of ignorance, greed, drug dependency, hopes for a better life, or other reasons. Many of them constitute no future threat to others. Nevertheless, all of them will be deported and face draconian sentences upon reentry. Still, the incentive of many deportees to return is often overwhelming, especially if their entire family is in the United States, they have no or little connection to their country of origin, do not speak the language dominant there, and are in a country geographically close to the United States.

Enforcement of the Law

Since the passage of the 1996 immigration laws, immigration authorities and law enforcement have increasingly cooperated to remove noncitizen offenders from this country. Many prisons and jails now screen convicts upon admission for their citizenship status, and the immigration authorities initiate removal hearings during the term of imprisonment, so that the offender can be deported at the end of her prison term. While such identification and removal procedures apparently work efficiently in many prisons, they do not everywhere. Moreover, noncitizens sentenced to probationary sentences—even for offenses labeled as aggravated felonies—will not have to undergo such a screening process. Unless reported by their probation officers or the prosecutors, they may not come to the attention of the immigration authorities. Although these individuals live in a legal limbo in which removal may occur at any point, unless and until it does, they are not threatened by the reentry penalties.

Whereas much of the current rhetoric focused on the removal of criminal offenders from the United States is based on public safety and risk assessments (U.S. Department of Homeland Security 2003),[5] the reason underlying the congressional legislation was different. The deportation provisions in the 1996 legislation were justified largely because noncitizens who committed criminal offenses were considered to have abused their privilege as guests in this country. Even though this rationale continues to be important, increasingly the focus appears to be on the removal of risks from the United States and on preventing the reentry of such alleged security risks. The assumption behind the enforcement of the reentry statutes is that deported offenders seek to reenter solely to victimize the resident population in the United States. In this respect, U.S. immigration law continues the incapacitative approach of recidivist statutes and drug and violent crime legislation, which justify long sentences on public protection grounds.[6] After all, reentering felons are recidivists since they have broken two sets of laws—the underlying felony offense and the criminal immigration laws.

In recent years, the federal government has begun focused operations to remove certain types of offenders from the United States. Since the terror attacks of 9/11, 2001, the emphasis has been on removing men from Middle Eastern or Muslim countries who remained in the United States without immigration authorization, upon having received deportation orders, or upon having committed crimes that made them removable. In the summer of 2003, the Department of Homeland Security (under which immigration authorities are now largely centralized) began Operation Predator to remove convicted sex offenders, undocumented and documented, from the United States (U.S. Department of Homeland Security 2003b). In the first week-long sweep, federal authorities arrested 89 foreigners convicted of sexual offenses who had not been removed from the United States.[7] Both enforcement efforts have been justified in terms of domestic security. The former deportations were focused on alleged terrorists, the latter on offenders currently considered to be the most heinous. Greater detection and removal of felons increases the number of individuals who are barred from the United States.

Unless deported felons obtain prior approval of the Attorney General to reenter, they are barred from the United States for ten years. A twenty-year bar applies to aggravated felons, again subject to the Attorney General's waiver. Nevertheless, many noncitizens reenter the United States upon removal without such authorization. Most of the individuals caught upon unauthorized reentry are Hispanic males with less than a high school education (Maxfield and Burchfield 2002). Presumably for this group reentry is cheaper and less risky than for individuals returned to countries geographically farther removed from the United States. Also, larger numbers of Hispanic males are being deported, more than individuals from other groups, because they constitute a substantially larger proportion of the immigrant population.

Those reentering do so for a variety of reasons: for some it is the only (or best) opportunity to provide for their families; for some it is the sole opportunity to reunite with those left behind; others might be motivated by opportunities to commit crime or rejoin their criminal companions. The motivation for such reentry, however, is irrelevant in prosecutions and sentencing. In *United States v. Saucedo-Patino* (2004), the district court granted a downward departure from the otherwise prescribed sentencing guideline to a reentering felon. The court justified its decision based on the nature of the prior conviction and the defendant's claim that he reentered the United States to support his family. On appeal, the Eleventh Circuit reversed the decision because the court had no authority to treat a crime of violence as if it had not been such a crime and because "Saucedo-Patino's motive for reentering the United States is simply irrelevant to the determination whether to depart" (Saucedo-Patino 2004: 795). This rationale predominates, especially since courts do not usually take the time to consider an offender's motivations to reenter.

Whereas in fiscal year 1997 2,124 previously removed aggravated felons were sentenced for unauthorized reentry, by fiscal year 2000 the number had doubled (Maxfield and Burchfield 2002; Maxfield 2002: 267). This number does not include individuals who reentered upon removal for a nonaggravated felony or a misdemeanor conviction. Since the information is based on sentencing data, it does not provide a clear picture of how many removed individuals attempt to return to the United States. Anecdotal evidence indicates that of younger Mexican men deported for criminal offenses, many return. The rise in reentry prosecutions between 1997 and 2000 supports this impression. The increase in deportations for criminal offenses combined with heightened border enforcement has dramatically increased the number of noncitizens who attempt to return to the United States, frequently overwhelming criminal justice resources, especially in border districts.

The twenty-year statutory limit provides the maximum sentence that can be imposed on reentry offenders, and the federal sentencing guidelines set the actual parameters for the sentencing of such offenders. Prior to a guideline change in November 2001, the guidelines enhanced the sentences of all aggravated felons who reentered by 16 points, so that most of them, depending on their criminal history, ended up within a guideline range of 37 to 96 months (i.e., three years one month to eight years) (Maxfield and Burchfield 2002).

However, in many districts—especially the Southern District of California—prosecutors cap the sentence of most reentrants at 24 months. They do so by charging reentrants with a plain violation of the reentry statute rather than a violation of the aggravated felon provision of that statute, in exchange for the noncitizens agreeing to deportation. Generally, offenders with a more serious prior criminal record—either in terms of severity or length—would not be able to benefit from such charging practice. Some districts, including the District of Arizona, reject such a practice, and instead grant downward departures to felon reentrants, so as to bring their sentences below the otherwise prescribed guideline range.[8] Courts that have heard challenges to such divergent charging practices have generally rejected them, at least at the circuit level (*United States v. Banuelos-Rodriguez* 2000; *United States v. Bonnet-Grullon* 2000).

The motivating factor behind such different charging practices is ambiguous. It might be that the pressing caseload in the district with the largest number of immigration cases, the Southern District of California, caused the creation of the fast-track program. Others have claimed, however, that such charging practices were results of the harsh penalties threatening reentrants. When provided with leeway in charging reentrants, prosecutors are able to calibrate sanctions based on the severity of the noncitizen's prior criminal record. The recent changes to the federal Sentencing Guidelines, made in November 2001, however, should render such prosecutorial discretion unnecessary, as the guidelines now allow for enhancements tailored more narrowly to the underlying criminal record. Aggravated felonies generally receive an eight-point enhancement, while drug offenses receive a twelve-point enhancement.[9] The maximum enhancement also applies to a select group of other offenses, including crimes of violence and firearms offenses. This modification might arguably have changed the views of many federal district court judges. Yet, in a judicial survey conducted early in 2002, more than half of the responding judges felt that the sentences imposed for unlawful entry offenses were longer than appropriate. Further, the judges appeared equally split as to whether these sentences provided adequate deterrence (Maxfield 2003). The attempts of some district courts to depart downward even after the guideline change (Saucedo-Patino 2004) seem to indicate that many continue to feel that some reentering felons are punished too harshly.

Although the reentry offense may create a sense of greater public security, it is likely to increase the suffering of offenders who have served their time in prison. Many have not lived in their so-called home country in decades. The recent calibration of reentry sanctions is commendable. Yet, the scheme, which still relies on broad classifications, remains based on an overinclusive collateral sanction—the deportation of all so-called aggravated felons.

A number of changes are advisable: First, the "aggravated felon" category should be drawn more narrowly so as to include only those offenders whose actions constitute a likely threat to the United States. Second, waivers should be available to offenders who themselves or whose families would suffer substantial hardship from their deportation.

Models in use elsewhere shed some light on the latter alternative: Canadian courts, for example, have held family considerations highly relevant in deportation cases. Citizen children create humanitarian and compassionate reasons against deportation, as do other close family ties (*Baker v. Canada* 1999; Aiken and Scott 2000). The same holds true in many European countries. National courts have rejected attempts to deport non-nationals based on criminal convictions if the center of their life, including their families, is in the country of immigration. France has gone yet a step farther: unless the offenses committed were against the state or were terrorism related, the new French immigration law makes it virtually impossible to remove "those who entered France before age 13; the spouses of French citizens or legal residents; the parents of children who are French citizens; those who have resided legally in France for at least 20 years" (Baldwin 2003).

In addition to national courts, the European Court of Human Rights (ECHR) has heard numerous deportation cases involving criminal offenders who challenged their removal under Article 8 of the European Convention on Human Rights. The Convention guarantees "the right to respect for [one's] private and family life. . . ." In its jurisprudence, the Court has generally focused on whether the state has "struck a fair balance" (*Dahlia v. France* 1998) between the right to family life on the one hand and the state's legitimate interest in the prevention of disorder or crime along with the guarantee of public safety on the other.[10] To ascertain the value of the family life at issue, the Court has looked toward the length and quality of the family relationships as well as the number and location of relatives

(Janis, Kay, and Bradley 2000: 258–59). Under the Court's jurisprudence, no per se deportable offenses exist, and any deportation must be tested against the right to family life.

The ECHR considers the impact of deportation on the potential deportee's family life in a pragmatic and realistic way. This is a far cry from current U.S. law, which allows deportation waivers only under limited circumstances. U.S. courts have developed a much more individualistic jurisprudence, which discounts the third-party impact of deportation.

The more discretionary European approach provides for a substantially more individualistic assessment of the gravity of the offenses committed and other values at stake in the removal of a noncitizen. Current U.S. disdain for discretionary decisionmaking, however, may require strict limitations on collateral consequences unless a more discretionary application of collateral sanctions becomes acceptable. As a side benefit, such a development would be cost-effective because it would focus law-enforcement efforts on those reentering who constitute a threat to public safety. This conclusion applies not only to deportation but also to the so-called felon-in-possession statutes.

Felon-in-Possession Statutes

The Omnibus Crime Control and Safe Streets Act of 1968 aimed at gaining greater control over firearms offenses. It has been codified in part in 18 U.S.C. §921 and related provisions. The aim of this Act and later legislation was to get control of firearms, which Congress considered an integral part of a host of violent and drug-related offenses.

The Firearms Owners' Protection Act codified and amended 18 U.S.C. §922(g)(1), which states that "[i]t shall be unlawful for any person who has been convicted in any court of, a crime punishable by imprisonment for a term exceeding one year ... [to] possess ... any firearm. ..." The goal of this provision was to keep dangerous weapons, especially firearms, away from convicted felons, who are more likely to recidivate and to constitute a substantial danger to the public.

Judicial interpretations of the statute require the government to prove the defendant's prior conviction, which will be "determined in accordance with the law of the jurisdiction in which the proceedings were held,"[11] to show that the defendant knowingly possessed a firearm and that the firearm traveled in or affected interstate commerce. Other sections of the statute also prohibit drug users and misdemeanor domestic violence offenders as well as those subject to some restraining orders from possessing firearms (Ginkowski 2000: 59–60).[12] Convictions will not be counted if the offender's civil rights were restored (18 U.S.C. §921(a)(20)).

The maximum possible penalty for a felon-in-possession is ten years (18 U.S.C. §924(a)(2)). Statutory relief from this collateral sanction applies only in situations where the firearms were issued for the use of "any State or any department, agency, or political subdivision thereof" (18 U.S.C. §925(a)(1)). This exception does not cover misdemeanor domestic violence convictions.

Under the Armed Career Criminal Act of 1984 (ACCA), should the defendant have been convicted of three violent felonies or serious drug-trafficking offenses, a mandatory minimum sentence of fifteen years in prison applies (18 U.S.C. §924(e)(1)). Violent felonies are statutorily defined as any offense punishable by more than one year imprisonment as long as it includes the use, attempted use, or threatened use of force against another, or consists of the crimes of burglary, arson, or extortion (18 U.S.C. §924(e)(2)(B)).

The ACCA has been interpreted broadly to include offenses that are connected temporally and physically as long as the three previous convictions arose out of distinct criminal episodes. Moreover, any generic burglary fits the definition of burglary under the section. Finally, there is no time limit to the prior convictions that will be counted so that even very old convictions may make an ex-offender eligible for the sentence enhancement (Montgomery and Chutuape 1998: 3–6).

Congress passed this legislation as a way to address the scourge of weapons offenses by focusing on the high recidivism rate and the danger that recidivists pose, especially in connection with drug offenses. This varies only in nuance from the *U.S. Attorney's Manual*, which highlights in its introduction to firearms charges how gang members regularly engage in gun purchases and sales and because of the easy availability of guns constitute a substantial threat to others (U.S. Department of Justice 1997: 112).

The *U.S. Attorney's Manual* suggests that "[f]irearms violations . . . be aggressively used in prosecuting violent crime." The reason is that "[t]hey are generally simple and quick to prove" (U.S. Department of Justice 1997: 112). The Department of Justice, in most cases, has no difficulty proving the statutory elements required for a conviction: possession of a firearm and a prior qualifying conviction. The direction given in the *U.S. Attorney's Manual* may partially explain the substantial increase in firearms prosecutions under 18 U.S.C. §922 in general and under subsection (g)(1) in particular. Between 1992 and 2002, the number of federal prosecutions resulting from criminal referrals by the Bureau of Alcohol, Tobacco, and Firearms (ATF) under 18 U.S.C. §922 doubled. Between 2000 and 2002, the prosecutions under 922(g)(1) alone rose from 2,371 to 4,110—the largest number of prosecutions from ATF referrals. These data count only prosecutions based on ATF criminal referrals[13] and not those that may have been investigated by other federal agencies or state law enforcement. In addition, in the 4,110 cases listed, a violation of 922(g)(1) must have been the lead charge, implying presumably that it was the most serious offense prosecuted in a case. Therefore, these figures do not constitute all federal prosecutions under this code provision but only those not tied to another, more serious offense.

Moreover, some violations may not be prosecuted or may not be prosecuted under the applicable statutory provisions. The *U.S. Attorney's Manual* indicates that because of the substantial and often mandatory penalties under the firearms provisions, they are particularly suited "as leverage to gain plea bargaining and cooperation from offenders." The same can be said for state firearms provisions whose penalties are also frequently used to entice firearms offenders to reveal who provided them with the guns or ammunition. However, because state felon-in-possession statutes often carry substantially lesser penalties than the federal statute, state prosecutors may refer state cases, especially when investigated by joint federal–state task forces, to federal court for prosecution. Project Safe Neighborhoods, a program of the federal government, focuses on the federal prosecution of convicted offenders who commit gun crimes.[14] This program is responsible, according to the Department of Justice, for the substantial increase in gun crime prosecutions, many of which have led to substantial penalties (U.S. Department of Justice 2003).

Even though the federal felon-in-possession statutes were justified on a risk-based assumption, they are overinclusive. The case of Paul Bradley VanLeer is instructive (*United States v. VanLeer* 2004). VanLeer had a history of nonviolent drug offenses, largely connected to his use of illegal narcotics. After being released, VanLeer tried to sell a 12 gauge shotgun, which he had possessed prior to his incarceration but temporarily given to a friend. During the transaction at the pawn shop, VanLeer gave his correct name and address. In the course of a regular records check, the city police department determined that VanLeer was a convicted felon and referred his case for prosecution to the federal government. Based on the federal sentencing guidelines, VanLeer faced 30 to 37 months (i.e., two and a half years to three years and one month) in prison.

VanLeer moved for a downward departure because his crime did not "threaten the harm or evil" ordinarily covered by the statute. Despite recent restrictions on the departure power of federal judges, the district court in this case granted such a departure and sentenced VanLeer to eighteen months in prison.

Even though VanLeer presumably does not constitute the typical felon-in-possession—after all, he tried to dispose of a gun legally—his case is not unique either. Other courts have also encountered cases in which they found the illegal possession of a weapon to be sufficiently harmless to allow for a downward departure (*United States v. Lewis* 2001; the gun in question was an heirloom, which the defendant retrieved from a pawnshop).

While the judges in those cases recognized their unique nature and departed downward from the guideline sentence, they still imposed substantial prison terms. VanLeer, for example, even after the downward departure, will serve one and a half years in a federal prison. Whether this is a useful allocation of public resources, let alone a good use of VanLeer's potential, is questionable.

Many ex-offenders, especially those with stale convictions, have attempted to regain their right to carry a firearm, often for hunting purposes or to gain employment. A few avenues are open to them: pardons, expungement or a similar procedure, or the ATF procedure specifically granting ex-offenders the right to carry a gun. Gubernatorial pardons, however, are frequently insufficient to eradicate federal firearms restrictions, unless they specifically reinstate a person's right to carry a firearm. Presidential pardons, on the other hand, are only available to federal offenders, and their number has declined substantially at the same time as the number of federal ex-offenders has risen dramatically. Expungement-type procedures may lead to the restoration of firearms privileges. The most direct route, however, would be the procedure that allows for the ATF to restore firearms privileges of ex-offenders (18 U.S.C. 925(c)). However, since 1992, Congress has refused to fund this part of the ATF's work (Pals 1998: 1099), and the U.S. Supreme Court held that federal courts lack jurisdiction to grant relief (*United States v. Bean* 2002).

The felon-in-possession statutes have many of the same shortcomings that characterize the reentry statutes. They carry relatively high sentences for behavior that may be a precursor to the individual's becoming a threat to the public. However, the underlying triggering offenses are drawn too broadly to allow for an accurate risk assessment and frequently lead to unjust penalties when measured against the risk the person poses and the social harm he has caused. Moreover, the use and enforcement of the provision appears to be more designed to increase cooperation, often with regard to unrelated offenses, and enhance the percentage of successful criminal prosecutions than meaningfully provide for public safety.

Focusing Enforcement

Narrowly drawn, risk-based collateral sanctions are useful as they may highlight and restrict the potential danger an ex-offender poses. For example, a sex offender convicted of sexual assault of a minor should not be permitted to work as a teacher in a daycare center or a school upon his release; an offender convicted of voting fraud may be barred from the ballot box for a limited period of time (Demleitner 2000).

However, many, if not most, of the collateral sanctions in place are too broadly drawn to serve effectively as a measure of public protection. As the deportation of aggravated felons indicates, the category currently encompasses a wide array of offenders, only some of whom constitute a substantial threat to public safety. Therefore, the deportation of all the others, as well as the punishment of all felons-in-possession, independent of the threat they pose, must be justified on other grounds.

Retributive considerations cannot be the guidepost as the courts have held that collateral sanctions, including a ban on firearms and deportation, are not akin to traditional punishment, such as imprisonment or fines. Therefore, they cannot be defended on such grounds.

Deterrence is also closely connected to criminal punishment though not required by it. Therefore, deterrence may play a role in such sanctions. However, the haphazard way in which deportation occurs and the uncertain likelihood of being arrested and prosecuted for illegal reentry or being a felon-in-possession makes deterrence, even if a goal, too uncertain to be successful.

Most likely, the incapacitative rationale animates collateral sanctions. They have become an extension of prison as they continue to limit an individual's participation in society. Even though they may be designed to prevent further unlawful activity, they restrict much lawful activity. In the case of deportations, the noncitizen is prevented from engaging in any lawful activity in the United States. While the felon-in-possession statute is not equally far-reaching, it may prevent an ex-offender from taking up various lawful employment opportunities in which he would be required or expected to carry a firearm. Moreover, it also limits his enjoyment of lawful leisure activities, such as hunting, even though his conviction for a nonviolent offense may be decades in the past.

For these reasons, these two collateral sanctions, like many others, are overbroad and do not promote public safety. To the contrary, they present obstacles to the full reintegration of offenders, albeit of a different magnitude, and therefore increase the likelihood of recidivism. This is especially true as the possibilities of avoiding or curtailing these two collateral sanctions are very limited. Even a fully rehabilitated offender will have difficulty regaining his right of access to the United States or to firearms.

Because of the breadth of collateral sanctions and the difficulties in overcoming them, it might not be surprising that some individuals either decide to disregard them intentionally or in some cases violate them inadvertently. Unintentional violations have occurred in the case of felons-in-possession with very old convictions who lacked information about the legislation and of some illegal reentrants who did not realize they were crossing into the United States. Intentional violations have been committed by ex-felons who opt to engage in hunting or buying a gun for personal protection despite their knowledge of the legislation as well as by the vast majority of aggravated felons who reenter the United States.

Any violation of the two sanctions discussed will be interpreted as a security threat. Therefore, substantial sanctions appear justified. However, because of the breadth of the underlying collateral sanction, the penalties often are disproportionate and unfair. Why should an ex-felon who retrieves an heirloom gun from the pawnshop spend any time in prison? Why should a noncitizen who grew up in the United States and whose entire family, including a citizen spouse and citizen children, lives here be deported and barred from reentry for a decade or longer after a theft conviction? Because of the increasing enforcement focus on felons-in-possession and on reentry offenses, growing numbers of offenders are being prosecuted under such statutes.

While judges and, in some cases, prosecutors will make charging and sentencing decisions based on their assessment of the public threat such individuals pose, such ad hoc decision making is discretionary, often impressionistic, and potentially decreases the deterrent value of such sanctions. More importantly, judges lack the authority to depart in some cases, especially when mandatory minimum sentences are involved. In those cases, the sole hope for proportionate punishment rests with the prosecution that makes the charging decisions. However, because of the Department of Justice's focus on reentry and felon-in-possession cases and their easy provability, such cases present a relatively straightforward way of boosting conviction figures.[15] For those reasons, administrative pressures may counsel against the exercise of discretion in individual cases.

A narrower drafting of collateral sanctions would allow for a more accurate public threat assessment once such sanctions are violated. Moreover, it would eliminate the need for individual discretion. This is particularly important in a climate where administrative pressures and rewards focus enforcement on the violation of collateral sanctions and the judiciary is unable to dispense individualized justice because of mandatory sentences and the restrictions of the federal sentencing guidelines.[16]

References

Aiken, Sharryn and Sheena Scott. 2000. "*Baker v. Canada (Minister of Citizenship and Immigration)* and the Rights of Children," *Journal of Law and Social Policy* 15: 211.

Baldwin, Carl R. 2003. "France's Immigration Reform Limits the 'Double Penalty' of Deportation After Time Served," at www.ilw.com.

Demleitner, Nora V. 2000. "Continuing Payment on One's Debt to Society: The German Model of Felon Disenfranchisement as an Alternative," *Minnesota Law Review* 84: 753–804.

Demleitner, Nora V. 2002. "'Collateral Damage': No Reentry for Drug Offenders," *Villanova Law Review* 47: 1027–54.

Fellner, Jamie and Marc Mauer. 1998. Human Rights Watch and the Sentencing Project. "Losing the Vote: The Impact of Felony Disenfranchisement Laws in the United States."

Ginkowski, Richard A. 2000. "Domestic Violence Misdemeanors: Firearms Prohibitions," *Criminal Justice* Winter: 59.

Janis, Mark W., Richard S. Kay, and Anthony W. Bradley. 2000. *European Human Rights Law: Text and Materials.* (2nd ed.). Oxford: Oxford University Press.

Maxfield, Linda Drazga. 2002. "Fiscal Year 2000 Update on Unlawful Entry Offenses," *Federal Sentencing Reporter* 14: 267–70.

Maxfield, Linda Drazga and Keri Burchfield. 2002. "Immigration Offenses Involving Unlawful Entry: Is Federal Practice Comparable Across Districts?," *Federal Sentencing Reporter* 14: 260–66.

Maxfield, Linda Drazga. 2003. Office of Policy Analysis. U.S. Sentencing Commission. "Final Report: Survey of Article III Judges on the Federal Sentencing Guidelines." at www.ussc.gov.

Montgomery, Pamela G. and Jeanne G. Chutuape. 1998. Office of General Counsel. U.S. Sentencing Commission. "Firearms: Selected Federal Statutes and Guideline Enhancements."

Nafziger, James A.R. and Michael Yimesgen. 2003. "The Effect of Expungement on Removability of Non-Citizens," *Michigan Journal of Law Reform* 36: 915–50.

Pals, Gregory J. 1998. "Judicial Review under 18 U.S.C. § 925(c): Abrogation Through Appropriations?," *Washington University Law Quarterly* 76: 1095–1119.

Travis, Jeremy. 2002. "Invisible Punishment: An Instrument of Social Exclusion." In *Invisible Punishment,* edited by Marc Mauer and Meda Chesney-Lind. New York: New Press: 15–36.

Travis, Jeremy, Amy L. Solomon, and Michelle Waul. 2001. "From Prison to Home: The Dimensions and Consequences of Prisoner Reentry." Urban Institute.

U.S. Department of Homeland Security. 2003a. Office of Immigration Statistics. *Yearbook of Immigration Statistics, 2002.* Washington, D.C.: U.S. Government Printing Office.

U.S. Department of Homeland Security. 2003b. "Protecting America's Children: Operation Predator; Secretary Ridge Announces Operation Predator."

U.S. Department of Justice. 1997. *U.S. Attorney's Manual,* Title 9, Criminal Resource Manual. at www.justice.gov/usao/eousa/foia_reading_room/usam/title9/crm00112.htm.

U.S. Department of Justice. 2003. "Attorney General Ashcroft Announces New Project Safe Neighborhood Records in Fighting Gun Crime." at www.usdoj.gov/opa/pr/2003/December/03_ag_685.htm.

Cases Cited

Baker v. Canada, [1999] SCR 817.

Dahlia v. France, 19 Feb 1998, Reports, 1998-I 76.

Ewing v. California, 538 US 11 (2003).

Fraternal Order of Police v. United States, 173 F3d 898 (DC Cir.), *cert. denied,* 528 US 428 (1999).

Matter of Rodriguez-Rodriguez, Int Dec 3411 (BIA 1999).

Matter of Small, Int Dec 3476 (BIA 2002).

Matter of Yanez, 23 I&N 390 (BIA 2002).

United States v. Atkins, 872 F2d 94 (4th Cir.), *cert. denied,* 493 US 836 (1989).

United States v. Banuelos-Rodriguez, 215 F. 3d 969 (9th Cir. 2000).

United States v. Bean, 537 US 71 (2002).

United States v. Bonnet-Grullon, 212 F3d 692 (2d Cir.), *cert. denied,* 531 US 911 (2000).

United States v. Gayle, 2003 U.S. App. LEXIS 26673 (2d Cir. 2004).

United States v. Lewis, 249 F3d 793 (8th Cir. 2001).

United States v. Saucedo-Patino, 358 F3d 790 (11th Cir. 2004).

United States v. VanLeer, 270 F Supp2d 1318 (D Utah 2003).

United States v. Winson, 793 F2d 754 (6th Cir. 1986).

Laws, Statutes, and Treaties Cited

18 U.S.C. §1326(b)(2).

2003 Federal Sentencing Guidelines Manual §2K2.1 (2003).

2003 Federal Sentencing Guidelines Manual §2L1.2 (2001, 2003).
Armed Career Criminal Act of 1984, codified at 18 U.S.C. §924.
European Convention on Human Rights, art 8.
Firearms Owners' Protection Act, codified at 18 U.S.C. §922.
Omnibus Crime Control and Safe Streets Act of 1968, codified at 18 U.S.C. § 921.
Violent Crime Control and Law Enforcement Act of 1994, Pub L No 103-322, Tit. XIII, 130001(b)(1)(A), 108 Stat 2023.

Endnotes

1. In this chapter I focus on "aggravated felonies." Even though they are not the only offenses making a noncitizen deportable, conviction of such felonies has the most dramatic consequences.
2. See, e.g., Matter of Yanez, 23 I&N 390 (BIA 2002); Matter of Rodriguez-Rodriguez, Int Dec 3411 (BIA 1999); Matter of Small, Int Dec 3476 (BIA 2002) (misdemeanor sexual abuse of a minor is an aggravated felony).
3. Legislation pending in the House of Representatives would substantially undermine even these limited protections.
4. While such allegations are frequently heard, including in congressional testimony, it is often difficult to track an offender's criminal record abroad. For that reason, the federal sentencing guidelines, for example, do not factor foreign criminal convictions directly into the calculation of an offender's criminal history, though they may be considered for departure purposes.
5. A critique of the definition of public safety as limited to the territory of the United States is beyond the scope of this chapter.
6. See, e.g., *Ewing v. California*, 538 US 11 (2003) (upholding California's Three-Strikes Law against an Eighth Amendment challenge).
7. For further information on Operation Predator, see www.dhs.gov.
8. It is unclear what impact recent congressional legislation mandating the U.S. Sentencing Commission to limit downward departures and the Department of Justice's restrictions on fast-track programs will have on these types of cases in border districts.
9. Unless the sentence imposed was longer than 13 months, in which case the maximum enhancement of 16 points applies.
10. State interference with family life is permitted if it "is in accordance with the law and is necessary in a democratic society in the interests of national security, public safety or the economic well-being of the country, for the prevention of disorder or crime, for the protection of health or morals, or for the protection of the rights and freedoms of others" (European Convention on Human Rights art. 8(2)).
11. 18 U.S.C. §921(a)(20)(B) (2003). The federal courts are split as to whether foreign convictions are covered under 18 U.S.C. §922(g). Compare *United States v. Ingram* 2003 (Canadian felony conviction does not qualify under felon-in-possession statute) with *United States v. Winson* 1986 and *United States v. Atkins* 1989.
12. For further discussion of domestic violence prohibitions, see www.atf.treas.gov/core/firearms/information/domes.htm. See also *Fraternal Order of Police v. United States* 1990.
13. The data are available on the TRAC Web site, which is managed by Syracuse University, trac.syr.edu/tracatf/trends/current/leadchgX.html.
14. For further information on the project, see www.psn.gov.
15. Some districts intentionally increase the investigation and prosecution of felon-in-possession cases when conviction numbers appear low.
16. Even though VanLeer 2004 was decided after Congress passed the so-called Feeney amendment, which limits downward departures, many other district judges may feel intimidated departing downward in a climate where Congress is likely to scrutinize their actions.

12

Lawyering at the Margins: Collateral Civil Penalties at the Entry and Completion of the Criminal Sentence

LUCIAN E. FERSTER AND SANTIAGO AROCA

One summer in the 1950s, in upstate New York, a boy named Lucian and his parents stayed in a house on a hill above a large swamp, known only as "the Bog." From the first day, there were parental warnings, "Stay away from the Bog." When the boy asked why, the response was always, "The Bog is a dangerous place." And, when he responded with yet another "why," his father's answer was something like, "It is easy to go down to the Bog and it is easy to get in there but it is hard to get out of the Bog. Many a little boy has been lost in that swamp." Of course, on his first opportunity, tempted by the chorus of bullfrogs, Lucian went down the gently sloping hill to explore the Bog. No "Posted: No Trespassing" or "Keep Out" signs greeted him. Unwisely, he chose the late afternoon to scout the swamp and, true to the warnings, he got lost. The rapid descent of darkness, compounded by an immediate loss of direction, led to a nasty couple of hours during which he was forced to tromp through mud until he found his way out. Once the boy came home muddy, covered with mosquito bites, and the stink of skunk cabbage in his nose, he had learned a bit about places where it is easy to enter but difficult to exit. He had also learned a thing or two about warnings.

Collateral civil penalties, or sanctions, are like that swamp: murky and unpleasant, and a place no one wants to be. It is a simple matter to enter the swamp of collateral sanctions; at the time of entry, it may seem to be a good idea. Exit may be difficult if not impossible. Moreover, warnings, although vague, are easily ignored and are rarely posted at the actual point of entry.

All collateral consequences are triggered by criminal convictions bestowed in one place only, a court of law, and usually by means of a plea agreement. When criminal convictions are meted out, procedures are followed, and constitutionally mandated due process rights are observed. Defense lawyers and judges have a clear duty to instruct defendants of the direct criminal penalties triggered by a conviction. However, it is clear that under Florida law defendants who plead guilty do not have to be warned, or even be made aware, of future collateral sanctions triggered by a plea agreement. It seems that the cornerstones of procedural fairness—the right to a fair hearing and the right to prior notice—do not apply.

For example, in Florida, the law mandates that civil rights, including voting rights, shall be permanently revoked upon a felony conviction and an adjudication of guilt.[1] The transformation from "full citizen" to "citizen with limited rights" usually happens to the accused without his or her knowledge. The right to vote is removed automatically by operation of law, yet it is considered a collateral, not a direct, result of a criminal conviction. Thus, there is no duty for a judge or a lawyer to warn a defendant. As a result, criminal defendants most often enter the swamp of collateral sanctions ill-advised and under stressful conditions.

If collateral sanctions, or consequences, are so burdensome, then why do criminal defendants submit themselves to these consequences? The short answer is that criminal justice systems require it. The efficiency, and even the survival, of criminal justice systems demands that defendants regularly accept negotiated plea settlements. If criminal defendants clearly understood the future collateral sanctions at the time of pleading guilty, then they would agree to negotiated pleas less frequently, or less readily. And, if fewer pleas were taken, or if they were taken more slowly, the machinery of justice might overheat and falter. Collateral sanctions are a murky and unpleasant surprise that are hidden until most defendants leave the courtroom. How do criminal defendants get caught in the swamp? And how do they get out?

This chapter is a study in two parts. The first part, Entry, is a general look at the courtroom dynamics of plea taking. Written by Lucian Ferster, a public defender, this part outlines the practical considerations and expectations that shape the plea-bargaining process and, hence, the application of collateral civil penalties. The second part, Exit, is written by Santiago Aroca, a critical journalist. It is a study of one defendant's nearly impossible struggle to exit the morass, a task reminiscent of Franz Kafka's *The Trial*. Focusing on the South Florida family of Chris di Franco's, it documents the long-term consequences of collateral civil penalties and the difficulties involved in efforts to undo them.

Part One—The Entry: From Citizen to Felon

Practical Considerations of Guilty Pleas

Examining collateral criminal sanctions in a criminal courtroom is much like examining a vacuum: the center is static and empty. All of the observable and meaningful phenomena take place outside the vacuum. Within criminal courtrooms, the majority of criminal cases are settled by plea agreements, which result in criminal convictions. Before the conviction, and outside the courtroom, someone formulated collateral penalties. After the conviction, and again outside the courtroom, someone—perhaps a bureaucrat or an election official—will enforce collateral penalties. But within the courtroom, at the time of pleading guilty, there is a procedural vacuum: almost no one discusses or seriously contemplates collateral sanctions.

Practical Considerations: How and Why Plea Agreements Occur

The collateral consequences of criminal convictions are generally functionally meaningless to the accused, particularly the indigent, at the time of conviction. This is not to say that the consequences are *actually* meaningless but that other priorities are more pressing. In the negotiations and attorney/client discussions that lead up to a guilty plea, future collateral consequences are little considered because direct criminal sanctions are *the* issue. Criminal sanctions, at this point, are urgent and concrete; collateral sanctions are abstract and seem far off in the future. In the struggle between the concrete and the abstract, the concrete wins the day.

Let us understand what happens in a courtroom. Under Florida criminal procedure rules, prosecutors must file formal felony charges at the arraignment, usually twenty-one days after the arrest. A large number of defendants take pleas at the arraignment. In fact, the majority of nonserious or nonviolent crimes are pled at arraignment, particularly if the defendant has not been "habitualized" or deemed a repeat offender under Florida's many enhancement statutes. This transition from a plea of not guilty at arraignment to a plea of guilty a few minutes later takes place quickly, under pressure and with a minimum exchange of important information.

Why Accept a Plea?: Factors That Motivate the Accused to Plead Guilty

Four main considerations bear upon criminal defendants considering a guilty plea early in the pendency of a case. Those considerations are present incarceration, risk of conviction at trial, the "hassle factor," and expectations of justice.

Present Incarceration

At arraignment, a defendant is either in jail or out of jail. If a defendant has been able to afford bail (or be accepted into a pretrial monitoring program), he may enter the court through the front door wearing clean clothes and be free to sit with the public. However, if unable to produce bail (for instance, because he is indigent or is charged with a serious felony), a defendant must enter the courtroom through the "secure" door wearing a musty jail jumpsuit. He will be seated in the jury box wearing handcuffs. For lawyers and defendants contemplating a plea at this early stage of the process, the much-quoted axiom is simple and brutal: "if a defendant is in jail, he wants to get out; if he is out of jail, he wants to stay out."

The mandate for early pleas is clear. First, judicial efficiency demands that the court settle a great many cases by pleas at arraignment. Without early pleas, the machinery of justice would falter: courtrooms would slow down and judges, lawyers, and staff members alike would overheat. Second, in order to settle cases early, the system must offer an incentive to the accused. The incentive is always a low and attractive early plea offer. Such offers are termed, in the parlance of retail sales, "blue light specials," or, in the parlance of home buying, "pre-construction bargains." Although much maligned, "plea bargains" persist because they are, in fact, bargains and because they benefit all: the defendant, the prosecutor, and the court itself.

If a defendant is in jail—and the plea will get him out—the defendant will almost always accept the plea. In fact, he will demand to take the plea. Consideration of the other factors—risk, hassle, or even justice—will be quickly dismissed. An admission of guilt will be overwhelmingly attractive if it provides liberation from jail, even if the agreement calls for probation or even house arrest. Who can refute this logic? Certainly not a defense lawyer who woke up in a soft bed that morning. The term *plea of convenience* is not a legal fiction; rather, it is a reality, if not a necessity. An admission to questionable facts that perhaps could not be proven at trial and a future exposure to collateral consequences are both meaningless if the jailhouse door swings open.

If, by the time of arraignment, a defendant has gotten out of jail, the plea dynamic changes. If the charge is not a serious felony and if a defendant is not burdened with a bad criminal record, then a plea of credit for time already served, probation, or house arrest may be offered. The chances are great that the accused will accept the plea offer. Here the risk factor, the hassle factor, and the justice expectation factor come into play.

Risk of Conviction at Trial

While contemplating a plea offer, defendants must weigh their risks. Defense lawyers have a legal and humane duty to explain that, if there is a trial, and if the jury finds the defendant guilty, then jail or prison will be the likely postconviction penalty. Judges, particularly, with one eye fixed on their caseloads, like to make this fact clear when a defendant rejects a plea offer at arraignment. At this point, a criminal defendant is seated uncomfortably on the horns of a nasty dilemma: to take the present offer (which may be taken off the table), with its relatively mild sanctions, or to demand a trial and risk incarceration. The practical consideration of risk, and its attendant fear, often overshadows all other considerations.

Hassle Factor
The hassle factor is also compelling at the time that an early plea is offered. Insightful defendants will ask, "How many times will I have to come back to court on this matter?" The defense attorney's honest answer may be something like, "You'll first have to make an appointment to come see me, then you will come back to court four or five times, and, yes, I am going to send you all the deposition transcripts. I want you to read them, and then, right before your trial, you will need to spend several hours in my office while we prepare." Translation: major hassle. The simple hassle factor is often sufficient motivation to "get it over with today," without further effort and loss of time.

Expectations of Justice
Finally, for a defendant to resist the temptations of an early plea, he must possess a high expectation of justice. To reject a mild plea offer and demand a trial, the accused must believe that our system of justice, and all its elements, can actually produce Justice. There is nothing more heartbreaking for a criminal lawyer, particularly a public defender, than to review a new and perfectly defensible case at arraignment and then discuss options with a new client who has no faith in the outcome. The lack of faith takes many forms. Alienation is one: "The criminal justice system will never do *me* any good," is often heard. Or, lawyers (particularly public defenders) being too inept or overburdened to really fight is another faithless attitude. Or, having a criminal record already, criminal defendants often feel that the court and "the system" will automatically convict. This thought (which is rooted in collateral sanctions) has a ring of truth to it. These attitudes can be overcome and a defendant can be aided in his quest for Justice, but this takes time and certain social skills that attorneys often lack.

Where, in all of this, is the consideration of possible collateral consequences of a plea agreement? They are not greatly considered. And why should they be? They are abstractions. How often, in a crowded, hurried, confusing, and hostile courtroom will legal abstractions withstand practical scrutiny? At the early stages of a criminal case, the main party—the defendant—wants out as quickly, as cheaply, and as painlessly as possible.

In such a mind-set, the direct consequences are more than enough to consider; the abstract collateral consequences, no matter how clearly explained, appear inconsequential. For a large portion of defendants who plead guilty early in the pendency of their cases, the collateral consequences of felony convictions are a dirty little secret: they are little addressed by judges and defense attorneys and they are little considered by defendants themselves.

There is a final courtroom scenario: serious cases that linger in the court system. In the case of defendants charged with serious crimes, or defendants who have extensive criminal records, the dynamic changes. In this situation, a defendant is almost always incarcerated while awaiting trial, and, unless a jury totally acquits, he will face substantial posttrial incarceration. Now the accused's expectations of justice, balanced against the risk of prison, are the prime considerations. Collateral consequences become almost meaningless in the light of the seriousness of the situation.[2]

Softening the Blow: Adjudication of Guilt

In Florida, civil rights will be revoked upon conviction of a felony and an adjudication of guilt. To some degree, adjudication of guilt is a matter of judicial discretion. Generally speaking, in Florida state courts in the Miami-Dade Circuit, judges generally withhold adjudication for the first conviction only. By statute, adjudication can only be withheld if an accused is sentenced to probation or house arrest rather than jail or prison (Florida Rules of Criminal Procedure 3.670). From time to time, judges may withhold adjudication of guilt for a second time if a previous withhold was granted in the distant past.[3] If a defendant is placed on probation and if he violates the terms of probation and the probation is revoked, he must be adjudicated guilty, thus losing civil rights (Florida Rules of Criminal Procedure, 3.790(b)). During the plea negotiations and colloquy, neither the court nor defense counsel has the duty to notify defendants of the potential collateral consequence—an adjudication of guilt—upon violation and revocation of guilt. Even though a judge may grant a withhold of adjudication, collateral consequences, notably immigration consequences, may take effect.

Notification: Who Has a Duty to Tell What to Whom

"You all took away my right to vote, and you never even told me," exclaimed a disgruntled former client, one day following the 2000 presidential elections. Defendants generally will hear precious little concerning collateral consequences. Neither judge nor counsel has a binding obligation to inform the accused of many material consequences before or during plea colloquies. Hence, defendants who face overpowering reasons to plead guilty early in the case are generally little advised of future collateral sanctions. Defendants who pay for and seek advice from paid counsel generally receive more instruction about unseen consequences. A defendant who retains private counsel is usually not indigent, and is apt to be employed and aware of employment-related licensing, testing, or other scrutiny. Conversely, indigent defendants, represented by a public defender, generally are less instructed in collateral consequences. This is due to several factors: public defender clients are more likely to be unemployed (or marginally employed); they are more likely to have already been convicted and adjudicated guilty; and public defenders, usually assigned the majority of a court's cases, often operate under oppressive time restraints when directed to convey plea offers the day of a client's arraignment.

Notification: Legal Considerations

Florida judges and lawyers have a limited duty to notify defendants of collateral consequences at the time of plea. Florida law, following federal case law, requires a showing that a plea was entered into "intelligently and voluntarily" (*Boykin v. Alabama*).

The Florida Supreme Court further addressed the rights at stake in the plea process in 1993 (*Ashley v. State*). The term *knowing and intelligent* was used and further clarified as follows: "In keeping with *Boykin*, this Court has ruled that in order for a plea to be knowing and intelligent the defendant must understand the *reasonable consequences* of the plea (Id. at 488; emphasis added). Thus, the trial judge is required to inform a defendant only of the direct consequences of a plea. A direct consequence is one that has a "definite, immediate and largely automatic effect on the range of the defendant's punishment" (*Zambuto v. State*).

The collateral sanctions triggered by a guilty plea have been held to be beyond the pale of reasonable consequences; thus, no warnings need be administered by a judge during a plea colloquy. In 1987, the Florida Supreme Court found that "[i]t is clear under both state and federal decisions that the trial court judge is under no duty to inform a defendant of the collateral consequences of his guilty plea" (*State v. Ginebra*). Florida District Courts of Appeal have consistently followed this thinking (see *State v. Fox; Bethune v. State*).

The Florida Rules of Criminal Procedure, in effect since 1977, prescribe the content of a judge's plea colloquy (*Florida Bar, re Florida Rules of Criminal Procedure*). Rule 3.172 calls for a judge to be assured that a defendant understands the following: 1) the charges and penalty; 2) the defendant has a right to counsel; 3) that he has a right to a trial, with all its procedural safeguards, and competent counsel; 4) that he is giving up his appellate rights; 5) the plea will end the proceedings; 6) the plea colloquy, taken under oath, may be later used against the defendant in a perjury proceeding; and 7) that the defendant understands "[t]he complete terms of any plea agreement, including specifically all obligations the defendant will incur as a result" (Id., at 1255).

The 1977 version of the Rules made no mention of collateral consequences or sanctions—not even immigration. Eleven years later, the Florida Supreme Court held that judges still had no duty to notify of immigration consequences and that a plea may be considered to be knowing and voluntary although a defendant was *not* instructed by counsel that the plea might result in deportation (*Ginebra*, at 961–62).

In 1988 the Court, belatedly, disregarded its previous ruling in *Ginebra* and adopted the following amendment to Rule 3.172:

> (c)(viii) That if he or she pleads guilty or *nolo contrendere*, the trial judge must inform him or her that, if he or she is not a United States citizen, the plea may subject him or her to deportation pursuant to the laws and regulations governing the United States Naturalization and Immigration Service. It shall not be necessary for the trial judge to inquire as to whether the defendant is a United States citizen, as this admonition shall be given to all defendants in all cases (*In re Amendments to Florida Rules of Criminal Procedure*).

Apart from this amendment, the Rule has not been further expanded in the quarter century since it was drafted.

Notification: Immigration Consequences

Of all collateral consequences, the fear of deportation (or the withholding of resident status or citizenship) is the most frequently addressed by defendants. In Miami, a city of immigrants from mostly poor or turbulent nations, "immigration" consequences are genuine consequences. Unlike other collateral consequences, they are often raised by defendants themselves, long before a judge refers to them in a plea colloquy. Like most collateral consequences, it is unclear from the standpoint of the courtroom at plea time what future sanctions the U.S. government will apply in any particular situation. Good practice dictates that a defendant should expect the worst.[4] Good practice also dictates that criminal defense attorneys must discuss immigration consequences, assess the risks, and search for possible alternative remedies to pleading guilty.

Most criminal defense attorneys, both private and government paid, are sadly uninformed regarding the changing and murky rules and procedure of immigration law. Uninformed, but still wise, criminal defense lawyers know enough to counsel that the INS (now absorbed into the Department of Homeland Security) or, more simply, *la migra*, will probably do great harm sometime in the future. Perhaps that is enough for the defense to know as a safe rule of thumb. Foreseeing future immigration consequences, defendant and lawyer have four strategic choices: try the case and win, opt for a diversion program, negotiate the actual charges, or take the plea and hope for the best.

Trying the Case: This, of course is the most risky of options. The outcome will never be clear till the jury speaks. The facts, the quality of lawyers, the law, the composition of the jury, and the vagaries of Lady Justice all will determine the trial's outcome.

Diversion Programs: In Florida's 11th Judicial Circuit (Miami-Dade County) there are several diversion programs that allow for the case to be *nolle prosequi*, or dropped after completion. Only the Office of the State Attorney can approve entry. Once the case has been dropped, there are no immigration consequences. The programs are intelligent alternatives, but entry requirements are strict. These programs merit a brief description, as follows.

Drug Court: Florida's 11th Circuit is blessed with an innovative, rigorous, and effective "drug court." If a defendant is charged with a narcotics case (possession or purchase only), and if he has no prior drug convictions, he can enter a year-long drug program. During the year the defendant reports to a special judge who monitors, encourages, and cajoles on a regular basis. If successful, defendants "graduate" from this special court at the end of the year and the prosecution will drop the case.

Pretrial Intervention: Pretrial Intervention (PTI) is a program, administered by a nongovernmental agency, which accepts people charged with certain crimes. Unfortunately, the doorway is a narrow one. Only first offenders are accepted. No drug charges are accepted. Usually only nonviolent charges are accepted. Property crimes where the amount of restitution is less than $5,000 are accepted. Pretrial Intervention, which charges a fee, often requires payment of restitution, community service hours, and/or an appropriate instruction such as a parenting course or anger management classes. Defendants, upon completing PTI requirements, return to court for one final hearing in which the prosecution "speaks Latin," announcing a *nolle prosequi*.

Firearms Intervention Program: The Firearms Intervention Program (FIP) is run by the State Attorney's Office and a local nongovernmental agency. Defendants must pay a hefty fee. The only defendants admitted are those who are charged with carrying a concealed firearm. Only people who have never been arrested before are accepted and the person must be gainfully employed. The FIP requires that defendants take a course and obtain a Florida permit to carry a concealed firearm. Upon completion, the prosecution will drop the case. By and large, the program is offered only when a defendant is actually employed in, or has concrete plans to enter, the field of security work.

Negotiate the Actual Charge: In rare cases, usually involving minor and nonviolent crimes, defense attorneys may negotiate the criminal charge so that the defendant pleads guilty to a revised and lesser charge in order to avoid immigration consequences. Only certain "aggravated" crimes or "crimes of moral turpitude" seem to alert the immigration authorities. If the offending charges can be substituted by negotiation, the defense lawyer has served his client masterfully. Usually this is only done where the defendant presents compelling equities: for example, he is a first time offender, a student, is supporting family members, or has escaped gross injustice in the home country. Unfortunately, the list of "aggravated" crimes or "crimes of moral turpitude" is depressingly long and fluid. Before negotiating the charges, it is wise to consult with a well-informed immigration lawyer to learn which criminal charges are currently benign in the eyes of the Department of Homeland Security.

Take the Plea and Hope for the Best: All too frequently, defendants and lawyers take this choice, hoping that the immigration authorities will never get around to seeking deportation. This is particularly true with noncitizen defendants born in Cuba; they know that the United States will not deport them under the current political situation. Miami's many Central American and Caribbean immigrants have no such choice.

Occasionally, under threat of deportation, defendants return to the original criminal court years later with an immigration attorney in tow and attempt to revoke the original plea agreement in hopes of reversing the conviction. The only permissible legal grounds are that during the original plea, the defendant was uninformed or misinformed of the (now pressing) immigration consequences. In such instances, judges usually order production of the original plea colloquy's transcript. If no transcript can be produced, judges may be forced to revoke the plea agreement. Upon revocation, all parties are left with an open case that is years old with unavailable witnesses and destroyed police reports. In this rare situation, prosecutors may be forced to drop the original charges. Thus, the lucky defendant's record is clean and the threat of his deportation eliminated.

Notification: Enhanced Penalties, Present and Future.
Cases addressing mandatory or enhanced sentences under Florida's complex habitualization statutes have held that with *future* enhancements predicated upon the current sentence follow federal decisions, there is no duty to notify (*United States v. Wood*; see also *Rhodes v. State*). An attorney's failure to notify the accused of potential future enhanced sentences is not subject to future claims of ineffective assistance of counsel; lack of knowledge

will not render a plea involuntary (see *Sherwood v. State*). The only concrete sentencing notifications that must be made by judge and lawyer are in regards to the maximum possible penalty provided by law and the effect of any mandatory minimum penalty provided by law (*Ashley v. State*).

Notification: Sexual Crimes, the Predators, and the Indefinitely Incarcerated

The same analysis holds true for defendants convicted of sexual crimes. Statutorily mandated consequences have been held as "collateral" even though they appear to be automatic requirements that will have a direct future effect upon the liberty of the convicted felon. The lifelong mandatory duty to register as a sexual offender need not be explained at the time of plea because it "is a collateral consequence of the plea, and therefore failure to inform the defendant of that requirement before he entered the plea does not render the plea involuntary (*State v. Partlow*).

Thus, the plea will not be vulnerable to later attacks on ineffective assistance of counsel claims. However, there are limits. If a defendant is misled by counsel as to whether the defendant will be subject to collateral consequences, then the plea agreement can be revoked or, at the least, an evidentiary hearing should be conducted to determine whether, and to what degree, he was misled. "The failure of the trial court or counsel to advise the defendant of a collateral consequence does not render the plea involuntary and does not provide a basis on which to withdraw the plea. However, affirmative misadvice about a collateral consequence of a plea provides a basis on which to withdraw the plea (*Gunn v. State*).

Florida, as well as many other states, provides for indefinite civil commitment of certain sexual predators. Likewise, it has been held that failure of the trial court and counsel to advise of that consequence did not render the plea involuntary or provide a basis on which to withdraw the plea. However, if trial counsel in error advised the defendant that he would be released almost immediately after pleading guilty, the defendant may be entitled to withdraw his plea (*Waterous v. State*). So it would appear that a defense lawyer has no real duty to inform the accused of a collateral consequence, but there is a duty to not *misinform* a client.

Efficiency vs. Justice: The Practical vs. the Ideal

Our criminal justice system, overloaded and ill-funded on the state level, has created a safety valve: plea bargains early in the pendency of cases. These pleas have become a systemic survival tool from which the system and all its participants reap benefits. Early pleas, particularly for the indigent, are contemplated and taken under real pressure to hurry and "take the opportunity to get it over with before the prosecutor (or judge) takes the deal off the table." Early pleas are often forged within an overheated crucible where factors of incarceration, risk assessment, practicalities, and faith in our justice system are weighed. Often, in haste, in fear, or in resignation, pleas are taken, rights are relinquished, and unforeseen collateral consequences are triggered.

Collateral consequences are rarely mentioned when early pleas are taken. If defendants were to be fully informed of future collateral sanctions, they might accept fewer early pleas or defendants might ask more time-consuming questions. If more questions were asked, no one could accurately answer them because collateral consequences are largely future-oriented, hidden, and unforeseeable. Fewer early pleas, more questions, and answers that might be subject to later legal challenges all would burden the engine of justice, not lighten its load. The law seems to have realized this fact, and thus courts have consistently ruled that neither judge nor lawyer has much duty to explain or even to forewarn of collateral sanctions.

Is this justice? Clearly it is not Justice, the *capital-J* justice of our ideals. What has developed is a practical, unattractive, and often unfair "system" that keeps the criminal justice system functioning. In Florida we all are complicit in the revocation of our fellow citizens' right to vote, as well as other important rights and opportunities, *without even informing the accused that we know it will happen!* What could be done to change this? Money would be a start. Criminal justice systems should not be starved so that they must make such drastic compromises. Moreover, courts should have the ability to create more diversionary programs that would be more accessible and more effective. Such programs would allow more minor offenders a side door out of the courthouse and out of the conundrum of early pleas for safety and convenience. Finally, Florida, and the few other southern states that have retained their permanent civil rights revocation statutes for felons, should adopt notions of justice, fairness, and decency more advanced than the 19th century, postbellum, Jim Crow rationale that entrenched felon disenfranchisement so long ago (see Goodnough 2004).

Part Two—The Exit: The Story of Chris di Franco's Restoration of Civil Rights

When U.S. District Judge Michael Moore sentenced Chris di Franco to a $50 fine and 5 years' worth of probation for possession of contraband, nobody in that Miami courtroom told him that he would be stripped of his civil rights for life, including the rights to vote and to hold professional licenses in Florida. Presently, some 600,000 Floridians are in that situation and thousands more join their ranks every year.[5] In a recently published study, two legal experts calculated a higher figure; according to them, on December 31, 2000 there were 827,207 disenfranchised citizens in Florida, or 7.03% of the voting-age population.[6]

Chris di Franco, a 49-year-old contractor, was indicted in 1993 as result of a federal investigation that had begun in 1985. In 1995, he pleaded guilty to conspiring to import marijuana, but he avoided jail time because he had no prior convictions and only a minor role in ground transportation of marijuana. "I admit I did wrong," says Chris di Franco, "I pleaded guilty and I told the judge I was sorry for what I had done. So when in 1995 the judge sentenced me to 5 years' probation, it was my understanding that my punishment would end in the year 2000. I thought that everybody felt the same way in the courtroom, including the judge, but it turned out that everybody was wrong because I was punished for life. As I would learn later on, in the year 2000, I had lost my civil rights and, unless I was willing to spend tremendous amounts of money and time to walk trough an extremely complicated administrative process to restore it, I would never recover them."

Chris di Franco lives in North Miami, Florida, with his wife and two cats, and he compares his fight to have his civil rights restored with the fight of an explorer against a huge snake that is entangled around his body and about to devour him. For Chris di Franco, to strip former felons of their civil rights is one of the reasons that explain the high rates of recidivism among Florida's inmates.

"I want to be clear that when I say that felons are stripped of their civil rights for life," he emphasizes, "I don't mean only the right to vote, I mean every civil right, including the right to be eligible to hold a professional license in a profession regulated by the State, as roofer, plumber, barber, or funeral embalmer. I don't understand, I don't know what kind of damage a felon can inflict upon a cold body but I have seen that when you do your time, in prison or in probation, nobody wants to hire you. So the only way to make a honest living is to buy some tools and start working yourself as contractor but the State comes and tells you, you can't. So to me it is a mystery why the State spends money teaching felons basic skills in plumbing or electrical engineering in its prisons to deny them a license to practice those skills when they have done their time and are out of prison. How are people supposed to make an honest living out of prison if they cannot work?"

That is a question that is not answered by either the Florida Constitution or the state statutes. Chris, like thousands of Floridians every single year, fell into a legal quagmire.[7] Chris had received a building contractor's license in 1993 and had renewed it annually. "Financially, I wasn't doing real well, so I went to work for a contractor in South Beach for over five years as project manager," he says. "I didn't need to be licensed. I maintained the license for two years but didn't use it. One year when the application came, we put it on inactive status." He shakes his head: "Big mistake. Big mistake. If I had known what you have to go through to reactivate it. . . ."

At the time of signing his plea, Chris di Franco did not know that in Florida, the application forms to every professional licensed by the State require an answer to the following question: "Have you been convicted or found guilty of, or entered a plea of *nolo contendere* (regardless of adjudication) of any crime (other than a traffic violation)?"[8] A positive answer carries a denial of the State license, under the pertinent statutory authority that says that grounds for sanction are to have been "convicted or found guilty of, or entering a plea of *nolo contendere* to, regardless of adjudication, a crime in any jurisdiction which relates to the practice of, or the ability to practice, a licensee's profession."[9] Furthermore, the prohibition from holding licenses applies to anyone who has been adjudicated guilty of any crime, even when the crime is not related in any manner to the licensed profession, and the sanction applies to almost every imaginable profession. The Florida Administrative Code provides a long list of professional activities regulated under these strict rules.[10] The reinstatement of civil rights is the only remedy available to those who are disenfranchised in Florida.

Chris di Franco discovered it the day he visited the Miami office of the Florida Department of Business and Professional Regulations. "I went there to have my license restored and several days later, I received a letter telling me that to get my license back I would have to restore my civil rights, and therefore I was not going to be eligible unless I had completed the clemency process," he remembers. Di Franco says that, at that time, it did not look like a very difficult process. Just some days later, he changed his opinion and realized that he was facing an almost insurmountable obstacle. Di Franco called his probation officer and was told that only the Governor, acting with the consent of his Cabinet, could restore his civil rights and the starting point was to fill in Application Form ADM 151A. "It looked quite simple, I believed it was going to be a couple of weeks. Not so," he says. "I mailed my application to the Governor's Office of Executive Clemency in Tallahassee but the office sent it back because I did not attach a copy of my release from the Probation Board. I obtained the certificate, sent it back to Tallahassee and then I received a letter telling me that my case had been assigned to two state agencies, the Investigative Division of the Office of Clemency Administration and the Florida Parole Commission. Both agencies were supposed to review the merits of my application. Then, I realized that the system is crazy: a $50 fine and 5 years of probation had deprived me of my civil rights that only could be restored by the Governor himself, with the consent of his Cabinet members and after my case had been reviewed by several state agencies and dozens of state officers! For God's sake, isn't it insane?"

The process was not supposed to be so complex and, in fact, there is a discretionary simpler and quicker procedure when a felon qualifies for "Restoration of Civil Rights Without a Hearing. . . ."[11] But, as di Franco learned, that provision is rarely applied because the members of the Governor's Cabinet[12] have discretion to object to the restoration without a hearing and their staff members do it by default.[13] Since the default objection process was initiated, Florida has accumulated a backlog of cases. In 1986, when it was common to get restoration without a hearing, 15,000 Floridians recovered their civil rights. In contrast, in 2000, when the objection by default started, the number of restorations went down to 927, although that year more than 15,000 people were released from prisons or ended their parole terms (see *Florida Executive Clemency Report of 2001*).

"Of course, my petition was objected to, so yes, I received a letter saying that I had to go to a hearing in Tallahassee too. Also the letter said that my presence there, at a date that would be notified later on, was compulsory. But before the hearing my record had to be checked and approved by the Investigative Division of the Florida Parole Commission, which in due time would contact me," di Franco says.

Weeks passed by. Di Franco needed his contractor's license to work, but nobody contacted him. "We, my wife and I, decided to be proactive. So we started calling and found what officer was in charge of my file. We called him. He confirmed us that he had received the file and assigned it the number 72. Well, we called him one week later, it was still number 72. We called him once a week for six months, it was number 72 always. It wasn't moving," he says.

One year later, it was still number 72 yet and di Franco did not want to work as an unlicensed contractor. "I knew that if I was caught, I would risk jail time, but I wanted my life back. I felt that I had paid my debt to society. So I wrote to my Parole Commission officer telling him that after one year in the process, I was getting nowhere and asking him what to do." The answer was a total surprise. "I got a letter saying that I had to start all over again. Attached to the letter, I found a 12 page application form."

Di Franco displays a copy of that form. Among the inquiries were the addresses, phone numbers, and occupations of siblings; age at which moved from parents' home; information on parents, including, if deceased, by what cause; children "born out of wedlock;" a complete marital history; and financial disclosures that exceeded those required for most mortgage loans. "I'm sorry, but if your parents die or you have a stepbrother, what relevancy does that have to clemency," Chris wonders.[14] He continued to wait but his wife, Robin, became impatient and began contacting friends and groups such as the ACLU. The Miami chapter of the ACLU agreed to help them and pushed forward his application for restoration. Through the calls the di Francos knew that they would eventually get a hearing. Finally, almost three years after initiating the process, the letter arrived. "We were notified that we had a hearing in Tallahassee." But through the network of friends they were unofficially informed that Chris's application had been labeled as "unfavorable" by the Clemency Office staff. "Why? Because somebody at the Parole Commission or at the Department of Corrections, or who knows where, forgot to state that I had completed all my court-ordered courses, including drug counseling. So we had to find my probation officer and beg him to write a letter to the Commission stating that I had completed all the required counseling, including of course drug counseling," di Franco remembers.

The anticipated day came and the di Francos bought plane tickets—around $500—and rented a car—about $125—and booked a hotel—almost $75—and paid for other expenses—for a total of almost $1500. At eight o'clock on the morning of the indicated day, the di Francos were at the gates of the building that houses the Florida Clemency Board. "We gave our names and we were told that we were number 82 on line. Well, it wasn't too bad. The worst is that we found that I was still listed as 'unfavorable' for restoration," di Franco explains and continues, "once you're 'unfavorable,' it's up to you to prove yourself 'favorable.'" He planned his attack. He had prepared a speech but "by the time they called me and I was given the opportunity to speak for five minutes, I had seen that there is only one path to succeed before the commission, that (don't forget) is formed by the Governor, Jeb Bush, and his Cabinet. That path is to show remorse, play the Christian Born Again tune. So, I did. I made a remorseful confession and I pleaded for mercy. Jeb Bush granted it." Chris di Franco reapplied for his license and went back to roofing and other construction-related work. "It took me more than three years and cost about $4,000. I was lucky. I know people that hired lawyers and spent $25,000 and after 5 years they are still in the process," he says. As a souvenir, di Franco keeps in his office six cardboard boxes filled with copies of faxes and letters. "You know, in Florida if you are convicted, you will be banned for life, unless you beat the system. It should not be that way because my punishment was $50 and 5 years on probation. Why should I be banned for life? Well, I guess I had the opportunity to question the Governor but I did not. May be another time I will, next time he comes to Miami and asks for my vote."

References

Amendments to Florida Rules of Criminal Procedure: 536 So.2d 992,994 (Fla. 1988).
Executive Clemency Report: 2001
Florida Rules of Criminal Procedure: 1977
Garcia, Manny and Jason Grotto. 2004. "Justice Withheld," *Miami Herald,* 25 January.

Goodnough, Abby. 2004. "Disenfranchised Florida Felons Struggle to Regain Their Rights," *New York Times*, March 28:1.
Uggen, Christopher and Jeff Manza. 2002. "Democratic Contraction? Political Consequences of Felon Disenfranchisement in the United States," 67 *American Sociological Review* 777, 797.

Cases Cited

Ashley v. State, 614 So.2d 486 (Fla. 1993).
Bethune v. State, 774 So.2d 4 (Fla. 2nd DCA 2000).
Boykin v. Alabama, 395 U.S. 238 (1969).
Gunn v. State, 841 So. 2d 629, 631 (Fla. 3rd DCA 2003).
Johnson v. Bush, (2003).
Rhodes v. State, 701 So.2d 388 (Fla. 3d DCA 1997).
Sherwood v. State, 743 So2d 1196 (Fla. 4th DCA 1999).
State v. Fox, 659 So.2d 1324 (Fla. 3rd DCA 1995).
State v. Ginebra, 511 So.2d 960 (Fla. 1987).
State v. Partlow, 840 So.2d 1040 (Fla. 2003).
United States v. Wood, 879 F.2d 285 (5th Cir. 1989).
Waterous v. State, 793 So.2d 6 (Fla. 2nd DCA 2001).
Zambuto v. State, 413 So.2d 461, 462 (Fla. 4th DCA 1982).

Laws Cited

Beverage Law.
Florida Bar, re Florida Rules of Criminal Procedure 343 So.2d 1247 (Fla. 1977).
Florida RICO (Racketeer Influenced and Corrupt Organization) Act.
Florida Sexual Predators Act.
The Florida Voter Registration Act (2002).
Voting Rights Act.

Endnotes

1. Florida Constitution (1968) Art. VI Sec 4. "No person convicted of a felony, or adjudicated in this or any other state to be mentally incompetent, shall be qualified to vote or hold office until restoration of civil rights or removal of disability."
2. There is one occasional exception. From time to time in Miami a defendant will opt for a trial because the prospect of deportation, particularly to Haiti, is a *worse* outcome than going to state prison.
3. In response to a recent newspaper series published in the *Miami Herald*, judicial discretion may be further limited by the Florida Legislature. Some observers have found some judges to be overly liberal in granting withholds of adjudication as a plea bargaining tool. See Garcia and Grotto 2004.
4. The exception to this rule is Miami's sizable Cuban exile population. Due to the tortured history of U.S. and Cuban relations during the four decades since the Cuban Revolution, few Cubans have been deported. However, in the future this "Cuban exception" may disappear if the political and diplomatic climates change.
5. See *Johnson v. Bush*, 353 F.3d 1287 (11th Cir. 2003). In what probably is the most important litigation, in present times, of Florida's disenfranchisement, eight plaintiffs, who had been convicted of felonies but had successfully completed all terms of incarceration, probation, or parole, sued Governor Bush alleging discrimination and imposition of improper poll tax and wealth qualifications, in violation of First, Fourteenth, Fifteenth, and Twenty-fourth Amendments and the Voting Rights Act. The U.S. District Court dismissed the action and found in favor of defendants as a matter of law. The Eleventh Circuit reversed partially. Plaintiffs for this action provided the figure of 607,000, which has not been contested by the government).
6. Uggen and Manza (2002); see also their chapter herein. The 827,207 estimated figure includes 71,233 who were incarcerated, 131,186 who were on probation, 6,046 on parole, 5,228 jail inmates, and 613,514 ex-felons who have completed their sentence and supervision

requirements. Indeed, 17.65% of all disenfranchised ex-felons in the United States live in Florida, and that number is rapidly increasing. The racial impact is highly disproportionate: 256,392 of these disenfranchised felons (30.99%) are African-American, 16.02% of the African-American voting age population in Florida cannot vote as a result of felon disenfranchisement.

7. Article VI, section 4 of the Florida Constitution provides that "[n]o person convicted of a felony . . . shall be qualified to vote or hold office until restoration of civil rights. Two statutes repeat this prohibition on voting by convicted felons. The Florida Voter Registration Act, §97.041(2)(b), Fla. Stat. (2002), provides that "[a]person who has been convicted of any felony by any court of record and who has not had his or her right to vote restored pursuant to law" is not entitled to register and vote even if otherwise qualified. Section 944.292(1), Fla. Stat. (2002), states that "[u]pon conviction of a felony as defined in s. 10, Art. X, of the State Constitution, the civil rights of the person convicted shall be suspended in Florida until such rights are restored by a full pardon, conditional pardon or restoration of civil rights granted pursuant to s. 8, Art. IV of the State Constitution." Also, other statutes provide that convicted felons, "unless restored to civil rights," are disqualified from certain rights and responsibilities of citizenship, applying by their terms to "persons." See, for example, §40.01(2) and §40.07(1), F.S. ("No person" convicted of a felony is qualified to serve as a juror unless restored to civil rights); and 75.13(1) and (5) ("Any person" convicted of a felony in any Florida court must, within 48 hours after entering any county, register with the sheriff thereof unless, *inter alia*, the person has received a full pardon or his civil rights have been restored). See also 12.011(1)(a) and (b) ("A person" convicted of a felony or first degree misdemeanor may be denied certain described employment if the crime was "directly related" to the employment or to the occupation, trade, vocation, profession, or business for which a license, permit, or certificate is sought), and 61.15(2) (no license may be issued under the Beverage Law to "any person" convicted of any felony within the past 15 years in Florida, or of any offense designated a felony by any other state or by the United States).

8. Instructions for completing initial licensure and change of status application DBPR ALU 4052-1 (Board of Asbestos consultants) Accessible at: http://www.myflorida.com/dbpr (Last accessed February 2004).

9. Fla. Stat. §455.227. Grounds for discipline; penalties; enforcement (1) The following acts shall constitute grounds for which the disciplinary actions specified in subsection (2) may be taken: (c) Being convicted or found guilty of, or entering a plea of *nolo contendere* to, regardless of adjudication, a crime in any jurisdiction which relates to the practice of, or the ability to practice, a licensee's profession. The sanctions contemplated in subsection 2 are: (a) Refusal to certify, or to certify with restrictions, an application for a license. (b) Suspension or permanent revocation of a license. (c) Restriction of practice. (. . .) (g) Corrective action.

10. See Fla. Stat. Chap 455. "Business and Professional Regulation: General Provisions," which mentions expressly the following professions and activities: architects and interior design; asbestos; athlete agents; auctioneers; barbers; building code; community association managers; construction industry; cosmetology; electrical contractors; employee leasing; funeral directors; geologists; landscape architecture; pilots commissioners; pilotage rate review; surveyors and mappers; talent agencies; veterinary medicine; education and testing; alcoholic beverages and tobacco; boxing; certified public accounting; hotels and restaurants; land sales; condominiums and mobile homes; pari-mutuel wagering; real estate.

11. The Governor and the Cabinet establish and amend the Rules of Executive Clemency. Rule 9. A sets forth the criteria for restoration without hearings. To qualify the individual must meet: "1. No outstanding detainers or pending criminal charges, or terms of supervised release; 2. No outstanding pecuniary penalties or liabilities if such penalties or liabilities are attributed to victim restitution, including, but not limited to, restitution pursuant to a court order or civil judgment, or obligations pursuant to Chapter 960, Florida Statutes; 3. No conviction for a capital or life felony; 4. The Clemency Board has neither restored the individual's civil rights nor granted the individual a pardon within the past 10 years; 5. No declaration that the individual is (i) a Habitual Felony Offender, (ii) a Habitual Violent Felony Offender, (iii) a Three-time Violent Felony Offender, (iv) a Violent Career Criminal, as those terms are used in section 775.084, Florida Statutes, or (v) a Prison Release

Reoffender, as that term is used in section 775.082(9)(a); 6. No felony conviction involving (i) prosecution by the Office of Statewide Prosecution under section 16.56, Florida Statutes; (ii) prosecution under the Florida RICO (Racketeer Influenced and Corrupt Organization) Act, Chapter 895, Florida Statutes; (iii) trafficking or conspiracy to traffic in a controlled substance under section 893.135, Florida Statutes; (iv) crime described as a "dangerous crime" under section 907.041, Florida Statutes; (v) conspiracy to commit a crime of violence; (vi) lewd, lascivious, indecent, or unnatural acts under Chapter 800, Florida Statutes; (vii) crime that required registration under the Florida Sexual Predators Act, section 775.21, Florida Statutes; (viii) sexual battery under Chapter 794, Florida Statutes; (ix) battery, aggravated assault, or aggravated battery of a law enforcement officer, firefighter, emergency medical care agent, or other specified officer under section 784.07, Florida Statutes; (x) DUI manslaughter or DUI classified as a felony under section 316.193, Florida Statutes; (xi) homicide; (xii) public corruption or violations of election laws; or (xiii) crime committed by an elected official; 7. The individual must be a citizen of the United States, if he or she is requesting restoration of civil rights. 8. If convicted in a court other than a Florida court, the individual must be a legal resident of Florida if requesting a restoration of civil rights. 9. The individual must be domiciled in Florida, if requesting Restoration of Alien Status Under Florida Law.B. Objection by Clemency" See Rules of Executive Clemency. Rule 9 A.

12. The Attorney General, the Chief Financial Officer and the Commissioner of Agriculture form the Florida Cabinet. See Fla. Stat. §20.03 (2003).

13. Rules of Executive Clemency. Rule 8.B "If three or more members of the Clemency Board object to the restoration of civil rights or alien status under Florida law without a hearing within 20 days of issuance of the preliminary list by the Coordinator, the objections will require the individual to pursue restoration of these rights by application pursuant to Rule 6. If there are no objections, the Coordinator shall, pursuant to an executive order, issue a certificate which grants restoration of civil rights or alien status under Florida law in the State of Florida, without the specific authority to own, possess or use firearms."

14. In 2003, Florida amended its Restoration of Civil Rights Application Form. The initial application has one page now and can be access at www.state.fl.us/fpc/exclem.htm See form ADM 1501A.

13
Claiming Our Rights: Challenging Postconviction Penalties Using an International Human Rights Framework

PATRICIA ALLARD

A Woman's Journey Through the Prison Industrial Complex

Please imagine that you are a young woman in your first year in college who works as a nurse's aide part-time to help pay your tuition. You meet a young man who is charming, caring, and who works in a factory in town. You fall madly in love with him, get married, and give birth to your first child. Now, based on the stories your mama read you as a child, you know that you will live happily ever after.

During the second year of your marriage the factory in town closes and relocates overseas. Your husband loses his job. He tries for months to find another job but has no luck because the economy has gone sour. He starts using and selling drugs. You quit school and go to work full-time to pay for the drug treatment your husband needs. He's in treatment, and you think your family is getting back on track. Unfortunately, one night a drug squad awakens you, and both you and your husband are arrested for possession of controlled substances. It seems that your husband has had a relapse, not uncommon in the early stages of drug treatment. Ten grams of crack are found in your home. The prosecutor tells you, "I'll cut you a deal if you give me some names." But you can't give him any names because you're not involved in the drug ring; you've never even used drugs. So, you're convicted and sentenced under a mandatory minimum sentencing law to a sentence lengthier than those received by the actual drug dealers your husband knew.

At the time of your conviction, you're expecting your second child. You receive no prenatal care while in prison, and give birth shackled to the hospital bed and surrounded by prison guards. During your prison term, your mother cares for your daughter but is unable to care for the newborn. So your brother and sister-in-law agree to care for your baby boy in addition to their four children. But because your sister-in-law has a three-year old drug conviction, she and your brother cannot be foster or adoptive parents, and so your son becomes a ward of the state. After the baby spends 15 consecutive months in the child welfare system, your parental rights to the baby are terminated, and the baby is placed on an adoption list. You may never see your child again.

When you leave prison, you decide to move in with your mother and your daughter, who live in Section 8 housing. But if you move in, they may be evicted because of your drug conviction. So you go to a woman's shelter and try to get your old job back as a nurse's aide. However, due to your drug conviction you're barred from the field of nursing. You figure you'll go back to college to get another degree. But because of your drug conviction you're denied federal financial aid.

Your mother falls ill and can no longer care for your daughter. You decide to apply for welfare benefits to provide for you and your daughter until you get back on your feet, but once again, because of your conviction, you're denied access to these benefits. Finally, you figure you'll register to vote so next election you can vote those stinking politicians out of office. But you can't register to vote, and now join the ranks of over 1.4 million Americans who have completed their felony sentence yet face taxation without representation (Allard 2002). Welcome to the revolving door of the prison industrial complex.

This story was first presented at a roundtable discussion on reentry sponsored by Illinois State Congressman Danny Davis during the Congressional Black Caucus Foundation's 2002 Legislative Conference. The purpose of the narrative is to illustrate the cumulative effect of post-conviction penalties on the lives of people coming in contact with the criminal punishment system. This narrative also serves to demonstrate the senselessness and dehumanizing impact of these penalties, and the need to claim many fundamental rights that have been denied for far too long in the United States.

This chapter is arranged in three sections. The first section traces the history of the "get tough on crime" crusade in the United States from the late 1960s to 2000, showing how criminal punishment policies arrived at punishing beyond prison walls through postconviction penalties. Second,

I identify the preliminary building blocks necessary for reframing rights in the United States, which would eventually lead to the elimination of post-conviction penalties. The third part of this chapter provides a brief history of human rights in the United States, concluding that the use of human rights principles to reframe the notion of rights in this country is not a radical proposal, but rather a necessary and inevitable development.

"Get Tough on Crime" Crusade

The experience of the young woman in the story is unfortunately a very common one, and is increasingly being experienced by a growing number of people leaving prison. Until the 1970s, the American sentencing system was characterized by indeterminate sentencing schemes in which there was greater judicial discretion in sentencing decisions. Rehabilitation was emphasized as a major objective of sentencing. This model came under attack in the 1960s from both the political left and right. Liberals came to view the broad discretion available to sentencing judges and parole boards as too fraught with opportunities for discrimination based on race, gender, and socioeconomic factors, among others,[1] whereas conservatives felt that people who came in contact with the criminal punishment system were not being treated harshly enough. As a result, in the early 1970s a shift toward determinate sentencing structures limiting judicial discretion began. The "get tough on crime" crusade was born. The series of Rockefeller Drug Laws represents one example of the early determinate sentencing structures. Under these draconian provisions, anyone convicted of selling two ounces, or possessing four ounces, of narcotics was subject to a 15-year prison term regardless of the individual's criminal history or the circumstances surrounding the offense. The movement toward determinate sentencing quickened in the 1980s and continues today, intimately intertwined with the War on Drugs.

The War on Drugs, declared by the Reagan Administration in the early 1980s as the second phase of the "get tough on crime" crusade, is one of the most significant contributing factors to the rapid prison population growth. The number of people in federal and state prisons has dramatically increased since the 1980s. In 1980, there were 315,974 people behind bars (Bureau of Justice Statistics 2000). There were over 1.4 million in 2002 (Harrision 2003). People of African ancestry and Latinos/Latinas have been significantly more affected by the "Race to Incarcerate"[2] than members of white communities.[3]

United States drug policy over the past 20 years has emphasized incapacitation over rehabilitation, leading to (1) a shift in police practices from responding to crime to seeking out criminal activity, and (2) more punitive sentencing schemes. In order to implement this criminal justice policy—incapacitation—two-thirds of the federal anti-drug budget was earmarked for law enforcement and incarceration, whereas only one-third was dedicated to prevention and rehabilitation. Unlike many European nations that emphasized rehabilitation in the 1980s and 1990s, especially for drug offenses, the United States embarked on an unprecedented penal experiment of mass incarceration during the same period.

Postconviction Penalties

Prior to the 1990s, persons convicted of certain criminal offenses, whether misdemeanors or felonies, were subjected to additional penalties upon completion of their prison term. These "civil" penalties included bars to obtaining certain types of occupational licenses and disenfranchisement, either temporary or permanent. Beginning in the mid-1990s, the U.S. Congress embarked on the third phase of its "get tough on crime" crusade, adding a new layer to the prison industrial complex that has had the effect of ensuring that people coming in contact with the criminal punishment system remain within its grasp even beyond prison walls. Between 1995 and 1998, the U.S. Congress enacted a number of laws imposing additional penalties beyond a term of incarceration on individuals convicted of drug offenses, essentially creating a number of postconviction penalties. A drug conviction can now result, in addition to a criminal sentence, in a lifetime ban on the receipt of cash assistance and food stamps, ineligibility for federal financial aid for postsecondary education, the denial of public housing, and the denial of the right to become a foster or adoptive parent. The denial of these basic socioeconomic rights to people with convictions is made possible in large part because they are not entrenched in the laws of the United States as fundamental and inalienable rights. To understand how such basic human rights—to employment, housing, family and education—can be denied in the United States, and what is necessary to reclaim them as inalienable, an examination and reframing of the notion of rights must be undertaken.

Framing Postconviction Penalties as a Human Rights Concern

The efforts of people of color, First Nations people, and low-income people to articulate what constitutes a right, define its parameters, and claim a particular right as fundamental and inalienable in the United States and around the globe, are documented throughout history. People around the world express the desire to be active participants in shaping principles and laws. Such expressions are not always possible due to their exclusion from mainstream politics. Nonetheless, people do take to the streets and, in some cases, overthrow their governments to have their say. Dr. Kly succinctly articulates in the *Anti-Social Contract*, the importance of recognizing how the laws in the United States have been constructed without input from communities of color, First Nations, and low-income communities:

> [T]he social contract that serves to legitimize the establishment of the U.S. government must be found not only in the Constitution, but also in the laws that sanctioned slavery and the settlers' right to land once used by the Native Americans, in Jim Crow laws, the laws that legitimized segregation, the Civil Rights Laws, [as well as the laws that sanction the criminalization of people of color, Native people, and low-income people,] etc., and most recently, the legal principles and court rulings that prevented quotes or an effective affirmative action program to overcome the present result of past injuries.
>
> There is one significant fact that must be incorporated into any sincere scientific analysis: when the U.S. Constitution (which would eventually serve as the basis for legitimate government) was written, more than 50% of the population, which was not Anglo-American and not European, did not participate in its construction (Kly 1989: 1–2).

Many non–Anglo-American and non-European communities are determined to redress this exclusion from a discourse of rights. There is an ever-growing need in the United States and globally to reframe our understanding of rights and recalibrate the balance between individual and collective responsibility (individual responsibility for one's actions and collective responsibility for society's actions), which contributes to the context in which each individual's choices are made. International human rights principles can be used to guide a discourse of rights that reflect the needs and desire of all U.S. residents, in which both individual and collective responsibility are defined and upheld.

The proposed guidepost to frame rights in the United States is based on one fundamental human rights principle—human dignity.[4] *Human dignity* is a condition in which federal, state, and local governments ensure respect for the bodily integrity of all members of the global community and equal access to the social, economic, political, and cultural conditions for all individuals in order to ensure the opportunity to achieve their fullest potential. Mere survival does not equate with human dignity.[5] The violation of bodily integrity or denial of any of the above-mentioned conditions is inhuman treatment. Once the principle of human dignity is accepted, inhuman treatment cannot be justified under any circumstances because such treatment impedes people's ability to reach their fullest potential, and, therefore, undermines human dignity.

The approach proposed here does not suggest the U.S. government incorporate international treaties and norms into its domestic laws.

Although U.S. "exceptionalism" with respect to international human rights standards is extremely problematic, and its eradication remains an important goal, the aims of this chapter are as follows:

1. To reframe the dialogue around rights and government accountability in a manner that is authentic to the needs of all community members
2. To offer human rights principles as tools through which communities of color and low-income communities can conceptualize and claim rights in their own image as well as means to revitalize our communities' organizing spirits
3. To move criminal punishment concerns into a broader movement of rights

The present trend of punishing beyond prison walls through postconviction penalties is incompatible with human dignity. Laws denying access to basic and fundamental human rights—political voice, education, housing, family unity, employment, and social assistance—to individuals convicted of certain types of crimes represent an intentional, state-driven effort to treat people inhumanly upon their return to their community following conviction. A postconviction penalty is inhuman treatment because it undermines the ability of U.S. residents, especially First Nations people, people of color, and low-income people, to reach their fullest potential. For human dignity to be realized, at least two critical elements of the American notion of "rights" must be reframed.

Right vs. Privilege

To eliminate any of the justifications for postconviction penalties, the American notion of "rights" must be reevaluated. Under the current U.S. system of so-called rights, citizens do not have actual rights but rather have privileges that can be taken away at the will of state agents. Rights grounded in the principle of human dignity ensure that each and every person is endowed with rights simply by virtue of being human, and under no circumstances can these rights be taken away. Privileges are provided to members of society as long as they follow the rules established by the dominant group: white, upper/middle class, male Anglo-Americans and Europeans. When predetermined actions are classified by the dominant group as breaches of the established rules, members of the community who are deemed guilty of committing the breaches are stripped of their privileges and alienated from society. Criminal convictions are increasingly used to justify stripping people of their "privileges": employment, parenting, social benefits, housing, education, and voting. The significance of shifting the dialogue from privileges to human rights is that an individual's criminal record could no longer be used as a justification for stripping that person's equal access to the social, economic, political, and cultural conditions that are integral to that person's ability to achieve his or her fullest potential.

Individual Responsibility Versus Collective Responsibility

A central point united Third World traditionalists of both stripes—that First World rights were based on excessively individualistic concepts of human nature and human needs. Such individualism, and the competitiveness, selfishness, isolation, and alienation it generated, were at odds with Third Word patterns of community, family, tribal, and other forms of group solidarity, with their inherent values of duty, obligation, belongingness, and mutual aid and protection. (Burns and Burns 1991: 441)

Many communities of color, as well as First Nations communities, continue to espouse principles that reinforce group solidarity, but struggle to do so in a society structured around individualism. The notion of individual responsibility as central to American society is manifested in such common expressions directed at people going through the criminal justice system as, "Take responsibility for your actions!" and "Pull yourself up by your boot straps!" Under the individual responsibility approach, each individual is assigned responsibility without regard to the socioeconomic conditions that may contribute to or dictate her criminal activity or to society's decision to punish certain types of conduct while condoning others. Meanwhile, society as a whole is not held accountable for its collective contributory inaction—the failure to address the socioeconomic conditions that compel people to crime. [6]

Examining the situations that push most members of our communities through the revolving doors of the prison industrial complex, it becomes clear that individuals are not acting in a vacuum. The Bureau of Justice Statistics's detailed surveys of prison populations, among many other sources of information on people going through the system, reveal a long list of social, cultural, and economic conditions—physical and sexual abuse, poverty, education, mental health challenges, and substance abuse—disproportionately affecting individuals in communities of color, low-income communities, and First Nations communities that hobble individuals' abilities to reach their fullest potential, and bring them in contact with the criminal punishment system. These conditions in turn arise in large part as a result of systemic conditions formed by racism, capitalism, sexism, homophobia, and xenophobia, which are constructed collectively by the dominant group in ways that benefit their interests, while

230 • Patricia Allard

detrimentally affecting not only individuals, but nondominant communities as a whole.

By individualizing responsibility, we have come to view each criminal act as the failing of an individual, and thus justify excessive punitive measures. However, the human rights principle of human dignity would compel balancing individual and collective responsibility for all social and economic problems, including criminal activity. Such a notion of responsibility would, once fully developed and implemented, undermine the justification for excessive punishment offered within an individual responsibility approach.

There is a need to shift criminal punishment concerns from a strictly criminal punishment realm, where only the individual is held accountable, to a broader context of inalienable rights, through which the collective, along with the individual, is held accountable for its actions and inactions. Criminal punishment concerns such as postconviction penalties must be incorporated into a human rights framework to ensure the following:

1. People who come in contact with the criminal punishment are not dehumanized, and are treated in a manner consistent with human dignity.
2. People who come in contact with the criminal punishment maintain fundamental and inalienable rights that permit them to reach their fullest potential in order to permanently exit the prison industrial complex.
3. Federal, state, and local governments implement laws and policies that facilitate and protect the exercise of inalienable rights.

The notion of shifting the rights debate in the United States is not new or without foundation. There is a long history of human rights advocacy in the United States, in which government officials, such as Eleanor Roosevelt, and many communities of color and low-income communities have played central roles.

Human Rights Movement in the United States

Since the early 1900s, leaders from First Nations communities and communities of color have used a human rights framework to advocate for the rights of their members. For instance, "Marcus Garvey submitted complaints to the League of Nations on behalf of the 'Negro Peoples of the World'. . . . Deskaheh, a chief of the Cayuga Nation and speaker of the Haudensosaunee Six Nations Confederacy, made his case to the League of Nations for the right of his people to live according to their own laws on their own lands"(Cho 2003: 5). In 1948, following global recognition that the social, political, and economic conditions that fueled the human suffering and atrocities of World War II must be eradicated, the United Nations adopted the Universal Declaration of Human Rights.

The drafters of the Universal Declaration faced numerous obstacles. One of the most significant conflicts, mediated by Eleanor Roosevelt, the U.S. delegate to the UN General Assembly, was one of ideological differences and tensions between individualism and collectivism, between the United States and the Soviet Union. This translated into a very practical balance between socioeconomic rights and civil and political rights, which is well summed up by Burns and Burns:

> "The American vision of an international declaration was, as a United States representative put it, "a carbon copy of the American Declaration of Independence and Bill of Rights," devoted to the individual's freedom from government. But the Soviets were determined to include an array of economic and social rights and the less said about freedom of speech, the right to a fair trial, etc., the better." (Burns and Burns 1991: 422)

In the end, the Universal Declaration addressed both sets of rights but "all enforcement powers had been stripped from it" (Burns and Burns 1991: 422). Two separate covenants were subsequently adopted, addressing civil and political rights in one document and social, economic, and cultural rights in the other.[7] The absence of enforcement mechanisms, both internationally and in the United States, for social, economic, and cultural rights, as well as many other human rights, persists to the present day, fueling a new human rights movement domestically.

Momentum for a U.S. Human Rights Movement

As the Reverend Martin Luther King, Jr., declared, "I think it is necessary to realize that we have moved from the era of civil rights to the era of human rights."

Since the early 1990s, human rights organizations such as Amnesty International and Human Rights Watch, which have traditionally focused on human rights abuses abroad, have increasingly been documenting human rights abuses in the United States[8] Many other U.S.–based organizations and individual advocates are using human rights tools in their litigation strategies, public education campaigns, organizing efforts, and documentation of domestic social injustices. In 2003, the American Civil Liberties Union convened a conference exploring the use of international law in U.S. courts. Later that same year, over 50 national organizations launched the U.S. Human Rights Network, which aims to "promote U.S. accountability to universal human rights standards by building linkages between organizations, as well as individuals, working on human rights issues in the United States. The Network also works towards connecting the U.S. human rights movement with the broader U.S. social justice movement and human rights movements around the world" (Cho 2003). A recent publication by the Ford Foundation documents the renewed enthusiasm and commitment to addressing social justice concerns in a more integrated fashion through a human rights framework in the United States:

> Across the American Indian, civil, women's, worker, gay, immigrant and prisoner rights communities in the United States, a powerful new politics of social justice is emerging—one that favors multi-over single-issue, compound rather than singular identities; that conceives of rights holistically rather than in terms of outmoded hierarchies; and finally, that situates those most affected at the center of advocacy. (Ford 2004: 7)

This more comprehensive and integrated understanding of social, economic, and political problems would mean that the examination of and reform of efforts directed at the criminal punishment system would be interwoven with such concerns as access to quality education, minimum wage, affordable housing, health care services, and quality child care. By incorporating criminal punishment concerns into the broader social justice framework of human rights, advocates may finally be able to force policymakers to get beyond the "tough on crime" rhetoric, and finally address some of the root causes of crime.

In addition to national, state, and local organizations' efforts to infuse a human rights analysis into their domestic work, policymakers and the judiciary are also exploring the possibility of incorporating human rights principles and international law into domestic decision-making processes. In August 2003, Justice Ruth Bader Ginsburg of the United States Supreme Court, extolled the value of a comparative perspective in constitutional adjudication, suggesting that the American judicial community's "perspective on constitutional law should encompass the world" (Ginsburg 2003: 2). Justice Ginsburg pointed out that since 1982, the Supreme Court of Canada has referred to international human rights instruments in at least 50 cases, whereas "the U.S. Supreme Court has mentioned [the Universal Declaration of Human Rights] a spare six times" since its adoption in 1948 (Ginsburg 2003: 24). However, she noted that the Court is "becoming more open to comparative and international law perspectives" (Ginsburg 2003: 24). During the Court's 2003 term, the justices referred to international human rights conventions in the Michigan affirmative action cases. The Court also cited legal precedent from the European Court of Human Rights in *Lawrence v. Texas* (2003), declaring unconstitutional a Texas statute prohibiting two consenting adults of the same sex from engaging in intimate sexual conduct. This decision overturned the Court's 1986 decision in *Bowers v. Hardwick* (1996), which had found no constitutional protection for consensual sex between gays or lesbians.

The judiciary is not the only branch of government through which the incorporation of human rights principles into domestic laws has become a possibility. Members of Congress are also signaling a willingness to embrace human rights principles. In 2001, Illinois State Congressman Jesse Jackson Jr. released a book entitled *A More Perfect Union: Advancing New American Rights.* Jackson brings renewed vitality to the notion of reframing rights in a way that would guarantee inalienable social and economic rights to U.S. residents, proposing "a radical economic strategy and program of new human rights." Jackson recommends several constitutional amendments that would preserve into domestic laws the right to full employment; affordable housing; universal and comprehensive health care; quality public education; fair taxes; and a clean, safe, and sustainable environment. Jackson clearly views the right to full employment as central to sustaining economic growth. He also recognizes, as did President Bush during the 2004 State of the Union Address,[9] that formerly incarcerated people must have a supportive economic environment in which they have a fighting chance to reach their fullest potential. Jackson points out that, "[w]hen we leave people unemployed and underemployed there are costs for our society, such as lost productivity and taxes. But it also burdens our society in other ways, including supporting a massive and rapidly growing prison-industrial complex" (Jackson and Watkins 2001: 260). Congressman Jackson's proposal seeks to address the collective responsibility that is so fundamental to human dignity. Unlike the Reagan, Clinton, Bush Sr., and Bush Jr. administrations, which have focused on punishing the individual without addressing the socioeconomic conditions that compel people to crime for survival, Jackson proposes concrete reforms to the U.S. economic structure. Jackson's proposal is particularly timely given the growing movement in the United States to address the needs of formerly incarcerated people as they return to their communities.

In 1999, the Urban Institute released a report documenting the fact that 650,000 people leave prison and reenter American society each year. An increasing number of states are beginning to fund reentry programs, and even the current Republican White House is now convinced of the importance of addressing reentry. One of the most perplexing aspects of the government's new commitment to reentry is the lack of a concomitant pledge to repeal the federal laws that create socioeconomic barriers for people with criminal convictions. During the 2004 State of the Union Address, Bush stated, "This year, some 600,000 inmates will be released from prison back into society. We know from *long experience* that if they can't find work, or a home, or help, they are much more likely to commit crime and return to prison" [emphasis added]. This assertion clearly demonstrates awareness that the current postconviction penalties, such as occupational licensing bans and the "One Strike and You're Out" policy, are likely to compel people to commit crimes. Nonetheless, the current reentry efforts have been limited to the development and implementation of programs geared at "fixing" the individual rather than addressing the socioeconomic barriers that hobble people's reentry efforts.

Although Congressman Jackson's proposed constitutional amendments are one of the most sensible approaches to readdress the socioeconomic issues currently plaguing the United States, he does not specifically speak about the rights of incarcerated or formerly incarcerated people. Nonetheless, his call for the implementation and protection of fundamental, inalienable rights should apply to people caught in the prison industrial complex. As the dialogue progresses around human rights in the United States, it is critical that the notion of inalienable rights apply to all regardless of their race, gender, sexual orientation, creed, religion, class, or criminal history, and that the application of exclusionary measures to people caught in the Prison Industrial Complex be avoided.

Conclusion

The current approach to addressing the reentry of formerly incarcerated people—"fixing" the individual without simultaneously addressing the social, economic and political structure of American society—demonstrates the continued strength of the individual responsibility approach in the United States, which serves to overshadow the collective responsibility that we all share in addressing the social, economic, and political concerns facing our communities. A human rights framework opens the dialogue to explore a new framework of rights that enables a more appropriate balance between individual and collective responsibility. An interest in international human rights is growing in various sectors of American society. Criminal justice advocates should work to ensure that oppressive and ill-conceived criminal punishment policies be framed as human rights concerns rather than allowing them to be limited to the criminal punishment arena. Framing postconviction penalties as infringements of fundamental human rights begins the process of joining other social justice movements under the new and integral framework of human rights.

References

Bader Ginsburg, Ruth. 2003. "Looking Beyond Our Borders: The Value of a Comparative Perspective in Constitutional Adjudication." Remarks for the American Constitution Society, 2 August, Washington, D.C.

Bureau of Justice Statistics. 2000. *Source Book of Criminal Justice Statistics 1999.* Washington, D.C.: U.S. Department of Justice.

Burns, James McGregor and Stewart Burns. 1991. *The People's Charter: The Pursuit of Rights in America.* New York, NY: Knopf.

Bush, George W. 2004. "State of the Union." January 24, 2004.

Cho, Eunice, Lisa A. Crooms, Heidi Dorow, Andy Huff, Ethel Long Scott, and Dorothy Q. Thomas. 2003. *Something Inside So Strong: A Resource Guide on Human Rights in the United States.* New York: U.S. Human Rights Network.

The Ford Foundation. 2004. *Close to Home: Case Studies of Human Rights Work in the United States.* New York: The Ford Foundation.

Harrison, Paige M., and Allen J. Beck. 2003. "Prisoners in 2002," *Bureau of Justice Statistics Bulletin.* Washington, D.C.: U.S. Department of Justice.

Jackson, Jr., Jesse L. and Frank E. Watkins. 2001. *A More Perfect Union: Advancing New American Rights.* New York: Welcome Rain Publishers.

Kly, Y.N. 1989. *The Anti-Social Contract.* Atlanta, GA: Clarity Press, Inc.

Mauer, Marc. 1999. *Race to Incarcerate.* New York: New Press.

Mauer, Marc, Cathy Potler, and Richard Wolf. 1999. *Gender and Justice: Women, Drugs and Sentencing Policy.* Washington, D.C.: The Sentencing Project.

Richie, Beth. 1996. *Compelled to Crime: The Gender Entrapment of Black Battered Women.* New York: Routledge.

The Sentencing Project. 1999. *Drug Policy and the Criminal Justice System.* Washington, D.C.: The Sentencing Project.

U.S. Human Rights Network. 2003. http://www.ushrnetwork.org.

Cases Cited

Bowers v. Hardwick, 478 US 186 (1986).

Lawrence v. Texas, 123 S. Ct. 2472 (2003).

Law Cited

Universal Declaration of Human Rights, United Nations, December 10, 1948.

Endnotes

1. The possibility for discrimination is a valid concern, but the removal of discretion has not addressed the discriminatory impact of sentencing laws. Any future sentencing reform efforts must address the issue of discretion and discrimination.

2. The term *Race to Incarcerate*, comes from a book so entitled and authored by Marc Mauer (1999).

3. It has been well documented that the War on Drugs has disproportionately affected people of African ancestry and Latinos, both in the United States and Latin America. What is less well-known is that the War on Drugs has not only resulted in women being incarcerated at double the rate of men, but has also resulted in Latinas and African American women being the most likely social group to be incarcerated for drug offenses. According to the Bureau of Justice Statistics, in 1997 44% of Latinas in state prisons were incarcerated for drug offenses, 39% of women of African ancestry, compared with 23% of white women, 24% of black men, 26% of Latinos, and 11% of white men.

4. The Universal Declaration of Human Rights encompasses fundamental rights that belong to all individuals by virtue of being human. Some of the enumerated rights include the right to equality, the right to be free from discrimination, the right to be free from slavery, the right to life, liberty, personal security, the right to be free from arbitrary arrest, the right to participate in government and free elections, the right to social security, the right to desirable work

and to join a trade union, the right to an adequate standard of living, the right to education, and the right to rest and leisure.

5. Article 25 of the Universal Declaration of Human Rights stipulates, "(1) Everyone has the right to a standard of living adequate for the health and well-being of himself and of his family, including food, clothing, housing and medical care and necessary social services, and the right to security in the event of unemployment, sickness, disability, widowhood, old age or other lack of livelihood in circumstances beyond his control. (2) Motherhood and child-hood are entitled to special care and assistance. . . ."

6. Beth Richie coined the concept "compelled to crime" in her book *Compelled to Crime: The Gender Entrapment of Black Battered Women* (Richie 1996).

7. International Covenant on Civil and Political Rights, adopted 16 Dec. 1966, GA Res. 2200 (XXI), 21 UN GAOR Supp. (No.16) and International Covenant on Economic, Social and Cultural Rights, adopted 16 Dec. 1966, GA Res. 2200 (XXII), 21 UN GAOR Supp. (No.16).

8. Human Rights Watch and Amnesty International have issued reports on a wide range of criminal punishment issues, including the right to voting of formerly incarcerated people, denial of public housing to people with criminal records, prison conditions, and the death penalty.

14

Prisoner Voting Rights in Canada: Rejecting the Notion of Temporary Outcasts

DEBRA PARKES

When Richard Sauvé walked into a Port Hope, Ontario, bar on October 18, 1978, he could not have anticipated that the events of that night would lead him to prison for 15 years, to Queen's University to obtain an B.A. in psychology and criminology while in prison, and to the center of a political and legal battle that one commentator has said "reflects a controversy about what kind of state Canada is" (Hampton 1998: 23). On October 31, 2002, the Supreme Court of Canada brought 20 years of litigation by Sauvé and other prisoners to a successful end when a majority of the Court decided that denying the vote to prisoners violates the Canadian Charter of Rights and Freedoms 1982. In striking down the prisoner voting ban, the Court explicitly rejected the notion that prisoners are "temporary outcasts from our system of rights and democracy" (*Sauvé v. Canada* [*Chief Electoral Officer*] 2002 at para. 40).

The Canadian government had defended prisoner disenfranchisement in the courts as a symbolic exclusion of people like Richard Sauvé from the law-abiding Canadian citizenry. Yet Sauvé fought for inclusion in society in a number of ways, and the voting rights litigation was just one way. The crime for which he was convicted, first-degree murder, is the most serious one in Canadian law. People convicted of murder are consistently cited by defenders of prisoner disenfranchisement as those least deserving of the franchise. However, Richard Sauvé's trajectory through the prison system as an activist, scholar, voter, and finally, advocate for prisoners from the outside, is at odds with the experience of most prisoners and with popular ideas about prisoners' relationships with the broader society. The case and its aftermath raise questions about the significance, and limits, of judicial recognition and enforcement of prisoners' rights.

This chapter suggests that the emerging opposition in the United States to postincarceration legal, social, and economic consequences of criminal conviction would benefit from attention to the way the continued construction of prisoners as temporary outcasts resonates positively in society, assisting to legitimate the myriad penalties and consequences imposed on prisoners' release. This chapter is divided into five sections; the first introduces contemporary Canadian penal policy and popular perceptions of crime and punishment, noting that Canada both reflects and departs from some of the attributes of modern "crime control cultures" (Garland 2001). The second section briefly describes the recent Canadian litigation over the constitutionality of prisoner disenfranchisement. This part discusses the court's rejection of the government's symbolic and expressive justifications for the voting ban, as well as the court's affirmation of prisoners' status as rights holders and members of broader communities. Even though positive, the *Sauvé* decision represents a departure from the usual judicial approach to prisoners' rights claims, an approach that gives those rights little meaningful content. The third section examines the often negative reaction to the decision by legislators and the popular media, paying attention to the strong popular appeal of the notion of prisoners as temporary outcasts and the dissonance between that popular conception and the one adopted by the court. The fourth section considers the vanishing concept of prisoners' rights and community membership in the United States, as exemplified by a recent U.S. Supreme Court decision upholding severe limits on, and even permanent denial of, prisoners' family visits. Finally, the fifth part makes the case that efforts to reform or repeal the civil penalties faced by ex-prisoners should begin by recognizing the link between those penalties and a conception of prisoners as temporary outcasts from society. The chapter concludes with some thoughts on promoting a culture of rights and citizenship that includes prisoners.

The Canadian Context: A Kindler, Gentler "Tough on Crime" Stance?
Canada's incarceration rate of 102 prisoners per 100,000 population seems low when compared with the United States's world-leading rate of 686 per 100,000 (Walmsley 2003). However, this simple comparison masks the degree to which Canada has adopted "tough on crime" policies, such as mandatory minimum sentences (Doob and Cesaroni 2001) and incarcerated

more of its people than comparable Western European countries (Walmsley 2003).[1] While it is tempting to dismiss American mass incarceration as another example of American exceptionalism, David Downes (2001) has argued that the modern American "macho penal economy" is influencing Europe, rather than remaining exceptional. Downes cites Canada as an example of a country that has resisted this influence (Downes 2001: 63). However, a closer look calls that conclusion into question. Canada's adult prison population rose in the early to mid-1990s (CCJS 1997) before declining somewhat from 1997 to 2001 (Canadian Centre for Justice Statistics 2001). Aboriginal people are increasingly overrepresented in the country's prisons and jails, a trend admittedly on a smaller scale, but with systemic characteristics similar to the mass incarceration of young black men in the United States. In 2001, 19% of Canada's provincial prisoners and 17% of federal prisoners were Aboriginal, compared to only 2% of the general population in Canada (CCJS 2001). The overrepresentation is even more pronounced in provinces such as Saskatchewan, where 76% of prisoners are Aboriginal, whereas Aboriginal people make up only 8% of the province's population (CCJS 2001). Various commissions of inquiry have found systemic racism against Aboriginal and other people of color within Canada's federal and provincial criminal justice systems (e.g., Commission on Systemic Racism in the Ontario Criminal Justice System 1995; Hamilton and Sinclair 1991). Although the incarceration rate has increased, Canada's crime rate has been declining or remaining steady since the early 1990s and, in 2002, stood at the same level it had in 1979. Nevertheless, the Canadian public mistakenly perceives that crime is on the rise (Environics 1998), making "tough on crime" laws and policies politically expedient (Doob and Cesaroni 2001).

David Garland (2001) has characterized late twentieth century "tough on crime" trends in the United States and the United Kingdom as part of a shift toward a "crime control culture" arising from anxieties about economic and social change, risks, and social order in the period he calls "late modernity." Garland argues that political, social, and economic restructuring associated with the neo-liberalism, social conservatism, and "post-welfarism" of the Reagan/Thatcher era gave rise to new social attitudes, fears, and resentments that had an outlet in increasingly harsh crime control policies. In addition to strict sentencing laws and rapidly increasing prison populations, Americans (and to a lesser degree, Britons) embraced the privatization of security and crime control in the form of gated communities, surveillance, and private policing.

While the analogy to Canada is not perfect, significant aspects of this crime control culture, present in the United States and the United

Kingdom, are also present in Canada. In popular discourse and policy making, a strategy of "punitive segregation" or expressive punishment has tended to replace the liberal "penal welfare" focus on due process rights, proportionate punishment, and rehabilitation. Like the United States and United Kingdom, Canada's penal law and policy have increasingly raised the profile of crime victims (Roach 1999), both actual and symbolic, as players in a zero-sum game in which any attention to the rights or welfare of people accused or convicted of crime amounts to disrespect for victims. Finally, the idea that "prison works" resonates with the Canadian public in a manner not unlike that in the United States and United Kingdom. Prisons are symbols of public order as places of incapacitation and punishment, meeting demands for public safety and harsh retribution. Canadian media stories often refer to federal prisons as "Club Fed" (Pemberton 2003; Rodriguez 2002), reflecting public acceptance of the view put forward by opposition politicians, "victims' rights" lobby groups, and police associations that prisoners live a coddled existence in cushy, resortlike surroundings. Prisoners are neither people in need nor products of disadvantaged social and economic circumstances. They are rational, responsible, dangerous, and undeserving of our collective concern.

One must be careful not to overstate the point. Many of the harsher measures of America's crime control culture (e.g., "three strikes" sentencing laws, chain gangs, and the death penalty) have not made their way into Canadian law. In fact, a considerable amount of the law and policy governing sentencing and imprisonment remains consistent with liberal, penal welfare concepts. For example, the Criminal Code requires sentencing judges to consider "all available sanctions other than imprisonment that are reasonable in the circumstances . . . for all offenders, with particular attention to the circumstances of aboriginal offenders," an effort to address Aboriginal overrepresentation in Canada's prisons and jails, as well as overincarceration more generally. The Federal Corrections and Conditional Release Act of 1992 has as one of its guiding principles that prisoners retain the rights and privileges of all members of society, except those rights and privileges that are necessarily removed or restricted as a consequence of sentence. Canada's penal law has also been developed by legislators and interpreted by courts over the past two decades in the shadow of the Canadian Charter of Rights and Freedoms, entrenched in the Constitution in 1982, which has given rise to a new, normative human rights framework that is increasingly at odds with public calls for more expressive and symbolic punitive responses to crime. Yet the Charter remains very popular among Canadians (Centre for Research and Information on Canada 2002). Canada's crime control culture and nascent "Charter culture" collided in the *Sauvé* case and its aftermath.

Sauvé v. Canada: Rejecting Prisoner Disenfranchisement

Prisoner disenfranchisement has been part of Canadian law since the country's colonial beginnings. Federal law disqualified all prisoners and jail inmates from voting until 1993, when Richard Sauvé, a prisoner serving a life sentence for murder, successfully challenged the law as an infringement of his right to vote guaranteed in the Charter: *Sauvé v. Canada (Attorney General)* 1993.[2] Section three of the Charter guarantees that "every citizen of Canada has the right to vote in an election of members of the House of Commons or of a legislative assembly and to be qualified for membership therein."

Having lost the battle to uphold a wholesale prisoner voting ban, the federal government quickly enacted a new, narrower law that disenfranchised only prisoners who were serving sentences of two years or more.[3] Richard Sauvé was soon back in court, challenging the new law that continued to deny him the right to vote. His claim was joined by a group of Aboriginal prisoners who argued that prisoner disenfranchisement violated not only their right to vote, but also their right to equality, due to systemic racism and chronic overrepresentation of Aboriginal people in Canada's prisons (Aboriginal Legal Services of Toronto 2001). In October 2002, a majority of the Supreme Court of Canada held that prisoner disenfranchisement laws, even those limited to longer-serving prisoners, unjustifiably infringed prisoners' right to vote, a right that is "fundamental to our democracy and the rule of law and cannot be lightly set aside." The decision was not unanimous. Four members of the court dissented, taking the view that the government's objectives were valid and that the Court should defer to legislative policy choices "based on reasonable social or political philosophy" and uphold the prisoner voting ban (*Sauvé* 2002 at paras. 79–121). These four judges also rejected the arguments made by the Aboriginal plaintiffs and prisoners' advocacy groups that the voting ban violated prisoners' equality rights.[4] However, the majority decision written by Chief Justice Beverly McLachlin meant that the prisoner disenfranchisement law was struck down.

The practical impact of *Sauvé* in Canada will extend beyond the federal law found unconstitutional. The fact that this was the second time the Supreme Court of Canada had rejected a prisoner voting ban, combined with the strong language used to denounce the government's purported objectives, makes it unlikely that any prisoner voting ban will pass constitutional muster, including a number of provincial disenfranchisement laws. The decision has also proved to be a persuasive precedent internationally. It was cited with approval in a recent South African Constitutional Court decision declaring that country's prisoner disenfranchisement law unconstitutional (*Minister of Home Affairs v. NICRO* 2004) and in an opinion of the European Court of Human Rights finding the United Kingdom's prisoner voting ban inconsistent with the right to vote (*Hirst v. United Kingdom (No. 2)* 2004).

The Supreme Court's interpretive framework for Charter claims requires the government to articulate clearly its objectives for infringing a right and to prove that the infringement is rationally connected to the objective and is the least-restrictive means for achieving that objective.[5] As a result, courts have subjected the normative arguments for prisoner disenfranchisement to clsose scrutiny. The Canadian government had defended the ban on prisoner voting by asserting that disenfranchisement (1) enhances the general purposes of the criminal sanction and (2) promotes civic responsibility and respect for the rule of law (*Sauvé* 2002 at para. 21). Neither of these goals appeared in the legislative history of the voting ban and even though the Chief Justice was prepared to accept the stated objectives, she pointedly observed that "[t]he record leaves in doubt how much these goals actually motivated Parliament; the Parliamentary debates offer more fulmination than illumination" (para. 21). In any event, the government's position had changed from the one it had adopted in the earlier *Sauvé* 1993 case, having argued there that excluding prisoners promoted a "decent and responsible electorate." Such an argument, based as it was on the moral character of voters, had been rejected as anachronistic and inconsistent with the values enshrined in the Charter (*Sauvé* 1993 at 650–51).

The majority in *Sauvé* 2002 viewed the new objectives of enhancing punishment and promoting civic responsibility as too symbolic and abstract to justify overriding a right as important as voting. Chief Justice McLachlin stated, "the government has failed to identify particular problems that require denying the right to vote" (para. 26) and expressed concern that judicial review would be rendered meaningless if the government could simply assert that it had symbolic objectives for any rights-infringing law (para. 23).

The government's defense of the prisoner voting ban relied heavily on the purported expressive power of disenfranchisement to educate prisoners about civic responsibility. One of the government's key witnesses, moral philosopher Jean Hampton, testified that through the imposition of disenfranchisement as additional punishment, crime victims and the community symbolically express that they will not tolerate the violation of trust and values that the criminal conduct represents (Hampton 1995: 11–15). Therefore, as part of the individual's punishment, he or she will not be entitled to participate in the decision-making process that is committed to those values. Hampton suggested that this process "morally educates" prisoners (Hampton 1998: 15). The majority in *Sauvé* agreed that disenfranchisement sent a message, but not a positive one:

> Denying citizen law-breakers the right to vote sends the message that those who commit serious breaches are no longer valued members of the community, but instead are temporary outcasts from our

system of rights and democracy. More profoundly, it sends the unacceptable message that democratic values are less important than punitive measures ostensibly designed to promote order (para. 40).

In describing disenfranchisement's second purported objective, promoting civic responsibility and respect for the rule of law, another government witness advanced the theory that criminal behavior indicated disrespect for the welfare of fellow members of society, for the rule of law, and for the electoral process (Pangle 1995). He then reasoned back from that proposition to conclude that denying the vote to people who have committed serious crimes makes the franchise seem more valuable both to those prisoners and to the general public, thereby promoting the virtues of responsible citizenship (Pangle 1995: 41).

Again, the Supreme Court majority disagreed, saying that the government gets the connection between obeying the law and having a voice in making the law "exactly backwards" (*Sauvé* 2002 at para. 21). The right of all citizens to vote is the basis of democratic legitimacy. Therefore, when the state disenfranchises a group of citizens, it undermines its ability to function as the legitimate representative of those citizens. In doing so, it "erodes the basis of its right to convict and punish law-breakers" (*Sauvé* 2002, para. 32–34).

Two things are noteworthy about the way the majority opinion conceives of prisoners. First, prisoners are unequivocally full rights holders under the Charter. They do not hold attenuated, weaker versions of the rights enjoyed by other Canadians. Whereas certain rights, such as liberty, are necessarily limited by the fact of incarceration, prisoners' rights claims are not subject to a lower standard of justification when the government infringes them. In addition, prisoners are members of communities and societies, sharing common interests with members of their communities outside prison. The decision takes it for granted that prisoners, and particularly the disproportionately high number of Aboriginal prisoners, should be encouraged to maintain stakes in their communities.

A clear conception of prisoners as rights holders animates the majority decision. Chief Justice McLachlin says that denying prisoners the right to vote "runs counter to our constitutional commitment to the inherent worth and dignity of every individual" (para. 35), and cites the South African Constitutional Court for the principle that the franchise is a "badge of dignity and of personhood" (para. 35; August 1999 at para. 17) belonging to all citizens, including prisoners. On the question of whether disenfranchisement is a constitutionally permissible form of punishment, the Chief Justice said,

> The argument, stripped of its rhetoric, proposes that it is open to Parliament to add a new tool to its arsenal of punitive implements—denial of constitutional rights. I find this notion problematic. I do not

doubt that Parliament may limit constitutional rights in the name of punishment, provided it can justify that limitation. But it is another thing to say that a particular class of people for a particular period of time will completely lose a particular constitutional right. That is tantamount to saying that the affected class is outside the full protection of the Charter (para. 46).

The decision is significant as a strong pronouncement that prisoners are full and equal rights-holders under the Charter.

Few prisoners' rights cases have made it to the Supreme Court of Canada since the Charter became part of the Constitution in 1982, due to unavailability of legal aid, mootness, or other barriers. Prisoners continue to have few meaningful avenues for redress, prompting Justice Louise Arbour (1996) to conclude in an inquiry into the strip-searching of women prisoners by a male emergency response team that "[t]he Rule of Law is absent, although rules are everywhere" (Id. at 181). A leading advocate has reported that most women prisoners either did not know they had Charter rights or thought the rights could be removed by prison officials as "discipline" (Pate 1998). When prisoners' cases have gone to court, judges have tended to continue a pre-Charter tradition of deference, meaning that the rigorous standard of government justification for infringing rights is effectively lowered in prison cases (Manson 1994). For example, a prisoner's challenge to a random urinalysis policy (compulsory, nonprivate urination without individualized suspicion) was prematurely rejected without requiring correctional authorities to demonstrate that the policy was, in the language of the Charter, "a reasonable limit demonstrably justified in a free and democratic society" (Manson 1994: 364). It remains to be seen whether the Supreme Court decision in *Sauvé* signals a shift from deference to a more rigorous review of prisoners' rights claims outside the relatively limited context of the political rights at issue in *Sauvé* where the government trump card of "public safety and security" was not in play.

Another potentially significant aspect of *Sauvé* is the affirmation of prisoners' membership in society and in particular communities, as well as the need for social inclusion and reintegration. The Chief Justice approved of the trial judge's finding that the voting ban adds to the alienation prisoners feel from the communities where their families live and to which they will one day return (para. 59). She pointed to the "need to bolster, rather than undermine, the feeling of connection between prisoners and society as a whole" (para. 38), noting that depriving marginalized individuals of their sense of community identity through voting is not likely to promote the government's stated objective of civic responsibility (para. 38).

The majority in *Sauvé* expressed particular concern about the negative and disproportionate impact of disenfranchisement on Aboriginal prisoners, and the communities to which they belong. The Chief Justice recalled the Court's holding in a previous case that the overrepresentation of Aboriginal people in Canada's prisons is a crisis that must be addressed (*Gladue* 1999 at para. 64; *Sauvé* at para. 60). The Court went further in *Sauvé*, noting that the overrepresentation is linked to high rates of poverty and "institutionalized alienation from mainstream society" and may not accurately reflect individual culpability (para. 60). In light of the reality that Aboriginal people in prison have "unique perspectives and needs" (para. 60), the majority found their exclusion from the ballot box unjustified.

Reaction to *Sauvé*: Prisoners and Public Opinion

Sauvé garnered considerable popular and media attention. Most news stories reported that the decision was historic and significant for prisoners' rights (e.g., Friscolanti 2002; MacCharles 2002; Makin 2002), but many also reported that "victims' rights" groups were angered by the ruling (e.g., Czekaj 2002; Mahoney 2002). A number of the news stories were accompanied by sensational headlines such as "Killers Win Vote Rights" (e.g., Gamble 2002b). A few editorials and opinion articles lauded the decision as positive step for rights and democracy (*Globe and Mail* 2002; Pruden 2002; Parkes 2003), but many more decried the decision as an example of undemocratic, liberal "judicial activism" (e.g., Morton 2002; Simpson 2002; Gibbons 2002) and radically out of step with public opinion (Harris 2002). Some characterized the right to vote as a privilege (*Hamilton Spectator* 2002; Toews 2003). Others raised the specter of notorious serial murderers running for elected office (Gibbons 2002; *London Free Press* 2002). Letters to the editor were also largely opposed to idea of prisoners voting, with many writers taking the view that recognizing prisoner voting rights was an affront to victims (Mills 2002; Woodford 2002).

In a similar vein, during the course of the *Sauvé* litigation, opposition politicians used the prisoners' success at trial as an opportunity to take the government to task for being "soft on crime." For example, on April 22, 1997, the government was criticized in the House of Commons by a member of the opposition for allowing prisoners to vote:

> Mr. Speaker, you see, it is election time again and enumeration has taken place in my riding, in particular at Matsqui Prison. A judge said prisoners should have the right to vote because "preventing prisoners serving more than two years from voting is too sweeping an infringement." This government must be really hard up for votes these days. . . . This is about the rights of criminals versus the rights

of victims and law-abiding citizens. That is what this is about.
(Hansard; House of Commons 1997)

Eager to shed the "soft on crime" label and in an attempt to prevent prisoners from voting in the 1997 election, the governing Liberal party immediately filed an application to stay the judge's order pending appeal. The application was unsuccessful, and on May 17, 1997, Reform Party leader Preston Manning held a press conference to announce that serial rapist and murderer, Paul Bernardo, the most notorious offender in Canada, was still on the voters' list at the infamous residence in St. Catherines where he had committed his crimes (Canadian Press 1997). On the day the Supreme Court decision came down in 2002, government House Leader Don Boudria told the House he was reviewing the decision with a mind to finding a way to continue the prisoner voting ban (J. Brown 2002).

The public backlash against the *Sauvé* ruling, like the government's approach in the *Sauvé* litigation, defended the prisoner voting ban as valid expressive punishment in a manner consistent with the values of Garland's crime control culture. The popular discourse surrounding prisoner-voting rights in Canada rejects the key premises of the majority decision in *Sauvé*—that prisoners are rights holders and members of our communities. It is likely that, over time, this issue will fade from public view as prisoner voting bans are repealed across the country (see e.g., Canadian Press 2003). However, advocates of penal reform and the reintegration of former prisoners into communities should not ignore public opposition to prisoner voting rights as simply ill-informed opinion. Arie Freiberg has described how Australian crime prevention strategies aimed at addressing the root causes of crime, such as poverty and inadequate education, tend not to resonate with the public in the emotive way that "law and order" policies do (Freiberg 2001: 265). He argues that crime prevention initiatives and reform efforts must "recognize and deal with the roles of emotions, symbols, irrationalism, expressionism, nonutilitarianism, faith, belief, and religion in the criminal justice system" (Freiberg 2001: 266).[6] Unlike most prisoners' rights cases, there was no utilitarian, public safety, or security basis on which the denial of voting rights could be defended. Instead, the insistence on denying prisoners the vote seemed rooted in a public need to create "deeper and longer lasting divisions between 'us' and 'them'" in the form of punitive, "no-frills" imprisonment and a marked, monitored existence upon release (Travis 2002: 33). Canada's prisoner voting ban was pure, expressive punishment.

The Supreme Court of Canada pronounced a limit on popular punitiveness in *Sauvé*, finding this particular form of expressive punishment inconsistent with Canada's normative human rights commitments and its growing "Charter culture." There is considerable dissonance between the Supreme Court's conception of prisoners and the one portrayed daily in the popular media. Despite early indications that the Canadian government might attempt to "legislate around" the *Sauvé* decision (J. Brown 2002), and despite calls by the opposition in Parliament for a constitutional amendment to permit prisoner disenfranchisement (Gamble 2002a), the government appears to have quietly accepted the decision and the reality of prisoner voting rights (Hansard; House of Commons 2003). The *Sauvé* decision and its aftermath reveal both the significance, and limits, of judicially enforced human rights norms.

The Case of the Vanishing Rights: Prisoners at the U.S. Supreme Court

It is safe to assume that the Canadian Supreme Court's decision to reject prisoner disenfranchisement will have little, if any, practical impact in the United States. Advocates and activists are concentrating their lobbying and litigation efforts on regaining the vote for the millions of Americans who are disenfranchised *after* being released from prison (Coyle 2003). However, as part of that struggle, and the struggle against the myriad penalties that follow former prisoners back to their communities, the official "truths" told by courts about prisoners' and ex-prisoners' rights and (non-) membership in communities become significant. There is a danger that in attempting to bring an end to the "invisible punishment" of postincarceration collateral punishment on the basis that ex-felons have "paid their debt to society" and are therefore entitled to full citizenship and rights, we may inadvertently strengthen the case for increasingly harsh treatment of prisoners. In a recent editorial advocating the repeal of ex-felon disenfranchisement laws, the editorial board made the point that "[m]ost states block felons from voting while they are in prison or on parole. That approach recognizes that those who commit felonies can be deprived legitimately of many of society's privileges" (*USA Today* 2003). In light of the mass incarceration Loïc Wacquant (2001) has compellingly described as "black hyperincarceration" and "the first genuine prison society of history" (Wacquant 2001: 121); we must interrogate our assumptions about the legal status and societal participation of prisoners.

A recent decision by the United States Supreme Court demonstrates the degree to which the concept of prisoners as rights holders has fallen out of favor, in the popular realm but also among judges charged with protecting constitutional rights. *Overton v. Bazzetta* 2003 is the most recent in a long line of U.S. Supreme Court decisions holding that any constitutional rights retained by prisoners may be infringed as long as the limitation is "rationally related to a legitimate penological objective" (*Turner v. Safely* 1987).

Michelle Bazzetta and a number of other prisoners in Michigan challenged state regulations that severely limited family and other visits by prisoners. In the case of prisoners with two or more drug infractions, the
regulations permanently denied *all* visits except those from lawyers or
members of the clergy. The challenge concerned the limit and denial of
noncontact visits (where prisoners and visitors are separated by glass),
which clearly raise fewer security concerns than do contact visits. At the
time of trial, over 1,000 Michigan prisoners were subject to a permanent
ban on prison visits. The Court of Appeals for the Sixth Circuit found the
regulations unconstitutional for falling "below minimum standards of
decency owed by a civilized society to those it has incarcerated," (*Bazzetta
v. McGinnis* 2002). However, the U.S. Supreme Court unanimously upheld
the regulations.

It is worth recalling that in *Turner* (1987), a case dealing with corre-
spondence between prisoners and with prisoners' right to marry, Justice
O'Connor had commented that "[p]rison walls do not form a barrier sep-
arating prison inmates from the protections of the Constitution" (*Turner*,
at 84), a pronouncement that sounds similar to the rejection of a concept
of prisoners as "temporary outcasts" in *Sauvé*. However, the notion that
prisoners are rights holders rings hollow in *Overton* where the Court fails
to recognize that prisoners have any right to, or legitimate interest in, family
contact. In addition, the links between prisoners and their communities are
minimized, and their reintegration is not contemplated.

Taking the harshest view against the prisoners' claim is Justice Thomas,
with Justice Scalia concurring, who states that the only right retained by
prisoners is the Eighth Amendment right to be free from cruel and
unusual punishment. As long as the punishment or prison conditions
imposed by states do not amount to "deliberate indifference" to the prisoners' health or safety (*Hudson v. McMillian* 1992), prisoners have no constitutional claim. In fact, Justice Thomas would have the Court revisit, and
sharply limit, its key precedents on prisoners' rights, even putting the word
"rights" in quotation marks to emphasize his point that prisoners are not
legitimate rights holders.

Rather than starting from the assumption that prisoners, like other
Americans, have rights to intimate association and familial relationships,
the majority opinion of Justice Kennedy went directly to the justification
stage, noting that "[m]any of the liberties and privileges enjoyed by other
citizens must be surrendered by the prisoner." He cited the now familiar
Turner test that any deprivation of prisoners' rights is constitutional so
long as it bears a "rational relation to legitimate penological objectives," in
this case, combating the illicit drug trade. His conceptual move shifted the
focus away from the premise that prisoners are rights holders at all.

Instead, prisoners "rights" are any interests that are "left over" after considering legitimate penological objectives and according broad deference to legislators and prison officials to meet those objectives. *Overton* revealed the complete inadequacy of the *Turner* test to limit harsh treatment of prisoners. Given the tone and scope of the decision, it seems plausible that the court would uphold a rule that banned all family visits for all prisoners at all times.

Justice Stevens wrote for himself and the three other "liberals," Souter, Ginsburg, and Breyer, yet his decision does not depart in any meaningful way from the restrictive view of prisoners' rights articulated by Justice Kennedy. Shortly after the decision was released, Georgetown Law Professor Mark Tushnet was quoted in the *New York Times* as lamenting the "absence of a liberal articulation" of rights in framing the issue before the Court (Greenhouse 2003). The view that prisoners' rights are but pale reflections of constitutional rights, and in any event, can be cast aside with little justification appears to have become commonsensical, even to liberals. Justice Stevens made a point of saying that "nothing in the Court's opinion today signals a resurrection of [the view once held by some state courts that prisoners are mere slaves]." However, that reassurance provided little comfort to the more than 2 million U.S. prisoners or the estimated 1.5 million children with at least one parent behind bars (Bureau of Justice Statistics 2000).

A conception of prisoners as members of communities was also absent in *Overton.* The Court's doctrinal analysis allowed it to avoid consideration of the reality that a majority of prisoners will return to a relatively small number of economically disadvantaged, often racialized, urban communities (Travis, Solomon, and Waul 2001: 41), as well as the uncontradicted evidence that family visits during incarceration correlated with reduced recidivism and improved prospects for successful release. One commentator noted the irony of the court's complete disregard for prisoners' family relationships in a culture purportedly committed to "family values" (Mariner 2003).

The opinions in *Overton* lead one to the unhappy conclusion that prisoners are, in fact, "temporary outcasts from our system of rights." As the other chapters herein demonstrate, the status of "outcast" follows prisoners back to their homes and communities upon release. The increased use of collateral penalties in the 1980s and 1990s (Travis 2002: 18) corresponded with longer sentences, prison expansion, an increasingly punitive approach to prisoners and a wholesale assault on any residual rights they may have held, including rights of redress in the courts (Prison Litigation Reform Act [1996]; Herman 1998). The only discernible constraint on the treatment of prisoners is the Eighth Amendment prohibition against cruel and unusual punishment, which apparently guards against only flagrantly inhumane treatment such as chaining prisoners to hitching posts for hours in admittedly "non-emergency" situations (*Hope v. Pelzer* 2002).

Prisoners' Rights and Citizenship in Crime Control Cultures

Garland has warned that "[a] government that routinely sustains social order by means of mass exclusion begins to look like an apartheid state" (Garland 2001: 204). The increasingly widespread opposition to ex-felon disenfranchisement (Coyle 2003), and awareness of its profound impact on the political participation of racialized groups, demonstrates that the public and policy makers are waking up to this problem. However, that opposition often reifies the distinction between prisoners and ex-prisoners in a way that may legitimate increasingly punitive treatment of prisoners and render their rights claims less significant. The modest goal of this chapter has been to urge consideration of the scope and meaning of public, political, and legal indifference to prisoners' rights claims and to spur debate about the possibility of moving toward meaningful rights, redress, and reintegration of prisoners into our communities.

The successful Canadian litigation over prisoner voting rights points to the importance of a well-functioning, normative human rights framework with rigorous review and meaningful remedies for the violation of rights. As significant as that is, it is not the whole story. Michael Jackson (2002), a leading scholar and advocate of prisoners' rights, has argued that "the principal benefit flowing from a constitutionally entrenched Charter of Rights and Freedoms is not to be found in the litigation it spawns, but rather in the climate and culture of respect it creates amongst both governments and citizens for fundamental human rights and freedoms." Reaction to the *Sauvé* decision reveals that the notion of prisoners as "temporary outcasts," as persons less than full citizens and rights holders, resonates strongly with members of the Canadian public. Perhaps it is time we confronted this reality and addressed some of our political efforts at promoting what David Brown (2002) has called "discursive citizenship." Brown advocates broadening our focus from the formal legal status of prisoners to consider the "necessary conditions under which prisoners might participate fully in a democratic citizenship" (Id. at 323). Discursive citizenship requires safe and healthy living conditions that promote participation in public discourse through access to education and work skills, the media, and the Internet, as well as forging links between prisoners and members of other social justice movements. Richard Sauvé's own story[7] demonstrates some of the possibilities of participation and engagement. Of course, securing these conditions necessarily implicates laws and rights, but it does so in a way that emphasizes participation and process over static, liberal notions of entitlement, a message that may have more currency in contemporary politics and culture.

References

Aboriginal Legal Services of Toronto. 2001. Intervenor Factum, *Sauvé* 2002. http://aboriginallegal. ca/docs/sauve.factum.final.htm.

Arbour, Louise. 1996. *Report of the Commission of Inquiry into Certain Events at the Prison for Women in Kingston*. Ottawa: Public Works and Government Services, Canada.

Brown, David. 2002. "Prisoners as Citizens," in *Prisoners as Citizens: Human Rights in Australian Prisons*, edited by David Brown and Meredith Wilkie. Sydney: The Federation Press: 308–25.

Brown, Jim. 2002. "The Supreme Court of Canada has struck down the law that barred penitentiary inmates from voting in federal elections, saying it violates the fundamental rights of prisoners," *Canadian Press Newsire* 31 October.

Bureau of Justice Statistics. 2000. *Special Report: Incarcerated Parents and Their Children* U.S. Department of Justice, Office of Justice Programs. August. NCJ 182335.

House of Commons. 2003. Canada. *Hansard*. No. 0098. 37th Parl., 2nd Sess. 8 May.

House of Commons. 1997. Canada. *Hansard*. No. 0161. 35th Parl., 2nd Sess. 22 April.

Canadian Centre for Justice Statistics. (CCJS) 2001. "Adult Correctional Services in Canada, 2000/01," *Juristat*. Ottawa: Statistics Canada 22(10).

Canadian Centre for Justice Statistics. (CCJS) 1997. "The Justice Factfinder 1997," *Juristat*. Ottawa: Statistics Canada 19(7).

Canadian Press. 2003. "A bill introduced Friday in New Brunswick will allow inmates to vote in provincial elections," *New Brunswick Telegraph-Journal* 4 April.

Canadian Press. 1997. "Ottawa keeps up fight to remove inmate vote," *Kitchener-Waterloo Record* 17 May: A4.

Centre for Research and Information on Canada. 2002. *The Charter: Dividing or Uniting Canada?* April. Montreal, Quebec.

Commission on Systemic Racism in the Ontario Criminal Justice System. 1995. *Racism Behind Bars: The Treatment of Black and Other Racial Minority Prisoners in Ontario Prisons*. Toronto: Government of Ontario.

Coyle, Michael. 2003. *State-Based Advocacy on Felony Disenfranchisement*. February. Washington, D.C.: The Sentencing Project.

Czekaj, Laura. 2002. "Controversy on the ballot," *Ottawa Sun* 4 November: 7.

Doob, Anthony, and Carla Cesaroni. 2001. "The Political Attractiveness of Mandatory Minimum Sentences," *Osgoode Hall Law Journal* 39:287–304.

Downes, David. 2001. "The *macho* penal economy: Mass incarceration in the United States: A European perspective," *Punishment and Society* 3(1):61–80.

Environics Research Group. 1998. *Focus Canada* Ottawa: Environics 1998-1.

Freiberg, Arie. 2001. "Affective versus effective justice," *Punishment and Society* 3:2, 265–78.

Friscolanti, Michael. 2002. "Convicts 'morally' fit to vote: Supreme Court ruling," *National Post* 1 November: A4.

Gamble, David. 2002a. "Alliance MP targets cons' voting rights," *Edmonton Sun* 11 December 2002: 29.

Gamble, David. 2002b. "Killers granted right to vote," *London Free Press* 1 November: A1.

Garland, David. 2001. *The Culture of Control: Crime and Social Order in Contemporary Society*. Chicago: Univ. of Chicago Press.

Gibbons, Rick. 2002. "Next, Cons will be running for office," *London Free Press* 5 November: A7.

Globe and Mail. 2002. Editorial, "Even prisoners may cast a ballot," *Globe and Mail*. 1 November: A14.

Greenhouse, Linda. 2003. "Will the Supreme Court Move Right? It Already Has," *New York Times*, 22 June 2003.

Hamilton, Alvin C. and C. Murray Sinclair. 1991. *Report of the Aboriginal Justice Inquiry of Manitoba*. Winnipeg: Aboriginal Justice Inquiry of Manitoba.

Hamilton Spectator. 2002. Editorial, "Convicts should lose precious right to vote," 2 November: D3.

Hampton, Jean. 1998. "Punishment, Feminism, and the Politics of Identity: A Case Study in the Expressive Meaning of Law," *Canadian Journal of Law and Jurisprudence* 11:23–45.

Hampton, Jean. 1995. "Disenfranchisement as a Punitive Response," expert report submitted in *Sauvé v. Canada*, [1996] F.C. 857. 18 April.

Harris, Michael. 2002. "One Felon, One Vote," *Ottawa Sun* 1 November: 15.

Herman, Susan. 1998. "Slashing and Burning Prisoners' Rights: Congress and the Supreme Court in Dialogue," *Oregon Law Review* 77:1229–1303.

Jackson, Michael. 2002. *Justice Behind the Walls: Human Rights in Canadian Prisons.* Toronto: Douglas & McIntyre.

London Free Press. 2002. Editorial, "Prison vote wrong-headed," *London Free Press* 5 November: A6.

MacCharles, Tonda. 2002. "Prisoner voting ban lifted," *Toronto Star* 1 November: A8.

Mahoney, Jill. 2002. "Victims' groups angered by ruling," *Globe and Mail* 2 November: A6.

Makin, Kirk. 2002. "Top court gives inmates right to vote," *Globe and Mail* 1 November: A1.

Manson, Allan. 1994. "Fieldhouse and the Diminution of Charter Scrutiny," *Criminal Reports* 33:358–64.

Mariner, Joanne. 2003. "Rhenquist Family Values," *Common Dreams* 27 June 2003. <http://www.commondreams.org/views03/0627-06.htm>

Mills, Wendy. 2002. Letter to the editor, *Ottawa Sun* 6 November: 14.

Morton, Ted. 2002. "Once again: Court-made law," *National Post* 2 November: A23.

Nicholovsky, Boris. 1994. "Lifer granted parole hearing after 15 years," *Toronto Star* 22 May: A16.

Pangle, Thomas. 1995. "Voting Rights of Inmates," expert report submitted in *Sauvé v. Canada*, [1996] F.C. 857. 18 April.

Parkes, Debra. 2003. "Even prisoners have right to vote," *Winnipeg Free Press* 18 February: A13.

Pate, Kim. 1998. *50 Years of Canada's International Commitment to Human Rights: Millstones in Correcting Corrections for Federally Sentenced Women.* Ottawa: Canadian Association of Elizabeth Fry Societies <www.elizabethfry.ca/50years/50years.htm>

Pemberton, Kim. 2003. "William Head exemplifies the 'Club Fed' approach," *Vancouver Sun.* 22 May.

Pruden, Jana. 2002. "More than psychopaths: Supreme Court gives convicts the right to vote," *Fort McMurray Today* 3 December: 4.

Roach, Kent. 1999. *Due Process and Victims' Rights: The New Law and Politics of Criminal Justice.* Toronto: Univ. of Toronto Press.

Rodriguez, Jose. 2002. "Mystery Bar None: Why we must question why prisoners treated better than poor," *Calgary Sun.* 1 November: A15.

Simpson, Jeffrey. 2002. "The court of no resort," *Globe and Mail* 22 November: A25.

Toews, Vic. 2003. "Inmate voting rights offend fundamental value," *Winnipeg Free Press* 6 March 2003: A13.

Travis, Jeremy. 2002. "Invisible Punishment: An Instrument of Social Exclusion," *Invisible Punishment: The Collateral Consequences of Mass Imprisonment,* edited by Marc Mauer and Meda Chesney-Lind. New York: New Press: 1–36.

Travis, Jeremy, Amy L. Solomon, and Michelle Waul. 2001. *From Prison to Home: The Dimensions and Consequences of Prisoner Reentry.* Washington, D.C.: The Urban Institute.

Wacquant, Loïc. 2001. "Deadly Symbiosis: When ghetto and prison meet and mesh," *Punishment and Society* 3(1):95–134.

Walmsley, Roy. 2003. *World Prison Population List* (4th ed.), London: United Kingdom Home Office Research, Development and Statistics Directorate. http://www.homeoffice.gov.uk/rds/pdfs2/r188.pdf.

Woodford, Joe. 2002. Letter to the editor, *Calgary Sun* 11 November:14.

Cases Cited

August and Another v. Electoral Commission and Others, (1999) 4 B.C.L.R. 363 (S.A. Const. Ct.).

Bazzetta v. McGinnis, 286 F.3d 311 (6th Cir. 2002).

Byatt v. Alberta (Chief Electoral Officer), [1998] A.J. No. 399 (C.A.).

Canada (Attorney General) v. Gould, [1984] 1 F.C. 1133 (C.A.), rev'g [1984] 1 F.C. 1119 (C.A.).

Driskell v. Manitoba (Attorney General), [1999] M.J. No. 352 (Q.B.).

Hirst v. United Kingdom, (2004) E.C.H.R. 74025/01.

Hope v. Pelzer, 536 U.S. ___ (2002).

Hudson v. McMillian, 503 U.S. 1 (1992).

Minister of Home Affairs v. National Institute for Crime Prevention and the Reintegration of Offenders (NICRO) and others, (2004) cct. 03/04 (S.A. Const. ct.).

Overton v. Bazzetta, 123 S.Ct. 2162 (2003).

R. v. Gladue, [1991 1 S.C.R. 688.

Re Jolivet and Barker and the Queen et al. (1983), 1 D.L.R. (4th) 604 (B.C.S.C.).

Sauvé v. Canada (Attorney General), [1993] 2 S.C.R. 438.

Sauvé v. Canada (Chief Electoral Officer), [2002] S.C.J. No. 66.

Turner v. Safely, 482 U.S. 78, 89-91 (1987).

Laws Cited

Canadian Charter of Rights and Freedoms Part I of the *Constitution Act, 1982,* being Schedule B to the *Canada Act 1982* (U.K.), 1982, c. 11.

Constitution Act (U.K.), 1791, 31 Geo. 111, c. 31.

Corrections and Conditional Release Act (Canada). S.C. 1992, c. 20, s. 4(e).

Criminal Code (Canada), R.S.C. 1985, C-46, s. 718.2(e).

Electoral Act (Canada), R.S.C. 1985, c. E-2, s. 51(e).

Prison Litigation Reform Act, Pub L. No. 104-134, 110 Stat. 1321 (1996).

Endnotes

1. Only the United Kingdom, Portugal, and Spain had higher rates (Walmsley 2003).

2. Federal prisoners had previously sought unsuccessfully to have the law declared unconstitutional. The British Columbia court in *Re Jolivet and Barker and the Queen et al.* (1983) based its decision to uphold the section on the ground that, by virtue of their incarceration, prisoners could not exercise a "free" political choice. Another early case, *Canada (Attorney General) v. Gould* (1984) saw the Federal Court of Appeal reverse an interlocutory order, which would have enabled one prisoner to vote in an upcoming federal election on the grounds that the law infringed his right to vote. These decisions were of limited precedential value. However, it is notable that the government justified the law in *Gould* on the basis that allowing prisoners to vote was too difficult for security and administrative reasons. In the Court of Appeal decision in *Sauvé* (1993), Justice Arbour commented that the government "wisely abandoned" that argument before that court. Prisoners have also successfully challenged a number of provincial disenfranchisement laws: *Byatt v. Alberta (Chief Electoral Officer)* (1998) and *Driskell v. Manitoba (Attorney General)* (1999).

3. That section provides, "The following persons are not qualified to vote at an election and shall not vote at an election . . . (a) every person who is imprisoned in a correctional institution serving a sentence of two years or more. . . . "

4. I am grateful to Allan Manson for pointing out that the Chief Justice's majority opinion left open the question of whether prisoner status may constitute an analogous ground of discrimination and, therefore, may provide the basis for a successful prisoners' equality rights case in the future.

5. Section 1 of the *Charter* provides the following: The Canadian Charter of Rights and Freedoms guarantees the rights and freedoms set out in it subject only to such reasonable limits prescribed by law as can be demonstrably justified in a free and democratic society.

6. Freiberg describes the restorative justice movement as somewhat successful at capturing the public imagination and attempting to address what he describes as the "three essential core elements that make up a response to crime: the instrumental, the emotional/affective and the production of social cohesiveness" (Freiberg 2001: 272).

7. During the eighteen years he was in prison, Sauvé started a "Lifers' Group" and a "Ten Plus Group," both of which aimed to represent the interests of long-term prisoners. He obtained his B.A. and did much of the work toward an M.A. in Criminology. He advocated for prisoners' rights and interests to the prison administration and politicians and was the Deputy

Co-ordinator of an annual sporting event that brought together mentally challenged children from across Ontario for a weekend of Special Olympic-style games in the prison yard. A jury of local citizens rewarded Sauvé for his high level of civic engagement by granting his application for an early parole hearing ten years before he would normally have been eligible (Nikolovsky 1994). He is currently employed as an in-reach worker with "Lifeline," a support organization for lifers.

15[*]

Civil Disabilities of Former Prisoners in a Constitutional Democracy: Building on the South African Experience

DIRK VAN ZYL SMIT

Introduction

As bearer of guaranteed fundamental rights to human dignity the convicted offender must be given the opportunity, after the completion of his sentence, to establish himself in the community again.[1]

One of the salient features of the apartheid legal order was the extent to which it used criminal law to suppress opposition to the government. Opponents were not only prosecuted for political offences but also subjected, after they had served their sentences, to various forms of civil disability, or *collateral civil penalties*, as they are sometimes called. In the most extreme case, this took the form of legislation allowing for their detention after they had served their sentences.[2] More often, the civil disability took the form of *banning orders*, which often included "house arrest".[3] Even those who had served full sentences were effectively removed from civil society. Former prisoners were denied the right to stand for parliament if they had been convicted of an offence involving imprisonment for more

*This chapter was originally published as "Civil disabilities of former prisoners in a constitutional democracy—Building on the South African experience." *Acta Juridica*, 2003: 221–37. It has been reproduced with the kind permission of the author and Juta Law Publishers.

than twelve months within the previous five years.[4] This was not necessarily a hardship, as the right to be a candidate for parliament was denied to the majority of the population on the basis of race.[5] More importantly, banning orders prevented their writings from being quoted in public, and even forbad meetings of more than one person at a time, effectively excluding the majority population from taking part in the life of civil society at all.

All this now has changed at the formal level. South Africa today is a constitutional democracy with a justiciable Bill of Rights. This chapter investigates the implications of these changes for the civil status of former prisoners. In the process of political change, there were developments, such as universal suffrage, that improved the general civil status of the majority of the population, including former prisoners, and that brought particular benefits to former political prisoners. These particular benefits could be pointers to how former prisoners ought to be treated.

The chapter goes on to state that, in practice, the position of most former prisoners has not improved significantly and that most, if not all, of the old legal disabilities remain intact. Nor has the new constitutional order engaged directly with the position of former prisoners. Nonetheless, the new South African Constitution does supply the basis for asserting the rights of former prisoners in a way that could diminish their civil disabilities. South African constitutional law should follow the lead of English and German law in this regard although the difficulties of converting such developments into practice must be acknowledged.

Former Political Prisoners Come to Power

In the transition to democracy after February 2, 1990, the overt restrictions on former political prisoners were removed with the lifting of the state of emergency and the unbanning of political parties and individuals. Yet many, if not most, of the leaders of the liberation movements were either already convicted prisoners or had committed offenses that could lay them open to prosecution. Some of these were political offenses in the narrow sense, such as joining an illegal organization or leaving the country without permission, but others were common-law offenses, including murder, allegedly committed with political motivation. The early 1990s were a somewhat confused period in which agreements were reached among the various parties about releasing offenders. These were cast in the form of indemnity legislation passed by the minority parliament then still in power. The purpose of this legislation was both to indemnify offenders who had not been prosecuted and to release those already in prison. Actual releases were affected by presidential exercise of the inherent constitutional power to pardon and the power of early release granted to the president by the Correctional Services Act.[6]

Little thought was given to the legal status of the released prisoners. It appears that many of them were pardoned outright. The result is that at law they have no criminal record and consequently none of the civil disabilities that may still flow from the status of being a former prisoner. The announced intention of the negotiating parties was to release only offenders convicted of "political offenses" defined according to strict criteria.[7] The process itself was not without flaws. For example, a bank robber, appropriately named Lucky Malaza, was released, even though his crime had no political connection at all. There was apparently no legal way of rectifying this error.

As the 1990s progressed, the government decided to speed up the process by deliberately releasing prisoners whose offences did not meet the strict political offense criteria. One method was simply to grant general reductions of sentence to all prisoners, which meant in practice that several prisoners whose status was disputed were also released early. Moreover, in 1992, the Further Indemnity Act (Act 151 [1992]) went beyond the strict definition by authorizing the total pardon of offenders (from both sides of the political divide), whose claim to immunity rested only on their subjective conviction that they were acting for political ends.

Although the status of political offenders and convicts remained in dispute, negotiations continued, and in late 1993 an interim constitution (Constitution of the Republic of South Africa Act 200 [1993]) was adopted that would serve as the basis for the new democratic South Africa that eventually emerged after the first democratic elections in 1994. The interim Constitution contained a justiciable Bill of Rights, which was largely reenacted in the final Constitution of 1996.[8] The Bills of Rights in both constitutions make extensive and explicit provision for the rights of prisoners. They provide that all detainees, including sentenced prisoners, have to be treated with dignity. The State has to provide publicly funded legal advice, if substantive injustice would otherwise arise, in addition to adequate accommodation, nutrition, reading material, and medical treatment (Section 25[1] of the 1993 Constitution and s 35[2] of the 1996 Constitution). Former prisoners are not specifically mentioned, but many of the fundamental rights could, it will be argued below, be held to be applicable to them.

In addition to the Bill of Rights, the 1993 Constitution contained an eloquent epilogue, which described the role that the Constitution was to play in national unity and reconciliation. It referred to the "legacy of hatred, fear, guilt, and revenge" and noted that "[t]hese can now be addressed on a basis that there is a need for understanding but not for vengeance, a need for reparation and not for retaliation, a need for *ubuntu* not for victimisation." The epilogue, which was a legally binding part of the 1993 Constitution (Section 232[4] of the 1993 Constitution), further provided for a mechanism to advance reconciliation and reconstruction by granting amnesties "in respect of acts, omissions, and offences associated with political objectives and committed in the course of the conflicts of the past." The mechanism that parliament eventually settled on was the Truth and Reconciliation Commission. One of the Commission's three key committees was the amnesty committee, which had to decide who qualified for "amnesty," more accurately described as a form of pardon. The effect of such amnesty on those already convicted and sentenced to imprisonment was that the person would be immediately released, the conviction would be expunged from all official documents and records, and "the conviction shall for all purposes, including the application of any Act of Parliament or any other law, be deemed not to have taken place . . ." (Section 20[10] of the Promotion of National Unity and Reconciliation Act 34 of 1995). Moreover, those who had been granted amnesty were exempted from civil liability for their past actions (Section 20[10] above). Although, of course, their conduct could still be subject to informal censure and "sanction" by disgruntled fellow citizens.

Family members of some famous political figures of the resistance struggle, who had been murdered by the state, challenged the constitutionality of the amnesty process and of its nullification of the criminal and civil liability of offenders. The Constitutional Court ruled, however, that the rights that victims might otherwise exercise to both see the convictions of offenders upheld and to collect civil compensation had to yield to the exigencies of the time. The court explained that "those who had negotiated the Constitution made a deliberate choice, preferring understanding over vengeance, reparation over retaliation, *ubuntu* over victimisation" (*Azanian Peoples Organization [AZAPO] v. President of the Republic of South Africa* 1996[4] SA 671 [CC] para 18). It further noted that the state would provide at least partial reparation to victims of political violence. On balance, therefore, victims' loss of the rights to civil compensation, directly from wrongdoers or vicariously from the State, was justified in the circumstances.

The amnesty process remained controversial. Only a minority of the offenders who applied for amnesty had been successful by the time the process was completed in 2001. A significant number of prisoners who regard themselves, and who are regarded by their supporters, as "political prisoners" remain in prison. Some of these prisoners applied for amnesty but were refused. The status of these remaining so-called political prisoners remains a political problem for the government. In 2002, President

Thabo Mbeki controversially used his wide general powers to pardon a small number of prisoners whose applications for amnesty had failed ("Pardons apartheid justice," *Mail and Guardian Online* 16 May 2002). They too have now had their criminal records expunged and are free of civil disabilities. The question of further amnesties and pardons continues to surface in public debate from time to time.

"Ordinary" Former Prisoners in the New South Africa

What has been the impact of the historic move to democracy and the tremendous changes in the legal and political order on the legal and social position of former prisoners in South Africa? It is important to avoid being starry-eyed about the social reality that prevails in South Africa. Not all the social benefits hoped for after the demise of apartheid have materialized. Neither the crime rate nor—in spite of the de facto abolition of the whole category of political prisoners—the imprisonment rate has declined in South Africa since 1994. Unemployment rates are still high. Massive socioeconomic differences remain between affluent and poor communities. The rise of the black middle class and the descent into poverty of a number of whites have not demonstrated that differences in the consequences of imprisonment between the affluent and the poor have ceased to follow broadly racial lines. Moreover, the rise of gated communities and the increased use of private security in the suburbs have exacerbated the social divide.

These divisions are still reflected in significant differences in the social consequences of imprisonment for people from different walks of life. For the relatively affluent on whom imprisonment is rarely imposed, the stigma of actually serving a term of imprisonment is inherently devastating. Kanyisile Mpuang,[9] the National Manager of the Offender Reintegration Programme at NICRO,[10] explains it as follows:

> People with money have ways of keeping themselves away from the government systems. For example, they use private clinics and hospitals, get lawyers, consult private psychologists, etc. So when they land in government systems it is scandalous!

In poorer communities, the response is more nuanced. Women who have been imprisoned are generally stigmatized more heavily than are men: for males, a period in prison is still often regarded as a rite of passage to manhood. Among men, the social consequences of being former prisoners vary according to the crime committed. Rapists and child molesters, particularly those who committed crimes in the community, are severely stigmatized, as are their families, including their children. The local community may even evict the entire family from an area. Such offenders are referred to as murderers, rapists, or molesters long after they have been released from prison. Economic crimes, by contrast,

> are not seen as bad. It is generally understood that a person who steals or robs does so to survive. The family may support the person . . . sometimes encouraging them to continue after release from prison.

The economic consequences of imprisonment vary also. Although professional people may be hard hit by restrictions that exclude them from certain forms of employment, they usually have the resources to move more easily to anonymous new communities or to fight such restrictions by legal or other means. One director of a large multinational company persuaded the courts that his conviction of price fixing was not a crime of dishonesty; consequently, he was not prevented from continuing as a director of a limited company (*Ex Parte Bennett* 1978[2] SA 380 [W]). In more tightly knit communities, by contrast, the informal economic effects of crimes to which great stigma is attached will be greater. Informal community mechanisms will be mobilized to ensure that such offenders are not employed again.

There has not been systematic effort to think through what the fundamental change to the constitutional order should mean for the legal disabilities imposed on former prisoners. Current disabilities are something of a neglected ragbag, typically relegated to a passing paragraph in the major legal textbooks dealing with prisoners' general legal status. Previous convictions of accused persons are routinely recorded and, with minor exceptions,[11] do not fall away through passage of time, unless, of course, the offender has been pardoned. Only in the area of public law has there been some change, as former prisoners are now no longer excluded from standing for parliament. Former prisoners had never been directly excluded from voting but, of course, the majority of them could not vote prior to 1994 because of their race.

The existing legal disabilities of former prisoners mostly affect their right to certain types of employment. Thus, offenders convicted of crimes of dishonesty may not be directors of companies (Section 218 [1][d][iii] of the Companies Act 61 of 1973), curators of insolvent estates (Section 55[1] of the Insolvency Act 24 of 1936), or executors of deceased estates (Section 54 [1][b][iii] of the Administration of Estates Act 66 of 1965). More widely, criminal records generally are used to determine whether someone is a "fit and proper" person to practice law (Section 15[1][a] of the Attorneys Act 53 of 1979; s 3[a] of the Admission of Advocates Act 74 of 1964) or to work in the security industry (Section 23[1] of the Private Security Industry

Regulation Act 56 of 2001), a large and burgeoning source of employment in South Africa. Another area in which a criminal history plays a crucial role is in citizenship and residence rights. Citizens who hold dual nationality may be stripped of their citizenship if convicted of offenses,[12] whereas all noncitizens may be declared prohibited persons and deported on similar grounds.[13] As there are a large number of immigrants in South Africa, this is a powerful tool of social control.[14]

Former Prisoners in Constitutional Jurisprudence

What principled guidance can be distilled from the new constitutional dispensation to reevaluate the law and practice in relation to the treatment of former prisoners? This issue has not been addressed directly, but it is certainly possible to give some indication of how the law could be developed. Given that the South African Constitution enjoins us directly to consider both international and foreign law (Section 39[1]), a comparative perspective may be of assistance. For analytical purposes in the next two subsections, it is useful to draw a distinction between (1) negative limits that the Constitution may set on the imposition of civil disabilities on former prisoners and (2) positive constitutional duties that there may be on the state to come to the assistance of former prisoners. The latter could take the form of defending former prisoners against interference with their rights and, more controversially, of offering them opportunities and services.

Constitutional Limits on Imposing Disabilities on Former Prisoners

There are significant constitutional limits on the disabilities that may be imposed upon former prisoners. One way to explore these limits is to contrast the position of former prisoners with that of currently serving prisoners. Prisoners retain all the rights of ordinary citizens except those necessarily taken away from them by the fact of incarceration (*Minister of Justice v. Hofmeyr* [1993][3] SA 131 [A], *Minister of Correctional Services v. Kwakwa* [2002][4] SA 455 [SCA] and the sources cited there). The key legal right that prisoners lose is that of liberty. More controversially, other rights, such as the right not to be compelled to work, may be restricted for sentenced prisoners as well. In contrast, such general restrictions have not been recognized in South African law in the case of former prisoners.

How would a South African court react to legislation that attempted to limit the right of former prisoners to vote, for example? In 1999, in the case of *August v. Electoral Commission* (1999 [3] SA 1 [CC]), the Constitutional Court ruled that it was unacceptable for the Electoral Commission to fail to make or enable prisoners to vote by taking practical steps to allow them to do so. In his judgment, Justice Sachs, with whom all the other members of the Court concurred, emphasized the importance of the right to vote in a constitutional democracy (*August* [n 31] para 17):

> Universal adult suffrage on a common voters' roll is one of the foundational values of our entire constitutional order. The achievement of the franchise has historically been important both for the acquisition of the rights of full and effective citizenship by all South Africans regardless of race, and for the accomplishment of an all-embracing nationhood. The universality of the franchise is important not only for nationhood and democracy. The vote of each and every citizen is a badge of dignity and of personhood. Quite literally, it says that everybody counts. In a country of great disparities of wealth and power it declares that whoever we are, whether rich or poor, exalted or disgraced, we all belong to the same democratic South African nation; that our destinies are intertwined in a single interactive polity. Rights may not be limited without justification and legislation dealing with the franchise must be interpreted in favour of enfranchisement rather than disenfranchisement.

Note, however, that the court did not exclude the possibility of a carefully crafted legislative restriction on the suffrage of prisoners. The Constitution explicitly allows limitation of constitutional rights by a law of general application, where such "limitation is reasonable and justifiable in an open and democratic society based on human dignity, equality and freedom" (Section 36[1]). As Justice Sachs explained:

> We recognise that, in a country like ours, wracked by criminal violence, the idea that murderers, rapists and armed robbers should be entitled to vote will offend many people. Many open and democratic societies impose voting disabilities on some categories of prisoners. . . . This judgment should not be read, however, as suggesting that Parliament is prevented from disenfranchising certain categories of prisoners.[15]

A limited restriction on the voting rights of prisoners convicted of crimes that target the integrity of the state or the democratic order, the category excluded in Germany, might possibly pass constitutional muster. Such restrictions are closely related to the direct threat to the democratic process posed by the individual offenders.[16]

The Supreme Court of Canada recently invalidated legislation that had sought to deny the right to vote in federal elections to all prisoners convicted of serious offences, defined as those serving sentences of more than two years (*Sauvé v. Canada [Chief Electoral Officer]* para 21). The government of Canada had claimed that the legislation "would enhance civic responsibility and respect for the rule of law; and . . . enhance the general purposes of the criminal sanction" (*Sauvé* [n 36] para 21). The majority of the court, however, rejected these objectives as "vague and symbolic" (*Sauvé* [n 36] para 22). Moreover, it found that the denial of the vote to all prisoners sentenced to terms of more than two years was a disproportionately intrusive infringement on a fundamental right.

In 2004, the South African Constitutional Court was faced with a similar challenge, for the 2003 Electoral Laws Amendment Act (Act 34 of 2003) sought to prohibit from voting all prisoners sentenced to imprisonment without the option of a fine. The South African Court responded much in the same way as did the Canadian Court in *Sauvé* and held that the disenfranchisement was unconstitutional, as the government had not justified the blanket removal of a fundamental constitutional right of all such sentenced prisoners (*Minister of Home Affairs v National Institute for Crime Prevention and the Re-integration of Offenders and Others* case CCT 03/04, 3 March 2004).[17] Arrangements had hastily to be made to allow them all to vote in the South African elections on 14 April 2004.

Had the Court not come to this conclusion, a further potential problem may have arisen. Were the loss of the right to vote to be seen as an additional punishment, it could be open to further objections. Disenfranchisement could be seen as an unconstitutionally retrospective penalty, if it were extended to prisoners to whom it had not applied at the time when they offended.

Even if restrictions on the right to vote were to be accepted for some classes of sentenced prisoners, the possibility that the Constitution would allow a voting disability to be extended to former prisoners seems very remote. The idea that former prisoners have violated the social contract and should therefore be prevented from voting for all time, or that the moral purity of the electorate must be protected from contamination, seem relatively weak counterarguments.[18] The constitutional guarantee of the right to vote is so fundamental that it must trump these countervailing considerations. Equality and dignity-based arguments combine to support this position. Former prisoners have, by definition, served their time and "paid their debt to society," and consequently are entitled to the same treatment as other citizens. Universal suffrage is essential for respecting human dignity, and is a cornerstone of the constitutional order.

There has been no systematic review in South Africa of the legal disabilities that various laws have imposed on former offenders. From a normative perspective, von Hirsch and Wasik have argued that civil disqualifications should be used only "when the occupation or activity is especially sensitive to abuse, and when the defendant's conduct is of a kind that is indicative of risk of that kind of abuse."[19] One may assume that such a normative framework will be applied when legal disabilities in South Africa are subject to close constitutional scrutiny. Consider, for example, the disqualification of a lawyer who has been sentenced to imprisonment on the basis that upon release he is not a "fit and proper" person to continue to practice law. In earlier cases, the courts adopted a surprisingly liberal attitude. Lawyers who were convicted of criminal offences were not automatically disbarred. Thus, the young Mandela, who was convicted of illegally agitating for the lifting of legal restrictions on blacks, was not found to be unfit to practice law, as the court found that his offence was not "dishonourable" (*Incorporated Law Society, Transvaal v Mandela* 1954 [3] SA 102 [T] 107). However, this attitude changed in the late apartheid years. A criminal offence was found to be presumptive evidence of unfitness to practice law and political motivation was downplayed (*Hassim (also known as Essak) v. Incorporated Law Society of Natal* 1977 [2] SA 757 [A] at 765-6). A review of the law in this area would need to reevaluate what "fit and proper" means today in the new South African context, balancing permissible regulation of a profession against the right of citizens to choose their trade, occupation, or profession freely.[20]

There is considerable skepticism about new restrictions such as the introduction of registries or of officially warning a community of sexual offenders in its midst. Having studied United States precedents, the South African Law Commission recently recommended against the introduction of a version of Megan's Law.[21] The Commission explained that:

> once a sexual offender has served his or her sentence (which should, in our opinion, include a substantial treatment portion) the offender has paid his or her dues to society and is a free person. To subject such a person to notification and registration requirements after the expiry of his or her sentence seems to be constitutionally suspect. Indeed, if such an offender still poses a threat to society after serving a prison sentence and receiving treatment, the criminal justice system has failed that person. We also warn of the danger and the false sense of security inherent in notification and registration systems. As previously stated, no notification or registration system can predict criminal behaviour. There is also a real threat that communities might take the law in their own hands and cleanse neighbourhoods from offenders, even on the slightest of rumours.[22]

Constitutional Duties to Limit the Social Disabilities of Former Prisoners
A notable feature of South African constitutional jurisprudence has been the extent to which the Bill of Rights has been found to impose specific duties on the state to provide positive benefits to its citizens. Cautious enforcement of socioeconomic rights has occurred in diverse fields

involving the medical treatment of prisoners (*Van Biljon v. Minister of Correctional Services* 1997 [4] SA 441 [C]), an adequate housing program (*Government of South Africa v. Grootboom* 2001 [1] SA 441 [C]), and health care interpreted as providing drugs for pregnant mothers who are HIV-positive (*Minister of Health v. Treatment Action Campaign* [No2] 2002 [5] SA 721 [CC]). In each instance, the courts have relied on specific constitutional rights and have required the state to act. They have also developed common-law actions at private law to extend the duty of the state to act positively to protect more general constitutional rights. An illustration of this last process is the decision in 2001 of the Constitutional Court in *Carmichele v. Minister of Safety and Security*, which maintained that the state could be held liable for the criminal conduct of a third party where the state had omitted taking reasonable steps to restrain it.[23]

There is no reason why private law remedies cannot be extended in a similar way to protect former prisoners. The South African law of delict (tort) already safeguards individuals against having their pasts raked up unnecessarily, long after they have served their sentences. The standard justification for publishing defamatory material, that the statement is true and disseminated in the public interest, does not apply in these cases, since there is no public benefit in repeating it. The underlying reasoning was explained in the old, but oft-cited, case of *Graham v. Kerr* ([1892] 9 SC 185. See also *Kemp v. Republican Press (Pty) Ltd* 1994 [4] SA 261 [E]):

> As a general principle, I take it to be for the public benefit that the truth as to the character or conduct of individuals should be known. But the worst characters sometimes reform, and some of the inducements to reformation would be removed if stories as to past transgression could with impunity be raked up after a long lapse of time. Public interest . . . would suffer rather than benefit from an unnecessary reviving of forgotten scandals.

Graham v. Kerr specifically found that recent offenders "stand on a different footing" (see *Graham*, above). A closer analysis in the light of the new constitutional realties may reveal that the public interest requires that recently released prisoners benefit from similar protection. A dramatic example is in the English case of *Venables v. News Group Newspapers Ltd.* (and *Thomas v. News Group Newspapers Ltd* [2001] Fam 430), in which the president of the family division of the High Court, Dame Elizabeth Butler-Sloss, developed the tort of confidentiality in order to issue a perpetual injunction forbidding the publication of any information that could lead to the identification, even after they reached the age of majority, of the two boys convicted of the sensational murder of the toddler James Bulger.

What makes this judgment particularly interesting for present purposes is that Dame Butler-Sloss reached this revolutionary conclusion by relying on the Human Rights Act, which effectively gives the European Convention on Human Rights quasi-constitutional status in the United Kingdom.[24] From the Human Rights Act and the European jurisprudence interpreting it, she derived a positive duty binding the state to protect the applicants' rights to life[25] and to be free of torture and inhuman or degrading treatment or punishment.[26] For these purposes, the courts are regarded as an organ of the state, empowered to grant injunctions to private individuals as a development of common law remedies. Where the fundamental rights of the applicants were threatened by the prospect of vigilantism, the judge was prepared to intervene by granting an injunction curtailing media rights to freedom of expression.[27]

In principle, such an injunction need not be restricted exclusively to former prisoners themselves, but could also protect members of their families where they faced a similar threat. In the case of the equally notorious child murderer, Mary Bell, the courts were prepared to safeguard the anonymity of Mary Bell's daughter, as well as of Mary Bell herself, through injunctive relief.[28] Initially, the injunction protected the daughter only until she reached the age of majority, but at the time of writing the courts were considering an extended injunction that would protect her indefinitely as well (Wilson 2002).

As far back as 1973, the German Federal Constitutional Court intervened on fundamental constitutional grounds to shield a prisoner, who was about to be released, against media reportage. In some ways, the justification for judicial intervention in this case was even more far-reaching. The (anonymous) applicant in the so-called *Lebach* case had been convicted of assisting in a terrorist attack, perpetrated by a homosexual gang, on a German army base. In the attack, four soldiers were killed. When the applicant was about to be released, after serving four years in prison, a national television station announced that it was planning to produce a dramatized documentary of this sensational crime. An actor would portray the applicant, but his name and the basis of his motivation for joining the gang would be revealed.

As in the *Venables* case, the court had to weigh the rights of the applicant against the media's freedom of expression. However, the rights that the applicant asserted were not as narrow as those on which the applicants had relied in *Venables*. Instead, the applicant alleged that publicity at the time of his release that would lend renewed prominence to his name and the homosexual basis of his involvement in the crime would make his successful reintegration into the community impossible. The court responded positively. Since the state had recognized that the objective of imprisonment was to allow the offender time to become socially responsible and lead a crime-free life, it followed that this policy needed to be supported by a similar policy at the stage when the offender was being released. The court explained the implications of this approach:

> Constitutionally this claim reflects the self-image of a society that places human dignity at the centre of its value system and is committed to the principle of the Sozialstaat. As bearer of guaranteed fundamental rights to human dignity the convicted offender must be given the opportunity, after the completion of his sentence, to establish himself in the community again. From the point of view of the offender, this interest in resocialization develops out of his constitutional rights in terms of article 2(1) in conjunction with article 1 of the Constitution [i.e., the right to develop one's personality freely in conjunction with the protection of human dignity]. Viewed from the perspective of the community, the principle of the Sozialstaat requires public care and assistance for those groups in the community who, because of personal weakness or fault, incapacity or social disadvantage, were retarded in their social development: prisoners and released prisoners also belong to this group. (*Lebach* [n 1] at 235–36)

The court found on the facts that the reintegration of the applicant would be harmed by publicity. Conversely, public interest in securing access to information about the case that included details about the applicant and his motivation for getting involved in the crime, which earlier had been sufficient, had much diminished at the release stage. Accordingly, under these circumstances, it was held that the individual rights of the applicant must take priority over the television station's right of freedom of expression.

A Constitutional Duty to Offer Former Prisoners Positive Assistance?

Although *Lebach*, like *Venables*, resulted in an injunction granted to protect the anonymity of released prisoners, *Lebach* is particularly significant because it constitutionalizes the interest that former prisoners have in being given a chance to live, following their release, in circumstances that give them the opportunity to lead useful and crime-free lives as full citizens.[29] This opens the way for arguing that, like prisoners,[30] released prisoners can require the state to take positive steps, in addition to protecting their anonymity, to enable them to integrate themselves fully and usefully into the community after release. Human dignity is crucial to this argument; otherwise, it might be said that the protection of the community could be achieved by restrictive measures constraining the freedom of former prisoners rather than seeking to facilitate their rehabilitation.

To what extent are constitutional systems around the world likely to follow the example of British and German courts by recognizing a positive duty of the state to assist released prisoners? Clearly, the case is strongest in relation to universally recognized rights, such as the right to life or the right not to be subject to cruel or inhuman punishment or treatment. Indeed, the precedent in the European Court of Human Rights on the question of positive duties of states with regard to these rights is so strong that other European states are likely, as a matter of law as well as through the force of logic, to decide in the same way as the English court in *Venables* (see Emmerson and Ashworth [no 45] at 535–44).

The German decision in the *Lebach* case should comport with other civilized constitutional traditions, insofar as it rests on the human dignity of the applicant. It is less common to draw inferences from the constitutional commitment to the *Sozialstaat*, loosely translatable into English as the "social welfare state." Where this concept is not incorporated directly into a national constitution, one needs to consider broader constitutional principles. Thus, for example, the finding by the German Federal Constitutional Court that the State has a particular duty toward former prisoners as members of one of "those groups in the community who, because of personal weakness or fault, incapacity or social disadvantage, were retarded in their social development," is echoed in the South African Constitution and the jurisprudence flowing from it.[31] In this respect the ideal of social solidarity captured in the concept of *ubuntu* in the epilogue to the Interim Constitution may be important, notwithstanding the somewhat vague nature of that concept.[32] In South Africa, moreover, the new Correctional Services Act (1998) provides in terms very similar to those of the German Prisons Act that "the implementation of the sentence of imprisonment has the objective of enabling the sentenced prisoner to lead a socially responsible and crime-free life in the future."[33] It flows from this objective, which the state has set itself, that the state should follow through at the postrelease stage by rendering whatever support to ex-prisoners that can realistically be offered.

Conclusion

Former prisoners may suffer legal and social restrictions placed upon them and resulting from malign neglect. The needs of this vulnerable group are easily overlooked in the clamor for state services from other, more socially acceptable, groups. The prognosis for limiting—and still less, reducing—the civil disabilities of prisoners in South Africa is mixed. The experience of liberation gives powerful indications of the extent to which it is possible to remove all restrictions on former offenders. Moreover, the liberation process has produced a constitution that offers released prisoners a degree of protection against further diminution of their rights and that can be interpreted as placing duties on state organs to assist them and to facilitate their rehabilitation.

At the same time, in contemporary South Africa there are also pleas for new restrictions to be imposed on certain classes of prisoners, even after they have served their full sentences. In a climate of popular punitiveness, attempts to argue that the state has a positive duty to provide material assistance to former prisoners are likely to be resisted with angry protestations that criminals are less eligible for benefits than other members of society. In the *Lebach* judgment, the German Constitutional Court forcefully observed:

> Last but not least resocialization serves to protect the community itself: the community has a direct interest of its own in ensuring that the offender does not become a recidivist and again harm his fellow citizens or society. (*Lebach* [n 1] at 236)

In my judgment, it is communitarian arguments such as this one, rather than claims rooted in individual rights, that are likely to be more successful in limiting the civil disabilities of former prisoners in South Africa. The political task is to demonstrate that positive results are more likely if former offenders are treated as responsible citizens and given appropriate support, rather than being hounded by the law, excluded by the community, and then left to their own economic devices. Whether the recent legal and political history of South Africa will allow this to happen remains to be seen.

References

Barrie, G. N. 2000. "A Comparative View of the Voting Rights for Prisoners: A Limitation Reasonable and Justifiable in an Open and Democratic Society?" *TSAR*, 92.

Demleitner, N. V. 1999. "Preventing Internal Exile: The Need for Restrictions on Collateral Sentencing Consequences." *Stanford Law and Policy Review*, 11: 153.

Demleitner, N. V. 2000. "Continuing Payment of One's Debt to Society: The German Model of Felon Disenfranchisement as an Alternative." *Minnesota Law Review*, 85: 753.

Dugard, C. J. R. 1978. *Human Rights and the South African Legal Order.*

English, R. 1996. "*Ubuntu*: The Quest for an Indigenous Jurisprudence." *SAJHR*, 12: 641.

Harvard Law Review. 1989. "Note: The Disenfranchisement of Ex-Felons: Citizenship, Criminality and the "Purity of the Ballot Box." *Harvard Law Review*, 102: 1300.

Kanstroom, D. 2000. "Deportation, Social Control and Punishment: Some Thoughts about Why Hard Laws Make Bad Cases." *Harvard Law Review*, 113: 1890.

von Hirsch, A. and M. Wasik. 1997. "Civil Disqualifications Attending Conviction: A Suggested Conceptual Framework." *Cambridge Law Journal*, 56:

Keightley, R. 1993. "Political Offences and Indemnity in South Africa." *South African Journal of Human Rights*, 9: 334–57.

Kutz, F. 2001. *Amenstie für Straftäter in Südafrika.*

Mathews, A. S. 1986. *Freedom, State Security, and the Rule of Law: Dilemmas of the Apartheid Society.*

Markesinis, B. 1986. "The Right to be Left Alone versus Freedom of Speech." *Public Law*. 67–82.

Naudé, B. C. 2002. "Legislative Expungement of Criminal Records." *South African Journal of Human Rights*, 15 287.

de Wet, E. 1995. "Can the Social State Principle in Germany Guide State Action in South Africa in the Field of Social and Economic Rights?" *SAJHR*, 11: 30–49.

Wilkins, K. B. 2003. "Sex Offender Registration and Community Notification Laws: Will these Laws Survive?" *University of Richmond Law Review*, 37: 1245.

Wilson, J. 2002. "Child Killer Mary Bell to Seek Permanent Order Hiding Identity," *The Guardian*, September 9.

van Zyl Smit, D. 1999. "Anchoring the Treatment of Prisoners in a Rights Discourse: The Example of the Rewards for Prison Labour in German Law." *SALJ*, 116: 613–23.

Cases Cited

Lebach case, in German Federal Constitutional Court, BVerfG 35 203, June 5, 1973.

Azanian People's Organization (AZAPO) v. President of the Republic of South Africa 1996 (4) SA 671 (CC).

Ex parte Bennett 1978 (2) SA 380 (W).

Minister of Justice v. Hofmeyr 1993 (3) SA 131 (A).

Minister of Correctional Services v. Kwakwa 2002 (4) SA 455 (SCA).

August v. Electoral Commission 1999 (3) SA 1 (CC).

Sauvé v Canada 2002 SCC 68.

Minister of Home Affairs v. National Institute for Crime Prevention and the Reintegration of Offenders (NICRO) and Others 2004 (5) BCLR 445 (CC).

Hirst v. United Kingdom no 2 (2004) 38 EHRR 825.

Incorporated Law Society, Transvaal v. Mandela 1954 (3) SA 102 (T).

Hassim (Essak) v. Incorporated Law Society of Natal 1977 (2) SA 757 (A).

Van Biljon v. Minister of Correctional Services 1997 (4) SA 441 (C).

Government of South Africa v. Grootboom 2001 (1) SA 46 (CC).

Minister of Health v. Treatment Action Campaign (no 2) 2000 (5) SA 721 (CC).

Carmichele v. Minister of Safety and Security (2001) (4) SA 938 (SCA).

Van Eeden v. Minister of Safety and Security 2003 (1) SA 389 (SCA).

Graham v. Kerr, (1892) 9 SC 185.

Kemp v. Republican Press (Pty) Ltd 1994 (4) SA 261 (E).

Venables v. News Group Newspapers Ltd [2001] FAM 430.

Osman v. United Kingdom (1998) 29 EHRR 245.

Z v. United Kingdom (2001) 34 EHRR 97.

S v. Makwanyane 1995 (3) SA 391 (CC).

Laws Cited

General Law Amendment Act 23 of 1963.

Suppression of Communism Act 44 of 1950.

Republic of South Africa Constitution Act 110 of 1983.

Further Indemnity Act 151 of 1992.

Constitution of the Republic of South Africa Act 200 of 1993.

Constitution of the Republic of South Africa Act 108 of 1996.

Promotion of National Unity and Reconciliation Act 34 of 1995.

Criminal Procedure Act 51 of 1977.

Companies Act 61 of 1973.

Insolvency Act 24 of 1936.

Administration of Estates Act 66 of 1965.

Admission of Advocates Act 74 of 1964.

Private Security Industry Regulation Act 56 of 2001.

South African Citizenship Act 88 of 1995.

Correctional Services Act 111 of 1998.

Aliens Control Act 96 of 1991.

Immigration Act 13 of 2002.

Electoral Law Amendment Act 34 of 2003.
General Law Amendment Act 37 of 1963.

Endnotes

1. Decision of the German Federal Constitutional Court in the *Lebach* case, 5 June 1973: BVerfGE 35 203 at 235-6. My translation, as are further translations from German below.

2. Section 4 of the General Law Amendment Act 37 of 1963, which inserted s 10(1)(a)bis into the Suppression of Communism Act 44 of 1950. This provision was enacted specifically to detain the leader of the Pan-Africanist Congress, Robert Sobukwe on Robben Island after he had served a three-year sentence arising from the Sharpeville shootings in 1961. He was subsequently released, but restricted to living in the city of Kimberley, see Dugard 1978: 113–14.

3. For a full description of the draconian list of restrictions that could be imposed on organisations or individuals, see Mathews 1986: 101–47.

4. Without the option of a fine: s 5(4) of the Republic of South Africa Constitution Act 110 of 1983.

5. All "non-whites" prior to 1983. Thereafter, election to separate chambers for "Coloureds" and Asians was possible, but still not for Blacks (Africans). An elaborate parliamentary system ensured that the majority in the white chamber could not be outvoted by a combination of the white minority and the other chambers: see the Republic of South Africa Constitution Act 110 of 1983.

6. Act 8 of 1959. For a full account, see Keightley 1993 and Kutz 2001.

7. The so-called Norgaard principles, named after the Danish diplomat who developed them for application in Namibia, from where they were adapted for South Africa.

8. The Constitution of the Republic of South Africa, Act 108 of 1996, which is still in force. Reference to "the Constitution" below is to the final Constitution unless the context indicates otherwise.

9. In the section that follows I have drawn heavily on the insights of Ms. Mpuang. I am very grateful to her for her assistance. The two quotations below are from notes, dated September 26, 2002, which she made at my request.

10. NICRO, the National Institute of Crime Prevention and the Reintegration of Offenders, is the major nongovernmental organizatoin dealing with former prisoners in South Africa.

11. Section 271A of the Criminal Procedure Act 51 of 1977 provides for "a conviction to fall away as a previous offence," where the offense was not one for which imprisonment of more than six months without the option of a fine could be imposed. A conviction also falls away for an offense that can be punished by imprisonment for more than six months without the option of a fine if the offender is merely cautioned and discharged, or if the passing of sentence is postponed for a period and the accused is charged at the end of that period or simply not called upon to appear in court again. See Naudé 2002.

12. Section 8(2) of the South African Citizenship Act 88 of 1995, which provides that "The Minister may by order deprive a South African citizen who also has the citizenship or nationality of any other country of his or her South African citizenship if (a) such citizen has at any time been sentenced in any country to a period of imprisonment of not less than 12 months for any offence which, if it was committed outside the Republic, would also have constituted an offence in the Republic. . . ."

13. Cf ss 39(d) and 45(1) of the Aliens Control Act 96 of 1991 (amended by the Immigration Act 13 of 2002).

14. For a detailed United States study of just how harsh such laws can be, see Kanstroom 2000.

15. *August v. Electoral Commission* (n 31??) para 31. A footnote in this passage briefly discusses the law in some democratic countries in which there are such restrictions. See also Barrie 2000.

16. Even this limited denial of the right to vote is controversial in Germany: See Demleitner 2000.

17. On March 30, 2004, the European Court of Human Rights ruled that a similar ban on sentenced prisoners voting in the United Kingdom infringed Protocol 1 of the European Convention on Human Rights, which guarantees the right to vote: *Hirst v. United Kingdom (No 2)* (Application 74025/01).

18. Harvard Law Review 1989.
19. Von Hirsch and Wasik 1997 and Demleitner 1999.
20. Cf. s 22 of the Constitution: "Every citizen has the right to choose their trade, occupation or profession freely. The practice of a trade, occupation or profession may be regulated by law."
21. For a detailed discussion of the origin and development of Megan's law, see Wilkins 2003.
22. South African Law Commission Report Discussion Paper 102 (Project 107) Sexual Offences: Process and Procedure (2002) Volume II para 42.7.7.7 at 774. The South African Law Commission has adopted a more progressive view than the European Commission of Human Rights, which has ruled that registration on a list of sexual offenders is not a penalty but a restriction on privacy acceptable in a democratic society: See *Welch v. United Kingdom* and *Adamson v. United Kingdom*.
23. *Carmichele v. Minister of Safety and Security (Centre for Applied Legal Studies Intervening)* 2001 (4) SA 938 (CC) in which it was accepted in principle that the plaintiff could sue the police in tort (delict) because she had been seriously assaulted by a man whom the police knew should be refused bail but had failed to advise the authorities accordingly. See also *Van Eeden v. Minister of Safety and Security* 2003 (1) SA 389 (SCA).
24. This case indicates the march of a more interventionist constitutionalism in an increasingly united Europe.
25. Cf. a 2 of the European Convention of Human Rights. Applied by the European Court of Human Rights in *Osman v. United Kingdom* (1998) 29 EHRR 245.
26. Cf. a 3 of the European Convention on Human Rights. Applied by the European Court of Human Rights in *Z v. United Kingdom* (2001) 34 EHRR 97. See B. Emmerson and A. Ashworth (n 45).
27. Cf. a 10 of the European Convention on Human Rights.
28. Re X [1984] WLR 1422; see also Markesinis 1986.
29. In *Venables*, the applicants also sought in the alternative to rely on the protection of their statutory right to rehabilitation. They argued that such a right could be derived from the requirement that there should be no interference in the statutory responsibility of a public body, in this instance, its responsibility to assist in their rehabilitation. The judge expressed "considerable reservations" (at 472c) about granting an injunction on this basis, but did not decide the point.
30. In German law, the impact of the *Lebach* judgment on prisoners' rights continues to be felt. This is apparent in the judgment of the Federal Constitutional Court of July 1, 1998, which ruled that prisoners who work must be rewarded adequately for their labor: discussed in van Zyl Smit 1999.
31. For example, the exception to the equality provision. Section 9(2) of the Constitution provides "Equality includes the full and equal enjoyment of all rights and freedoms. To promote the achievement of equality other measures designed to protect or advance persons, or categories of persons, disadvantaged by unfair discrimination may be taken." For an early study that finds the German Sozialstaat approach applicable in South Africa, see de Wet 1995.
32. English 1996. English points out that apart from its function as a "marketing device" designed to put an African imprimatur on a set of civil liberties and freedoms forged largely out of Western instruments," *ubuntu* has been linked to ideals of restorative justice and to community values. Leaving aside the first cynical reflection, there is support for the latter two meanings in the jurisprudence of the Constitutional Court. In the case in which capital punishment was found to be unconstitutional, the concept of *ubuntu* was invoked by a number of judges to mean "humaneness, social justice, and fairness" in a community context. (See, for example, *Madala J in S v Makwanyane* 1995 (3) SA 391 (CC) 484A.) The restorative justice usage of *ubuntu* is prominent in the Azapo case (n 15).
33. Section 36 of the Correctional Services Act 111 of 1998. Compare s 2 of the German Strafvollzugsgesetz 1976.

List of Contributors

As associate counsel at the Brennan Center for Justice at New York University School of Law, **Patricia Allard's** research and advocacy efforts focus on the impact of criminal justice policy on low-income women and women of color. She is currently involved in building an advocacy base from which to reform the Census Bureau rule that enumerates incarcerated people in prisons instead of in their home communities, as well as developing a collaborative research project, documenting the impact of current parental rights policies on incarcerated and formerly incarcerated mothers and their children. Pat is also a coordinating committee member of the U.S. Human Rights Network, where she co-chairs the Criminal Punishment Caucus. Pat is the author of several national reports, including "Life Sentence: Denying Welfare Benefits to Women Convicted of Drug Offenses," and co-author of "Racing the Police: Race, Police Brutality, and International Human Rights in the United States of America," and "Regaining the Vote: An Assessment of Activity Relating to Felony Disenfranchisement Laws." Pat is a graduate of Queen's University Law School (1996) and received her master's in criminology from the Center of Criminology at the University of Toronto (1999).

Santiago Aroca was born in Madrid. He graduated from the Universidad Complutense (Madrid) and the London School of Economics. For more than twenty years he has been a journalist writing for *El Mundo* in Madrid and has published books on the Cuban Revolution, on the Middle East, on human rights issues in Guatemala, as well as a novel. Also he has covered news events on the Balkans, Caucasus, Africa, Latin America, and Middle East, including Iraq for radio, TV, and print media. For his television reporting on Univision, he received two Emmy Awards for his coverage of the war in

Colombia and the plight of Cuban Mariel refugees. He is a 2004 graduate of St. Thomas School of Law, where he was a Merit Scholar. After taking the Florida Bar Exam in July, he will begin a clerkship for a U.S. District Judge in Miami.

Gabriel J. Chin is Chester H. Smith Professor of Law, Professor of Public Administration and Policy, and Co-Director of the Law, Criminal Justice and Security Program, University of Arizona James E. Rogers College of Law. A graduate of Michigan and Yale law schools, he has been a public defender and prosecutor, and served as reporter for the American Bar Association's *Standards for Criminal Justice on Collateral Sanctions and Discretionary Disqualification* (3d ed., 2003). His research interests include legal history, race, and the criminal justice system.

Elizabeth Curtin is the department director for Adult Correctional Services at Community Resources for Justice in Boston, MA. She has extensive experience in providing technical assistance in the community corrections field for projects with the National Institute of Corrections, the National Institute of Justice, and the McConnell Clark Foundation. Ms. Curtin has taught at several Massachusetts schools, and is currently an adjunct faculty member for the criminal justice graduate program at Suffolk University in Boston.

Nora V. Demleitner is professor of law at Hofstra University School of Law on Long Island, New York. She joined the Hofstra Law faculty in 2001 from St. Mary's University School of Law in San Antonio, where she had taught since 1994. She teaches and has written widely in the areas of criminal, comparative, and immigration law. Her special focus is on sentencing and collateral sentencing consequences. Professor Demleitner is a managing editor of the *Federal Sentencing Reporter*, and serves on the executive editorial board of the *American Journal of Comparative Law*. She is also a coauthor of *Sentencing Law and Policy*, a major casebook on sentencing law, published by Aspen Law & Business in 2004.

Lucian E. Ferster has been an assistant public defender in Miami for the past fifteen years. He is a graduate of Union College and the University of Miami Law School and is proud of having attended Antioch School of Law before the lights went out. During his tenure in the public defender's office, he has defended juvenile, DUI, and felony clients. He has spent two years training young lawyers. Currently he specializes in major felony crimes. He has tried nearly 200 cases and has pled many thousands of clients. The cumulative collateral effects of his work are staggering; it could be argued that he alone is responsible for so many Florida voter disenfranchisements, that without his body of work, George Bush would have lost the Florida general election.

Stephanie S. Franklin is an attorney and activist who resides in Baltimore, Maryland. She currently represents children in abuse and neglect proceedings and parents in termination of parental rights cases. Mecca presents nationally on the intersection of child welfare and the criminal justice system and serves as a board member for the American Friends Service Committee Mid-Atlantic Region. She also facilitates empowerment workshops in prisons, serves as a member of the National Advisory Board with the NuLeadership Policy Group and is a member of the Maryland Sentencing Reform Coalition to end excessive sentences.

Amy E. Hirsch is a supervising attorney at the North Philadelphia office of Community Legal Services, Inc. She has worked in legal services, representing low-income people on family, welfare, and health law issues since 1979. She has taught welfare law as an adjunct at the University of Pennsylvania Law School and at the Bryn Mawr College Graduate School of Social Work and Social Research. She frequently writes on the interaction of welfare and family law, and of welfare reform and the criminal justice system.

Daniel Kanstroom is the director of the Boston College Law School International Human Rights Program and clinical professor of law. He was the founder and is also the current director of the Boston College Immigration and Asylum clinic, in which students represent indigent noncitizens and asylum seekers. Professor Kanstroom has published widely in the fields of U.S. immigration law, criminal law, and European citizenship and asylum law. His work has appeared in such venues as the *Harvard Law Review*, the *Yale Journal of International Law*, the *Georgetown Immigration Law Journal*, and the French *Gazette du Palais*.

Jeff Manza is an associate professor of sociology and political science and associate director of the Institute for Policy Research at Northwestern University. His research is in the area of political sociology, social stratification, and public policy. In addition to his collaborative work with Christopher Uggen on felon disenfranchisement, he is the coauthor (with Clem Brooks) of *Social Cleavages and Political Change: Voter Alignments and U.S. Party Coalitions* (Oxford University Press, 1999), which received a distinguished book prize from the political sociology section of the American Sociological Association.

Christopher Mele is associate professor of sociology at the University at Buffalo, where he teaches courses in urban and community sociology. His current interest is in social regulation and control of public housing communities. He is the author of *Selling the Lower East Side: Culture, Real Estate, and Resistance in New York City* (2000) and co-editor (with John Eade) of *Understanding the City: Contemporary and Future Perspectives* (2002).

Teresa A. Miller is an associate professor of law at the University at Buffalo Law School, State University of New York. She teaches courses on criminal punishment, prisoner law, and most recently, immigration law. She has written articles analyzing legal and gender issues raised by cross-sex searches in prison. More recently, her interest in punishment has led her to document the growing use of detention as a policy within the immigration system, and to examine the broader issue of how the "severity revolution" within the criminal justice system has influenced immigration policy. Her interest in collateral civil penalties evolved from research on immigration reforms mandating the deportation of non-U.S. citizen ex-offenders, and through discussions with prisoners and ex-offenders in Western New York.

Debra Parkes is an assistant professor of law at the University of Manitoba. She teaches and researches in the areas of constitutional law, criminal law, and employment law. Her current research examines trends in, and barriers to, the adjudication of prisoners' rights claims. She is a member of a national coalition of lawyers, activists, former prisoners, and academics participating in a review by the Canadian Human Rights Commission of systemic discrimination experienced by women prisoners.

William G. Staples is professor and chair of the Department of Sociology at the University of Kansas. He has interests in social control, surveillance, and historical sociology. His books include *Castles of Our Conscience: Social Control and the American State, 1800–1985* (1991), *Everyday Surveillance: Vigilance and Visibility in Postmodern Life* (2000), and *Power, Profits, and Patriarchy: The Social Organization of Work at a British Metal Trades Firm, 1791–1922* (with Clifford L. Staples; 2001).

Christopher Uggen is an associate professor of sociology and McKnight Presidential Fellow at the University of Minnesota. He studies crime, law, and deviance, with current projects involving felon voting rights and responses to sexual harassment. With Jeff Manza, he is coauthor of *Locking Up the Vote: Felon Disenfranchisement and American Democracy* (Oxford University Press, forthcoming).

Dirk van Zyl Smit holds joint appointments as professor of international and comparative penal law at the University of Nottingham and professor of criminology at the University of Cape Town. His books include *Taking Life Imprisonment Seriously in National and International Law* (2002), and *Prison Labour: Salvation or Slavery? International Perspectives* (1999) and Imprisonment Today and Tomorrow: International Perspectives on Prisoners' Rights and Prison Conditions (1991, 2nd ed. 2001), both edited together with Frieder Dünkel. In South Africa, he has been actively involved in law reform and in drafting the Correctional Services Act of 1998. In 2002 and 2003, he advised the government of Malawi on new prison legislation. He is currently an expert consultant to the Council of Europe on the redrafting of the European Prison Rules.

Index

A

Absconder Apprehension Initiative, 60–61

Adoption and Safe Families Act (ASFA) of 1997, 18, 32, 87, 99–110
  affect of incarcerated populations, 101
  Congressional spending on, 103–104
  Constitutional considerations, 106–108
  financial incentives, 103–105
  implementation of, 100–101
  recommended changes in, 108–109
  timelines of, 101–103
  waivers, 105–106

"aggravated felon" designation, 47–65, 188, 191
  reform in, 193–194

Al Qaeda, 170

American Civil Liberties Union (ACLU), 231

Amnesty International, 231

Anti-Drug Abuse Act of 1988, 17, 18, 53–55, 123, 125, 127, 130, 134

Anti-Terrorism and Effective Death Penalty Act (AEDPA) of 1996, 19–20, 54

apartheid, 255

Armed Career Criminal Act (ACCA) of 1984, 195

Ashcroft, John, U.S. Attorney General, 166, 170, 172, 179n28, 179n29, 179n30

C

Canada, 237–254
  civil rights, 240, 242, 244, 250–251
  criminal justice system, 238–240
  perceptions of prisoners, 245–247

Canadian Charter of Rights and Freedoms, 240, 244, 253n5
  interpretations of, 242

Census Reduction for Ex-Offenders (CREO) program, 117

child welfare policies, 99–110; *see also* Adoption and Safe Families Act (ASFA) of 1997

civil rights (felons and ex-felons)
  in Canada, 240, 242, 250–251
  and clemency, 216–218, 220n11
  employment and licensing, 215–216
  in Florida, 220n7
  restoration of, 214–218
  suspension of, 247–250

collateral civil penalties
  ad hoc imposition of, 28–29
  in Canada, 237–254
  definitions of, 1–2, 9–12, 25n2, 161–162, 185–186
  as deterrence, 198
  as incapacitating, 198
  invisibility of, 12, 208–213
  reform of, 22–23, 223–236, 237–254
  and restoration of civil rights, *see* civil rights
  as retribution, 198
  as social policy, 3, 14–22
  in South Africa, 255–272
  as techniques of management and social control, 20–22
  as technique of racial discrimination, 28

collateral civil penalties, related to
  adoption laws, 5, 99–110
  criminal defense procedures, 6, 203–221
  deportation of non-US citizens, 5, 47–65, 161–183; *see also* deportation
  disenfranchisement and voting rights, 4, 29, 32, 67–84, 237–254
  drug laws, 27–46, 225–226
  employment, 10, 11, 26n3, 32
  firearms, 194–197
  higher education, 33
  house arrest, 5, 139–159
  housing, 5, 33, 18, 111–120, 121–138